Development and Regional Stability in Africa

Adeoye O. Akinola · Emmaculate Asige Liaga
Editors

Development and Regional Stability in Africa

Unlocking Potential

palgrave
macmillan

Editors
Adeoye O. Akinola
Institute for Pan-African Thought
and Conversation
University of Johannesburg
Johannesburg, South Africa

Emmaculate Asige Liaga
Institute for Pan-African Thought
and Conversation
University of Johannesburg
Johannesburg, South Africa

ISBN 978-3-031-56694-3 ISBN 978-3-031-56695-0 (eBook)
https://doi.org/10.1007/978-3-031-56695-0

Cover credit: Maram_shutterstock.com

This Palgrave Macmillan imprint is published by the registered company Springer Nature Switzerland AG
The registered company address is: Gewerbestrasse 11, 6330 Cham, Switzerland

Acknowledgements

This edited volume is part of the research outputs of the African Union Studies Annual Symposium titled, *"The African Union @20: Progress, Problems and Prospects Towards Agenda 2063"*, organised by the Institute for Pan-African Thought and Conversation (IPATC) at the University of Johannesburg in South Africa, in collaboration with the TrustAfrica in Dakar, Senegal. The 3-day symposium, in November 2022, was sponsored by the Open Society Initiatives for West Africa (OSIWA). We sincerely appreciate the generosity and support of OSIWA.

Contents

Notes on Contributors

Dr. Adiat Abiodun is a Nigerian Academic and Researcher. He holds a Bachelor's Degree in Political Science and a Master's and doctorate in International Relations from the Obafemi Awolowo University, Ile-Ife, Nigeria. He teaches in the Department of International Relations, Faculty of Administration, Obafemi Awolowo University. His research interests include security studies, international relations, development studies, foreign policy of great powers, and African studies.

Dr. Adeoye O. Akinola is Head of Research and Teaching, and Head of Unit: African Union Studies, Institute for Pan-African Thought and Conversation, University of Johannesburg, South Africa. He obtained a doctorate from the University of KwaZulu-Natal, South Africa. He specialises in African political economy, African Union Studies, migration, conflict, and peace studies. Among his recent book publications *are IGAD and Multilateral Stability in the Horn of Africa: From the Lens of Somali Conflict* (Palgrave, 2024), *Contemporary Issues on Governance, Conflict and Security in Africa* (Palgrave, 2023), and *Worlds Apart? Perspectives of Africa-EU Migration* (Jacana Media, 2022).

Dr. Olawale Akinrinde currently a Lecturer I, holds a permanent position in the Department of Political Sciences at Osun State University, Nigeria. He is also a Postdoctoral Research Fellow at the Johannesburg Business School (JBS), University of Johannesburg, South Africa. He is an accomplished published scholar with over 50 articles published in refereed university-based journals across the globe, including publication of articles in Scopus-indexed journals. He is a recipient of several local and international fellowships and grants.

Professor Fidelis Allen holds a Ph.D. in Political Science from the University of KwaZulu-Natal, South Africa. He was the former head of the Department of Political and Administrative Studies at the University of Port Harcourt, Nigeria. He was a two-term director of the University's Centre for Conflict and Gender Studies and held a Visiting Fellow position at the Institute for Pan-African Thought and Conversation, University of Johannesburg, in 2022. In 2024, he held a Visiting Fellow position at the Institute of Environmental Futures, University of Leicester, United Kingdom, and is currently an Honorary Visiting Fellow at the School of Criminology and Sociology of the same university.

Dr. Gallous Atabongwoung holds a doctorate in Anthropology Development Studies and a Master of Arts in African and European Cultural Relations from the University of Pretoria, South Africa. His research interests include the political economy of development, state-society relations in Africa, Africa and European relations, democracy and good governance, migration, informal migrant entrepreneurship, and xenophobia. He is a member of the Canada Anthropology Society, Anthropology Southern Africa, the University Association for Contemporary European Studies, and the International Memory Studies Association.

Gabriele Casano is a Ph.D. Student in Security, Risk and Vulnerability at the University of Genoa and a Research Fellow at the Einstein Center of International Studies (C.E.S.I.) in Turin, Italy. He is a member of the Early Career Scholars of the University Coordination for Development Cooperation (CUCS—Italy). He specialises in issues related to international cooperation between Europe and Africa, dynamics of supranational integration, and climate change challenges at both local and global levels through the interpretative lens of political and economic geography.

Farai Joseph Chidhume is a Lecturer in the Department of Peace and Security Studies at Midlands State University, Gweru, Zimbabwe. He holds a Masters in International Affairs and is currently a doctoral candidate in International Relations at the University of KwaZulu-Natal, South Africa. He specialises mostly in security, diplomacy, and peace studies.

Dr. Siphumelele Duma is a Senior Postdoctoral Research Fellow at the Institute for Pan-African Thought and Conversation, University of Johannesburg, South Africa. He holds a doctorate in International Relations from the University of Pretoria, South Africa. His research areas include regional integration, African political economy, and south-south cooperation. He has authored a recent book entitled, ***Developmental Integration and Industrialisation in Southern Africa*** (UJ Press, 2023).

Dr. Ganiyu Lai Ejalonibu is a Research Fellow in the Department of Democracy & Governance at the National Institute for Legislative and Democratic Studies, Abuja, Nigeria. He previously worked as a Legislative Research Officer in the Oyo State House of Assembly, Nigeria. He was educated at Lagos State University and holds Masters and doctorate degrees in Public Administration. His areas of research interests are political economy of regional integration, public policy, election administration, development, and gender studies.

Habdisalan Mohamud Habib was born in Mogadishu, Somalia. He is the Executive Director and founder of Somali Weyn Development Organisation, a local non-governmental organisation (NGO) whose main areas of work include peacebuilding, education, health, and advocacy for marginalised communities in Somalia. He started writing in 2016. His research focuses on socio-politics and peacebuilding. He is a humble, country-loving patriot and Pan-Africanist who always aspires to be a voice for the voiceless communities in Somalia, Africa, and the global community.

Dr. Omowumi Omodunni Idowu is a Senior Lecturer in the Department of Economics at the Ekiti State University, Ado-Ekiti, Nigeria. She obtained a doctorate in the same Department of Economics. She is a 2015 recipient of the WARC Travel Grant from the West Africa Research Association (WARA), Boston. She is a fellow of the Lagos Studies Association. Her research interest revolves around issues relating to women, particularly in an African context. Her articles have appeared in several local and international journals.

Dr. Emmaculate Asige Liaga is a Postdoctoral Research Fellow at the Institute for Pan-African Thought and Conversation, University of Johannesburg, South Africa. She obtained a doctorate from the University of Pretoria, South Africa. Her research investigates the strategies of peacebuilding employed by both local and international organisations of peace operations in post-conflict communities, analysing the top-down and bottom-up approaches by both foreign intervention and local-level organisations.

Dr. Rich Mashimbye is a Postdoctoral Research Fellow at the Institute for Pan-African Thought and Conversation, University of Johannesburg, South Africa. He obtained a doctorate in International Relations from the University of Pretoria, South Africa. He authored a recent book titled, *The Southern African Development Community in Zimbabwe* (Cambridge Scholars Publishing, 2023).

Tendai Shephard Mbanje is a doctoral candidate in International Human Rights Law at the Centre for Human Rights, University of Pretoria, South Africa. He is a governance, election, and legal scholar whose research focuses on the activities of the African Union (AU) and the Regional Economic Communities (RECs). He has written extensively on the subject and regularly comments on international media platforms (including television stations) on the work and performances of the AU and the RECs particularly on electoral and governance processes.

Dr. Zainab Monisola Olaitan is a Postdoctoral Fellow at the Centre for Human Rights, Faculty of Law and an Assistant Lecturer in the Department of Political Sciences, University of Pretoria, South Africa. She is also a Research Associate at the Institute for Pan-African Thought and Conversation, University of Johannesburg, South Africa. She is an avid researcher with published articles in journals and edited book projects, as well as produced policy briefs across different themes on African politics, gender and representation, conflict and peace studies.

Eleonora Panizza is a Researcher in the Department of Political and International Science (DISPI) at the University of Genoa, in collaboration with the CIMA Research Foundation in Savona, Italy. With a background in international and diplomatic studies and a Masters in Politics and International Cooperation, her research focuses on displacement in the context of disasters. She has expertise in East Africa, particularly the IGAD region.

Dr. Mandiedza Parachi is currently working as the Chairperson for the Peace Studies Department at the Midlands State University in Gweru, Zimbabwe. She holds a Ph.D. in Media and Gender. She also holds Masters in Gender and Policy Studies; and another one in Peace, Leadership and Conflict Resolution. She also holds a Postgraduate Diploma in Tertiary Education. She also holds a Postgraduate Diploma in Media and Communication studies as well as a B.A. of Arts Honours in Theatre Arts.

Naledi Ramontja is a research assistant at the Institute for Pan-African Thought and Conversation, University of Johannesburg, South Africa. She is currently a Masters candidate in (Africa and Caribbean) at the University of Johannesburg. She holds a B.A. Hons in International Relations and Foreign Affairs and a Bachelor's Degree in International Relations and National Security Studies.

Arushi Singh has a Master's in Geopolitics and International Relations. She has domain experience in the geopolitics of West Asia, the geopolitical implications of great power competition in Africa, Russia's foreign policy orientations, and emerging technologies. She currently serves as a researcher at the Consortium of Indo-Pacific Researchers and a geopolitical risk analyst for a private consulting firm based in the Middle East.

Michael Washaya is a doctorate candidate in Peace, Leadership and Governance, at the College of Business, Peace, Leadership and Governance at Africa University, Mutare, Zimbabwe. He holds a Masters in Human Rights, Peace and Development and a B.A. in Economic History. His research interests are human rights, peace, security, conflict, and governance.

Divine K. Yamulamba is a doctoral candidate in Political Science at the University of Pretoria, South Africa. She obtained a Masters in Diplomacy and currently teaches French at the University of Pretoria. She was a research intern at the Institute for Pan-African Thought and Conversation, University of Johannesburg, South Africa.

List of Figures

List of Tables

CHAPTER 1

In Search of Governance, Development, and Peace in Africa

Adeoye O. Akinola and Emmaculate Asige Liaga

The Conundrum of African Stability and Development: An Introduction

Africa is always associated with conflict and underdevelopment. In the last few years, the continent has witnessed the resurgence of military coups and the emergence of non-conventional forms of violent conflict, including Afrophobia. Thus, conflict in Africa is transforming and conforming into a shape and space that was not the norm in the two decades after the Cold War. Contemporary trends of conflict, and by extension violent conflicts, have developed to be more complicated, complex, and protracted, thereby involving divergent non-state and state actors. Conflict and instability have both been linked to various causes—core or conventional and peripheral or recurrent issues—which have threatened the statehood of many African countries.

A. O. Akinola (✉) · E. A. Liaga
Institute for Pan-African Thought and Conversation, University of Johannesburg, Johannesburg, South Africa
e-mail: aoakinola@uj.ac.za

A. O. Akinola and E. A. Liaga (eds.), *Development and Regional Stability in Africa*, https://doi.org/10.1007/978-3-031-56695-0_1

The conversation and discourses on conflict are continuously abandoning simplistic rhetoric and embracing deeper, historical, and non-exclusive approaches. For instance, while there has been rhetorical support for women's empowerment and integration of the youth into national and continental agenda, there has not been a significant change in their status. Indeed, the vulnerable groups, women and the youth, have been the major victims of violence and underdevelopment in the continent. Even though women suffer the most in conflicts and make up more than 50 per cent of the African population and despite the reality that Africa has become a continent with the youngest population of the youth (about 60 per cent are under the age of 25), their participation in economic productivity, peacebuilding processes, and political leadership remains very minimal.

Despite the efforts of the continental body, the African Union (AU), and Regional Economic Commissions (RECs), conflict and insecurity continue to present one of the biggest challenges to Africa's quest for socio-economic and political development. Peace and security are considered a necessity and precondition for development, as contained in both the AU Agenda 2063[1] and the United Nations (UN) Sustainable Development Goals (SDGs).[2] The lack thereof has stunted developmental initiatives and restricted the flow of beneficial foreign direct investment (FDI), including democratic consolidation on the continent. These have also impeded the required progress in attaining the goals of the continental and global blueprints for development and security—Agenda 2063 and SDGs.

The AU plays a pivotal role in fostering peace, security, and development across the continent. Established in 2002, the AU succeeded the Organisation of African Unity (OAU), signalling a paradigm shift towards a more integrated and proactive approach to addressing the multifaceted challenges facing Africa. One of the primary mandates of the AU and other RECs, such as the Southern African Development Community (SADC) and Economic Community of West African States (ECOWAS), is to prevent and resolve conflicts within member states and implement policies for continental economic growth and development.

[1] For more understanding of the agenda, see https://au.int/en/agenda2063/overview.

[2] For a full understanding of the goals, see https://sdgs.un.org/goals.

The AU has undertaken peacekeeping missions in various countries, such as in Sudan, Somalia, and Mali, showcasing its commitment to resolving conflicts and promoting stability. Since the socio-economic crisis experienced by post-colonial African states in the 1970s, leading to the adoption of the Lagos Plan of Action for the Development of Africa, 1980–2000, national and continental political elites have acknowledged the important place of multilateral actions in fostering sustainable development on the continent. These understanding and other factors motivated the transformation of the OAU into the AU. The AU recognises that sustainable development is integral to ensuring sustainable peace and security.

Thus, Agenda 2063, the AU's strategic framework for socio-economic transformation, outlines a vision for Africa's development over the next five decades. This ambitious agenda emphasises self-reliance, integration, and inclusive development, aiming to eradicate poverty, promote gender equality, and build resilient economies. Continental actors further place a strong emphasis on human rights and good governance, as essential components of peace, security, and development. Many continental and regional instruments were established to protect the lives and human rights of citizens in continental Africa. For instance, the African Charter on Human and Peoples' Rights serves as a cornerstone for promoting and protecting human rights across the continent. Additionally, the AU supports efforts to strengthen democratic institutions, combat military coups and corruption, and enhance the rule of law.

Recognising the complexity of contemporary challenges, the AU actively engages in partnerships with the RECs, and other strategic partners, including the European Union (EU) and the UN, to amplify the AU's efforts and contribute to a more coordinated and effective approach to peace, security, and development. Despite the moderate achievements of the AU after 20 years of its establishment, the continental intergovernmental organisation faces monumental challenges in fully realising its goals. Insufficient funding, limited institutional capacity, and geopolitical complexities pose hurdles to the effective implementation of its programmes and Agenda 2063. Additionally, the AU grapples with the need to balance state sovereignty with interventions in the internal affairs of states, particularly in cases of violent conflicts, humanitarian crises, and unconstitutional changes of governments. The AU and its agencies, including the RECs, have the responsibility to evolve in their response to emerging threats, ensuring that their strategies remain adaptive and effective in the pursuit of a peaceful, secure, and prosperous Africa.

Objectives of the Book

As the AU celebrates its twenty years of existence in 2022, this book takes a critical standpoint of knowledge to engage the development-security nexus in contemporary Africa. Despite the rhetoric and literature on the 'Africa Rising', some indicators of economic growth on the continent, and the efforts of the AU, most African states continue to experience dwindling economic fortunes, violent conflict, and democratic reversals. The efforts by regional actors to harness the gains of regionalism to drive Africa's socio-economic and political development and ensure peace and security have yielded fewer results. Therefore, this edited volume interrogates the vexed issues that impede sustainable efforts at security and economic regionalism in Africa. Navigating the intricate interplay between regional stability and development in Africa presents a complex conundrum. The continent grapples with diverse challenges, including political instability, violent conflicts, economic disparities, and social fragmentation. Regional stability remains elusive due to factors such as ethnic tensions, governance deficits, tenure elongation and unconstitutional governments, and external influences.

While many studies have focused on conventional issues around conflict and development, this book exposes the reality of emerging threats to national and regional stability and development, such as the resurgence of military coups and Afrophobia. Thus, balancing the pursuit of individual state interests with the collective advancement of the region is a crucial consideration that the book attempts to unravel. Through a critical standpoint of knowledge, the book adopts a case study approach to locate Africa's challenges in both historical and contemporary contexts and thereby offers sustainable policy options for the myriads of gaps in Africa's peace, security, and governance architecture. The book holds the key to unlocking Africa's potential for development and regionalism, as well as providing practical recommendations for a prosperous and harmonious 'Africa We Want'.

Synopsis of the Book

The first chapter by the book editors, Adeoye O. Akinola and Emmaculate Asige Liaga, presents the objectives and synopsis of the book. In Chapter 2, *African Union and the Quest for Peace and Security in Africa: A Critique*, Adiat Abiodun undertakes a critical reflection on the African Union (AU) peace and security architecture on the continent since the inception of the continental organisation. It examines the performances of the AU as a security actor and reveals the successes of the AU in the aspect of conflict management while noting its reliance on external funding and lack of political will as some of its greatest obstacles. It further describes the AU as a nominal security actor because of its inability to match capability with its aspiration. It concludes by emphasising that a periodic and persistent appraisal of AU security architecture is essential for AU's optimal performance and admonishes member states for their failures to comply with the organisation's norms, principles, and protocols.

In Chapter 3, *Operationalisation of the Abuja Treaty (1991) and the Impact of Economic Regionalism on the African Union's Peace and Security Architecture*, Michael Washaya interrogates the AU peace and security mechanism architecture, highlighting its prospects and myriad operational challenges in its mandate to ensure the security of the continent. The chapter identifies the financial capacity conundrum as the Achilles heel of the AU peace and security agenda. It interrogates the 1991 Abuja Treaty and links it to the AU's attempt at economic and security regionalism. The author argues for an urgent need to fast-track the operationalisation of the Abuja Treaty, particularly the quest for monetary integration.

Chapter 4, *A Critical Assessment of the Challenges of the African Union Transition Mission in Somalia (ATMIS)*, by Habdisalan Mohamud Habib and Emmaculate Asige Liaga, explores the effectiveness of the African-led peacekeeping initiative in Somalia. Somalia has experienced protracted violent conflict that destroyed the socio-cultural, economic, and political fabric of the society, prompting a multilateral intervention, led by the AU. Authorised in March 2007, the African Union Mission in Somalia's (AMISOM) mandate officially ended on 31 March 2022, giving way to a newly established African Union Transition Mission in Somalia (ATMIS) which came into effect on 1 April 2022. The chapter identifies the operational differences between AMISOM and the newly established ATMIS, and their roles in Somali stability and security. The authors note that Somali stability and state-building efforts must be matched internally with meaningful advances towards political and national reconciliation, which should include all the main parties to the conflict. The chapter concludes by stressing the need for a critical reflection on AMISOM's experiences, to avoid repeating the mistakes or shortcomings of the past fifteen years, which will then make it difficult for ATMIS to perform effectively.

In Chapter 5, *African Union at 20: Taking Stock of the AU's normative and institutional frameworks on Human Rights and Governance,* Tendai Shephard Mbanje takes a reflection on the establishment and institutional performance of the 20-year-old AU. Since its establishment in 2002, Africa has recorded modest gains in deepening a culture of democratic and participatory governance, respect for human rights, constitutionalism, justice, and the rule of law. These gains were founded on robust normative and institutional frameworks the AU has developed for the protection and promotion of the human rights of African peoples. Despite this appreciable record, numerous governance challenges persist, thereby significantly impeding the consolidation of human and people's rights in Africa. However, there is optimism that the continent can achieve its aspirations enshrined in the instruments it has adopted through the continental institution.

Chapter 6 exposes the misconceptions about youth's political participation in Nigeria. The chapter, *EndSARS Protest and Political Participation of Youths in Nigeria*, by Zainab Monisola Olaitan interrogates political engagement by young people, via social media and non-elective means, which has often been seen as irrelevant to the actual operations of the Nigerian political terrain. The magnitude of the 2020 *#EndSARS* protests in Nigeria and the role of social media in the protest signified that youth participation in politics needs to be evaluated in a new light. This chapter therefore explores how the *#EndSARS* movement symbolises a new approach to youth participation in politics through their engagement in protest and use of social media platforms. Using a qualitative methodology and a case study research design, this chapter delves into the *#EndSARS* protest and its significance for youths' political engagement in Nigeria.

In Chapter 7, *Women-focused Legislation, Economic Empowerment and Sustainable Development in Africa*, Omowumi Omodunni Idowu discusses the important place of women in continental development projects. The author argues that women constitute a great spring of manpower for sustainable development and a powerful but untapped economic resource, due to their exemptions from economic productivity.

While various local and international conferences, protocols, and treaties are geared towards women's rights and empowerment, as well as gender equality in Africa, they are faced with several forms of discrimination and economic marginalisation. Thus, progress for women has been slow and superficial on the continent, except for Rwanda. This chapter provides descriptive statistics on women's economic empowerment and highlights some positive changes in education and politics while discussing negative growths in labour participation and employment between 1990 and 2020. The author draws lessons from Rwanda to recommend how to sustain progress in regions where positive strides have been made, while simultaneously intensifying efforts in countries with challenges in the implementation of gender-free developmental initiatives.

In Chapter 8, *SADC Peacekeeping Missions, and the Quest for Regional Security: From Congo to Mozambique*, Naledi Ramontja and Adeoye O. Akinola assess the performances of the Southern Africa Development Community (SADC) in the security of the conflict zones in the region. The region had enjoyed peace and stability and was considered one of the most peaceful regions in Africa; however, since 2017, the eruption of terrorism in Mozambique's Cabo Delgado resource community and the resurgence of violent conflict in the Eastern part of the Democratic Republic of the Congo (DRC) have distorted regional peace and compelled SADC to respond through military interventions. The chapter reflects on the root causes of regional insecurity in the Southern African region, contends with SADC's peace and security architecture, and examines the role of SADC's peacekeeping missions in enforcing peace and order in the region. The chapter draws from the cases of Mozambique and DRC to explore the performance of SADC in security regionalism and finds how the divergent complexity of the conflict in the region has affected the capacity of SADC to intervene effectively. It thus offers recommendations for peace and stability in the Southern Africa region.

Chapter 9, *African Union and the Consequences of Coup d'états in West Africa,* by Arushi Singh interrogates the vexed waves of unconstitutional changes of government in Africa, particularly the reaction of the regional institution, the AU. As coups profligate on the continent and especially in the West African region, there has been intense criticism of the AU's actions or inactions. In several instances, the AU has not been proactively involved in a manner that befits the posture of the continental organisation or its aspirations of attainment of Agenda 2063. The chapter attempts to decipher the organisational prerogatives of the AU regarding coup d'états and examines the contemporary geopolitical context of coups d'états in West Africa. It further assesses the response of AU and its organs to coups and critically explores the challenges and prospects for future AU actions against coup d'états in Africa.

In Chapter 10, *Regionalism, Trade, and the Development of Member States: A Perspective of ECOWAS Trade Liberalisation Scheme in Nigeria,* Ganiyu Lai Ejalonibu explores the importance of regionalism and trade on the growth and development of West Africa. Indeed, the role of trade as an engine of growth and development is well acknowledged by regional organisations across the world. However, the case of West Africa seems different. The ECOWAS Trade Liberalisation Scheme (ETLS), a regional trade mechanism designed to boost intra-ECOWAS trade, has been struggling to adequately respond to the economic development of member states. This chapter assesses the performances of the ETLS, identifies the challenges for a successful implementation of ETLS in Nigeria, and provides practical measures to transform the ETLS into an effective mechanism for growth and development.

In Chapter 11, Siphumelele Duma and Rich Mashimbye examine, *The Role of RECs in Mitigating the Impact of Natural Disasters in Africa: The Case of SADC.* Using the case of the SADC, one of the eight Regional Economic Commissions (RECs) recognised by the AU, the chapter analyses the frequency and severity of ecological and climate change-related disasters in Southern Africa since 2000 and explores the role of SADC in mitigating their impacts. In recent years, the region has been struck by natural disasters like cyclones, floods, and droughts, which disrupted and destroyed people's lives, property, and livelihoods, including the economies of SADC member states. Despite the interventions of the regional organisation through several instruments and initiatives, the results and performances have been less convincing. The chapter thereby offers insights into the effectiveness of SADC and its member states in managing and curtailing the effects of natural disasters.

Chapter 12, *The Global Gateway Africa: Europe Investment Package and the Future of EU -AU Relations,* by Gabriele Casano and Eleonora Panizza, discusses the importance and the potential opportunities for a stronger partnership between the European Union (EU) and the African Union (AU). The chapter notes the mutual satisfaction at the end of the 6th EU-AU Summit; however, there are genuine doubts about how '*The Global Gateway Africa: Europe Investment Package*' will be successfully implemented to benefit all parties. The 150-billion-euro package, which remains an ambitious financing plan for development, was operationalised in the 'Joint Vision for 2030'. It aims to support Africa to achieve the lofty objectives in the AU's Agenda 2063. The main challenge appears to be the realisation of adequate tools for its implementation, as well as how to mobilise, manage, and monitor such huge resources, as explicitly highlighted in the development plan. Thus, this chapter explores the possibility of accessing resources from the General Allocation of Special Drawing Rights (SDRs) of the International Monetary Fund (IMF), through the creation of an ad hoc instrument that would allow for their rechannelling from the EU to Africa.

In Chapter 13, *Peace and Security: The Question of 'Reunification' or 'Unification' of Cameroon,* Gallous Atabongwoung argues that the unification of Cameroon created the marginalisation of Anglophone Cameroonians, who were citizens of former British Southern Cameroons. This marginalisation established a strong sense of 'Anglophone consciousness', which led to the rise of Anglophone separatist movements and the consequent deadly civil war that has militarised a section of the country since 2016. The 'avoidable' violent conflict has led to the death of more than 3000 people and the destruction of over 200 villages, while more than 750,000 people have been internally displaced, including about 1.3 million people in need of humanitarian assistance. While there is an urgent need to resolve the conflict in Cameroon, the chapter argues for a return to the two-state federation, as the most practicable and sustainable solution to the crisis in the country.

In Chapter 14, *MNCs, Conflict and the Contradictions of Resource Extraction in the DRC,* Divine K. Yamulamba and Adeoye O. Akinola critically engage the complicit activities of Multinational Corporations (MNCs) in African resource communities. Indeed, foreign MNCs have been heavily criticised for exploiting Africa's natural resources and the unethical treatment of citizens of the resource communities. This chapter adopts a desktop research methodology to demonstrate how the corporate activities of MNCs in the DRC's Kivu region have militarised the resource zones and undermined the enduring peace and sustainable development of the country. Founded on an Afrocentric approach, the chapter argues for a harmonised response, where national government, MNCs, and other non-state decision-makers such as local community leaders, commit to regional peace, protect the rights of artisanal miners, and alleviate the pervasive corruption that has become the norm in the country.

Chapter 15, *Pan-African Integration: Afrophobia Conundrum and Migration Politicking in South Africa*, by Farai Joseph Chidhume, Olawale Akinrinde, and Mandiedza Parichi, situates anti-migration sentiments and acts in both South African historical and contemporary realities. Afrophobic Violence has consistently unfolded in post-apartheid South Africa since the attainment of majority rule in 1994, undermining the African Union's quest for African Unity. Episodes of Afrophobic violence have severed South Africa's diplomatic relations with its neighbouring counties and beyond. Multiple scholars have cited economic situation deterioration, bad governance, civil wars, and political instability in African countries. However, the high number of migrants from the African continent has prompted migrants' politicking and violent protests in the country Africa in recent years. The conundrum of Afrophobia has been catalysed by failed political transitions and governance in Africa resulting in migration to South Africa. This chapter examines Afrophobic violence and explores the diplomatic implications for the country and AU member states. This study argues that economic and governance deficits prevalent among South African blacks and the continued neglect of the economic and social needs of the black South Africans by the post-apartheid South African government relatively deprive indigenous black South Africans of socio-economic capital.

In Chapter 16, *Insights from Niger Delta Coastal Communities on Decolonial Climate Adaptation*, Fidelis Allen highlights the importance of high vulnerability and decoloniality in tackling the global climate crisis and development. Using the experiences of six communities in three Niger Delta states, the chapter explores the role of decolonisation in climate adaptation. The chapter further analysed qualitative data obtained through observation, focus group discussions, and interviews with coastal communities. There was a reinforcement of positions in the literature about decolonial climate adaptations. Communities are adopting legitimate adaptive measures such as migration, alternative sources of livelihood, shoreline embarkment, skill development, vocations, and infrastructure development. Maladaptive measures such as piracy, kidnapping, illegal oil refining, and gangsterism are commonplace at the same time. These antisocial behaviours complicate climate change.

CHAPTER 2

African Union and the Quest for Peace and Security in Africa: A Critique

Adiat Abiodun

Introduction

Regional integration as a collective self-reliance strategy for promoting political and economic development in Africa has a long history as it predates Africa's contact with European imperialism (Ake, 1981). Regional integration in Africa has undergone three different historical phases: Islamisation and Arab colonialism, diaspora colonialism and European colonialism, and Pan-Africanism and colonialism (Okafor & Aniche, 2017). In post-colonial Africa, the reconstitution of the Organisation of African Unity (OAU) to the African Union (AU) about 20 years ago was underlined by the need to improve the security profile of the continent which has been ravaged by different forms of insecurity from military to non-military threats (Makinda & Okumu, 2008; Murithi, 2012). After the end of European colonialism, Africa was engulfed in an infernal internal crisis across different states of the region while OAU's major

A. Abiodun (✉)
Department of International Relations, Obafemi Awolowo University, Ile-Ife, Nigeria
e-mail: adiatbdn7@gmail.com

A. O. Akinola and E. A. Liaga (eds.), *Development and Regional Stability in Africa*, https://doi.org/10.1007/978-3-031-56695-0_2

focus was on the safety of the newly independent African states from the vestiges of colonialism and neo-colonial influence (Aniche, 2020).

The focus on the liberation of African states under colonial power accounted for the neglect of the security and developmental needs of the people, while the prevalence of authoritarian regimes across the continent continued unabated. Indeed, OAU focuses more on state security rather than human security. Specifically, the OAU during this period was criticised for its minimal effort at protecting the fundamental rights of African citizens from their national governments, which necessitated the dubbing of the organisation as a dictator's club (Reynolds, 2002). Because of this, there were cycles of insecurity across different states of the region.

Scholars on African regionalism have expressed differing views about the impact of regional frameworks in addressing the political, social, and economic problems of the continent (Aniche, 2020). These differing views are classified into three groups which include Afro-pessimists, Afro-optimists, and Afro-realists. The Afro-pessimist group focused on the militating factors against regionalism on the continent (Nathan, 2010) while the optimist group acknowledged the progress made by the regional organisation. The Afro-realists are more concerned about the reality of the existence of the African Union by noting its achievements without neglecting its defects.

However, 20 years after its formation, peace and security is still elusive on the continent while African states continue to provide harbour to different forms of violent and criminal activities as well as interstate and intrastate crises. Many African states are plagued by intrastate armed conflicts, Jihadist terrorism, and other forms of violent and criminal activities (Grieger, 2019). The civil war in Ethiopia and the military takeover in countries like Mali, Burkina Faso, and Guinea Conakry are some of the political instabilities in the Post-OAU Africa that threaten its continental peace.

This chapter adopts in-depth interviews and secondary materials to critique the AU's security and development architecture for ensuring peace and stability on the continent, since its establishment. The primary data were obtained through the conduct of unstructured interviews. The participants were purposively selected to include two scholars each from the Department of International Relations at the Obafemi Awolowo University, Ile-Ife, Osun State; and the Department of Political Science, University of Lagos, Lagos State, in Nigeria, who have done extensive research on the AU. These universities were selected because of the large concentration of studies on regionalism in Africa.

Furthermore, three senior officers at the AU Commission's Department of Peace and Security and the Ministry of Foreign Affairs, who are familiar with AU's efforts on Peace and security in Africa, were also selected as participants. In all, 10 interviews were conducted. Secondary data were sourced from published documents, including articles in refereed journals, and books. Data were also sourced from AU's documents and protocols, and the Internet. Data obtained will be analysed using descriptive and content analyses. Specifically, it examines the credibility of the AU as a security actor with the capacity to provide peace and security on the African continent. This is to provide an insight into the significant challenges and successes of the AU in its 20 years of existence and to further reveal how it can be more successful as a competent regional security actor.

Conceptual Clarification

Security

The concept of Security originated from the Greek word *se-cura*, which means to be in a state of no fear (Akindele & Ossymen, 2015). Generally, it refers to the absence of threats to a referent object. A referent object or factor in this context refers to the things that are seen to be existentially threatened which has a legitimate claim for survival (Buzan et al., 1998). In its classical formulation, security is about how states use their military power to manage threats to their territorial integrity, their autonomy, and their domestic political order, primarily from other states. This was because the greatest threat to the state was the invasion of its territory by other states and most mportantly nuclear race among the superpowers during the Cold War era. This was also the focus of classical regionalism in Africa, which concentrates on the security of newly independent African states against the influences of capitalism, racial discrimination, and other forms of inhuman treatment from European colonialists (Awofeso & Udokang, 2015).

However, the collapse of communism in the 1990s and the end of nuclear and ideological rivalry between the Soviet Union and the United States brought about a shift in focus to other non-military threats. These threats are not new, but they received less attention during this period.

For instance, during the Cold War era, scholars such as Buzan (1983), Thomas (1987), and recognised that non-military phenomena can also threaten states and individuals. They argued that the concept of security should be expanded to include topics such as poverty, environmental hazards, trade, health issues, and drug abuse among many others (Brown, 1989; Buzan, 1983; Thomas, 1987).

Security in this context is perceived in line with the paradigmatic shift of the post-Cold War era which focused on humans as the primary referent of security as well as the recognition of both military and non-military threats. Human security in this context is defined as the freedom from fear and freedom from want (UNDP, 1994). This perspective is a clear intellectual departure from the Cold War era as it focuses on threats to human lives, including military and non-military threats. Security in this era was redefined as human security with advocacy for a more broadened and comprehensive understanding of humans as the referent of security and the description of security threats beyond physical violence as the only relevant threat to human life (Commission on Human Security, 2003).

It is also defined as the institutional approach to assist member states in identifying and addressing widespread and cross-cutting challenges to human survival, livelihood, and dignity of their people (United Nations Trust Fund for Human Security, 2012). This definition advocates for an approach to security that is a people-centred, comprehensive, context-specific, and prevention-oriented response that strengthens the protection and empowerment of the people. In another context, human security is also described as an approach to national and international security with greater primacy for human beings as well as their complex and social interactions (Catia, 2023). These definitions represent a departure from orthodox security studies, which have a greater primacy for the state as the referent of security. This perspective is more relevant to post-colonial African security needs as the people have been the direct victims of intrastate conflicts, terrorism, banditry, and other forms of violent and criminal activities. However, the use of the term security here will focus more on violent security threats, which are considered prerequisites for the non-violent threat category.

Security Actor

In security discourse in the study of International Relations, threats, and vulnerabilities have been treated or considered as synonyms without any attempt at differentiation between the two concepts in their usage. Consequently, the post-Cold War security definition has focused on the security of human life from vulnerabilities such as poverty, environmental degradation, and autocratic governance (Waltz, 1991). However, it is important to note that there is a great distinction between threats and vulnerabilities (Holsti, 1995). Without this distinction, it will be difficult to conceptualise what a security threat is and what constitutes a security actor. Vulnerabilities are mostly a derivative of geographical characteristics while threats are progenies of vulnerability (Buzan, 1991).

The implication is that a security referent's implicit or explicit susceptibility is an important area that an adversary can exploit, eventually resulting in threats. For instance, lack of money can be described as vulnerability while hunger and other forms of deprivation are threats that can occur because of this vulnerability. In this regard, the ability of a security actor to develop capabilities to manage its vulnerability is what determines its credibility as a security actor. This means that a credible security actor must be able to march aspiration with capability. Hence, a security actor in this context can be defined as an actor who can actualise its aspirations in protecting itself from internal and external security threats. Within the context of the theoretical framework for the study, a security actor possesses a strong level of cohesiveness among three causal factors. This includes strong and growing economic interdependence among its member states, the capacity to resolve disputes and develop an effective international regime, as well as efficient enforcement of supranational market rules.

Theoretical Analysis

This study utilises Neo-Functionalism, a theory of regional integration developed by Earns Haas and consequently used to explain and predict European integration in 1958 (Sabine, 2014). It is based on the description and explanation of the process of regional integration among states regarding how three causal factors interact (Wayne, 1997). According to Haas (1961), these include:

1. Growing economic interdependence among states.
2. Organisational capacity to resolve disputes and build international regimes.
3. Supra national market rules that replace national regulatory regimes.

According to the theory, the actors of the integration are member states, but with more focus on the 'secretariat' or the international organisation itself (Schmitter, 2002).

Integration in this context is the process whereby political actors in several distinct national settings are persuaded to shift their loyalties, expectations, and political activities to a new larger Centre, whose institutions possess or demand jurisdiction over the pre-existing nation-states (Haas, 1961). The partial ceding of their sovereign power to the supranational body is with an expectation of collective security that their collective action can better respond to their interest because of the similarities of their problems. The positive interaction among these three factors can be used to describe the extent to which an international organisation can be described as a security actor.

Previous studies on regional integration in Africa have utilised the theory to explain why regionalism is not producing the required results in Africa. For instance, Muhudin (2018) used the theory to examine the dynamics of decision-making and AU's capacity to attain aspiration three of Agenda 2063 with a focus on African Peace and Security Architecture (APSA). Similarly, Muzee and Enaifoghe (2019) adopt the theory to explore the possibility of incorporating the functionalist and federalist approaches into an inclusive model for African regional integration. This theory as demonstrated in the previous studies is relevant to the subject matter of this study. This is because of its capacity to provide answers to the following research questions that are very critical to the study: What factors led to the formation of the AU as a successor to OAU? What are the present violent security threats that are rocking Africa? Is the AU a credible security actor, and how effective is the APSA? In this regard, the subsequent discussion provides an insight into the capacity of the AU as a continental and global security actor.

The Formation of the African Union

The historical antecedent of the AU can be traced to the initial congress of newly independent African states which took place in Accra, Ghana between 15 and 22 April 1958. This congress serves as a precursor to the establishment of the OAU which was a parent organisation to the AU. The OAU, according to its summit in 1963, was established with a major objective to "rid the continent of the remaining vestiges of colonisation and apartheid; promote unity and solidarity amongst African States; coordinate and intensify cooperation for development; to safeguard the sovereignty and territorial integrity of Member States and promote international cooperation".

These objectives form the basis of the activities of the OAU in its 39 years of existence as a regional international intergovernmental organisation. During this period, OAU was instrumental in the decolonisation struggle in Africa and most especially in Southern Africa. However, OAU has been criticised majorly for its little effort at safeguarding the fundamental liberties of African citizens from their national government (Reynolds, 2002). The initiative to establish the AU was revived in the mid-1990s by the former Libyan head of state Muammar Gaddafi (Adebajo, 2011).

During the period of its existence, the OAU had some relative success such as the provision of a common front on African issues such as decolonisation and apartheid regimes. It was also instrumental to the resolutions of many interstate and intrastate crises. Some of these include the Chadian Civil War, the Ethiopia and Somalia conflict, and Morocco and Algeria. However, the organisation, in its more than three decades of existence, was characterised by a myriad of challenges. This greatly threatens its objective of promoting unity and solidarity among African states and the people of Africa. Despite forming a united front against apartheid and colonialism after its formation, unity among its member states in addressing socio-political and economic problems in Africa remains elusive. Thus, the OAU existed without apparent unity among its member states. There were a lot of explicit and manifest conflicts between and among African states. Some of these, as captured by Nathan (2010), include:

> Apartheid South Africa's military occupation of Angola and its support for Renamo in Mozambique, attacks on neighbouring countries in the 1980s;

> the war that began in the Democratic Republic of Congo (DRC) in 1998 and drew in Angola, Burundi, Chad, Namibia, Rwanda, Sudan, Uganda, and Zimbabwe as state belligerents; the heavy fighting between Uganda and Rwanda inside the DRC in 2000; and Angola's military assistance to General Sassou-Nguesso in his coup against President Pascal Lissouba of Congo (Brazzaville) in 1997. (Nathan, 2010)

Apart from the direct military confrontations among these states, there are also instances of proxy wars among them, such as Sudan's support for the Lord's Resistance Army in Uganda and rebels in Chad and the Central African Republic, Liberian support for rebels in Sierra Leone, Guinea, and Côte d'Ivoire as well as the Liberian supports for rebels in Sierra Leone, Guinea and Côte d'Ivoire (Furley & May, 2001).

These instances of political instabilities posed enormous challenges for the organisation because it lacked a standing army to independently tackle these problems while they worsened the level of unity and solidarity among its member states. Apart from the issue of political instability, other factors as identified by Salam and Usman (2019) that challenge the existence of the OAU and necessitated its eventual replacement include:

1. Incapacity, outright refusal, and the reluctance of its member states to fulfil their financial obligation.
2. Ideological differences among its member states which further fuel suspicion among them.
3. Foreign influence from the erstwhile colonial masters most importantly in African conflicts
4. The indifference of the OAU to the internal affairs of the member states.

These numerous challenges coupled with the challenges of the new millennium, such as the spread of terror organisations, climate change, and other human security threats were associated with globalisation and its processes necessitated the transformation of the OAU into the AU for the organisation to maintain its relevance in the changing global context (Vanheukelom, 2017). Consequently, its leaders met at a summit in Lome in 2000 to discuss the rebranding of the organisation. In 2000, an OAU Extraordinary Summit was convened in Sirte, Libya where the AU was officially proclaimed and eventually, it was officially launched on 9 October 2002 in Durban, South Africa (Salam & Usman, 2019).

The eventual establishment of the AU drove what Moller (2009) described as a grandiose plan which eventually posed a very big challenge to the success of the newly established organisation. According to Moller, the Pan-African view was the desire to create a larger community of people devoid of any form of discrimination on cultural, ideological, ethnic, and national basis (Ronen, 2002). Thus, the challenge of both unity of purpose and its people and government has become an albatross in the existence of the AU as a security actor. This is because the AU at its formation involves a mixture of three different ideas, preventing it from functioning as a system. These divergent ideas include the Libyan quest for Pan-African unity, Nigeria's desire for a Conference on Security, Stability, Development, and Cooperation in Africa (CSSDCA), and South Africa's idea of an African Renaissance (Tieku, 2004).

Violent Security Threats in the Post-OAU Africa

In the 1960s when the OAU which was a predecessor to the AU was formed, the main security issues were threats from state actors who were massively threatening people's rights across different countries on the continent. The multi-party democracy at the independence of many African states was replaced by a party system and eventually a strong military dictatorship (Onah, 2010). The military eventually replaced the civilian authoritarian regimes as Africa became the theatre of military coup and counter-military in the first decade of independence from the early 1960s.

The authoritarian nature of the civilian and military regimes caused and worsened the level of disunity among African states and the high-handedness of the regimes was a clear threat to the political and economic security of the people. For instance, the authoritarian military regime of General Idi Amin of Uganda was removed largely with the support of the Tanzanian Government under Julius Nyerere who were both members of the Organization of African Unity (Tony & Martha, 1983). The mass killings in Burundi and Rwanda between 1993 and 1994 were another instance that threatened African unity which eventually necessitated the replacement of the OAU by the African Union (Williams, 2009).

However, since its formation, the AU in addition to security threats from state actors has been confronted with violent security threats from non-state actors such as terrorist groups, arms traffickers, ethnic chauvinism, secessionist groups, banditry, and kidnapping among many others.

The emergence of different non-state armed groups has been described as a grave challenge to the African Union's peace and security architecture (Fafore, 2020). This is because APSA is the major security strategy of the African Union for addressing conflict and insecurity in Africa. While the security threats from the non-state actors are emerging and worsening, security threats from state actors have persisted. Despite the absence of interstate conflict among African states which makes Franke (2009) describe the AU as a security community, there have been a lot of proxy wars and massive repression of human rights in many African states which has resulted in intrastate conflicts in countries like Ethiopia, Sudan, South Sudan, and Mali among others. According to Williams (2015), violent and conflict trend in Africa is characterised by the following types of violent conflicts:

1. Non-State Armed Conflicts
2. One-sided Violence
3. Military Coups
4. Electoral Violence
5. Livelihood struggles
6. Intrastate Armed Conflicts
7. Interstate Armed Conflicts.

These different categories of organised violence according to him trends across many African states. While there has been a lull in interstate wars, intrastate wars have continued to be on the increase. The conflict in Somalia, Congo DRC, and Sudan to mention a few has been on for several decades while countries such as Libya, Ethiopia, and South Sudan have also added to the profile of intrastate conflicts in Africa. The problem with many of the intrastate conflicts is that they usually have spillover effects. In the year 2019, there was a drastic increase in state-based conflict in Africa which was four times more than what was recorded in 2018 (Palik et al., 2020).

Apart from intrastate wars, violent and criminal activities from non-state armed groups have also become very rampant. Terror groups like Alshabab (Somalia), Boko Haram, and ISWAP in Nigeria have become deadlier in their local area of operation and elsewhere in Africa with spillover effects. In 2019, eight different non-state conflicts were recorded in both South Sudan and Nigeria, while six different non-state conflicts occurred in Congo DRC, Somalia had four, and Libya recorded three (Palik et al., 2020: 25). Non-state-based armed conflict from 2011 to 2019 increase dramatically as a different type of armed groups sprang up across different African states (Pettersson et al., 2019). These violent security threats have resulted in numerous battle-related deaths and non-battle-related deaths from violent conflicts.

African Union as a Security Actor

The status of the African Union as a security actor can be viewed from the perspective of whether it's a security alliance or security institution or a combination of both. Security alliance in this context refers to the measures and techniques adopted by states and international institutions to ensure their survival and protection from violent and military threats (Marshall, 2017). Within the context of the theoretical framework for the study, the status of AU as a security actor can be determined by the extent or level of cohesiveness among three causal factors. This includes strong and growing economic interdependence among its member states, capacity to resolve disputes, and effective international regime as well as efficient enforcement of supranational market rules. In this regard, military and political measures are the basic instruments used by states and international institutions to provide security (Taylor, 2004).

To assess the security status of an actor in this context, the focus will be on the actors' military capability and political will to provide security. Security institution, on the other hand, refers to the ability of an international organisation that is considered a security actor to provide integration, democratisation, conflict resolution, and the rule of law as a strategy for providing security (Williams, 2013). The credibility of a security actor in this context can be accessed by its ability to provide collective norms, norm compliance, and military and non-military means as a strategy for providing security for its constituents. These two views represent the neo-realist and neoliberal approaches to the conceptualisation of what constitutes an international security actor. Another view that is worthy of consideration is the broadened conceptualisation of security by Critical Security Studies and the inadequacy of military capabilities as a strategy for conflict prevention in the post-Cold War era (Weiss, 2008). The implication of this is that a security actor's credibility is determined by its capability to respond to military and non-military threats. However, the chapter assesses the ability of the AU to respond to critical violent and military security threats.

Going back to our major research question for this study which stated that: Is the AU a credible regional security actor with the capacity to provide peace and security on the continent? As an international organisation, the African Union in the Constitutive Act of 2001 establishes certain norms which are common values to be shared and protected by its member states. Some of these include its charter on Democracy and human rights, Anti-corruption fight, and commitment to good governance. However, norm compliance has been a major problem facing the organisation; this is because many of its member states do not comply with most of these norms (Interview, August 5, 2022).

The lack of compliance with the AU constitutive act of 2001 is evident in the pervasiveness of military takeover in many African states as well as increasing cases of human rights violations. For instance, there were military takeovers in 4 African states in 2021 which include the Republic of Guinea, Chad, Mali, and Sudan (Sany, 2022). In the following year, Burkina Faso also experienced a military coup where Captain Ibrahim Traore declared himself as head of state (African Center for Strategic Studies, 2022). These instances of political instabilities constitute a threat to the AU's efforts at democratic consolidation on the continent. The decline of democracy on the continent is also hurting the continent's corruption perception index. Out of the 50 most corrupt countries in the world, 26 of them are in Africa (Transparency International, 2022). The prevalence and pervasiveness of corruption have been described as one of the major causes of insecurity in West Africa and other parts of the continent (Transparency International, 2020).

Another problem with the AU's status as a security actor is its inability to effectively use military and non-military means to address the problems of non-compliance to its norms by its member states. For instance, there have been economic sanctions through RECs against the military junta that grabbed power in Sudan, Mali, and Guinea Conakry. This is to force them to hand over power back to the civilians. Despite this, the military still holds on tight to political power in these countries. Another problem is the ineffectiveness of the African Standby force in the conflicts across the continent and in preventing emerging ones like in the case of Ethiopia recently.

More significantly, the ASF has been criticised as lacking consensus among its member states which significantly affects its ability to mandate a mission (Aboagye, 2012). This lack of political will among its member states to respond to a violent military threat shows the weakness of the AU as a security alliance and consequently as a credible regional security actor. Another significant criticism of the ASF is the fact that the regional economic communities (RECs), such as the Southern African Development Community (SADC) and Economic Community of West African States (ECOWAS), have very different perceptions of whether the AU or the United Nations (UN) should mandate the employment of the ASF (Aboagye, 2012). These two RECs in most cases prefer UN Security Council authorisation over those authorised by the AU. Apart from these defects associated with the ASF, the fact that most of the member states are politically and economically weak also renders it ineffective as a security actor.

However, the AU at its best can be described as a nominal security actor with limited capability and influence to manage its security threats. A Nominal Security Actor (NSA) is a type or form of security actor with institutional provision for security arrangement but without actual military capability or political will to march its aspiration with capability.

African Union Peace and Security Architecture: A Critique

Since its establishment in 2002, the AU has been able to make an institutional arrangement for conflict prevention and conflict management on the continent. Most of its human and financial commitment since its establishment has been towards ensuring peace and security on the continent (Vanheukelom, 2017). Its main institutional mechanism is the APSA, which is comprised of several instruments including:

1. Peace and Security Council
2. Continental Early Warning System
3. Panel of the Wise
4. African Standby Force
5. Peace Fund
6. Common African Defense and Security Policy.

The most important of all these instruments is the Peace and Security Council (PSC). This is because it is the major pillar of the APSA (African

Union, 2004). The effectiveness of others is anchored on the versatility of the PSC itself and the willingness of its members to authorise necessary actions. This is because the primary objective of the PSC is the prevention, management, and resolution of conflict. Hence most of the discussion in this section will be based on the capacity of the PSC and other subsidiaries of APSA to provide peace and security in Africa since its establishment in 2004. According to the African Union Protocol (2004) that establishes the AU Peace and Security Council, Article 5(3) makes it clear that APSA is to serve as a conflict prevention and resolution mechanism with powers to mount and deploy peace support operations. It is also responsible for the implementation of the union's common defence policy as well as the promotion of democracy and human rights.

Based on the powers allocated to the PSC by the African Union, it can be described in theoretical terms as a powerful security mechanism with the capability to achieve its targeted mandate. However, in two decades of its existence, Africa continues to harbour different forms of violent and security threats from both state and non-state actors. The views of the respondents for the study differ on the assessment of the extent to which the African Union PSC has been able to promote peace and security on the continent in the last 20 years. According to one of the participants who is a Nigerian diplomat with intensive familiarity with the workings of the AU being a former desk officer, he stated,

> The African Union has been active in responding to the security challenges on the African continent through training in best practices around the world as well as the provision of modern weapons and an increase in personnel for the ASF. However, the political will to make critical decisions and funding has been identified as its major challenges. (Interview, August 22, 2022)

The implication of this is that the African Union PSC is been adjudged a success in its effort to provide peace and security since its establishment in 2004. This view was also echoed by another respondent who noted that:

> The African Union in more than a decade since its establishment has adopted several instruments and mechanisms in policy documents to augment its conflict prevention capacity as a security actor. Hence, Africa is well equipped within the APSA as its blueprint for promoting peace and security in Africa. (Interview, August 29, 2022)

The views of these participants and many others like them demonstrate that the AU despite its numerous challenges has achieved some milestones in its effort to promote peace, security, and stability in Africa. Since its creation, it has been able to order 13 peace support operations with only one of them not deployed (Interview, August 22, 2022). The only one that was deployed but not authorised was the PSO in Burundi in 2015 which was objected to by its President (Karuhanga, 2015). Most of these PSOs have been deployed in conjunction with global contingents of the UN and sub-regional contingents from the RECs. The complex nature of the operation usually determines the effect of each of these operations and their ability to bring about peace in troubled areas. For instance, the African Union Mission in Burundi (AMIB) between 2003 and 2004 was replaced by the UN mission with stronger response capability.

The same scenario also occurred in the Central African Republic between 2013 and 2014 when the AU PSC mission ended with the transfer of authority from the African-led Support Mission to the Central African Republic (MISCA) to the United Nations Multidimensional Integrated Stabilisation Mission in the Central African Republic (MINUSCA) on 15 September 2014 (African Union, 2022). Most of these aborted authorised missions are usually determined by the conflict's intensity and complexity, which requires a superior intervention. Opposing views to the PSC's efforts at promoting peace and security on the continent have described the framework as a paperweight with no real capability to solve Africa's numerous security problems. One of the participants who is an expert on regionalism from Obafemi Awolowo University noted that:

> Despite the change in the name of the OAU to the African Union and its consequent establishment of APSA with its various components as a conflict prevention mechanism, old problems that were associated with the OAU remain, while the African Union appears to be ill-equipped to confront emergent security challenges such as banditry, terrorism among others from non-state actors in the continent. Even older problems such as coup de tat that appear to have faded away are reoccurring while intrastate crises have not abated. The obvious reality is that the AU as a security actor is weak with little or zero norm compliance. (Interview, August 20, 2022)

Embedded in this view is the fact that the African Union despite its establishment of several conflict prevention mechanisms which include the PSC and other frameworks, its enforcement capacity remains very weak to address many of the security challenges bedevilling the continent. For instance, since it imposed sanctions on military rulers in Sudan, Mali, and Guinea Conakry, its deterrence effort has not been enough to compel the military rulers to organise elections and return power to civilians. This is against the backdrop of the fact that authoritarian regimes are responsible for most of the cases of human rights violations on the continent. Importantly, there is usually a conflict of misunderstanding between the AU and the RECs over the superiority of the United Nations deployment and AU-authorised mission. This lack of consensus between the AU and the RECs who are integral components of the PSC has often resulted in the inability on the part of the AU to mandate a successful mission (Aboagye, 2012).

The major factor responsible for the prioritisation of UN deployment over that of the AU by the RECs can be linked with the financial incapability of the AU. For instance, in 2015, about 95% of the total AU budget was financed by external partners such as the European Union (EU) member states, Japan, and China, while in 2016, external funding of the AU budget was estimated at 52% of the total budget (African Union, 2016). In 2017, AU member states contributed 27% of the budget while the remainder was funded by foreign donors who increased their commitment to projects, programmes, and Pan-African organisations (Pharatihalihe & Vanheukelom, 2019).

In his critique of the APSA, Williams (2015) argued that the African Union mechanisms in theory are supposed to function independently, but they have not been functioning that way. He further noted that for APSA to be able to function effectively, it needs a lot of support from development partners for capacity building. Apart from the financial problem as a major challenge of the AU, he also noted that the AU remains divided on a lot of issues that require collective support to be able to confront its challenges effectively. Some of these include:

1. Leadership in Peace Support Operations whether the lead role should be taken by the African Union or the RECs.
2. Value of Democratic governance structure in solving security issues.
3. Decision on whether to invest in the ASF or the APSA's immediate capacity for crisis response.

While this statement was made about seven years ago, AU member states remain divided on most of these issues and many others. The AU's conflict prevention mechanisms are expected to function as a collective security system while the AU itself is expected to enjoy commitment to the regional organisation for the progress of the continent.

However, African states usually demonstrate a lack of political will to implement many of its protocols that border on development and security issues. Another important issue to be noted here is that APSA as security architecture is anachronistic. This is because it was not designed to address emergent security issues such as non-military threats like climate change, poverty, and epidemic diseases. These are other categories of security threats that have been described as both a cause and a consequence of insecurity. Aside from this, the PSC is also not well positioned enough to address security threats from non-state actors such as terrorist and insurgent groups while most of its member states have little or no capacity to deal with this global menace.

It is on this ground that Nathan (2010) has described the African Union and the RECs in Africa as communities of insecurity because of their lack of expectation of a peaceful change. The AU and its security architecture are argued to be constructed on the expectation of conflict rather than that of peaceful change. This is in contrast with what is obtainable in the European Union where conflict has been absent for several decades and peaceful change has been the norm. A major cause of this is the persistent and obvious lack of unity among African states. Despite the existence of the AU, African unity remains elusive (Murithi, 2017). The overall implication of this is that a continuous lack of unity among the AU member states will continue to invalidate its efforts through the PSC and its other conflict prevention mechanisms to ensure peace and stability in Africa.

Conclusion

This article explored the African Union and its efforts at promoting peace and security on the continent through the African Peace and Security Architecture since its inception about two decades ago as a regional security actor. The APSA has been identified to comprise several components: Peace and Security Council, Peace Fund, African Standby Force, Panel of the Wise, Continental Early Warning System, and Common African Defense and Security Policy. The PSC has been described as the major mechanism that gives life to others because it has the primary responsibility of preventing, managing, and resolving conflicts on the continent. Since its inception, the PSC has resulted in ordering thirteen peace operations while only one was ordered and not deployed. This represents one of its success areas. However, the issue of funding, political divisions among the AU member states, and as well as conflicting authority between the AU and the RECs remains major impediment to the success of the organisation.

Based on this, the African Union can thus be described as a nominal regional security actor. This is because; it cannot actualise its aspirations of promoting unity among African states for peace and security. In the aspect of norm compliance, the AU does not function like a system while many of its member states usually prioritise their national interest at the expense of regional interest. This is coupled with the fact that its decisions on erring states are neither implemented nor ineffective because of a lack of capacity to enforce effective compliance to its norms when violated.

The chapter concluded that effort should be made to ensure the member state's compliance with the organisation's norms for greater efficiency and its excess reliance on external funding for its activities should be curbed. This will continue to tie the AU and its member states to the apron string of the donors. This can be cited as a major reason for late deployment or no deployment in crisis-prone areas. There is also a need for periodic and persistent appraisal of AU security architecture (PSC) to capture the immediate and future security needs of the continent with an integrated focus on violent and non-violent security threats.

References

Adebajo, A. (2011). *The Man Who Would Be King of Africa*. http://www.thegurdian.com/commentisfree/2011/aug/26/gaddafi-legacy-meddling-africa

Akindele, A., & Ossymen, G. (2015). Small Arms and Light Weapons Proliferation and the Problem of National Security in Nigeria. *International Affairs and Global Strategy, 29*, 12–20.

Aboagye, F. (2012). *A Stitch in Time Would Have Saved Nine*. http://www.issafrica.org/uploads/ASFPolBrief.pdf

African Center for Strategic Studies. (2022). *Understanding Burkina Faso's Latest Coup*. http://www.africacenter.org/spotlight.htm

African Union. (2004). *Protocol Relating to the Establishment of the Peace and Security Council of the African Union*. http://www.au.int>psc.html

African Union. (2016). *African Union Executive Council 26th Ordinary Session*. https://web.archive.org/web/20160305185920/http://www.au.int/en/sites/default/files/decisions/9666-ex_cl_dec_851_-_872_xxvi_e.pdf

Ake, C. (1981). *A Political Economy of Africa*. Longman.

Aniche, T. E. (2020). From Pan-Africanism to African Regionalism: A Chronicle. *African Studies, 79*, 70–87.

Awofeso, O., & Udokang, C. U. (2015). *Political Ideas: An Introduction*. MacGrace Publisher.

Buzan, B. (1983). *People, States and Fear: The National Security Problem in International Relations*. Harvester Press/Chapel, North Carolina University Press.

Buzan, B. (1991). *People, States, and Fear: An Agenda for International Security Studies in the Post-Cold War Era*. Nova Scotia.

Buzan, B., Waever, O., & De Wilde, J. (1998). *Security: A New Framework of Analysis*. Lynne Rienner.

Catia, C. (2023). *Political Science: Human Security*. http://www.britannica.com/topic/human-security

Commision on Human Security. (2003). *Human Security Now: Protecting and Empowering People/Commission on Human Security*. https://digitallibrary.un.org/record/503749?ln=en&v=pdf.html

Fafore, O. (2020). The African Union's Collective Security Mechanisms and the Challenge of Armed Non-state Actors. *Journal of African Union Studies, 9*(3), 87–109.

Franke, B. (2009). *Security Cooperation in Africa: A Reappraisal*. First Forum Press.

Furley, O., May, R. (2001). *African Interventionist States*. Routledge Publication.

Grieger, G. (2019). *China's Growing Role as a Security Actor in Africa*. EPRS: European Parliamentary Research Service. https://policycommons.net/artifacts/1337678/chinas-growing-role-as-a-security-actor-in-africa/1945642/ on 3 August 2022. CID: 20.500.12592/nkr5xf.

Haas, E. B. (1961). International Integration: The European and the Universal Process. *International Organisation, 15*(3), 366–392.

Holsti, K. J. (1995). *International Politics: A Framework for Analysis*. Prentice-Hall.

Karuhanga, J. (2015). *What Next After AU Authorizes Deployment of African Force in Burundi*? https://www.newtimes.co.rw/section/read/195435

Makinda, S. M., & Okumu, F. W. (2008). *The African Union: Challenges of Globalisation, Security and Governance*. Routledge.

Marshall, A. (2017). *The EU as a Security Actor: A Comparative Study of the EU & NATO Between 2006 and 2014* (A Master Thesis Submitted to the Department of Political Studies). University of Malmo.

Moller, B. (2009). *The African Union as Security Actor: African Solution to African Problems* (Working Paper No. 57). Development Studies Institute.
Muhudin, M. (2018). *Decision-Making and AU's Capacity to Attain Aspiration 3 of the Agenda 2063: The African Peace Security Architecture*. https://www.grin.com/document/470533?lang=en
Murithi, T. (2012). The African Union at Ten: An Appraisal. *African Affairs, 111*(445), 662–669.
Murithi, T. (2017). *The African Union: Pan-Africanism, Peace-Building and Development*. Routledge.
Muzee, H., Enaifoghe, A. O. (2019). Towards an Inclusive Model of African Regional Integration: How Effective has the Linear Model been so Far? *Journal of Economics and Behavioral Studies, AMH International, 11*(1), 55–65.
Nathan, L. (2010). The African Union and Regional Organisations in Africa: Communities of Insecurity. *African Security Review, 19*(2), 106–113.
Okafor, J., & Aniche, E. (2017). Deconstructing Neo-functionalism in the Quest for a Paradigm Shift in African Integration: Post-neo-functionalism and the Prognostication of the Proposed Continental Free Trade Area in Africa. *IOSR Journal of Humanities and Social Sciences, 22*(2), 60–72.
Onah, F. N. (2010). The Electoral Process and Succession Challenges in Nigeria: The Case of 2007 General Election in Enugu State. *Nigerian Journal of Political Economy, 4*(1 & 2): 76–94.
Palik, J., Rustard, S. A., & Methi, F. (2020). *Conflict Trend in Africa: 1989–2019*. Peace Research Institute.
Pettersson, T., Högbladh, S., & Magnus Öberg, M. (2019) Organised Violence, 1989–2018 and Peace Agreements. *Journal of Peace Research, 56*(4), 589–603.
Pharatihalihe, K., & Vanheukelom, J. (2019). *Financing the African Union on Mindsets and Money* (Discussion Paper No. 240). http://www.ecdpm.org/dp240/.htm
Reynold, P. (2002). *African Union Replaces Dictator's Club*. http://www.bbc.co.uk/2/hi.africa/2115736.stm
Ronen, Y. (2002). Libya's Diplomatic Success in Africa: The Reemergence of Qadhafi on the International Stage. *Diplomacy and Statecraft, 13*(4), 60–74.
Sabine, S. (2014). *Theoretical Approaches to European Integration*. Palgrave Macmillan.
Salaam, N. F., Usman, S. A. (2019). *Rudiments of Governemnt and Politics*. Concept Publications.
Sany, J. (2022). *A Sixth Coup in Africa? The West Needs to Up Its Game*. http://www.usip.org/publication
Schmitter, P. C. (2002). *Neo-Neo-Functionalism*. Oxford University Press.

Taylor, O. (2004). Challenges and Opportunities for Defining and Measuring Human Security. *Disarmament Forum*, 14–24.
Thomas, C. (1987). *In Search of Security: The Third World in International Relations*. Wheatsheaf Books.
Tieku, T. K. (2004). Explaining the Clash and Accommodation of Interests of Major Actors in the Creation of the African Union. *African Affairs, 103*(411), 249–267.
Transparency International. (2020). *The Common Denominator: How Corruption in the Security Sector Fuels Insecurity in West Africa.* http://www.transparency.org
Transparency International. (2022). *Corruption Perception Index 2022.* http://www.transparency.org/cpi
Tony, A., & Martha, H. (1983). *War in Uganda: The Legacy of Idi Amin.* Tanzania Publishing House.
United Nations Development Programme. (1994). *Human Development Report.* http://www.hdr.undp.org/en/content/human-development.html
United Nations Trust Fund for Human Security. (2012). *What Is Human Security?* http://www.un.org/humansecurity/what-is-human-security
Vanheukelom, J. (2017). *Understanding the African Union: How to Become Fit for Purpose.* http://www.ecdpm.org/publications/African-union-become-fit-purpose/.html
Waltz, S. M. (1991). The Renaissance of Security Studies. *International Studies Quarterly, 35*(2), 211–239.
Wayne, S. (1997). European Integration and Supranational Governance. *Journal of European Public Policy, 4*(3), 297, 317.
Weiss, M. (2008). The "Political Economy of Conflicts": A Window of Opportunity for CFSP? *Journal of Contemporary European Research, 4*(1), 1–17.
Williams, P. D. (2009). The Peace and Security Council of the African Union: Evaluating an Embryonic International Institution. *The Journal of Modern African Studies, 47*, 603–626.
Williams, P. (2013). *Security Studies—An Introduction* (Vol. 2). Routledge.
Williams, P. D. (2015). *Peace Operations in Africa: Challenges and Solutions.* http://www.youtube/k8Np_yXt7wc

CHAPTER 3

Operationalisation of the Abuja Treaty (1991) and the Impact of Economic Regionalism on the African Union's Peace and Security Architecture

Michael Washaya

Introduction

Financing peace and security in Africa on a sustainable basis is not only an African priority but a global strategic imperative, given the complex and interconnected nature of threats to international peace and security today (Africa Union, 2017). Financial incapacity has been cited in a wide body of peace and conflict literature and discourse as the foremost albatross around the African Union's (AU) Peace and Security counter-conflict objectives. Despite the injection of substantial financial aid into the AU Peace and Security operations by external partners, particularly

M. Washaya (✉)
College of Business, Peace, Leadership and Governance, Africa University, Mutare, Zimbabwe
e-mail: mwashaya@africau.edu

A. O. Akinola and E. A. Liaga (eds.), *Development and Regional Stability in Africa*, https://doi.org/10.1007/978-3-031-56695-0_3

the European Union (EU), Africa continues to be haunted by a malignant of perpetual and obstinate conflicts. The major disadvantage of the donor-recipient marriage is that the recipient is always at the mercy of the donor. If the EU bursts out due to the vicissitude of its own socio-political and economic environment, then the AU's Peace and Security counter-conflict operations would certainly feel the shockwaves, with far-reaching ramifications for the continent's peace endeavours.

The operationalisation of the Abuja Treaty of 1991 provides a real opportunity for African Peace and Security Architecture (APSA) to extricate itself from the shackles of donor syndrome and catapult it to financial self-reliance and self-sufficiency. The treaty provides for the creation of an African Economic Community (AEC) through a gradual process of coordination, harmonisation, and progressive integration of the activities of existing and future Regional Economic Communities (RECs) in Africa. This will be done in six successive stages over 34 years. However, it is the sixth (6th) stage of the treaty, which provides for the setting up of an African Monetary Union through the establishment of a Central Bank and a single African currency that forms the fulcrum of this submission. The operationalisation of the African Monetary Union (AMU) will offset the continent on a financially self-reliant and sustainable trajectory much to the benefit of APSA's objectives.

APSA and Its Operational Challenges

One of the most important institutions of the AU is the APSA. The APSA is a set of institutions, legislation, and procedures designed to address conflict prevention and promote peace and security on the African continent (European Union, 2018). The Constitutive Act of the African Union lays down the legal basis for the APSA (European Union, 2018). It is designed as a system of institutions, norms, and policies, whose threefold purpose is to deal with conflict dynamics, tackle security challenges, and promote sustainable development on the continent (Eric & Amegan, 2019). These include the Peace and Security Council (PSC), the Panel of the Wise (PoW), the African Standby Force (ASF), the Continental Early Warning System (CEWS), and the AU Peace Fund (Chekol, 2019). The APSA is at the centre of the AU's peace and conflict agenda, including conflict prevention, early warning and preventive diplomacy, peacemaking, and peacebuilding, encouraging and promoting democratic practices and intervention, and humanitarian action and disaster management (Chekol, 2019).

The AU considers peace from a comprehensive perspective, as illustrated in the Agenda 206 vision for "an integrated, prosperous and peaceful Africa, driven by its citizens representing a dynamic force in the international arena" (Eric & Amegan, 2019). One of the novel principles introduced by the APSA is the right of the AU "to intervene in a Member State under a decision of the Assembly in respect of grave circumstances, namely: war crimes, genocide and crimes against humanity" (in Article 4 of the AU Constitutive Act) (Eric & Amegan, 2019). This was an important novelty as it provided a legal basis for the intervention of the regional organisation to resolve inter-state disputes and internal conflicts that Africa often faces (Eric & Amegan, 2019).

Besides, the AU launched in May 2013 a flagship initiative called 'Silencing the Guns', whose main purpose was to promote a peaceful resolution of wars within the region and contribute to the achievement of Sustainable Development Goals (SDGs), as well as reinvigorate the spirit of Pan-Africanism and the African Renaissance (Eric & Amegan, 2019). Indeed, the PoW is a relevant component of the APSA as it is based on the African tradition of mediation entrusted to elders. It includes five prominent African leaders and can act on its initiative (Eric & Amegan, 2019).

According to the African Union (2017), the major challenge facing the AU is the lack of funds which has important unintended consequences. High levels of donor dependency have weakened ownership in this critical area of the AU's mandate and led to strategic drift, as the AU Commission increasingly focused on externally financed activities (Africa Union, 2017). There is general agreement that the current financing arrangements for peace support operations are neither reliable nor predictable, especially in the context of high-tempo combat operations (Africa Union, 2017). While partners have demonstrated much flexibility and innovation, there is consensus that the current financing arrangements are unsustainable (Africa Union, 2017).

One such area where the AU has exhibited gross financial incapacity is the AU-led Peace Support Operations (PSOs). In Africa, Peace Support Operations (PSOs) are increasingly tasked with broad and complex mandates including protection of civilians, stabilisation, counterterrorism and counterinsurgency, and long-term post-conflict reconstruction operations (Amani Africa, 2019). The AU has mandated, managed, and/or authorised some ten PSOs since its first mission to Burundi (Amani Africa, 2019). The largest, most deadly, and expensive mission of the AU to date is the AU Mission to Somalia (AMISOM) since 2007 (Amani Africa, 2019). However, the delivery of these mandates highly depends on the financial and technical partnership of the UN and other multilateral and individual partners (Amani Africa, 2019). The protracted nature of the deployment timeline of PSOs is the other factor that is posing a challenge in securing sustainable funding (Amani Africa, 2019). The human and capital cost of such counterterrorism operations is also very high (Amani Africa, 2019). Challenges related to resources and funding have mainly contributed to the decision of drawdown and the eventual exit of peacekeeping operations such as UNAMID and AMISOM (Amani Africa, 2019).

Indeed, APSA suffers from a serious financial dependence, which leads to a complex relationship with its external partners (Eric & Amegan, 2019). Due to weak financial ownership of the APSA by the African Union, the APSA has been for many years heavily dependent on the support of donors (European Union, 2018). The APSA is still largely funded by external regional and global institutions, particularly the European Union (Eric & Amegan, 2019). The EU provides financial support for the development of the APSA through the European Development Fund (EDF) (European Union, 2018). The main channel of EDF support comes through the African Peace Facility (APF), established by the EU in 2003, as well as through the Regional Indicative Programmes (RIPs) (European Union, 2018). Consequently, the shortfall in contributions by the AU member states to the AU budget and the Peace Fund left the APSA underfunded (European Union, 2018). AU–EU relations reflect how complex it is for the former to achieve its ambitions without strong autonomy (Eric & Amegan, 2019).

Acknowledging the problems associated with relying on donors, the AU member states decided in July 2016 on a new mechanism for financing the AU's operational budget and the Peace Fund (European Union, 2018). The EU has supported this initiative, imposing a 0.2% levy on all eligible goods imported into Africa, starting in 2017 (European Union, 2018). By January 2018, 14 member states had started collecting the levy, the Peace Fund was beginning to operate, and it had a governance structure (European Union, 2018). At the AU Summit in July

2016, the rule of a 0.2% levy on all acceptable imported goods on the continent was agreed upon, so that the AU could finance 100% of its operational budget from 2017 onwards (Eric & Amegan, 2019).

The July 2016 AU Assembly Decisions on the Peace Fund was a powerful demonstration of the AU's and its members' determination and commitment to assume primary responsibility for funding the Organisation's peace activities. However, this objective remains a theoretical ambition (Eric & Amegan, 2019). Against this backdrop, this research submits to the need for sustainable and homegrown peace funding solutions hence the strategic significance of the full operationalisation of the Abuja Treaty (1991). According to the foregoing, adopting a Single African Currency could provide viable options for the AU to extricate itself from the doldrums of financial quagmire currently bedevilling its peace and security obligations.

Theoretical Perspectives on Regional Integration

The Neo-functionalism Theory

This article applied the neo-functionalism theory to decipher how and why African nations chose to integrate into AEC as enunciated by the Abuja Treaty (1991). Among regional integration theories that have evolved since the 1960s, neo-functionalism remains one of the essential tools to understand why nations decide to put together their economic and political destinies and how a regional integration process unfolds (Insight Turkey, 2017). The EU remains the most advanced integration case so far, but integration movements may emerge in other parts of the world, as well (Insight Turkey, 2017). Manboah-Rockson (2021) articulates that Neo-functionalism was developed during the 1950s as a 'classic' among grand theories and narratives of European integration. It is a theory of regional economic as well as political integration building on the work of Ernest Haas (1958) and Leon Lindberg (1963) (Manboah-Rockson, 2021).

The basis of neo-functionalism is the concept of 'spillovers'—a process that refers to an initial decision by a government of a country to place a certain sector under the authority of a central institution, which creates pressure to extend the authority of the institution into neighbouring areas of policy (Manboah-Rockson, 2021). Neo-functionalists believe that cooperation in one field has a knock-on effect on the next field of cooperation which leads to another as in the modular construction of a house (Manboah-Rockson, 2021). Therefore, making further commitments towards a full-fledged political unification or integration is unstoppable or inevitable (Manboah-Rockson, 2021). This resonates well with the idea of a stagiest African Economic Community integration envisaged by its proponents who prescribed that for it to be realised, it had to begin at the regional integration level and then move to the continental level on a stage-by-stage basis.

The neo-functionalist model, which prioritises common actions and concrete achievements among state actors, preferably neighbouring ones that are willing to create an integrated entity, is based on "common solidarity" among those states (Insight Turkey, 2017). Members of such an integration movement must create common institutions towards which they are supposed to transfer progressively more competence (Insight Turkey, 2017). Africa has five (5) Regional Economic Communities (RECs) that have constituted united economies through closer economic and political ties. By devolving more authority to the supranational organisations they have created, states make sure that their citizens will begin shifting more and more of their expectations to the "union". The economic and social integration will then 'spillover' into political integration (Insight Turkey, 2017).

Pan-Africanists who birthed the Organisation of Africa Unity (OAU) that later transformed into the AU envisaged the eventual spillover of the African Economic Area into a political integration called the United States of Africa (Insight Turkey, 2017). The positive spillover effect is the notion that integration between states in one economic sector will create strong incentives for integration in further sectors to fully capture the perks of integration in the sector in which it started (Insight Turkey, 2017). The process of establishing an AEC was designed in such a way that because of the need for greater incentives, the RECs would further integrate into a continental economic community and if need be, into the United States of Africa (Insight Turkey, 2017).

The progress and the success of political integration depend on the success of economic integration and the willingness of—supposedly rational—political elites to persuade their nations to move forward (Insight Turkey, 2017). In this regard, political will has often been cited in the literature as one of the impediments to the full realisation of the Abuja Treaty (1991)'s objectives. However, the neo-functionalism theory fell short of explaining either implicitly or explicitly how the APSA would benefit from such integration in addressing its operational challenges. This gap was bridged by applying the optimum currency area theory.

The Optimum Currency Area Theory

Optimum Currency Area (OCA) theory was developed in 1961 by Canadian economist Robert Mundell based on earlier work by Abba Lerner (Mitchelle, 2021). OCA theory posits that implementing currencies by geographic and geopolitical region, instead of by country, leads to greater economic efficiency (Mitchelle, 2021). In other words, geographic regions may be better off using the same currency instead of each country within that geographic region using its currency (Mitchelle, 2021). Stage six (6) of the implementation of the Abuja Treaty (1991) proposes an integration of all sectors, the establishment of a Central Bank and a single African currency and setting up an African Monetary Union (Oppong, 2020). In this vein, the envisaged Single African Currency is poised to assume the role of the flagship currency of the African Economic Union.

The OCA literature has examined both one-off and permanent benefits and costs of participating in a currency area (Mongelli, 2002). According to Mongelli (2002), the main benefits of the OCA accrue from microeconomic efficiency and macroeconomic stability. Benefits from improvements in microeconomic efficiency result principally from the increased usefulness of money. For instance, the liquidity services provided by a single currency circulating over a wider area as a unit of account, medium of exchange, standard for deferred payments, and store of value. In such arrangements, greater price transparency will discourage price discrimination, decrease market segmentation, and foster competition (Mongelli, 2002). Mongelli (2002) further highlights that the more concentrated trade is in a currency area, the greater the savings in transaction costs are likely to be and resultantly this will strengthen the internal market for goods and services, foster trade, lower investment risks, and promote cross-area foreign direct investments (FDI) and enhance resource allocation.

Benefits from increased macroeconomic stability (and growth) resulting from improved overall price stability includes access to broader and more transparent financial markets increasing the availability of external financing; reputational gains for those members with a history of higher inflation that benefit from an anti-inflationary anchor; the reduction of some types of fluctuations of output and employment across the currency area due, possibly, to different economic policies (Mongelli, 2002). Microeconomic efficiency and macroeconomic stability across Africa would no doubt result in immense benefits to APSA's peace efforts. Firstly, microeconomic efficiency and macroeconomic stability in Africa would intrinsically improve financial inflows into the coffers of the Peace Fund from the contributions of member states of the Africa Economic Area. Secondly, microeconomic efficiency and macroeconomic stability across Africa would naturally and most likely result in the reduction and suppression of conflicts particularly those related to economic problems hence indirect benefits to APSA's financial conundrums due to reduced workload.

The Nexus Between Regional Economic Integration and Peace and Security

There is ample evidence both in literature and precedence linking regional economic integration with peace and security efforts. In literature, this relationship is rooted in the Peace-Security-Development nexus discourses. Peace, security, and development are also inextricably interlinked with regional integration and cooperation (Slocum-Bradley & Felício, 2006). While regional integration can contribute to economic development, regional cooperation is a prerequisite to the attainment of, as well as dependent upon, peace and security (Slocum-Bradley & Felício, 2006). As argued by Basri (2022), economic integration plays a critical role in promoting peace and security as the opportunity cost of interdependence reduces the likelihood of war. Involvement of different countries, people, and territories in similar integration processes, also on regional and sub-regional levels, with proper legal, institutional, and financial arrangements, can result in a long-term perspective in the creation of a firm ground for the prevention and peaceful settlement of both inter- and intra-state disputes and deadly conflicts (Voronkov, 1999).

The European regional economic integration, founded on a vibrant EU with its flagship currency (Euro), remains one of the classic examples of how peace and security matters can derive immense benefits from regional economic integration. In the immediate post-World War II era, the primary consideration was how to prevent inter-state wars in Europe, create a conducive environment for regional peace, order, and security, and build cooperation among the states and communities that would ensure interdependence (Francis, 2006). Consequently, when the European Coal and Steel Community was created in 1951 and the European Economic Community (EEC) in 1957, they were based on the notion of sharing regional collective resources in development and security terms (Francis, 2006).

Between 1960 and 2003, the EEC expanded to 25 member states in a European Union (EU), with a common 'European community identity'—a supranational institution in the form of a European Commission with a parliament and a common currency, the Euro (Francis, 2006). War has become unthinkable among the countries of the EU (Voronkov, 1999). The deep and broad interdependence of the EU member states made the risk of violent resolution of inter-state disputes and contradictions, within the EU, irrational and non-existent (Voronkov, 1999). Further, Leininger and Ritcher (2012) allude to the fact that it has been recalled that Europe's transformation from a continent of war to one of peace has been the greatest accomplishment of the European Union (EU) as evidenced by the fact that former archenemies as France and Germany have become permanent friends and close partners, and the division into East and West has been overcome.

In another case, the Association of Southeast Asian Nations (ASEAN), an association for regional cooperation among the countries of Southeast Asia, formed on 8 August 1967, has over the years demonstrated how regional economic integration can foster regional peace and security. According to the Thai Embassy (2022), since its inception in 1967, ASEAN has made several achievements towards regional peace, stability, and prosperity by advancing its agenda to cover three main pillars: political/security, economic, and socio-cultural. As pointed out by Basri (2022), ASEAN has been able to play an important role in maintaining Southeast Asia's peace since its formation.

During the Cold War, for example, ASEAN attempted to mitigate the negative impact of geopolitical tensions between the United States, the Soviet Union, and China (Basri, 2022). The development of the ASEAN cooperative framework has also led to a series of significant results: the Zone of Peace, Freedom, and Neutrality (ZOPFAN) declaration in 1971; the conclusion of the Treaty of Amity and Cooperation in Southeast Asia (TAC) in 1976; the establishment of the ASEAN Regional Forum (ARF) in 1994; and the conclusion of the Treaty on the Southeast Asia Nuclear-Weapon-Free Zone (SEA-NWFZ) in 1995 (Tomotaka, 2008).

The foregoing is a demonstration of the critical milestone achieved by ASEAN around regional peace and security since its formation.

The Abuja Treaty (1991)

According to Fasan (2019), Africa's quest for a single market dates back to the establishment of the Organisation of African Union (OAU) in 1963. The OAU, which brought together Africa's newly independent nations, had at its heart intra-Africa economic integration (Fasan, 2019). It aimed to emulate Europe by creating an African Economic Community, encompassing a single market and a customs union (Fasan, 2019). In 1980, the OAU adopted the Lagos Plan of Action for economic development of Africa through the formation of an African common market (Fasan, 2019). This was the precursor to AEC was signed in Abuja on 3 June 1991 and came into force in May 1994. In formulating the Treaty, African leaders recognised the various factors which hindered the development of the continent and seriously jeopardised the future of its people and took into account the various resolutions and declarations at previous summit meetings (In 1968, 1970, and 1973) which provided that economic integration was a prerequisite for the realisation of the objectives of the OAU (Mukisa & Thompson, 1995). It was aimed therefore at fostering the social, economic, and cultural development of the African continent through the integration of the economies of the various countries.

The treaty provides for the creation of an African Economic Community through a gradual process of coordination, harmonisation, and progressive integration of the activities of existing and future RECs in Africa. The proposed approach towards pan-African unity and continental industrialisation was to be by the division of the continent into RECs that would, through closer economic and political ties, constitute a united economy—the AEC (de Melo et al., 2017). This notion is buttressed by Oppong (2020) who highlights that rather than start from scratch, the AEC uses existing RECs as the building blocks of the AEC. In other words, progress by the RECs is progress for the AEC and a step closer to the actualisation of the AEC (Oppong, 2020). This was to be done in six successive stages over 34 years. Table 3.1 presents the stages and the required activities.

Table 3.1 The African Economic Community roadmap

Stages	*Activity*
Stage 1	Strengthening and creating RECs, like SADC, and ECOWAS, within the first 5 years
Stage 2	Stabilisation of tariffs and other barriers to regional trade and the strengthening of industry and energy (next 8 years) sectorial integration particularly in the fields of trade, agriculture, finance transport, and communication
Stage 3	Establishment of a free trade area (further 10 years)
Stage 4	Harmonisation of tariff and non-tariff systems (2 years)
Stage 5	The establishment of a Common Market and the adoption of a common policies (4 years)
Stage 6	Integration of all sectors, the establishment of a Central Bank and a single African currency, setting up an African Monetary Union, and creating and electing the first Pan-African Parliament

See Oppong (2020)

African Monetary Union and the Single African Currency: APSA Game Changer

The African Monetary Union (AMU) is an economic and monetary union, which looks to introduce a currency like the Euro (Osterholt, 2011). The plan to introduce a common currency is based on the Abuja Treaty that was signed on 3 June 1991 in Abuja, Nigeria (Osterholt, 2011). As contained in the treaty, there was a provision to set up an African Central Bank, and an AEC, with a single currency by around 2020 (Osterholt, 2011). The idea of a single African currency became clearer when OAU member states in 2001 agreed to transform the intergovernmental organisation into the AU (African Union Commission, 2010).

Shortly afterwards, in August 2003, the Association of African Central Bank Governors agreed to develop plans to establish a common central bank that would manage a single continental currency by 2021 (African Union Commission, 2010). This plan is poised to offer an African market with no internal frontiers in which the free movement of goods, persons, services, and capital is ensured (African Union Commission, 2010). This push for a single currency stands for an Africa of unity, integration, and strength (African Union Commission, 2010).

The single African currency is poised to revolutionise the AU's peace and security agenda in a significant way, especially given the current financial conundrum bedevilling APSA. In its press release of 27 January 2017, the Africa Union (2017) noted that the July 2016 AU Assembly Decisions on the Peace Fund was a powerful demonstration of the determination and commitment of the AU and its members to assume primary responsibility to fund the Organisation's peace activities. The AU noted, however, that the complexity of the issues, ranging from funding to crafting new partnerships with the UN, cannot be underestimated and will demand political will and a paradigm shift (Africa Union, 2017). In light of the above, this paper concurs with the AU's position and submits that the political will to fully operationalise the Abuja Treaty (1991) could be the paradigm shift that the AU needs to address its counter-conflict financial challenges.

As a follow-up to the Abuja Treaty (1991), in August 2003, the Association of African Central Bank Governors agreed to develop plans to establish a common central bank that would manage a single continental currency by 2021. This agreement resonates with the aims and objectives of the Abuja Treaty (1991)'s 6th stage plan of action. This research argues that the implementation of the 6th stage of the Abuja Treaty (1991), which could be regarded as the climax of the treaty's overall objectives, has the potential to catapult Africa into a prosperous and peaceful continent. Assuming that all economic fundamentals are in place, the benefits of a single African currency to the AU's Peace and Security counter-conflict objectives would be undoubtedly profound, realistic, and immense.

The success of the single European currency (Euro), which has become very central to many recent economic signs of progress in Europe by offering more efficient means of transacting businesses and using the human and institutional capabilities of the continent to foster more prosperity, has shown the power of integrated monetary structure in a globalised world (Ekekwe, 2010). A single African currency, if realised, would radically redefine Africa's social, political, and economic landscape and position the continent on a solid footing to tackle the enormous challenges of the twenty-first century (Ekekwe, 2010). A helicopter view of the EU attests to the accrued geopolitical and socio-economic benefits to the European continent brought about by using a single currency.

Vourexakis (2012) buttresses this assertion by pointing out that there's much more transparency between states not only on the obvious monetary affairs side but also on the political, with political allegiances becoming ever more strengthened by a continental monetary policy. States must work together on common policy where one might be left-wing and the other right (Vourexakis, 2012). This shared capitalism through fiscal federalism has seen and proved that political relationships and diplomacy are much more subject to flexibility for the advantage of the wider community than they are for domestic national interest (Vourexakis, 2012). By the same token, if implemented, the African Monetary Union would no doubt motivate member states to contribute more towards a common goal of continental interests ahead of national interests. Nations would be compelled to think and act "African" rather than "nationally". The shared unity of purpose would energize Africa to confront its challenges with sheer determination and sagacity.

Also, a unified currency will improve fiscal and monetary cooperation among member states (Ekekwe, 2010). Indeed, it is the lack of fiscal and monetary cooperation among AU member states that has among other factors impacted the efficient operationalisation of the Peace Fund. According to ISS/PSC (2021), obstacles remain to the implementation of the Peace Fund in a way that provides sustainable and predictable financing. The Peace Fund is tasked with the mammoth role of ensuring the availability of funds. However, Mystris (2020) notes with concern that most AU members struggle to meet their membership dues, and self-financing of the AU has yet to prove possible. This means that the fund struggles to secure support from African states (Mystris, 2020). The fund is financed from the AU's budget, fundraising, and voluntary contributions from AU members, individuals, civil society, international partners, and the private sector (Mystris, 2020).

The assessment of countries' contributions and the fund replenishment strategy has divided member states (ISS/PSC, 2021). States in Central, Eastern, Western, and Southern AU regions have agreed to use the general assessment scale for the fund's regular budget but most northern African countries, including Algeria, Egypt, Tunisia, Mauritania, Western Sahara, and Libya, have objected to the decision (ISS/PSC, 2021). Instead, they advocate a regional scale, through which the central African region would contribute 10% and other regions 22.5% of the expected total of US$325 million (ISS/PSC, 2021).

According to the Africa Union Peace and Security Council (PSC), the Northern region has not been paying its assessed contributions on time, but there are other defaulters. In 2018, sanctions were imposed on 18 non-paying member states but were, however, lifted in February 2021 (ISS/PSC, 2021). Unification of currency would more likely reduce bickering and non-compliance by member states thereby improving cash inflows into the Peace Fund.

It is imperative to highlight that the current standard working currency of the AU is the United States Dollar (USD). Essentially, member states have to contribute to the Peace Fund in the USD currency, and this presents a huge challenge to most member states that have to navigate their way through the exchange rate conundrum. Faced with the vicissitudes of microeconomic efficiencies and macroeconomic stabilities, most member states are found wanting when it comes to fulfilling their obligations to the Peace Fund. Thus, Sheehan (2022) contends that a single currency will help to address the region's monetary problems like the difficulty in converting some of its currencies.

There are some indirect benefits that APSA's counter-conflict agenda would derive from a Single African Currency. The single currency-development-peace nexus validates this notion. A single currency boosts development and consequently development contributes to peace and security. There is evidence that some conflicts in Africa are poverty and deprivation-induced as a result of underdevelopment among other factors. In any case, economy and peace are intimately linked (Vernon, 2016) and competition over access to resources is at the heart of most conflicts. The Arab Spring was sparked by the public suicide of a chronically jobless young man in Tunisia who had simply lost all hope (Vernon, 2016).

Long-term peace within and between societies is only possible when people have fair opportunities for a sustainable livelihood and the accumulation of assets, combined with general well-being, justice, and security, in a context of good governance (Vernon, 2016). A single African currency has the propensity to transform the overall economic fortunes of the continent. In the best-case scenario, the common currency union increases trade within the member states, this would make the African Union members more independent from other countries and therefore more sustainable development might happen (Osterholt, 2011). Buttressing the foregoing, Ekekwe (2010) alludes to the fact that a single African currency has many promises in terms of boosting trade and increasing economic cooperation among AU member states, increasing

Foreign Direct Investment (FDI) opportunities, expanding industrialisation and stimulating faster development efforts across the continent.

The AU believes that having a single currency will facilitate a stable currency for the continent's economic development, and more trade among member states can be ignited (Enaifoghe & Maduku, 2021). Stable currencies are argued to attract investment and more investment can benefit Africa by reducing poverty, thereby allowing economic development to take proper shape through integration (Enaifoghe & Maduku, 2021). Human and economic development would no doubt have some profound effects on peace on the continent. With good jobs and higher trade volume in the continent, member states will witness improved consumer welfare, and stronger political and mutual security ties (Ekekwe, 2010). Development and stronger political and mutual security ties would significantly reduce not only the number of conflicts in Africa but also the budget of the Africa Union's Peace and Security Council. A reduced AU counter-conflict expenditure would also go a long way in weaning Africa from donor dependency and moving towards self-sufficiency.

Conclusion

Operationalisation of the Abuja Treaty (1991) provides a realistic opportunity for APSA to self-fund and sustain its counter-conflict obligations on the continent and to disentangle itself from the opprobrium of a perennial beggar. As envisaged by its architects, the rationale behind the proposed Africa Economic Area, bolstered by a single currency, would result in microeconomic efficiency and macroeconomic stability for Africa. This economic trajectory will have ripple effects on the continent's institutional objectives including APSA's. Microeconomic efficiency and macroeconomic stability will result in the improved financial capacity of member states to contribute to the Peace Fund, thereby achieving financial self-sufficiency. Suffice it to say, this does not mean to undermine the contributions of other partners such as the EU and UN, but to complement them more sustainably. It is now incumbent upon the AU leadership to speed up the processes of merging the RECs as well as implementing the proposed Africa Free Trade Area as these are regarded as important precursors to the realisation of the Africa Monetary Area.

The study offers the following recommendations: the AU should expedite negotiations of a merger of the RECs without any ambiguity. Oppong (2020) suggests that negotiating a merger protocol should start now given the complexity and size of the undertaking. It should address inter alia issues relating to: the post-merger legal status of the RECs; their assets and liabilities after the merger; whether the merger is compulsory or voluntary and, if compulsory, how that is going to be enforced; when the merger is to occur (simultaneously for all the RECs or incrementally after each reaches the needed stage of integration); the status of their personnel; and the status of active (Oppong, 2020). It is imperative to take cognisance of the fact that remarkably, although the RECs are the building blocks of the AEC, they are not members of the AEC or parties to the AEC treaty. It is the individual African states that are parties to the AEC treaty and the treaties creating the RECs; hence, states are often parties to more than one of the RECs (Oppong, 2020).

The need and urgency to activate the promise of an African Free Trade Area (AFTA) cannot be overemphasised. AFTA is widely viewed as a precursor to the successful establishment of the African Monetary Area. Thus, the recently established African Continental Free Trade Area Agreement (AfCFTA) is the first step to realising a single currency (Sheehan, 2022). This all-important multilateral agreement is viewed as the catalyst for long-term continental prosperity and integration (Sheehan, 2022), including sustainable peace and security.

References

African Development Bank. (2014). *Bank Group Post-Conflict Assistance Policy Guidelines*. https://www.afdb.org/en/documents/document/bank-group-post-conflict-assistance-policy-guidelines-27092

Africa Union. (2017). *Africa Union*. https://au.int/en/pressreleases/20170127/main-successes-au-peace-and-security-challenges-and-mitigation-measures-place

African Union Commission. (2010). *Towards a Single African Currency*. https://au.int/sites/default/files/documents/31782-doc-congress_article_volume_2.pdf

Amani Africa. (2019, May 23). *Insights on the Peace and Security Council (PSC)* Report on the Challenges Faced by AU-Led Peace Support Operations. https://amaniafrica-et.org/insights-on-the-psc-report-on-the-challenges-faced-by-au-led-peace-support-operations/

Basri, M. C. (2022). Can Economic Cooperation and Integration Promote Regional Peace and Security? *East Asia Forum*. https://www.eastasiaforum.org/2022/05/02/can-economic-cooperation-and-integration-promote-regional-peace-and-security/#:~:text=Economic%20integration%20plays%20a%20critical,them%20to%20engage%20in%20conflict

Chekol, Y. G. (2019). Major Successes and Challenges of African Peace and Security Architecture (APSA). *International Journal of Political Science, 5*(2), 1–8.

De Melo, J., Nouar, M., & Solleder, J. (2017). *Integration Along the Abuja Road Map*. United Nations University.

Ekekwe, N. (2010). *Towards a Single African Currency*. https://au.int/sites/default/files/documents/31782-doc-congress_article_volume_2.pdf

Enaifoghe, A., & Maduku, H. (2021). Regional Policy Convergence and the Quest for a Single Currency Possibility for Africa. *African Journal of Public Affairs, 12*(2), 85–100.

Eric, D. D., & Amegan, C. K. (2019). The African Peace and Security Architecture: An African Response to Regional Peace and Security Challenges. In A. Kulnazarova & V. Popovski (Eds.), *The Palgrave Handbook of Global Approaches to Peace* (pp. 393–409). Palgrave.

European Union. (2018). *The African Peace and Security Architecture: Need to Refocus EU Support*. https://www.eca.europa.eu/en/Pages/DocItem.aspx?did=46676

Fasan, O. (2019). *AfCFTA: Africa Is Moving Too Slowly Towards Economic Integration*. International Growth Center. https://www.theigc.org/blogs/afcfta-africa-moving-too-slowly-towards-economic-integration. Accessed 16 August 2022.

Francis, D. J. (2006). Linking Peace, Security and Developmental Regionalism: Regional Economic and Security Integration in Africa. *Journal of Peacebuilding & Development, 2*(3), 7–20.

Insight Turkey. (2017). *Insight Turkey*. https://www.insightturkey.com/articles/neo-functionalist

ISS/PSC. (2021, December 1). *Peace Fund Lies Dormant as Member States Discuss Its Use* (Report, PSC). ISS, Pretoria.

Leininger, J., & Ritcher, S. (2012). *Peace in the World: What Can the EU Achieve?* https://www.idos-research.de/en/the-current-column/article/peace-in-the-world-what-can-the-eu-really-achieve/

Manboah-Rockson, J. K. (2021). Grabbing the 'Bull' by the 'Horns': A Critical Analysis of the Establishment of AfCFTA. *Open Journal of Political Science, 11*(2), 301–315.

Mitchelle, K. (2021). *What Is the Optimum Currency Area (OCA) Theory?* https://www.investopedia.com/terms/o/optimum-currency-area-theory.asp

Mongelli, F. P. (2002, April). *"New" Views on the Optimum Currency Area Theory: What Is EMU Telling Us?* (Report for European Central Bank. Working Paper Number 138).

Mukisa, R. S., & Thompson, B. (1995). Prerequisites for Economic Integration in Africa: An Analysis of the Abuja Treaty. *The Politics of Economic Integration in Africa, 42*(4), 56–80.

Mystris, D. (2020). *The AU's Peace and Security Architecture: Filling the Gaps*. https://theconversation.com/the-aus-peace-and-security-architecture-filling-the-gaps-144554

Oppong, R. (2020). The African Union, the African Economic Community, and Africa's Regional Economic Communities: Untangling a Complex Web. *African Journal of International and Comparative Law, 18*(1), 92–103.

Osterholt, K. (2011). *Is It Beneficial for the African Union to Introduce a Common Currency?* GRIN Verlag Publishers.

Sheehan, J. K. (2022, March 18). Africa Needs to Move to Single Currency to Boost Intra-continental Trade. *Namibian Economist*. https://economist.com.na/69044/columns/africa-needs-to-move-to-single-currency-to-boost-intra-continental-trade/#:~:text=A%20single%20currency%2C%20even%20if,prospects%20of%20the%20African%20market

Slocum-Bradley, N., & Felício, T. (2006). *The Role of Regional Integration in the Promotion of Peace and Security* (Working Paper for UNU-CRIS. Working Paper Number O-2006/2). UNU-CRIS, Bruges.

Thai Embassy. (2022). *ASEAN at 55: Achievements and Challenges Ahead*. https://lisbon.thaiembassy.org/th/content/asean-at-55-achievements-and-challenges-ahead?

Tomotaka, S. (2008). *ASEAN Security Community: An Initiative for Peace and Stability* (NIDS Security Reports).

Vernon, P. (2016, February 2). Bread and Peace: Linking Economic Development with Peacebuilding. *Ecdpm*. https://ecdpm.org/work/prosperity-for-peace-volume-5-issue-1-february-2016/bread-and-peace-linking-economic-development-with-peacebuilding

Voronkov, L. (1999). Regional Cooperation: Conflict Prevention and Security Through Interdependence. *The International Journal of Peace Studies, 4*(2). https://www3.gmu.edu/programs/icar/ijps/vol4_2/cover4_2.htm

Vourexakis, A. (2012). *The Benefits and Challenges of Economic & Monetary Union*. https://www.e-ir.info/2012/08/08/the-benefits-and-challenges-of-economic-monetary-union/

CHAPTER 4

A Critical Assessment of the Challenges of the African Union Transition Mission in Somalia (ATMIS)

Emmaculate Asige Liaga and Habdisalan Mohamud Habib

Introduction

Preceded by other regional peace interventions including the African Mission in Burundi (AMIB, 2003), the African Union Mission in Sudan (AMIS, 2004), and Africa-led international support to Mali (AFISMA), the establishment of the African Union Mission in Somalia (AMISOM, 2007) was certainly one of the most significant and challenging African Union-led peace support operations. Authorised in 2007 by the African Union (AU) through its Peace and Security Council's Communiqué of 19th January and United Nations (UN) through Security Council resolution 1744 of 20 February under Chapter VII (United Nations, 2008) of the UN Charter, AMISOM was given the task of implementing a

E. A. Liaga (✉)
Institute for Pan-African Thought and Conversation, University of Johannesburg, Johannesburg, South Africa

H. M. Habib
Somali Weyn Development Organization (SOWDO), Mogadishu, Somalia

A. O. Akinola and E. A. Liaga (eds.), *Development and Regional Stability in Africa*, https://doi.org/10.1007/978-3-031-56695-0_4

peace enforcement mandate aimed at bringing peace and stability in Somalia. After decades of lawlessness, instability, and a longstanding political vacuum following the end of Mohamed Siad Barre's totalitarian clan-based regime in 1991, which led to the total disintegration of the State, the legal system, and security forces, AMISOM emerged. This was when an Islamic Shari'a-based system became prominent, with the rise and ascension of the Islamic Courts Union (ICU) in 2006 (Dias, 2010).

Furthermore, in the aftermath of the 9/11 terrorist attacks in the United States, the establishment of AMISOM was influenced by geopolitical and national security interests both at global and regional levels; the US-led Global War on Terror (GWOT); and the evolving partnership between the AU and UN in peace and security. Indeed, the establishment of AMISOM was the first kind of arrangement in which the UN broke the ground by authorising the funding of a regional force for an active combat operation through Resolution 1863 of 2009. This created the standalone UN Support Office for AMISOM (UNSOA), later renamed as UN Support Office in Somalia (UNSOS), whose mandate was to provide logistical and financial support to the AU forces fighting the war against al-Shabaab and other radical groups in Somalia (United Nations, 2009).

The main aim of the chapter is to highlight the challenges of AU policy in Somalia as it transitions its peace support mission from AMISOM to ATMIS while also highlighting the salient and challenging task for the still weak Federal Government of Somalia (FGS). The prospects for peace and security in the most conflict-ridden nation of the Horn of Africa how the new ATMIS mission can meet its achievements without leaving negative consequences to the recovering Somalia and the positive expectations of brotherly AU inputs in the past two decades.

Mandate Implementation

The assessment of how AMISOM went about carrying out the tasks assigned by the African Union Peace and Security Council (AUPSC) and United Nations Security Council (UNSC) through successive resolutions over the past fifteen years is twofold. On the one hand, aspects such as logistical and operational challenges had a significant impact on mandate implementation which revealed some design flaws and operationalisation of a regional peace support operation of this nature. As noted earlier, AMISOM's logistical support was provided by UNSOA. However, UNSOA struggled to overcome the clash of organisational cultures between the UN and AMISOM. The central problem was that UNSOA was based on UN procedures, mechanisms, and frameworks designed for more traditional UN peacekeeping operations in relatively benign environments but tasked with supporting a war-fighting mission.

As expected, UNSOA was simply overwhelmed and could not keep up with AMISOM's more intense tempo of operations, especially once the mission was expanded beyond Mogadishu. In addition, the UNSOA-AMISOM partnership broke one of the cardinal rules of war: commanders should always be in control of their logistics. While generally sympathetic to UNSOA, several senior AMISOM commanders saw their separation from their logistical support as fundamentally problematic and ill-advised, as would most military commanders. UNSOA's principal weakness was its structural design and the political terms on which it was established (Williams, 2018).

Another major challenge that was widely recognised and influenced AMISOM's ability to effectively implement its mandate was the issue of command and control. UN Security Council Resolution 2628 (2022) mandates the AU to put in place the necessary structures for command and control of the mission and ensure operational coordination between its contingents, in addition to coordinating operational decision-making under a Force Commander and Sector Commanders, among others.

As per the AUPSC communique issued on 8 March 2022, ATMIS was to be led by a Special Representative of the Chairperson of the African Union Commission, to whom each component—military, police, and civilian shall report separately. The Force Commander, who would come from the largest Troop Contributing Country (TCC), would have clear command and control over all the forces for the mission. The UN peacekeeping doctrine provides clear guidelines and policy on authority, command, and control in UN-led peacekeeping operations. This binding policy applies to all UN peacekeeping operations authorised by the UNSC and defines and describes the strategic, operational, and tactical levels of authority, command, and control. The policy also defines the tasking authorities for both military and civilian logistics units within the integrated logistics system of the UN peacekeeping operations. Clear command and control arrangements support greater cohesiveness among all mission elements, allow for efficient and effective implementation of mandates, and strengthen the mission's preparedness to handle crises (United Nations, 2008).

However, in the case of AMISOM, there is overwhelming evidence that points out the structural fault lines regarding the issue of command and control. For example, a major incident of a gun battle, which exposed the absence of a unified command and control structure in AMISOM, took place in September 2013 following a night-time raid by al-Shabaab militants (Horn Bulletin, 2022). The militants were engaged by Somali troops commanded by the regional administration (partnered closely with AMISOM), repelled the attack, and sustained causalities. Unfortunately, the request made by Somali officials for medical evacuation. the establishment of AMISOM was the first kind of arrangement in which the UN broke the ground by authorising the funding of a regional force to an active combat operation through Resolution 1863 of 2009—Reshaping the African Union Mission in Somalia (Horn Bulletin, 2022).

From AMISOM to ATMIS combat operation through resolution 1863 of 2009, which created the standalone UN Support Office for AMISOM (UNSOA), later renamed as UN Support Office in Somalia (UNSOS) whose mandate was to provide logistical and financial support to the AU forces fighting the war against al-Shabaab and other radical groups in Somalia (United Nations, 2009). Therefore, given the potential implications on the ground, in its resolution 2297 of 2016, the UNSC specifically called for the strengthening of command and control within AMISOM, cross-sector operations, and the generation/deployment of quick reaction forces (QRF) as well as force enablers and multipliers under the central command of the mission's Force Commander.

On the other hand, a critical assessment of AMISOM's fifteen years presence in Somalia has also revealed major fault lines that are consequential in regional peace support operations. This emerged in the form of pre-existing conditions reflecting the geopolitical and national security interests pursued by state actors involved both at the global and regional levels. For instance, in 2016, a prominent former Somali diplomat and political analyst, Abukar Arman argued that Somalia needed a strategic partner that was willing to pressure the neighbouring tag team—Ethiopia and Kenya—to step aside; to weigh in and put economic pressure on key actors to engage in genuine Somali-led reconciliation; and to help rebuild the National Army and security apparatus that is capable of keeping al Shabab at bay (Arman, 2016).

Through such pronouncements, Abukar Arman was certainly expressing his concerns and focusing on the interference by Somalia's neighbouring countries in the peace efforts and the apparent pursuit of their national security interests, while playing an active role in the implementation of the AMISOM mandate. Yet, both countries have been concerned with the dangers to States' survival which is consistent with the realist tradition (Keohane, 2012).

Furthermore, as Somalia and the Horn of Africa (HoA) in general became more and more the focus of attention in the post-9/11, 2001 coupled with the confluence of developments in the global geopolitical and geostrategic landscape, the overall AMISOM operating environment was inevitably shaped by other foreign interventions which also impacted on the implementation of its mandate. Thus, the prospects and purpose of external intervention changed dramatically in 2006 when the ICU took over power in Mogadishu. This introduced new dynamics and raised the interests of Western powers concerned about the threat of international terrorism and the situation in Somalia, particularly the United States increasingly renewed its strategic interests in the Horn of Africa (HoA).

The United States feared the threat of terrorism in the region and had accused the ICU of harbouring international terrorists associated with the 1998 East African simultaneous embassy bombings in Nairobi and Dar-es-Salaam. These US security concerns at the time, coincided with those of the most powerful regional states (Kenya, Ethiopia, and to some extent Uganda) in the sub-region. This is because the emergence of Islamism as a political force in Somalia gave the conflict a regional dimension with implications for Ethiopia and Kenya, which both have sizeable Somali communities within their borders (Healy, 2009). Meanwhile, the ever-growing influence of some Gulf Cooperation Council (GCC) countries and Egypt, particularly Saudi Arabia and Qatar who, on the one hand, have been engaged in the pursuit of an Islamist agenda.

Despite Qatar's relatively small size and population with a foreign policy impetus and objectives characterised as something of a black box and its long history in Somalia, the Gulf nation has played a powerful role in the country's politics since 2006 which was prompted by the rise of the ICU, their short-lived rule, and the subsequent atomisation of Islamist movements in the country. Doha used personal and religious networks to seriously engage with Islamist factions and former ICU members to influence politics in Somalia. Crucially, after Ethiopia invaded Somalia and ended the ICU's rule in 2006, Qatar hosted some of the ICU leadership members which included Sheikh Sharif Ahmed whose subsequent election as President in 2009 was possibly funded by Qatar despite later falling out with Doha when it insisted on expanding the government to include violent Islamists such as Hassan Dahir Aweys and his Hisbul Islam (Cannon, 2019).

The rivalries among members of the GCC—referred to earlier—had further complicated the situation in Somalia. Competition between the United Arab Emirates (UAE), Saudi Arabia, on the one hand, and Qatar and, by extension, Turkey, on the other hand, has aggravated longstanding intra-Somalia disputes. Notably, this has been the case between factions in the capital; between Mogadishu and the regions; and between it and the self-declared Republic of Somaliland. Abu Dhabi's relations with the government of the current President Mohamed Abdullahi Mohamed 'Farmajo' have tanked. Farmajo's government accused the Emiratis of funding its rivals and stoking opposition, particularly in Somalia's federal states. Emirati officials denied meddling and instead accused Farmajo of falling under Doha's and Ankara's sway (Crisis Group, 2018) aimed at promoting Wahhabism in Somalia while Egypt, on the other hand, sought to promote the Salafi views of the Muslim Brotherhood there was not a welcomed development by everyone, especially Ethiopia. Indeed, the expansion of radical Islam in Somalia may explain why more than ever, Ethiopia has continuously felt the need to adopt policies capable of influencing the political and security landscape inside Somalia (Ali, 2011).

The animosity, diplomatic tensions, and political rivalry that erupted in June 2017 within the GCC have had a spill-over effect reaching and significantly influencing the security dynamics and political shifts underway across the HoA region. Also, the impact of the Saudi-led intervention in Yemen has added to the complexity and volatility of the region which not only has challenged Somalia's federalism process but further complicated an already intricate situation with the balance of power shifting among the countries involved such as Qatar and UAE. These factors have altered old alliances in the region, eased access to weapons, and more importantly led to further militarisation which adds to the complexity and volatility of the region (Ali, 2011).

In summary, the various factors considered demonstrate the extent of complexity that surrounded the implementation of AMISOM's mandate between 2007 and 2022. Besides internal divisions and political dynamics, the analysis also shows that the competing international and regional interests of the actors involved in the peace efforts in Somalia have the potential to dictate the outcome and developments on the ground. While the African Union (AU) forces were engaged in the implementation of the peace enforcement mandate and fighting the war against al Shabab, the political process, consolidation of peace, and state-building efforts were being overshadowed by ongoing internal divisions and constant political tensions between the central Federal Government and federal member states, lack of meaningful progress towards political reconciliation and rebuilding of match needed government institutions across Somalia.

While there was a successful transfer of power in 2012 and 2017, the elections were also marred by widespread allegations of lack of transparency, procedural irregularities, and meddling in the electoral process by outsiders. Qatar's attempt to influence the political landscape did not stop with the withdrawal of support for Hassan Sheikh. Instead, it extended its financial support to Mohamed Abdullahi Mohamed 'Farmaajo' in the 2017 Somalia presidential election, the UAE reportedly also tried to influence the outcome of the election but ultimately failed in its bid to locate a suitable candidate (Cannon, 2019).

Faced with the failure to influence the outcome of the elections, Abu Dhabi has made strategic moves to remain an influential actor in the country including in the breakaway Somaliland where it has expanded its sphere of influence. To do so, it has used two main instruments: control of the ports and the establishment of military bases. The semi-autonomous regions of Somaliland and Puntland welcomed the Emirati initiative and allowed the UAE military to operate in these regions despite the explicit complaints from the Federal Government that Emirati activities have undermined its national unity (Ajú, 2022).

It is, therefore, not surprising that progress on security has been hampered by the political wrangling which has been in the spotlight recently and resulted in a power struggle at the highest level of the government between Prime Minister Mohamed Hussein Roble and the incumbent President Mohamed Abdullahi Mohamed 'Farmaajo'. As the Federal Government continued to be divided into the next steps in the electoral process and election deadlines were missed amid continued manipulation of the process, with state and federal leaders manoeuvring to install loyalists in parliamentary seats, al Shabab has not only exploited and increased attacks to derail the process but also launched large-scale attacks on strategic locations. In March 2022, al-Shabaab launched a twin suicide attack on an election venue in Hirshabelle state's Beledweyne city killing at least 48 people including MP Amina Mohamed Abdi. Militants also breached the highly fortified Mogadishu's Halane Airport perimeter for the first time since 2014, killing at least six people, including five foreign nationals. In another attack, al Shabab killed two electoral delegates in the Lower Shabelle region (Southwest State) and Mogadishu, respectively (Crisis Group, 2022).

It is within such a political and security landscape that Somalia's international and regional partners including the AU and UN will continue to rally support towards the rebuilding of strong state institutions, especially the security forces that will take over from ATMIS which is expected to withdraw by the end of December 2024 as stipulated in the Somalia Transition Plan (2021–2023). One thing is evident though, the plan has raised the stakes for AU's policy in Somalia and scepticism among Somalis including analysts. As the maxim says, *whoever wishes to foresee the future must consult the past*. Indeed, human events have a way of repeating itself. This stems from the reality that these outcomes are driven by individuals who have always been and will always be, motivated by the same passions, leading to inevitable similarities in results.

The closing of one page and opening of another by the AU, with the transition from AMISOM to ATMIS, warrants some reflections, particularly, on the successes and shortcomings that marked its one-and-a-half decade-long presence in Somalia. But first, it is worth noting that as an AU-led peace support operation, the AMISOM intervention fits within the mantra of African-led solutions to African problems (AfSol) in addressing the many challenges faced throughout the continent, particularly armed conflicts, and terrorism.

As a concept, AfSol has been used by some scholars in their assessment of AMISOM's successful or unsuccessful record in the past fifteen years. For example, Sebastiano Rwengabo has presented a positive argument regarding the success of the mission, suggesting that it supports the growing optimism in both scholarly and policy circles about Africa's ability to address its peace and security challenges through regionally focused approaches. In contrast to interventions not centred on Africa, AMISOM adopted the AfSol approach, built on pillars of genuine commitment, shared Pan-African values, and a collective sense of responsibility. Faced with the challenge of influencing election outcomes, Abu Dhabi strategically positioned itself to maintain influence in the country, including the breakaway region of Somaliland, where it expanded its sphere of influence through ownership and successfully encouraged states to bear the mission's costs while actively mobilising foreign support. Moreover, the willingness to undertake a risky operation and suffer large numbers of casualties without withdrawing reveals a sense of ownership, which was absent in previous interventions in Somalia (Rwengabo, 2016).

Meanwhile, as part of the lessons learned at the tenth anniversary in 2017, a strategic review of the mission conducted by the AU both praised AMISOM for its good work done under extremely challenging circumstances and criticised it for not having done enough in its 10-year presence in Somalia (Dessu & Mahmood, 2017). This introspective assessment is quite revealing in that it illustrates the cautious optimism in hailing the mission as having fulfilled its mandate successfully and highlights the fact that the success story emanating from an AfSol perspective is not shared by all. Another major strategic task assigned by the mandating principals to AMISOM was the re-establishment and training of all-inclusive Somalia's Security Forces (SSF) that would eventually assume the security responsibilities after the AU withdraws its troops from the country. However, there is evidence to suggest that the lack of a common agenda among key stakeholders undermined the attainment of this critical objective. African Union Mission in Somalia.

As it turned out, trained entirely independent of both AMISOM and the Somali National Army (SNA) leadership, and in general contradiction to the international community's agenda, several hundred Somalis were being trained and paid by the Ethiopian forces. In this way, different groups of armed Somalis—which may or may not be presented as SNA members—were supported with one aim in mind: the establishment of border security. This situation exposed the obvious weakness of the FGS and by extension the SNA. More importantly, it questioned the willingness of the TCCs to support, and thus AMISOM's ability to fulfil, the mandate of the mission. It also shows the limited room that the broader international community in Somalia can manoeuvre. While it holds that none of the above should detract from the successes that AMISOM has had over the years, it has become evident that realism, not idealism or liberalism, should be the mantra guiding expectations of the mission (Albrecht, 2015). In analysing AMISOM, the 'African solutions for African problems' motto has been branded as one of the most confusing phrases in Africa today. Therefore, it is not surprising that the interventions from neighbours have not brought Somalia the promised peace (Arman, 2014).

African solutions are often problematic and riddled with hidden agendas and tagged as traditional interventions. While African solutions sound more legitimate, interventions by African states are often no less controversial than international ones. For example, Ethiopia's and Kenya's interventions in Somalia in 2006 and 2011, respectively, have been deeply problematic and have had less to do with stabilising that country and more to do with their national concerns, even after the two countries were integrated as part of AMISOM (Ero, 2013).

In summary, there is no doubt that the overall security situation in the country improved significantly since AMISOM was established. It is also evident that AMISOM's ability to A map showing alleged territorial control by terrorist groups in Somalia as of December 2021 effectively implement its mandate was impacted by the global geopolitical interests and security dynamics of the regional countries involved which intersect with their national security interests in the whole sub-region of the Horn of Africa due to the centrality of Somalia. However, while AMISOM has undoubtedly laid the operational and strong security foundation, it remains to be seen how ATMIS will carry out the implementation of its mandate to eradicate and ultimately defeat al-Shabaab.

The Challenges of Transition

"The future of Somalia depends on the defeat of al-Shabaab, but it is also very clear that our success in this battle is of importance to the whole world" (Sharmarke, 2010). Much has happened since the above sentiment was expressed and most certainly echoed by Somalis and those who wish to see a peaceful and stable Somalia today. The reality is that not much has changed since then although the AU, together with international partners, has remained resolute in the quest for peace and stability through AMISOM which has now been transformed into 9 ATMIS on 1 April 2022.

This transition comes at a time when several assessments and lessons learned about AMISOM have highlighted a few operational, strategic, and tactical flaws during its fifteen years of existence in Somalia. Based on the experiences with AMISOM, several challenges would impact the transition to ATMIS and subsequently into the SSF. First, the mission's success and exit are expected to rely on the handover of military responsibilities to an effective Somali replacement. But the Somali National Army remains as politicised and clan-divided as it has ever been, and at present, little improvement seems likely in the short to medium term. Secondly, the al Shabab, the extremist Islamic insurgency, may continue to be a major threat. Third, there is the issue of TCC countries to AMISOM who have, to some extent, been fighting their separate wars for their reasons under the AMISOM banner and finally, the almost deliberately unsettled divisions of power and responsibilities between the FGS in Mogadishu and the federal member states.

Fourth, the absence of the required space for civil society organisations (CSOs), especially for those working in the field of peacebuilding awareness raisings will demean the impact of the mission as most of the society still regards ATMIS as having the same role as the former AMISOM mission. Fifth, ATMIS should be managed carefully and has to confirm a Somali National Force (SNA) free from clan bias, as this may lead to another civil war when the National Army is just from one clan or most of them are from Clan A, which might lead to clan clashes that have defined Somalia's conflict. Finally, the ATMIS mission should have the continental leadership for ensuring the 'Silencing of Guns' initiative, as members of the Somalis strategic committee. Indeed, almost all ordinary Somalis are armed except the farming and agricultural communities. The strategic committee plays a crucial role in facilitating comprehensive awareness initiatives involving the FGS and CSOs to promote the disarmament of the Somali population, contributing to the goal of a peaceful and secure nation.

AMISOM's Replacement and the Prevalent Political Tensions

Divisions among Somalia's elites over the distribution of power and resources are at the centre of all the problems. Moreover, with the political impasse and protracted power wrangling sometimes boiling over into armed clashes, the country's future remains unpredictable. Therefore, if it is to be anything different from AMISOM, ATMIS' mandate and force reconfiguration should include robust political engagement to support reconciliation among the country's divided political groups. Otherwise, the exercise simply renames the mission—which will not help the country much (Dessu, 2022).

Moreover, the bulk of the SNA remains a collection of clan-animated militias with few effective military characteristics that Westerners recognise. Foreign military assistance aimed at rebuilding a strong SSF has regrettably become deeply entangled with vested interests, helping to aid various political players against each other. The result is foreign-supported, and semi-detached parallel forces like the US-supported

Danab (probably the most effective military force in southern Somalia), the Turkish-supported Gorgor, the police Haram'aad, the intelligence agency's Gashan, and the newer Eritrean-trained forces.

Looking ahead, the challenge for the transition involves meeting specific targets and timelines. This includes collaboration between the Federal Government of Somalia and federal member states to establish a total of 3,850 security forces by December 2022, 8,525 by September 2023, and 10,450 by June 2024, as outlined in the Somalia Transition Plan (STP) and National Security Architecture (NSA) (United Nations, 2022). From the above, it is evident that stakes for peace and stability have once again been raised with the underlying security implications within Somalia and across the region. Finally, at the heart of finding durable security solutions lays an imperative that compels ATMIS to avoid falling into the same pattern of AMISOM's shortcomings, otherwise lasting peace and stability will remain an elusive grand ambition in the war-torn nation of the Horn of Africa.

Conclusion and Recommendations

The transformation of AMISOM into ATMIS illustrates the reshaping of the AU's policy in Somalia amidst the challenges highlighted in this article. This change also reflects the Federal Government of Somalia's transition plan (2021–2023), built upon national perspectives and policy objectives. Whereas AMISOM's legacy has arguably been associated with mixed results, the transition may prove to be rocky for several reasons. First, from AMISOM to ATMIS then gradually from the latter to the Somali Security Forces (SSF), which is fragmented and ill-prepared.

Second, while it attempts to build from AMISOM's legacy, the FGS continues to battle with a myriad of issues including a lack of progress towards security nationwide, political reconciliation challenges, and weak state institutions coupled with other external factors. Third, the envisaged counter-insurgency battle against al Shabab in the phased transition may prove to be the quagmire that will define the success or failure of the policy. Regardless of what happens, Somalia's stability and state-building efforts must be matched internally with meaningful advances towards political and national reconciliations, which perhaps should contemplate the inclusion of al-Shabaab as part of the process. Finally, without a critical reflection on AMISOM's experiences, there is a risk of repeating the mistakes or shortcomings of the past fifteen years which will then make it difficult for ATMIS to succeed in its mission.

References

Ajú, M. M. (2022). Reshaping the African Union Mission in Somalia: From AMISOM to ATMIS. *The Horn Bulletin*, *5*(3).

Albrecht, P. (2015, November). *Regional Interests Define the African Union Mission in Somalia. Danish Institute for International Studies* (*DIIS Policy Brief*). http://www.jstor.com/stable/resrep13237.

Ali, N. M. (2011). Ethio-Somaliland Relations Post-1991: Challenges and Opportunities. *International Journal of Sustainable Development*, *4*(4), 1–10.

Arman, A. (2014). *Somalia: African Solutions for African Problems?* https://www.aljazeera.com/indepth/opinion/2014/05/somalia-african-solutions-africa-20145812280255662.html

Arman, A. (2016). *Ethiopia and US Strategic Interests in Somalia on a Collision Course*. Tesfan News. https://www.tesfanews.net/ethiopia-usa-somalia-interest-on-collision-course/.

Cannon, B. J. (2019). Foreign State Influence and Somalia's 2017 Presidential Election: An Analysis. *Bildhaan: An International Journal of Somali Studies, 18*, 20–49.

Crisis Group. (2018). *Somalia and the Gulf Crisis*. available at https://www.crisisgroup.org/africa/horn-africa/somalia/260-somaliaand-gulf-crisis

Crisis Group. (2022, March). *Crisis*. Watch Tracking Conflict Worldwide. available at https://www.crisisgroup.org/crisiswatch/aprilalerts-and-march-trends-2022

Dessu, M. K. (2022). *Is the AU Mission in Somalia Changing in Name Only?* Institute of Strategic Studies (ISS). https://issafrica.org/iss-today/is-the-au-mission-in-somalia-changing-in-name-only#:~:text=The%20African%20Union%20(AU)%2C,to%20the%20Somali%20Security%20Forces

Dessu, M. K., & Mahmood, O. S. (2017). *London Conference May 2017: 'Somalia NEEDS More Action, Less Lip Service'*. Institute for Security Studies. https://issafrica.org/iss-today/somalia-needs-more-action-less-lip-service.

Dias, A. M. (2010). A Trajectória de Um Movimento Islamita na Somália. *Questões Islâmicas, Relacões Internacionais, 26*, 083–093.

Ero, C. (2013). *The Problems with African Solutions*. https://www.crisisgroup.org/africa/problems-african-solutions

Healy, S. (2009). Peacemaking in the Midst of War: An Analysis of Peace Processes in Colombia. *Journal of Conflictology, 1*(1), 27–40.

Keohane, R. O. (2012). Twenty years of institutional liberalism. *International Relations, 26*(2), 125–138.

Rwengabo, S. (2016). *AMISOM and African-centred solutions to peace and security challenges*. Available at https://www.researchgate.net/profile/Sabastiano-Rwengabo/publication/308898703_AMISOM_and_African-Centred_Solutions_to_Peace_and_Security_Challenges/links/59ae4242458515d09ce57170/AMISOM-and-African-Centred-Solutions-to-Peace-and-Security-Challenges.pdf

Sharmarke, O. A. A. (2010). Somalia dilemmas Changing security dynamics, but limited policy choices. https://www.academia.edu/download/30921341/Paper218.pdf

Shibutse, G., & Mwangi, J. (2020). Mediating Political Transitions in Fragile States: The African Union Mission in Somalia. *Journal of Contemporary African Studies, 38*(1), 58–73.

The HORN Bulletin. (2022, May–June). Reshaping the African Union Mission in Somalia: From AMISOM to ATMIS. *The Horn Bulletin, V*(III).

United Nations. (2009). *Security Council Resolution 1863 (2009).* https://undocs.org/S/RES/1863(2009)

United Nations. (2008, February). Department of peacekeeping operations department of field support. *Policy Authority, Command and Control in United Nations Peacekeeping Operations*. https://police.un.org/sites/default/files/authoritycommandandcontrolinunpkos_2008.pdf

Williams, P. D. (2018). *Fighting for peace in Somalia: A history and analysis of the African Union Mission (AMISOM), 2007–2017*. Oxford University Press.

CHAPTER 5

African Union at 20: Taking Stock of the AU's Normative and Institutional Frameworks on Human Rights and Governance

Tendai Shephard Mbanje

Introduction

The African Union (AU) commemorates its second decade in 2022. The AU was established in 2002, after the transformation of the Organisation of African Unity (OAU) to a new continental body, in Durban, South Africa. The AU aimed at promoting the unity and solidarity of African states, spur economic development, and promote international cooperation. This milestone of its commemoration presents an opportunity to reflect on the founding aspirations of the body, assess the current progress, and provide practical suggestions on how to achieve the AU aspirations.

T. S. Mbanje (✉)
Centre for Human Rights, University of Pretoria, Pretoria, South Africa
e-mail: mbanje.tendai@up.ac.za

A. O. Akinola and E. A. Liaga (eds.), *Development and Regional Stability in Africa*, https://doi.org/10.1007/978-3-031-56695-0_5

The continent has recorded modest gains in deepening a culture of democratic and participatory governance, respect for human rights, constitutionalism, justice, and the rule of law. Various organs and frameworks have been established to fulfil these objectives. These include the African Governance Architecture (AGA) and the African Peace and Security Architecture (APSA), to assist the AU in entrenching democracy on the continent (Lindiwe, 2021). As such, this chapter set out from the onset to achieve two important goals: to highlight the normative and institutional contributions and achievements of the AU, and to reflect on the persisting challenges of the AU.

The AU has developed a robust normative and institutional structure, otherwise called the African Human Rights System (AHRS), to promote and protect human and people's rights on the continent. This framework and structure have their roots in the OAU, the predecessor of the AU. First, the African Charter on Human and Peoples' Rights is the foundational human rights instrument upon which the system is established (OAU, 1986). The establishment of the AU is founded on the aspirations to realise the rights and values enshrined in the Charter. The Charter is Africa's most widely ratified human rights instrument, having been ratified by all except one member state (All African states have signed and ratified the Charter except Morocco). In several countries such as Benin and Nigeria, the provisions of the Charter form parts of domestic law. For example, the Constitution of the Republic of Benin 1990 recognises the constitutional status of the Charter, while Nigeria has domesticated its entirety.

The Charter is supported by various supplementary protocols such as the Protocol on the Rights of Women in Africa, 2003; the Protocol on the Rights of Persons with Disabilities, 2018; the Protocol on the Rights of Older Persons in Africa, 2016; and the Protocol establishing an African Court on Human and Peoples' Rights, 1998. Most of these supplementary protocols were adopted after the AU was established, which is an important achievement of the AU.

Other relevant regional human rights instruments that guarantee human rights and prohibit violations include the African Charter on the Rights and Welfare of the Child, 1990, known as the African Children's Charter; the African Charter on Democracy, Elections and Governance, 2007; the African Convention on the Conservation of Nature and Natural Resources, 2003; the Convention on Preventing and Combatting

Corruption, 2003; the OAU Convention on the Prevention and Combatting of Terrorism, 1998; the AU Convention for the Protection and Assistance of Internally Displaced Persons, 2009; and the OAU Refugee Convention, 1969. The totality of these regional human rights instruments forms the normative framework upon which the African human rights system is built. It is argued that the establishment of the AU to some extent has given an effect to the values and rights enshrined in these instruments (Lindiwe, 2021).

The African Human Rights System

The African human rights system, which has its roots within the OAU, has been advanced and sustained by the establishment of the African Union in 2002. In its quests for a democratic and prosperous Africa, the AU through its organs particularly the African Commission has, repeatedly, made states and African citizens aware of their rights enshrined in the African Charter (Lindiwe, 2021). The African Charter on Human and Peoples' Rights (1986) makes a unique normative contribution to the international human rights system in several ways. For instance, the Charter recognises the indivisibility and interdependence of all categories of human rights namely: civil and political rights, economic, social, and cultural rights, and solidarity rights in one document.

Second, the Charter does not make room for any derogations. To illustrate this, in the case of *Media Rights Agenda v Nigeria, (2000)*,[1] it was found that "the African Charter does not contain a derogation clause and emergencies and special circumstances cannot justify those limitations on the rights and freedoms enshrined in the Charter". Third, the Charter imposes duties on both states and individuals. In the preamble, the Charter declares that "the enjoyment of rights and freedom also implies the performance of duties on the part of everyone". For this reason, Articles 27 to 29 of the Charter stipulate the duties of individuals to the family, community, and state (OAU, 1986).

Finally, the Charter recognises the fundamental rights of both individuals (in Articles 2 to 17) and of peoples (in Articles 19 to 24). It affirms the right of peoples to self-determination within the existing structure of the state, (the African Charter art 20; *Gunme v Cameroon (2009)*; African

[1] See, AHRLR 200 (ACHPR 1998) para 67.

Human Rights Law Review (HRLR) 9 (ACHPR 2009) para 191; see also, *Katangese Peoples' Congress v Zaire* (2000); AHRLR 72 (ACHPR 1995) paras 4–5) the right of peoples to freely dispose of their natural resources, the right of people to economic, social, and cultural development, (Art 22, African Charter), the right of peoples to national and international peace and security (Art 23, African Charter), and the rights of people to a generally satisfactory environment suitable to their development (Art 24, African Charter). It is based on the recognition of these collective rights that the African Commission noted, in the case of *Centre for Minority Rights Development and Another v Kenya* (*Endorois* case), ((2009) AHRLR 75 (ACHPR 2009) para 149) that:

> The African Charter is an innovative and unique human rights document compared to other regional human rights documents in placing special emphasis on the right of "peoples". It substantially departs from the narrow formulations of other regional and universal human rights instruments by weaving a tapestry that includes the three 'generations' of rights: civil and political rights; economic, social, and cultural rights; and group and peoples' rights.[2]

It is therefore important to note that the establishment of the AU has given effect to most of the rights enshrined in the African Charter. The AU has also proactively put mechanisms in place to protect these rights. The discussion below articulates this in detail.

The African Human Rights Institutions: A Guardian of Human Rights within the AU

Since its establishment, the AU continues to safeguard human rights norms and standards, particularly those related to the monitoring institutions, to ensure that the rights and freedoms recognised in the various regional human rights instruments it has adopted are guaranteed and observed by the state and non-state actors. Currently, the three regional human rights institutions responsible for monitoring compliance with the various regional human rights instruments, continue to do incredible work on the continent. These are, namely the African Commission on Human and Peoples' Rights, created under Article 30 of the African

[2] See, https://www.achpr.org.

Charter on Human and Peoples Rights; the African Committee of Experts on the Rights and Welfare of the Child, established under Article 32 of the African Children's Charter; and the African Court on Human and Peoples' Rights, created under Article 1 of the Protocol to the African Charter establishing an African Court on Human and Peoples' Rights.[3]

These institutions have made several decisions and resolutions in the advancement of, protection, and promotion of human rights. The level of compliance with the decisions of these institutions varies among African states. Some states have demonstrated a high level of compliance with the decisions of these institutions, while others have shown reluctance to comply. In general, and as contained in a report by the Office of the United Nations High Commissioner for Human Rights, 2007,[4] compliance with the decisions of these institutions has been hindered by factors such as lack of political will, resource constraints, and institutional weaknesses.

Furthermore, it is worth noting that the AU has taken steps to improve compliance with the decisions of these institutions, including the establishment of a system for monitoring and reporting on compliance with decisions of the AU Commission and the African Court. Additionally, some states have taken measures to improve compliance, by incorporating the decisions of these institutions into their domestic laws and policies (Lindiwe, 2021). Overall, while there is room for improvement, these institutions play an important role in promoting and protecting human rights in Africa, and their decisions have had a positive impact in some cases.

Moreover, it should be noted that these three mechanisms are the main bodies that make up the institutional framework of the African human rights system. With the establishment of the AU, these mechanisms are supported by other policy-making bodies of the African Union such as the Peace and Security Council (PSC), the AU Department of Political Affairs (DPA), the Pan-African Parliament (PAP), the African Peer-Review Mechanism (APRM), the African Union Commission on International Law (AUCIL), the AU Women, Gender and Development Directorate (WGDD), the African Union Advisory Board on Corruption (AUABC),

[3] See, https://au.int/en/treaties/protocol-african-charter-human-and-peoples-rights-establishment-african-court-human-and.

[4] See, https://www.ohchr.org/sites/default/files/Documents/Press/OHCHR_Report_07_Full.pdf.

the Executive Council, and the Assembly (Lindiwe, 2021). Assessing the effectiveness of the policy organs of the AU is generally a complex issue, as it involves evaluating the performance of various bodies with different mandates. These organs are responsible for setting policies, making decisions, and implementing programmes that enhance the AU's objectives of promoting peace, security, and development on the continent.

While analysts are of the view that the AU policy organs have made some progress in achieving their objectives, there are also significant challenges that they face. Several obstacles hinder their effective mandate execution, such as constrained resources that limit their capabilities, restricted implementation capacity resulting in slow progress towards AU objectives, insufficient political will from certain member states not fully endorsing Union policies and decisions, and occasional limitations in public participation, leading to a lack of support from citizens and civil society organisations (Lindiwe, 2021). Though the AU policy organs have made some progress, there is a need to improve their effectiveness and ensure that they serve their purpose in promoting peace, security, and development on the continent.

The Impact of the AU's Treaty Monitoring Bodies on Human Rights and Democracy in Africa

The African Commission on Human and Peoples' Rights

The African Commission on Human and Peoples' Rights continues to usher landmark decisions and resolutions in protecting and promoting human rights.[5] Under Article 45 of the Charter, the Commission was created as the primary treaty monitoring mechanism responsible for promoting and protecting human and peoples' rights, redressing violations, and interpreting the provisions of the Charter and its supplementary protocols as well as any other international human rights treaty ratified by a state party. Over the last three decades, the Commission has firmly established itself as the principal human rights body on the continent by regularly engaging states through the reporting process and its monitoring of state party compliance, and the adjudication of communications containing allegations of human and peoples' rights violations, and interpretation of the Charter. The Commission has continued to offer

[5] For more information, see, https://achpr.au.int/en/about.

guidance to state parties on their obligations under the Charter and its supplementary protocols.

Under Article 62 of the Charter, state parties are required to submit periodic reports to the Commission on the legislative and other measures taken domestically to give effect to the rights and freedoms enshrined in the Charter. Similarly, Article 26 of the Protocol on Women's Rights in Africa, Article 22(1) of the Protocol on the Rights of Older Persons, and Article 34(1) of the Protocol on the Rights of Persons with Disabilities, all also require state parties to give periodic reports on compliance with their obligations under the respective thematic protocols. As a matter of practice, the content of the report includes information on the measures adopted to implement the Charter and its supplementary instruments domestically, the progress made so far, and the challenges affecting their implementation in the state concerned. Based on this process, states have responded favourably to the Concluding Observations and Recommendations of the Commission, even though there remain implementation challenges within member states.

Besides the reporting process, the Commission also adjudicates communications received from individuals or groups (or even state parties) who allege that there has been (or is likely to be) a violation of the Charter or other relevant international human rights instruments. However, such communications need to comply with the conditions laid down in Article 56 of the Charter, including the requirement that local remedies be exhausted. The conditions for receiving communications exist to afford the state party concerned ample opportunity to utilise its domestic system of justice to address grievances and prevent the Commission from acting as a tribunal of the first instance.

In its over 30 years of existence, the Commission has considered and determined numerous communications presented to it, including notable communications like the *SERAC* case; the *Endorois* case, *Jawara v the Gambia*, (2000); *DRC v Burundi, Rwanda, and Uganda*, (2004); *Open Society Justice Initiative v Cote d'Ivoire*, (Communication 318/06); and *Institute of Human Rights and Development in Africa v DRC*, (Communication 393/10 2016); to name a few. However, it is worth noting that decisions made by the Commission are recommendatory in nature. Under the AU, the Commission continues to receive support to fulfil its mandate.

In dispensing its role of interpreting the provisions of the Charter, the Commission adopts resolutions, principles and guidelines, general comments, and model laws. Through these declaratory and interpretive instruments, the Commission gives clarity to the textual content of the rights and freedoms recognised in the Charter and its supplementary protocols. At present, the Commission has adopted over 400 resolutions, 11 guidelines, six general comments, and one model law (Centre for Human Rights, 2020). Most of these have been adopted in the last two decades of the AU establishment.

In carrying out its mandate of promoting rights, the Commission operates through what is called 'Special Mechanisms'. Special mechanisms comprise experts or a body of experts assigned to deal with specific thematic issues under the African human rights system. At the Commission, there are two categories of special mechanisms—special rapporteurs and working groups. Special rapporteur is a single mandate holder usually, a commissioner, assigned to work on a particular thematic human rights area, while a Working Group is a body of experts in a particular field of human rights led by one of the Commissioners. So far, the Commission has undertaken numerous country visits and investigative missions to the territory of state parties, whenever human and people's rights issues are involved. As part of its promotional mandate, country visits to the territory of state parties are usually at the request or approval of the state concerned. Such country visits and missions are often led by a special rapporteur or the Chairperson of the Commission (Lindiwe, 2021). In the past two decades, most of these visits have been successfully conducted by the Commission.

Overall, the work of the body has had a significant impact on the normative development of human and people's rights in Africa. In its decisions on communications and thematic resolutions, it has given clarity to the tenor of the Charter rights and provided a framework for the development of human rights in domestic law. This impact is more evident in its adoption of the Principles on the Freedom of Expression 2002; the Robben Island Guidelines on Torture (2002); the Principles and Guidelines on the Right to a Fair Trial (2003); Access to Health and Needed Medicines in Africa (2008); the Principles and Guidelines on the implementation of Economic, Social, and Cultural Rights in the African Charter on Human and Peoples' Rights (2011); and more recently the Guidelines on the Right to Water in Africa (2019). The Commission has undertaken research studies expounding on the contents of the rights recognised in the Charter and has covered several thematic issues including climate change, land reforms, extractive industries, illicit financial flows, and pastoralism in Africa (Lindiwe, 2021).

The legal institution has also contributed to the growth and development of a progressive human rights culture in member states, through the active support for National Human Rights Institutions (NHRIs), and a vibrant civil society on the continent. In recognition of the work that NHRIs and CSOs play in the promotion and protection of human rights at the domestic level, the Commission endeavours to promote their involvement in the development of the African human rights system and also consult Africa's civil society and ensures their participation in all its processes. Today, no less than 30 NHRIs have affiliate status with the Commission and 535 CSOs enjoy observer status with the Commission (Centre for Human Rights, 2021). The participation of civil society in the Commission's activities is one of the biggest achievements of the work of the Commission.

Administratively, the Commission is composed of eleven Commissioners selected from among African personalities of the highest reputation, recognised for their high morality, integrity, competence, and impartiality in matters of human and people's rights. Although they perform an official function, members of the Commission serve in their capacities for a period of six years and are eligible for re-election (African Charter Arts 31 & 36). The Secretariat of the Commission is hosted in Banjul, the Gambia. The African Commission elects a Bureau from among the Commissioners, made up of a Chairperson and Vice Chairperson. They are eligible for re-election once. To carry on business and make decisions, a quorum is formed by seven members of the Commission. Annually, the Commission organises its public meetings in the form of Ordinary and Extraordinary Sessions. So far, the Commission has held 68 Ordinary Sessions and 32 Extraordinary Sessions.

African Committee of Experts on the Rights and Welfare of the Child

The second treaty monitoring an important body in the African human rights system is the African Committee of Experts on the Rights and Welfare of the Child (African Committee of Experts or ACERWC) (African Union, 2001). The African Committee of Experts although established in 2001 after the coming into force of the ACRWC on 29 November 1999. It draws its mandate from Articles 32–46 of the African Charter on the Rights and Welfare of the Child (African Union,

1990). The ACERWC is the first and only child rights treaty body in the world with the competence to receive complaints against States. Much like the Commission, the African Committee of Experts is the primary treaty monitoring mechanism responsible for promoting and protecting the rights and welfare of children in Africa.

The mandate and operations of the Committee are as prescribed in Article 42 of the African Children's Charter. The Secretariat of the Committee is in Maseru, Lesotho. The Committee is composed of eleven members "of high moral standing, integrity, impartiality, and competence in matters of the rights and welfare of the child" (ACRWC Article 33.1) who are tasked with the duty of monitoring the implementation processes of the ACRWC on the African continent. They serve in their capacity. These members are elected by the Assembly of Heads of State and Government from a list of persons nominated by the State Parties to the ACRWC.

The ACERWC came into existence to complement the efforts of the already existing human rights mechanisms, such as the UN Committee on the Rights of the Child, the African Commission, and the African Court. The first Communication was filed in 2005 by Michelo Hunsungule on behalf of children in Northern Uganda against the Government of Uganda and was declared admissible by the Committee (Fawole, 2020). The Committee rendered its decision (*Decision on the Communication submitted by Michelo Hunsungule and others (On Behalf of Children in Northern Uganda) against the government of Uganda*) the Committee found that the Government of Uganda violated some provisions of the African Charter.

The Second Communication was in 2009. The IHRDA and Open Society Justice Initiative (OSJI) filed a communication before the African Committee of Experts on the Rights and Welfare of the Child (ACERWC). The communication was filed on behalf of children of Nubian descent in Kenya, whose Kenyan nationality was denied at birth. This was the second communication considered by the ACERWC and was the first to reach the merits stage. In its decision (002/Com/002/09 IHRDA and OSJI on behalf of children of Nubian descent in Kenya v Kenya),[6] the Committee found Kenya to have violated the rights of

[6] See, https://www.refworld.org/cases,ACERWC,4f5f04492.html.

Nubian children to non-discrimination, nationality, and protection against Statelessness.

In addition, most recently, the IHRDA filed a communication against the Government of Malawi alleging the Constitution of the Republic of Malawi, excludes children of 16–18 ages from the protection of several international human rights instruments—most notably the African Charter on the Rights and Welfare of the Child. An Amicable settlement was reached under the auspices of the Committee and Malawi amended its Constitution to align the definition of the child with Article 2 of the Charter (Mezmur, 2019). These are some of the notable decisions of the ACERWC in the advancement of children's rights and are constantly promoted and achieved within the African Union. The AU and its partners continue to ensure the availability of resources for the work of these mechanisms.

The African Court on Human and Peoples' Rights

Finally, the African Court on Human and Peoples' Rights was established to complement the protective mandate of the African Commission on Human and Peoples' Rights.[7] The Protocol establishing the Court was adopted in Ouagadougou, Burkina Faso, on 9 June 1998 and came into force on 25 January 2004, under the auspices of the AU. The jurisdiction of the Court extends to all cases and disputes submitted to it regarding the interpretation and application of the Charter, its Protocol, or any other international human rights treaty ratified by the state party concerned. The Court also has jurisdiction to resolve any question on whether it has jurisdiction in any matter before it. In the future, the jurisdiction is set to be expanded to include jurisdiction over AU affairs and international crimes. The Court is composed of 11 judges with a six-year fixed term which is renewable once.

The Court is an independent and impartial body of the AU and judgements made by the Court are final and binding on the state parties concerned (The African Court Protocol Arts 28 and 30). Ordinarily, where a state has only ratified the Court's Protocol but has not yet made a declaration permitting individuals and non-governmental organisations to lodge direct complaints, it is only the African Commission or state

[7] See, https://www.african-court.org/wpafc/.

parties that can lodge direct complaints before the Courts. Under such circumstances, individuals and non-governmental organisations (NGOs) are not competent to bring direct cases before the Court. However, they can do so indirectly, by requesting the African Commission to do so on their behalf, and the African Commission has brought several cases before the Court on behalf of victims of human rights violations, following both the Rules of the Court and its own Rules of Procedure (African Court Protocol Arts 5 & 34(6)).

AU at 20: Persisting Human Rights Challenges

Despite the normative and institutional advances, numerous challenges yet persist that significantly impede the enjoyment of human and people's rights in Africa. More prominently, the problems of endemic poverty, unemployment, and lack of access to potable water, food, shelter, education, electricity, healthcare, and other basic social amenities like public transportation continue to deprive a large percentage of Africa's teaming population of a better life (Lindiwe, 2021). These have been attributed to poor governance in many parts of the continent. In the socio-political sphere, bad governance, a lack of gender mainstreaming in public and private spaces, gender-based discrimination, sexual harassment in the workplace, domestic violence, and rape, poor labour conditions, human trafficking, child labour, and child abuse, and mismanagement of public funds, are each precipitating various degrees of human rights challenges.[8] These are all connected to poor governance and leadership crisis on the continent.

In some countries, armed conflicts, terrorism, violent extremism, land grabs, environmental pollution in the extractive industries by multinational corporations, and development-induced displacement of local communities often lead to forced migration within and across local and international borders. In other cases, the non-accountability of government institutions, pervasive corruption of public officials, excessive use

[8] See, https://www.ohchr.org/sites/default/files/Documents/Press/OHCHR_Report_07_Full.pdf.

of force by security services, the lack of access to information, non-consultation of vulnerable and marginal communities (including indigenous populations) in development projects, electoral irregularities, and ethnic domination tend to threaten the stability of nations.[9]

In the context of natural resource extraction, historical patterns of human, labour, health, and environmental rights violations by foreign multinational corporations—including Chinese companies—present even bigger challenges for the economic, social, and cultural development of the continent and its people. More so, in the wake of the climate crisis, the increased vulnerability of the continent and its people to rapid and, sometimes, extreme weather changes suggests that domestic and foreign companies cannot continue to conduct business as usual in an abusive and unsustainable.[10]

On democracy, the continent continues to experience democracy regression, particularly the recurrence of military coups, and disputed electoral outcomes to mention a few. The resurgence of military coups in Africa raises questions as to whether the reaction by the AU and the Regional Economic Communities (RECs) and the international community are effective and commensurate with the scale of the problem. Focussing on Africa, various democracy indicators, such as Freedom House and Afrobarometer, provide evidence of how democracy in Africa is in a speedy decline (Freedom House, 2021).

AU at 20 and the Recurrence of Governance Deficits

The recurrence of military coups, "popular uprisings against long-serving dictators have provided an opportunity for the return of coups in Africa" (Freedom House, 2021). It is argued that military coups in Africa are on the rise amidst increased economic hardship and insecurity. Many of these coups are triggered by bad leadership and poor governance, economic hardship and rising insecurity seem to be driving the recent wave of coups. Ndubuisi Christian Ani argues that "popular uprisings against long-serving dictators have provided an opportunity for the return of coups in Africa" (Nile Post, 2023). For example, a popular people-driven

[9] See, https://www.ohchr.org/en/publications/annual-report/ohchr-report-2021.

[10] Ibid.

revolution in Sudan led to the ouster of military dictator Omar al-Bashir in April 2019.

Similarly, in Zimbabwe in 2017, the military takeover received popular support from the masses. In Guinea Conakry, the military takeover that ousted former President Alpha Condé—led by Colonel Mamady Doumbouya, was welcomed by the people. Most people were happy to see Condé leave, with some even expressing a little optimism that Doumbouya's coup might represent a rare opportunity for a fresh start (Courtright, 2022). The coup in Mali and Burkina Faso were both widely supported by the people (Courtright, 2022).

The AU and the RECs, such as the Economic Community of West African States (ECOWAS), have been unable to convince military leaders to re-establish civilian rule in the affected countries. Additionally, many citizens in countries where military takeovers have supported and welcomed coup leaders positively, especially those promising radical change. Where military takeovers have occurred, civilians have been seen kissing, hugging, and taking pictures with soldiers in jubilation. A study by two US researchers, Jonathan Powell, and Clayton Thyne, has identified over 200 such attempts in Africa since the 1950s. About half of these have been successful (see Nile Post, 2023). Although the AU having a 'zero-tolerance' approach to military coups, the enormity of these persisting challenges necessitates that the AU must be adaptive and responsive to the task of promoting and protecting human rights wherever and whenever it is called upon to do so.

Coups have also paved a fertile ground for disputed electoral outcomes where coup leaders are not trusted to hold free and fair elections. There are numerous examples where coup leaders have been accused of failing to hold free and fair elections. Research shows that an increasing number of Africans have stopped believing that elections alone can install the leadership they deserve. Support for elections has weakened among Africans, according to a 2019/2020 Afrobarometer survey. Many see elections as ineffective in holding leaders to account. Across the 18 African countries surveyed, only four (4) in 10 respondents believed that elections enable voters to remove non-performing leaders. Although most respondents supported multiparty elections, only 43% said that their countries' most recent elections had been completely free and fair. As revealed by Adekoya (2021), "It is not that Africans no longer want to choose their leaders via elections. It is simply that many now believe that their political systems are gamed". Other analysts argue that despite increasing mistrust in elections, Africans still prefer democratic forms of government. The AU at 20 is characterised by democratic governance deficits.

AU at 20: Lessons and Reflections

The lessons and reflections of the AU establishment are a mixed bag. Successes and failures characterise the reflections of AU at 20. Africa is yet to achieve more from the normative and institutional framework the AU has established. The AU has demonstrated and continues to demonstrate its great vision for the development of Africa. The AU has adopted Agenda 2063, a strategic framework for the continent's socio-economic transformation over the next 50 years (African Union, 2015). It builds on and seeks to accelerate the implementation of past and existing continental initiatives for growth and sustainable development. The goals and priority areas of Agenda 2063 include decent income, creation of jobs and decent work, eradication of poverty, inequality, and hunger. It also aimed at the provision of increased social security and protection including persons with disabilities, as well as modern and liveable habitats and basic quality Services. The Agenda 2063 is one of the achievements of the AU, though it is yet to be fully realised.

The AU continues to adopt resolutions that are thematic and appropriate to African human rights responses. These are making a difference in the human rights landscape on the continent. Finally, the future of the AU on governance is exciting when the Malabo Protocol (2014) comes into force (also known as the Protocol on Amendments to the Protocol on the Statute of the African Court of Justice and Human Rights) this protocol will strengthen the protection of human rights. There is hope for the African people, the AU despite its challenges, deserves credit at 20. It has demonstrated goodwill and some potentials, which can be built upon.

Conclusion

This chapter has presented the AU's successes and challenges in the past two decades. The chapter argued that the AU has achieved modest gains in deepening a culture of democratic and participatory governance, respect for human rights, constitutionalism, justice, and the rule of law. Furthermore, the chapter highlighted the normative and institutional contributions and achievements of the AU notwithstanding the persisting challenges that the AU faces. Although some institutional factors continue to be a threat to peace and security and democracy on the continent. The successes of the AU remain unmatched considering it's a young continent and many of its member states are at the formative stages of the establishment of representative democracy.

However, there is a need for increased cohesion among the organs of the AU to curb these challenges on the continent. The future of the AU depends on the creation of opportunities and prospects for deepening good democratic governance, the rule of law, and deepening human rights standards across the continent. The continent continues to make moderate progress in improving the livelihoods of the African people, despite the prevalence of complex historical and contemporary challenges. There is an optimism that, over time, the continent will make further strides in realising the goals outlined in the instruments it has embraced. As the AU reaches the milestone of two decades, it is an opportune moment for constructive critique, recognising numerous successes that often go overlooked by many scholars.

References

Adekoya, R. (2021, September 13). Why Are Coups Making a Comeback in Africa? *CNN*. https://edition.cnn.com/2021/09/12/africa/africa-coups-resurgence-intl-cmd/index.html

African Union. (1990). *African Charter on the Rights and Welfare of the Child*. https://au.int/sites/default/files/pages/32903-file-african_charter_on_the_rights_welfare_of_the_child_english.pdf

African Union. (2001). *The African Committee of Experts on the Rights and Welfare of the Child*. https://au.int/en/sa/acerwc

African Union. (2015). *Agenda 2063: The Africa We Want*. https://au.int/sites/default/files/documents/36204-doc-agenda2063_popular_version_en.pdf

Centre for Human Rights. (2020). *African Human Rights Yearbook*. Pretoria University Law Press.

Courtright, J. (2022). *Popular Support for Guinea's Coup Is Real*. https://www.icwa.org/support-for-guinea-coup/

Fawole, C. (2020). Revisiting Michelo Hansungule and Others (on Behalf of the Children of Northern Uganda) v Uganda: A Case Commentary. *African Human Rights Yearbook*, *44*, 415–435.

Freedom House. (2021). *Democratic Trends in Africa in Four Charts*. https://freedomhouse.org/article/democratic-trends-africa-four-charts

Lindiwe, K. (2021, September 10). *Introduction to the African Human Rights System*. African Commission on Human and Peoples' Rights' Third African Union-China Human and Peoples' Rights Dialogue.

OAU. (1986). *African Charter on Human and Peoples' Rights*. https://au.int/sites/default/files/treaties/36390-treaty-0011_-_african_charter_on_human_and_peoples_rights_e.pdf

Mezmur, B. D. (2019). No Second Chance for First Impressions: The First Amicable Settlement Under the African Children's Charter. *African Human Rights Law Journal, 9*, 62–84.

Nile Post. (2023, August 1). *Are Military Coups on the Rise Again in Africa?* https://nilepost.co.ug/2023/08/01/are-military-coups-on-the-rise-again-in-africa-2/

CHAPTER 6

EndSARS Protest and Political Participation of Youths in Nigeria

Zainab Monisola Olaitan

Introduction

The youths are often referred to as the 'future'; however, the bulging youth population in Africa makes it imperative for the youth to be seen as the present, as well as the future. Population Reference Bureau (2023) notes that by 2030 Africa's youth population aged 35 years and younger will make up 75% of its population, this growing youth population on the continent has created a new focus on how the youths are viewed concerning development, particularly with policies specifically addressing them as a separate demography. Youths have often been accused of political apathy due to their low numbers when it comes to voting during elections or their underrepresentation in contesting political positions. This view is supported by Kingsley (2013), who asserts that the youths are often one of the most excluded age groups in political engagement in Nigeria. This view espouses the dominant narrative that youths are often not participating in the political system. The danger is that it does not

Z. M. Olaitan (✉)
Centre for Human Rights, University of Pretoria, Pretoria, South Africa
e-mail: Zainab.olaitan@up.ac.za

A. O. Akinola and E. A. Liaga (eds.), *Development and Regional Stability in Africa*, https://doi.org/10.1007/978-3-031-56695-0_6

recognise the low underrepresentation of youth across the African political system, which is a function of the deliberate exclusion of young people from the polity.

Apart from women who are discriminated against from participating in the public spheres, the youth are the second most cohesive demography to suffer this exclusion. Hence, whatever discourse is geared towards the political participation of the youth in Africa, and specifically in Nigeria, must acknowledge the political exclusion that youth face (Kingsley, 2013), rather than sustain the argument that they are politically apathetic. Another reason why the narrative that youths are politically apathetic gains ground is due to the myopic understanding of what it means for citizens to participate or engage in politics. Akinyetun (2021: 8) notes that political participation is about having the wherewithal and opportunity needed to influence decision-making, as well as engaging in actions and activities to contribute to building a better society.

There are expanded discussions concerning what political participation means and the varying effects on democracy. Thus, rather than limiting political participation to just traditional means of voting and contesting for political positions, it is important to start broadening the horizon of the meaning of political participation. This is particularly relevant in a country like Nigeria where the arena of politics has been dominated by individuals who do not fall within the youth bracket (15–29 years), with the current president Bola Ahmed Tinubu in his 80s and the average age of the national legislators was 50 years. It becomes imperative for alternative forms of political participation to be identified to foster the inclusion of the youth in the political process, while also recognising other activities, which they engage in to influence the course of politics. While there has been a focus on the participation of youths in activities like voting and contesting for political positions, their engagements in political actions such as protests, demonstrations, and political commentary cannot be overemphasised. A notable demonstration of youth mass involvement in a protest and unconventional political participation is the October 2020 *#EndSARS* protest that rocked Nigeria.

The *#EndSARS* movement was a resistance against the brutality of young Nigerians by the Special Anti-Robbery Squad (SARS) in Nigeria (Olaitan, 2024). The movement was instrumental in demonstrating the power of the Nigerian youth when they assembled around a common goal. This protest majorly weaponised social media in reaching a global audience to pass its message across while enjoying the support of the international community. It was a movement against police brutality, endemic harassment, and profiling of young people by the notorious Special Anti-Robbery Squad across the country. However, this protest against SARS became something much more than just police brutality, it became a manifestation of the youth's long-harboured dissatisfaction with the Nigerian political system and particularly the ***modus operandi*** of the security operatives in the country, noted for extortion and brutalisation of the youth.

This movement also brings to the fore the realisation that peaceful protests and social media engagement are some of the foremost ways Nigerian youths have been delimited to participate in politics. Rather than waiting to be finally included in the political process by the gerontocrats running the affairs of the country, they decided to carve a niche for themselves. Thus, this chapter examines how the *#EndSARS* movement symbolises a new approach to youth participation in politics through their engagement in political activism and weaponisation of social media. This chapter employs a qualitative methodology and a case study approach to present its argument on how the *#EndSARS* movement should be perceived as a form of youth participation in the Nigerian political system This is in a bid to evaluate how the youth participate in politics while establishing the significance of protests and social media activism as important aspects of political participation.

Youth's Political Participation in Nigeria: Issues

The notion of youth has been defined in several ways in literature. For instance, while the United Nations (UN) defined the youth as anyone between the ages of 15–24 years, the World Bank framed them as individuals between 12–24 years. These categorisations have become very popular; however, some definitions do not allocate numerical age to the identification and categorisation of youth. For example, Galaytan (2019: 3) maintains that youth is a transitory stage from dependency to independence. Rather than presenting a rigid construct of youth based on age, Hilker and Fraser (2009) hold that youth is a transitional stage between childhood and adulthood.

Due to the political, sociocultural, and economic realities in Africa, the highlighted age brackets have been described as too narrow. As a result, Nigeria's 2009 National Youth Policy defined youth as persons between the ages of 18 to 35 years (Galstyan, 2019: 3; Hilker & Fraser,

2009; UNDP & UNDESA, 2013). This chapter adopts the constitutional delimitation of what a youth is in Nigeria. The population of Nigerians between the age of 15–35 years is around 70% of the total population of Nigeria. A total of 42% of the total population of Nigeria is below the age of 15 years (Akinyemi & Mobolaji, 2022). In absolute terms, there are more young people in Nigeria currently than any other segment of the population, and this comes with its peculiar social, political, and economic implications.

Due to many factors, the youth find it difficult to permeate the political space in Nigeria. The restrictive age limit for contesting certain political offices makes youth participation in politics difficult. It is also important to pay attention to individual capacity to contest for positions, for youth, it is difficult for them to contest positions in the current Nigerian polity due to the huge financial and social capital needed. The capacities of organisations and the degree to which an environment enables individuals and institutions to participate in political processes should be given utmost consideration. In theory, the age requirement for the Senate and House of Representatives in Nigeria starts at 25 years, while it is 35 years for the presidency. However, this does not reflect reality, as the average age of past presidents in Nigeria since the transition to democracy in 1999 is over 50 years, with the youngest being 53 years of age, while the other four Presidents have been over 60 years. This practice continues even though Nigeria has a youthful population with the percentage of young people below 30 years standing at 70%. However, this youthful population has not translated into a commensurate representation of youth in the political system of the country (Akinyemi & Mobolaji, 2022).

The Nigerian political system is saturated with older individuals, thus, leaving little space for the youth. Ibezim (2019) asserts that youth participation in Nigerian politics is bedevilled by several challenges, which stem from a lack of understanding of the benefits that youth political participation holds. He further notes that unemployment, social exclusion, limited capacity, resources, and tools are some of the obstacles facing youth participation in politics. About 70% of Nigeria's 80 million youth population are unemployed even after obtaining relevant work experience and acquiring other qualifications for the job (Ibezim, 2019). According to Lührmann (2013), the significance of the 2011 Arab Spring[1] was that it

[1] The Arab Spring was a wave of protest championed by young people clamouring for political and social change across the Middle East.

demonstrated that youth inclusion in the political system cannot be overstated. Nigeria, as a struggling democracy, needs its youth for creative ideas and innovative leadership that can help bring the needed change and development. Hence, Olufowobi (2018) opines that providing an enabling environment for the youth to operate is needed to improve their participation in politics.

The active participation of the youth during the liberation movement in pre-independence Nigeria is a testament to a long history of youth engagement in politics. Individuals, such as Nnamdi Azikwe, Obafemi Awolowo, and Anthony Enahoro, were students when they championed the cause of Nigerian Independence. They started their agitation for independence as Student Union Activists and mobilised formidable groups that challenged colonial rule. For instance, Anthony Enahoro was around twenty-one years old when he moved the motion for the Independence of Nigeria. Yakubu Gowon was twenty-nine years old when he became the Head of State in Nigeria between 1967 and 1976. Isaac Adaka Boro, from the University of Nigeria, Nsukka, was in his thirties when he formed the Niger Delta Volunteer Force (NDVF) and later fought for the emancipation of his people in Eastern Nigeria. A brief historical context into youth political participation is needed to counter the narrative that youth in Nigeria are politically apathetic or 'lazy' as peddled by the older generation prominent of them is the former president General Muhammed Buhari.

Badmus (2018) attests that Nigerian youth are ready to be actively involved in politics, especially as the world is beginning to beam its light on youth activities in the country. Many young people are organising fluid social movements across borders and around issues of common concern. In Nigeria and beyond, young people will generally be more likely to participate and to see value in their participation if it is structured around meaningful opportunities to change material conditions, decisions, policies, or other concrete outcomes than general participation efforts not linked directly to solving actual problems in people's lives. To corroborate this, Zohdy (2017: 9) posits that,

> The most effective citizen participation efforts tend to be those that design participation not as an end in and of itself. A broader base of both citizens and government officials are more likely to participate and see value in such efforts if they are targeted toward solving specific, concrete, and

tangible lived problems, for example, poor quality basic services like education, health, sanitation, and transportation. This principle should also be applied to inform youth political participation efforts.

Thus, political leaders should recognise and adapt to this shift to better support powerful, organic, youth-led efforts for social change and good governance (Dougherty et al., 2016).

O'Toole (2015) argues that despite youths' seeming lack of interest in formal political activities, they are attracted to, and often engage in informal and alternative modes and styles of political participation. Thus, even though there is a decline in youth participation in formal and active politics, young people are increasingly self-organising informal movements and activities. It is also essential to note that youth political participation transcends voting but involves several politically related activities undertaken by youth both online and offline. Therefore, the next section discusses the various ways citizens can participate in democracy, which often transcends the traditional forms like voting and contesting for political offices.

Variants of Political Participation

Political participation is relevant for any political system, as it is an indispensable feature of democracy. It is often understood as a voluntary activity by the government, politics, or the state. Political participation derives from the freedom to speak out, assemble, and associate; the ability to take part in the conduct of public affairs; and the opportunity to register as a candidate, to campaign, to be elected, and to hold office at all levels of government (United Nations, 2005). Political participation involves much more than just voting or standing for election, participation in the electoral process is seen as a major determinant. Socially and politically, participation refers to the platform and the mechanisms for the public to express opinions and ideally exert influence regarding political, economic, management, or other social issues. Democracy has tremendously enhanced people's political participation in Nigeria and all over the world. This is why democracy is seen as the best form of government, at least around participation.

In the 1950s, political participation was understood from an electoral perspective in terms of voting and attending political meetings (Sabucedo & Arce, 1991). Rapid social and political developments in the late 1960s and early 1970s demystified the operations of the political system, making it clear that political participation is not restricted to broadly accepted or institutionalised actions. Dissent, disapproval, rejection, and provocation are expressions of interests and opinions, which should be included as forms of political participation in a democratic system (Barnes & Kasse, 1979). However, recent developments have shown that voting is only one of how the electorates can attempt to influence the course of politics (Sabucedo & Arce, 1991: 93).

There has been an increase in various forms of political actions that are alternatives to voting, which reveals a new trend in the politicisation of participation. It becomes important to understand that categorisation varies from conventional to unconventional; direct to indirect, and traditional to non-traditional. The most common classification of political participation is between conventional and non-conventional methods (Sabucedo & Arce, 1991). Most of the processes involved in conventional political participation are related to the electoral process, while non-conventional participation processes focus on activities such as legal demonstrations, boycotts, and illegal strikes. Verba and Nie (1972) argue that conventional political participation is made up of the following four distinctive factors: voting, electoral campaigns, community activities, and contact with political administration.

Milbrath's (1981) listing of conventional participation is more detailed while that of non-conventional is much more general. With non-conventional activities, further classification is legal and illegal acts. Illegal activities include violent and non-violent demonstrations. Considering this shift away from conventional participation, almost every activity by some citizens can somehow be understood as a form of political participation. Reinforcing this assertion, van Deth (2016) maintains that such activities should aim to influence the course of politics. There is a positive correlation between more traditional forms of political participation and those of an aggressive or resistance-oriented nature (Muller, 1982). There are various ways citizens may participate in politics: active political participation, passive political participation, and becoming indifferent.

Hansen (2016) differentiated between traditional and non-traditional participation by classifying activities conducted using traditional and official channels, such as election or voting as customary, while non-customary activities are organised separately from these channels, including demonstration and industrial actions. Non-traditional participation was often observed to be an activity undertaken by the insubordinate few against government activities (Soloman, 2008). However, in recent times, the engagement of protests, demonstrations, picketing, and boycotts, for example, has turned out to be significantly more common (Hern, 2017). Non-traditional participation is known to have a considerably bigger scope of aim, they often involve organisations, and they try to influence popular belief and conduct.

Additionally, the use of internet-based technologies as a form of political engagement has made it almost impossible to recognise political participation. The agencies of engagement have turned out to be more varied than previously assumed due to modern technology, and its boost for communication and association. The changes in the approach by which citizens participate politically suggest a holistic conceptualisation of what activities constitute political engagement and the need to re-evaluate what falls outside this. In addressing the differences in political participation, Bouma (2014: 4) clarified the roles in a political society that comprise the central foundations of political parties, rules of elections, voting, and political agendas. According to this differentiation, it is only those activities that are political that should become operative in a political society (Beeri, 2013).

The role of citizens' engagement in the political system was the essence of state civilisation in ancient Greece, particularly looking at the direct democracy as practised in Athens, where all citizens directly choose their leaders. This form of democratic participation enhanced the full engagement of interested citizens in policy formations (Fielding, 2016). The procedural democratic theory of governance posits that citizenship engagement ought to be limited to voting participation or representation of the electorate (McCaffrie & Akram, 2014).

However, from the 1980s, there were calls for more dynamic and active citizenship participation in democratic governance (Ebeling, 2015). Beyond the conventional forms of political participation such as voting, campaigning, membership, voluntary work, civic responsibility, demonstrations, and community participation (Galstyan, 2019), new forms of participation have been documented. They include hacking and distributed denial of service (DDOS) attacks, which is a form of protest aimed at shutting down online servers and restricting access to internet services. It could sometimes be voluntary, online campaigning, because social networks are increasingly becoming popular for their use in starting a cause and gaining followership, crowdsourcing, and crowdfunding (Pleyers & Karbach, 2014).

The youth in Nigeria have found solace in engaging more within the unconventional form of political participation for some reasons, the most notable is their exclusion from the political system. This system mostly rewards people outside the youth category, with the average age of lawmakers in Nigeria being over 50 years old. This reality makes it imperative for the youth to carve a separate niche where they can actively engage with the political system. With the different ways citizens can participate in the democratic system beyond the traditional forms and the shift towards unconventional forms, this chapter adopts the *#EndSARS* protest in Nigeria as a case. This becomes necessary to contextualise the argument that youth participation in Nigeria should be viewed from a different lens, while also re-evaluating what it means for citizens to participate in the Nigerian political system.

Overview of the *#EndSARS* Movement

SARS was a branch of the Nigeria Police Force (NPF), under the State Criminal Investigation and Intelligence Department (SCIID). It was founded in late 1992, as one of the 14 units in the Force Criminal Investigation and Intelligence Department, to detain, investigate, and prosecute people involved in crimes like armed robbery, kidnapping, and other violent crimes. The squad was created as a masked police unit to perform undercover operations against violent crimes, like armed robbery, car snatching, kidnapping, cattle rustling, and the bearing and use of illegal firearms (Loudtips, 2020). This unit has been accused of several human rights violations, illegal 'stop and searches', illegal arrests and detentions, extrajudicial killings, sexual harassment of women, and brutalisation of young men (Ogundipe, 2017).

A 2016 report by Amnesty International indicted SARS and accused the squad of human rights abuses, cruelty, degrading treatment of Nigerians in their custody, and widespread torture of detainees and other victims. Specifically, some of the human rights abuses by SARS include shooting detainees in the leg, mock executions, threats of execution, hanging of victims, and physical assaults (Amnesty International, 2021). These human rights abuses were documented in trending videos on social media platforms.

There have been several protests against the brutality meted out on young Nigerians by SARS before the 2020 mass protest against the existence of the unit in Lagos. In 2017, Nigerian youths across the nation took to the streets in a peaceful protest to spread awareness of SARS brutality and extortions, and to demand its immediate disbanding. The protests also moved to social media using the hashtag *#EndSARS*. The government failed to respond to the public outcry against SARS. However, the most impactful demonstration against the infamous SARS was held in October 2020 which ended with the government-sponsored massacre of the protesters on 20 October 2020.

In October 2020, young people across Nigeria took to the streets calling for the disbandment of SARS and ending its brutality against the youth, through a movement tagged *#EndSARS* (Human Rights Watch, 2021). This movement was triggered by viral videos of police brutality that documented decades-long patterns of violence perpetrated by SARS. Though these demonstrations began as an outcry against the SARS police unit but evolved into a larger protest against bad governance (*New York Times*, 2021). On 3 October 2020, a video showing a SARS officer shooting a young Nigerian in front of Wetland Hotel, Ughelli, Delta State in Nigeria, trended on the Internet (Okon, 2020). Allegedly, the police officers confiscated the victim's car. This video caused public outcry on social media, especially on Twitter, with the *#EndSARS* hashtag.

The hashtag gained more momentum on Twitter starting on 5 October 2020, after another report surfaced, showing details of how SARS officers killed a 20-year-old rising artiste in his neighbourhood. He was reportedly in the company of a friend when the SARS officers assaulted and brutalised both. Lambo (2020) narrates that the SARS officers wrongly accused the two individuals of theft before shooting the artiste. Following these two shootings, by 8 October 2020, nation-wide protests on *#EndSARS* started along with agitations through social media, with the youth decrying the endemic SARS brutality, harassment, and extortion in Nigeria.

The protests were led predominantly by young Nigerians in different cities, alongside activists and notable personalities (Busari et al., 2020). The NPF disrupted the protests in some cities, throwing teargas, using water cannons, and shooting at unarmed peaceful protesters across the country. This resistance by the police led to the death of another young man in Ogbomoso, Oyo State. By Wednesday, 14 October 2020, the *#EndSARS* protests had attracted the attention of the international community to the agitations against police brutality in the country, as the youth kept intensifying their calls for reforms and accountability in police operations.

Twitter served as a tool through which the protest was facilitated, updating people about the protest action and its impacts in different locations. It was strategically and effectively used to mobilise the youths through hashtagging that made emotive messages go viral and impactful. The 2020 *#EndSARS* protest was largely effective due to the use of digital technology, particularly the internet. Nigerian youths, tagged the 'soro soke' generation, started the protest on Twitter before taking it to the streets. 'Soro soke', a Yoruba phrase that means 'speak louder', was used on social media and in physical or oral communication to encourage people to speak up in protest (Amnesty International, 2021). Due to the massive force of the protesters, the *#EndSARS* hashtag trended globally on social media.

A report analysis by NENDO in October 2020 showed that the online protest attracted 48 million mentions and tweets from 5 million unique authors on Twitter, between 5 and 14 October 2020. The protests, which were recorded in all major cities of Nigeria, attracted international mainstream media, like the BBC, CNN, and Al-Jazeera. It brought to the consciousness of the world the injustice meted out to Nigerian youth by SARS officers and kept the Nigerian government on its tiptoes. The protest was cut short on 20 October 2020 due to the shootings at the Lekki Tollgate in Lagos by the Nigerian Military and Nigerian Police Force, which was confirmed by the Lagos Judicial Panel of Inquiry (Redress, 2022). Nonetheless, it lasted that long due to the role of social media. Mobilisation of protesters, communication, and real-time updates took place via social media. Twitter was used to raise funds to sustain the protest and the funds were mostly in the form of cryptocurrency. The Feminist Coalition (FemCo) played a major role in providing food, funds, and other support services to the protesters across Nigeria. In discussing the significance of the protest, Okunna (2021: 4) notes that,

> The reality and true significance of the #EndSARS Protest dawned on Nigerians and the global community that #EndSARS was not just a protest against police brutality but a desperate lashing out by the Nigerian youth against a long history of government's failures to make Nigeria a livable society generally and to achieve genuine youth development in particular.

According to George (2020), the 3 October 2020 video caused an immediate trigger that made the hashtag *#EndSARS* go viral on social media platforms, which then resulted in massive street protests to call for the dissolution of SARS and to end police brutality, injustice, and maltreatments of the youth. The arrest of the young man who posted the video fuelled the anger of the youths (Gladstone & Specia, 2020) and further popularised the spread of the hashtag *EndSARS* nationally and globally. It also accounted for youth-inspired physical demonstrations in major cities like Lagos and Abuja.

Meanwhile, Vega (2020) observed that the hashtag *EndSARS*, indeed, started as far back as 2017 when Nigerians were using it to share their experience on extortion, harassment, torture, illegal arrest, and other violating behaviours of SARS officials. It only led to street demonstrations in 2020 when youths saw the need to take their online protests to the street for greater impact on to condemn the government's handling of the SARS unit within the Nigerian police system. Like the protests during the Arab Spring in North Africa, young people used social media to coordinate protests on a scale that frightened the state authorities, which are accustomed to being in control.

Any discourse on the *#EndSARS* protest must feature the impact it had on the Nigerian economy and if achieved its intended aim. First, the 2020 protest puts a halt to economic activities resulting in tremendous loss to the economy. The Lagos Chamber of Commerce estimated the loss at 700 billion naira while the Nigerian Insurers Association reported that insurers paid about 11 billion naira over property damage (*Premium Times*, 2020; *The Cable*, 2022). The protest was also impactful as there was a strong response from the Presidency on the status of SARS. At the height of the protest, former President General Muhammed Buhari made a statement that they had disbanded SARS.

Additionally, the protest shed light on the systemic dysfunctionality of the Nigerian Police Force, creating a shift in how they interacted with young Nigerians. While the Lagos *EndSARS* protest ended due to the Lekki Tollgate Shooting on 20 October 2020, the protest continued in other parts of the country and around the world. The *EndSARS* protest can be deemed as largely successful because of the impact it had on the economy, and operations of the country, the prompt response by the government and finally the setting up of panels of enquiry to investigate the atrocities of SARS. An interesting impact was the political awakening it created amongst young people to influence the operations of the Nigerian polity in preparation for the 2023 general elections.

Establishing Protests and Social Media Engagement as New Forms of Political Participation

From an overview of the *#EndSARS* protest, two issues need to be expanded on concerning the different forms of political participation: first, the mass mobilisation of youth culminated in protest action against police brutality, and by extension bad governance in Nigeria; second, the usage of social media as a platform for political engagement, considering its role in the global reach of protesters and its impact on the *#EndSARS* movement.

Protest as Political Participation

Eesuola (2015) defines protest as an expression of dissent, ventilation of anger, or resistance against a particular phenomenon. He clarifies that demonstration is the most popular manifestation of protest across the world. Auvinen (1996: 78) argues that protest includes activities such as "riots and strikes which have an expressed political target and/or involve conflict behaviour against the political machinery". In establishing protest as a form of political participation, Hollander and Einwohner (2004) and Olafsson (2007) note that protest is a non-conventional form of political participation. Charles (1996) considers protest as one of the forms of interacting with the elites, opponents, or the state. Hartington and Dominguez (1975: 11 cited in Eesuola, 2015) see protest as an activity executed by "private citizens to influence government decision-making".

Schussman and Soule (2005: 1084) attest to the assertion that protests, as well as social movements, are normal and inherently political because they are the medium through which citizens react to political activities. They observe that resistance, political protest, and other contentious activities increase as voting and other forms of political participation decrease. Thus, analysis of political participation should not be limited to voting and electoral activities. Bowman and Boyton (1974: 205) assert that "electoral activities are not the only form of political participation that is open to citizens". They further maintain that citizens can respond to government policies by expressing their opinions either via writing letters or group demonstrations. Eesuola (2015) criticised the process of elections as very ritualistic and periodised, as citizens often have no choice but to follow its rituals and periodisation before they can achieve any political or social changes. However, protest provides citizens with the opportunity to demonstrate their need for political change or express their frustrations on certain political issues that they might not approve. He further clarifies that "quite often they do this through means ranging from rallies, strikes, street marches, sit-ins and so on" (Eesuola, 2015: 30).

Although some scholars think that political participation must be backed by laws. Indeed, Verba and Nie (1972: 34) position it as "those legal activities by private citizens which are more or less directly aimed at influencing the selection of government personnel and, or the actions they take". However, Eesuola (2015: 33) contends that people are getting more and more involved in politics, while protest demonstration is quite central to the involvement creating grounds for legitimising it. He notes further that "protest demonstration is fast becoming an entrenched symbol of political participation amongst all nations of the world. It is perhaps the most used means of participation now, probably because it does not have age or gender restrictions, and it demands no known protocol" (Eesuola, 2015: 38).

The acknowledgement that a protest is a form of political participation creates a new lens through which to view the participation of Nigerian youths in the 2020 *#EndSARS* protest. This lens provides new grounds for discussing youth political participation in Nigeria considering the narrative that youth do not participate in the political system. The protest surely demonstrated that the youths were desperate to make their voices heard in the polity and the only practical way they could do that was through mass mobilisation of the group for a purpose. The menace of police brutality provided the needed impetus for the citizens to convey their dissatisfaction with the system and raise their discontent against bad governance. Therefore, recognising protest as a legitimate form of political participation establishes the *#EndSARS* movement and other activities of the youths in the polity as forms of political participation.

Social Media as a Platform for Political Participation

Isike et al. (2022) argue that the development of social media as a new form of media allows for cross-cutting engagement across the public and private spheres. They note that this new media connects the private with the public space, without the physical sites and structures significantly impacting the sort of engagements that take place. Jenkins and Nico (2013) argue that social media, which is part of cyberspace has solidified the grounds for wider citizenry participation outside of what traditional media can offer. This allows for a new era of media democratisation. Traditional media, which has often been described as the fourth pillar of democracy, due to its role as a watchdog, fosters accountability within the government. However, the evolution of social media ensures that citizens can demand this accountability directly without the traditional media acting as an intermediary. Thus, social media platforms have become very important spaces in recent times, spurring several governmental regulations and control, as seen in Nigeria with the banning of Twitter in 2021 (Isike et al., 2022).

The role of social media as a new platform for engagement enables it to contribute to fostering social change. In the past, non-governmental organisations and civil societies were the main actors in advocating social justice and inclusivity; but presently, social media has become the fourth space where social movements are mobilised. This has allowed the formation of new communities, as well as the aggregation of interest across physical structures to effect social change. Scott and Maryman (2016) note that the use of social media has enabled the creation of connected relationships via social media linkages often transcending national, tribal, disability, or gender status, thus, positioning it as an effective instrument in advocating for social change, justice, and inclusion. The communities developed on social media are often seen as cyber social movements, which organise themselves to achieve their aggregated interest. For instance, the Arab uprising that took place in Egypt, Tunisia, and Libya, was initiated by cyber social movements (Miladi, 2016). In this case, the citizens were able to connect online and join voices to advocate for democratic changes.

In Nigeria, youth with lived or acquired experience of police brutality formed social movements across social media platforms to agitate for the banning of SARS. Olaitan (2024) attests that the *#EndSARS* protest was dominated by youth who had firsthand experience of SARS torture, arrest, and brutality, while some of the participants were associated with people with similar experiences. This manifested in the weaponisation of platforms like Twitter and Facebook in driving the key messages of the protest. Hence, social media served as a platform to mobilise youth with common experiences into a social movement to protest against police brutality. This shows that while political activism and engagements with political office holders have come under threat in the traditional media due to incessant governmental regulations and broadcasting limitations, the evolution of social cyber movements has allowed unfettered and strong demand for accountability, justice, and improved governance via online protests.

Twitter and Facebook are the two notable social media platforms often used for social activism and protests against bad governance in Nigeria. The platform offered by Twitter, in particular, has been used to organise and execute social protests such as the 2012 *#OccuppyNigeria* protest on the removal of fuel subsidy, and the 2020 *#EndSARS* protest. These platforms are intriguing in the way they have provided the required access to widely disseminate the protest message beyond national borders and physical barriers. This is due to the fluidity provided by these platforms in ensuring that political messages travel across different spaces with unimaginable immediacy (Ibezim-Ohaeri, 2017).

Thus, social media "are increasingly playing the role of the public sphere where public issues are debated outside the control and dominance of government" and people come together as 'equals' in a public debate (Hari, 2014: 37). Twitter especially has become the new medium through which Nigerians freely express their opinions and feelings about government corrupt practices and status of governance; hence, gaining increased awareness and recognition globally. The use of this platform for political purposes goes beyond online protests and aggregating citizens' dissenting views concerning government actions. It has often been used by the government to communicate state policies to the citizens further entrenching its role as a space for political participation (Hari, 2014).

There are various examples of protests that engage the use of platforms such as Facebook and Twitter to demonstrate the impact social media has on political processes. Some are the Arab Spring of 2010–2011, which saw the youths revolutionise the political terrain of most North African countries, including the protest against electoral fraud in Iran, as well as the *#OccupyNigeria* protest in 2012 (Soriano, 2013). In the case of 2020 *#EndSARS* protection, social media served as a tool for organising the protest and updating people about the protest's locations and plans. It also provided a space for protesters to express their demands and share their experiences and opinions on political activities.

The way social media was used during the *#EndSARS* protest has positioned social media activism as a form of political participation, outside of the conventional electoral form of participation. This asserts the notion that social media has become a new instrument for political participation, embodying traits of unconventional political participation. Furthermore, social media enhances democratic sustainability in Nigeria, as the youths championed the cause to end police brutality and demand for policing reforms and good governance. They thereby validate its usefulness as a transformational platform in driving change and promoting democracy.

Re-thinking Youth Political Participation in Nigeria

In using the *#EndSARS* protest as a case to re-evaluate the political participation of youths in Nigeria, this section focuses on two themes: social media as a platform for political activism and engagement, and protest as a form of political participation. Over the years, youth participation in politics has often been low or adjudged to be low due to the limitations several studies have placed on what it means to participate in politics and its link to traditional forms of voting and contesting for elective positions. Studies that decry the low political participation of youth often employ conventional means of political participation as their metric, without making concerted efforts to discuss the reason behind the low participation of youth in active participation such as voting.

Understanding why they do not feature prominently in electoral contestation or vying for political offices places at the forefront, the deliberate exclusion of youth from the political system. This manifests in the Nigerian political system, which is dominated by people who fall above the youth categorisation, as with most countries in Africa, where old people between the age of 50–80 continue to occupy elective positions. Since Nigeria has a predominantly youthful population with 70% of the total population composed of the youth, it remains a puzzle why the inclusion of youth in politics has not gained nationwide attention.

There have been many attempts by the youth to actively participate in the political system with the efforts of individuals to contest political positions. The Nigerian government have been able to respond to the quests to integrate the youth into active politics through different initiatives such as the *#NotTooYoungtoRun* bill and the 2019 National Policy on Youth. All these aimed to foster the increased political participation of youth to address their low participation. However, as has been constantly pointed out, merely understanding conventional political participation will often lead to the erasure of an important demographic, who are engaging in unconventional political participation.

What the *#EndSARS* protest signifies is that there is ample evidence that Nigerian youth are participating in politics via political activism and using social media as a platform for engagement. Therefore, there is a need to expand our definition and understanding of what it means to participate in politics. This expansion also enables us to paint an accurate picture of youth's political participation in Nigeria rather than regurgitating the narrative that they do not engage in politics. While also broadening the discourse on the significance of social media to the political system and how it can be used to mobilise and aggregate dissent.

The relevance of social media to the *#EndSARS* protest is very significant, hence the need to include social media in the discourse. The youths explored the platform to register and better articulate their disapproval of police brutality in Nigeria, and demand for better governance. The weaponisation of social media by the youth validates their inability to operate in traditional politics due to the possibility of government crackdowns and other limitations. Hence, social media provides an alternative platform that allows for the sharing of individual and group viewpoints to a wider and much more global audience. The youth consider this as a vital means of expressing their freedom of expression, thereby participating in the political system.

The protest has often been seen as a form of demonstration that aims to influence government policies or influence the course of politics. The *#EndSARS* protest rightfully sought to influence government policies by clamouring for the ban of the special anti-robbery squad and other demands that would result in better policing in the country. Compared to voting which Eesuola (2015) conceived as a periodic ritual, protest is spontaneous, drastic, and quite effective at getting a message across. This is because it often has an impact on economic activities, public order, and political stability of the state, which is why protests are often not tolerated in the country. Nigeria has experienced cases where the government crackdown on protesters because they are seen as rebellion against the government, rather than citizens expressing their views or citizens displaying their freedom or rights to participate in the political system.

The *#EndSARS* movement helped to legitimise protest as a form of youth political participation owing to the massive appeal it enjoyed amongst the youth. The government, at both national and state levels, also recognised this demonstration as a clamour against police brutality and a call to improve governance. However, there were accusations by certain governmental officials that the movement amounted to treason and an attempt to overthrow the ruling government. This accusation stems from the government's disapproval of protest as a legitimate form of political participation. The Nigerian government failed to see the protest as one of the human rights enjoyed by citizens, and the government officials, as usual, displayed their political intolerance by using their condemnation of the protesters as justification for unleashing terror on the peaceful protesters.

Conclusion

This chapter attempted to explore how the *#EndSars* movement symbolises a new approach to youth participation in politics through their engagement in protest and the use of social media. The significance and impact of the *#EndSARS* movement need to be documented and analysed for future generations because of the galvanising effect it had on the Nigerian youth, as well as the world in light of the prevalence of police brutality across the world. The protest action also debunks the illustration that Nigerian youths are not 'lazy' or apathetic, as has been publicised by some government officials, they just needed the right environment to channel their voices towards a cause they could identify with. The joint experience of police brutality, extortion, and harassment by SARS created the much-awaited moment for Nigerian youths to create a platform for political activism through the social movement. This mass mobilisation not only led to the 2020 *#EndSARS* protest but also showed that the subject of youth political participation needs to be viewed in a different light.

Therefore, this chapter has located the youths' political participation within the unconventional form of involvement, using the *#EndSARS* protest as a case to contextualise the arguments. It noted that most studies often argue that Nigerian youths are apathetic, which accounts for their low participation in politics, rather than acknowledge the difficulty youth encounter in participating in a gerontocratic political system. Second, the chapter argues that democratic or political participation takes different forms such as 'conventional' and 'unconventional', and 'direct' or 'indirect'. However, it is interesting to note that the traditional form of participation (voting, contesting for elective positions) is dominant in discourse concerning democratic participation. This brings up the need to normalise activities like protests, boycotts, social media engagement, and political commentary, as well as forms of political participation.

The chapter underscores a key argument that conventional participation involves the elected and appointed ruling class, policymakers, and decision-makers. In contrast, unconventional participation encompasses individuals who, though not elected or not directly involved in decision-making, exert influence on decisions through diverse forms of engagement such as protests and activism. The youths fall into the latter as they seek to influence decisions through unconventional means of political participation.

It is on that note that this chapter argues that the massive youth participation and weaponisation of social media in the *#EndSARS* protest signifies political participation. That is, the chapter acknowledges that social media is a new platform for political activism and engagement in recent times and legitimatise protest as a form of political participation. This chapter concludes that by expanding the conceptualisation of what it means to participate in politics beyond the traditional lens, legitimising the youth's political participation becomes more apparent. This emerging understanding fosters the inclusion of the youth in the Nigerian political system as this chapter has studied the youth within the new niche of political participation, they have carved out for themselves.

References

Akinyemi, A. I., & Mobalaji, J. W. (2022, July 18). Nigeria's Large, Youthful Population Could Be an Asset or a Burden. *The Conversation*. https://theconversation.com/nigerias-large-youthful-population-could-be-an-asset-or-a-burden-186574

Akinyetun, T. (2021). Youth Political Participation, Good Governance and Social Inclusion in Nigeria. *Commonwealth Youth and Development, 18*(2), 1–15.

Amnesty International. (2021). *#ENDSARS Movement: From Twitter to Nigerian Streets*. https://www.amnesty.org/en/latest/campaigns/2021/02/nigeria-end-impunity-for-police-violence-by-sars-endsars/

Auvinen, J. (1996). IMF Intervention and Political Protest in the Third World: A Conventional Wisdom Refined. *Third World Quarterly, 17*(3), 337–400.

Badmus, B. (2018, June 4). Nigerian Youths more than Prepared for Leadership—Young Alliance. *Nigerian Tribune*. Retrieved from https://tribuneonlineng.com/2019-nigerian-youths-more-than-prepared-for-leadership-%E2%80%95young-alliance/

Barnes, S., & Kaase, M. (1979). *Political Action: Mass Participation in Five Western Democracies*. Sage.

Beeri, I. (2013). Governmental Strategies Towards Poorly-Performing Municipalities: From Narrow Perceptions to Ineffective Policies. *Lexlocalis-Journal of Local Self-Government, 11*(1), 33–51.

Bouma, H. (2014). Vappu Taipale: Tireless Advocate of Gerontechnology in the Political Arena. *Gerontechnology, 12*, 4–10.

Bowman, L., & Boynton, G. R. (Eds.). (1974). *Political Behavior and Public Opinion: Comparative Analyses*. Englewood Cliffs, N. J. Prentice-Hall.

Busari, S., Orji, S., & Salaudeen, A. (2020, October 9). Nigerians Take to the Streets in Protests Against Controversial Police Unit Accused of Brutality. *CNN*. https://edition.cnn.com/2020/10/09/africa/nigeria-police-sars-police-brutality-intl/index.html

Charles, A. (1996). Political Movement and Social Change: Analyzing Politics. *American Political Science Review, 90*(4), 874–884.

Dougherty, R., Mazursky, E., Nguyen, A.-T., & Ordonez, H. (2016). *The New Global Citizen: Harnessing Youth Leadership to Reshape Civil Society*. http://www.rhize.org/newglobalcitizen/

Ebeling, M. (2015). Epistemic Political Egalitarianism, Political Parties, and Conciliatory Democracy. *Political Theory, 44*(5), 629–656.

Eesuola, O. (2015). Protest Demonstration, Political Participation, and the Law in the Era of Terrorism: Nigeria's Public Order Act and the United States' HR347 in Perspectives. *International Journal of Arts and Humanities, 4*(2), 28–41.

Fielding, M. (2016). Why and How Schools Might Live Democracy as an Inclusive Human Order. In S. Higgins & F. Coffield (Eds.), *John Dewey's Democracy and education- A British tribute*. UCL IOE Press.

Galstyan, M. (2019). *Youth Political Participation: Literature Review*. European Commission and Council of Europe. https://pjpeu.coe.int/documents/42128013/47262631/Youth-Politicalparticipation_Lit+review_BRIEF_FINAL.pdf/1ff0bb91-a77b-f52e-25b4-5c8bd45a0c36

George, A. (2020, October 20). The Roots of the #EndSARS Protests in Nigeria. *The Washington Post*. https://www.washingtonpost.com/outlook/2020/10/25/roots-endsars-protests-nigeria/

Gladstone, R., & Specia, M. (2020). Nigeria's Police Brutality Crisis: What's Happening Now. *The New York Times*. https://www.nytimes.com/article/sars-nigeria-police.html

Hansen, J. M. (2016). Mobilisation, Participation, and Political Change. *Party Politics, 22*(2), 149–157.

Hari, S. (2014). The Evolution of Social Protest in Nigeria: The Role of Social Media in the "#OccupyNigeria" Protest. *International Journal of Humanities and Social Science Invention, 3*(9), 33–39.

Hern, E. (2017). Better Than Nothing: How Policies Influence Political Participation in Low-Capacity Democracies. *Governance, 30*(4), 583–600.

Hilker, L., & Fraser, E. (2009). *Youth Exclusion, Violence, Conflict and Fragile States* (Report Prepared for DFID). http://www.gsdrc.org/document-library/youth-exclusion-violenceconflict-and-fragilestates/SocialDevelopmentDirect

Hollander, J., & Einwohner, R. (2004). Conceptualizing Resistance. *Sociological Forum, 19*(4), 533–554.

Human Rights Watch. (2021). *Nigeria: A Year On, No Justice for #EndSARS Crackdown*. https://www.hrw.org/news/2021/10/19/nigeria-year-no-justice-endsars-crackdown

Ibezim, E. (2019). The Philosophy of Youth Inclusion in Nigerian Politics: Trend, Challenges and Prospect. *Journal of Religion and Human Relations, 11*(1), 119–136. https://www.ajol.info/index.php/jrhr/article/view/190041

Ibezim-Ohaeri, V. (2017). Confronting Closing Civic Spaces in Nigeria. *SUR-26, 14*(6), 129–140.

Isike, E., Olaitan, Z., & Isike, C. (2022). Cyberspace Xenophobia in South Africa. In C. Isike & E. Isike (Eds.), *Conflict and Concord: The Ambivalence of African Migrant/Host Relations in South Africa* (pp. 85–108). Palgrave Macmillan.

Jenkins, H., & Nico, C. (2013). Theorising Participatory Intensities: A conversation about Participation and Politics. *Convergence. The International Journal of Research into New Media Technologies*, 225–286.

Kingsley, P. (2013). NGOs, Doctors, and the Patrimonial State—Tactics for Political engagement in Nigeria. *Critical African Studies, 6*(1), 6–21.

Lambo, D. (2020, October 18). Lagos #ENDSARS Protesters Arrest Man for Stealing Phone. *Punch Newspaper*. https://punchng.com/lagos-endsars-protesters-arrest-man-for-stealing-phone/

Loudtips (2020, October 11). *A History of Police Brutality in Nigeria: A Case study of SARS 1992–2020*. Edu Project Topics. https://eduprojecttopics.com/product/a-history-of-police-brutality-in-nigeria-a-case-study-of-sars-1992-2020

Lührmann, A. (2013). *Enhancing Youth Political Participation throughout the Electoral Cycle: A Good Practice Guide*. United Nations Development Programme.

McCaffrie, B., & Akram, S. (2014). Crisis of Democracy? Recognizing the Democratic Potential of Alternative Forms of Political Participation. *Democratic Theory, 1*, 2–30.

Miladi, N. (2016). Social Media and Social Change. *DOMES: Digest of Middle East Studies, 25*(1), 36–51.

Milbrath, L. (1981). Political Participation. In S. Long (Ed.), *The Handbook of Political Behavior*. Plenum Press.

Muller, E. (1982). An Explanatory Model for differing Types of Participation. *European Journal of Political Research, 19*, 1–16.

Okon, D. (2020, October 4). Nigerians Insist on Disbandment of SARS as IGP Bans Killer Police Unit for Third Time. *Business Day Newspaper*. https://businessday.ng/features/article/nigerians-insist-on-disbandment-of-sars-as-igp-bans-killer-police-unit-for-third-time/

Ogundipe, S. (2017, December 5). #EndSARS: Nigeria Police Threaten Leader of Campaign Against Notorious Anti-robbery Squad. *Premium Times*. https://www.premiumtimesng.com/news/top-news/251453-endsars-nigeria-police-threaten-leader-of-campaign-against-notorious-anti-robbery-squad.html?tztc=1

Okunna, S. (2021). *#EndSARS Protest: Re-thinking Nigerian Youth and Government Policies* (Enugu: African Heritage Policy Working Paper).

Olafsson, J. (2007). Defiance: A Comment on the Logic of Protest. *Trames, 11*(61), 432–442.

Olaitan, Z. M. (2024). Women of EndSARS: Understanding Women's Participation in Protests in Nigeria. *International Journal on Law and Politics*, *2*, 25–49.

Olufowobi, S. (2018, June 4). Nigerian Youths Ready for Leadership—Young Alliance. *Punch*. https://punchng.com/nigerian-youths-ready-forleadership-young-alliance/

O'Toole, T. (2015). Beyond Crisis Narratives: Changing Modes and Repertoires of Political Participation among Young People. In K. Kallio, S. Mills, & T. Skelton (Eds.), *Politics, Citizenship and Rights, Geographies of Children and Young People* (Vol. 7, pp. 1–15). Springer. https://doi.org/10.1007/978-981-4585-94-1_2-1

Pleyers, G., & Karbach, N. (2014). *Young People Political Participation in Europe: What Do We Mean by Participation*? Strasbourg: Council of Europe.

Population Reference Bureau. (2023). *Africa's Future: Youth and the Data Defining Their Lives*. Available at: https://www.prb.org/resources/africas-future-youth-and-the-data-defining-theirlives/#:~:text=By%202030%2C%20young%20Africans%20are,under%20age%2035%20in%20Africa

Premium Times. (2020, November 10). *EndSARS: Businesses Count Losses Weeks After Chaos*. https://www.premiumtimesng.com/business/425429-endsars-businesses-count-losses-weeks-after-chaos.html?tztc=1

Redress. (2022). *Two Years On: No Accountability for the Lekki Tollgate Massacre*. https://redress.org/news/two-years-on-no-accountability-for-the-lekki-toll-gate-massacre/#:~:text=In%20November%202021%2C%20the%20Lagos,the%20recommendations%20of%20the%20JPI

Sabucedo, J.-M., & Arce, C. (1991). Types of Political Participation: A Multidimensional Analysis. *European Journal of Political Research, 20*, 93–102.

Schussman, A., & Soule, S. (2005). Process and Protest: Accounting for Individual's Protest Participation. *Social Forces, 84*(2), 1083–1108.

Scott, T., & Maryman, J. (2016). Using Social Media as a Tool to Complement Advocacy Efforts. *Global Journal of Community Psychology Practice, 7*(1S), 1–22.

Soloman, V. (2008). Participation of Youth Associations in Community Development Activities: A Case Study of Oron Local Government Area. *Bowen Journal of Agriculture, 1*(2), 100–107.

Soriano, M. T. (2013). Internet as a Driver of Political Change: Cyber-Pessimists and Cyber-Optimists. *Revista Del Instituto Español de EstudiosEstratégicos, 1*(7), 333–352.

UNDP & UNDESA. (2013). *Youth, Political Participation and Decision-Making*. https://www.un.org/esa/socdev/documents/youth/fact-sheets/youth-politicalparticipation.pdf

United Nations. (2005). Political Participation. https://www.un.org/womenwatch/osagi/wps/publication/Chapter3.htm

van Deth, J. (2016). *What Is Political Participation?* Oxford University Press.

Vega, P. (2020). Nigerian Activists Created #EndSARS in 2017. Now, It's Resurfaced and Sparked a Social Media Movement. *Los Angeles Times*. https://www.latimes.com/world-nation/story/2020-10-21/nigerian-activists-created-endsars-in-2017-now-its-resurfaced-and-sparked-a-social-media-movement

Verba, S., & Nie, N. (1972). *Participation in America: Political Democracy and Social Equality*. Harper & Row.

Zohdy, N. (2017). *Examining Why and How to Engage Young People in Global Development: A Literature Review*. World Bank Group. https://www.youthpower.org/resources/examining-why-and-how-engage-young-peopleglobal-development-literature-review

CHAPTER 7

Women-Focused Legislation, Economic Empowerment and Sustainable Development in Africa

Omowumi Omodunni Idowu

Introduction

Empowering women is central for all national policies needed for continuous improvement in life quality both for current and future generations (Bayeh, 2016). Women's empowerment is crucial for achieving gender equality and sustainable development. Achieving women's empowerment is integral to each of the 17 Sustainable Development Goals (SDGs). Only by ensuring the rights of women and girls across all the goals we will get to justice and inclusion, economies that work for all, and sustaining our shared environment now and for future generations.

Women's empowerment is important for achieving social development, pro-poor growth, and sustainable economic growth (Organisation for Economic Cooperation and Development, 2011). This includes

O. O. Idowu (✉)
Ekiti State University, Ado Ekiti, Nigeria
e-mail: omowumi.idowu@eksu.edu.ng

A. O. Akinola and E. A. Liaga (eds.), *Development and Regional Stability in Africa*, https://doi.org/10.1007/978-3-031-56695-0_7

equal participation in existing markets, access and control over productive resources, access to decent work, and meaningful participation in economic decisions at all levels. Increasing women's and girls' education enhances women economic empowerment and as more women work the economy improves and there is inclusive growth. Women and girls' empowerment drives economic growth as it improves health outcomes and creates a more peaceful and stable society. Women can be empowered socially, educationally, and economically.

Economic empowerment is an important component of women's empowerment that propels gender equality, poverty eradication and inclusive growth. Women's economic empowerment is defined as a transformative process that helps women and girls from being dependent to being independent, and from limited power, voice and choice, to having skills, opportunities and resources that are needed in all markets (Gate Foundation, 2022). Having skills, opportunities and resources empower women to compete equally with their male counterparts, and it also enables them to control and benefit from economic gains.

Everyone has the right to education, health services, to stay safe from violence and for their voices to be heard, so also are the women. Women economic empowerment is women's rights and in our contemporary world, discrimination has no place. Secondly, empowering the female folks makes families healthier and it creates a multiplier effect on productivity, efficiency and sustained economic growth. Women when economically empowered invest in their children well-being, education and in their communities. Evidence shows that children welfare, particularly in poor households, improves when income is in women's possession rather than men's (Ernst & Young, 2011).

Moreover, it was revealed that the survival probability of a child increases by about 20% when income is in the hands of the women because women invest more of their income in health and nutrition (World Bank, 2019). Moreso, women's economic empowerment has beneficial effects on family planning, nutrition, and maternal and child mortality. According to Idowu (2019), this also provides a springboard for families to move out of poverty and consequently the whole economy. It is believed that if women's labour participation was the same as men's, global gross domestic products (GDP) would amount to an annual $28 trillion in 2025 (Madgavkar et al., 2016). It is also the right and smartest thing to do given that women constitute about half of the world's population and an untapped human resource. This will promote a healthier and more prosperous economy.

While gender equality is women's right and women's rights are human rights (United Nations, 2014), it is important to say that cultural norms and belief systems majorly prevent the experience of women's rights and empowerment in Africa. In addition to these are educational barriers, issues of security, and lack of access to credit and finance and legal barrier, which can be found in Africa constitutional law, family law, property law, and labour law (IMF, 2022). Others are lack of political will on the part of the government, religious norms and values, urbanisation, women's productive years coinciding with their reproductive years, non-availability of childcare facilities and other forms of discrimination against women (Tsani et al., 2012).

African countries have endorsed and incorporated the sustainable development goals into their national and development plans for the implementation of sustainable development agenda. For most countries, these SDGs targets are prioritised, and adequate attention has been given by identified government units. Notwithstanding, while women constitute about 50.2% in sub-Saharan Africa (World Bank, 2023), only Rwanda and Namibia were able to close at least 80% of their gender gaps. Specifically, out of 146 countries assessed and among the top 10 countries that have considerably closed their gender gaps, Rwanda was in 6th position and Namibia 8th position with 81.1% and 80.7%, respectively (World Economic Forum, 2022).

This global commitment to implement the SDG 2030 agenda brought into the limelight the importance of investing in human resources of women in achieving these goals. What is surprising is that despite several programmes and policies geared towards bridging the gender gap, such as the United Nations (UN) Charter of 1945, the UN Convention on the Elimination of all Forms of Discrimination Against Women (CEDAW), 1989 UN Convention on Child's Rights, the Beijing Conference of 1995 and other numerous female-focused legislations. Also, with evidence from the International Monetary Fund (IMF) and World Bank data, there are about 280 legal reforms that have been enacted to improve the gender gap (Gonzales et al., 2015).

However, despite all these legislations and movements, progress for women has been slow and superficial, except for a country like Rwanda. This raises some pertinent questions: What is the state of women in the face of numerous women-friendly legislations and policies in Africa? What factors account for the ineffectiveness in the implementation of women-focused legislation in the continent? What is Rwanda doing differently? What lessons can be learned? This chapter investigates the state of women's economic empowerment in Africa, examines the factors militating against the implementation of women-focused legislation, explores Rwanda's approach to women's empowerment, and suggests solutions or policy recommendations.

Theories on Women Empowerment and Economic Development

Over the years, studies have tried to establish the relationship between women's economic empowerment and economic development. Some of these schools of thought include:

Economic Modernity—Modernisation theory describes and explains the transformation processes from traditional societies to modern societies. It believes that modern societies are more productive, children are well educated, and the less-privilege receive more welfare (Reyes, 2001). Modernisation takes place economically, politically, and socio-culturally. Economic modernisation implies a change of outlook towards earning profit, rational economic, the use of sophisticated technology, and persistent efforts in bringing about innovations in the production system. This is a transition from an agrarian economy which was only consumption-oriented to an industrial economy. This is otherwise known as classical modernisation, and it can be explained as the process of transformation from traditional societies to modern societies.

Economic modernisation was developed by Walt Whitman Rostow in the 1960s to provide answers as to why some countries were developed while others were not (Rostow, 1959). It focuses on how past and present premodern societies become modern. According to this theory, for a country to be developed it must drop its traditional attitudes, beliefs, values and institutions. A country's economy grows faster when people embrace attitudes and values that favour efficiency and entrepreneurship, and this can only be found in a modernised society. The theory posits that a country remains underdeveloped for as long as it holds on to its traditional beliefs, customs and culture that impede human capacity development. Invariably, development brings about changes in democracy and human choice. Economic development is important in increasing the number of women for power positions. Economic development is associated with a broad base distribution of educational and occupational resources. Thus, greater access to educational resources by women increases the chances for their professional development, thereby creating a larger pool of women eligible for political office.

U-shaped Hypothesis—This theory was propounded by Claudin Goldin in 1995. The theory states that female labour force participation is U-shaped during development process. It describes the relationship between female labour force participation rate and economic development (structural shifts in economic activity and changes to household labour supply and attitudes about women working outside the home). In basic term, the hypothesis states that at the early stage of economic development, when incomes are very low and when agriculture dominates, women are in the labour force to a great extent. They are sometimes paid labourers but are often unpaid workers on family farms and in family businesses, often engaging in family workshop production. Fertility rates are high because their economic engagements allow them to combine it with child rearing. As the society becomes richer, the structure of the economy shifts towards industrial production and a formal sector-based economy emerges. Thus, income rises in most societies often because of the expansion of market of the introduction of new technology, female labour force participation falls.

As a result of this low level of female participation and the incompatibility of wage work and childcare as well as socio-cultural restrictions on female employment outside of the home, women are not able to benefit from the new opportunities in the manufacturing industry and other formal sectors, leading to low rate of fertility among married women or the termination of employment after marriage or the birth of a child. This is often reinforced by social stigma, and even formal restrictions against female industrial workers or generally outside the home (Goldin, 1994). This hypothesis has been used to analyse different sorts of female labour force participation and development within and among countries (Robinson, 2005; Tsani et al., 2012). Intuitively, it means that gender equality is a spur to sustainable development particularly where the well-being of children is concerned.

Emancipation Hypothesis—Literally, emancipation means liberation, the process of being free as an individual or as a group from economic, social, legal, political, and cultural limitations (Booth, 2007). Kolasi (2019) opines that the emancipation movement is closely associated with the struggle for social transformation to promote human freedom and welfare. It denotes the elimination of all forms of restrictions and oppressions that prevent people from seeking and reaching self-actualisation, happiness, and fulfilment. The emancipation hypothesis was propounded by Alfred Adler in 1975 as one of the feminist theories of criminology. According to this hypothesis, there is a direct relationship between industrialisation and increasing employment and freedom for women. This implies that industrialisation fosters a new mentality and disintegration of patriarchal ideology. The hypothesis stipulates that when women become more economically independent, there is a tendency to engage in criminal activities. It also posits that emancipative cultural changes give rise to gender egalitarian attitudes and self-expression values that emphasises autonomy and human choice. This includes choices and autonomy of women (Inglehart & Welzel, 2005). In some sense, rising emancipative values lead to improvement in women empowerment in the society.

Constancy Hypothesis—This hypothesis posits that there are a lot of data related issues that present women as being less productive. It believes that women have been working and always work, and the curvilinear relationship is related to statistical artefact of women under counting during industrialisation (Rau & Wazienski, 1999). Census and data collection on women was inconsistent until 1982 when International Labour Organisation (ILO) provided a standard definition of what labour activity means. In early and mid-industrialisation stage, women are often under-represented in labour force activities because their activities during these periods were ignored.

Other schools of thought include historical perspective that cultural and political traditions impact women empowerment and development.

Enhancing Gender Equality and Women Empowerment in Africa

This section discusses different instruments for the promotion of gender equality. They are as follows:

The Convention on the Elimination of all Forms of Discrimination Against Women (CEDAW)—Prominence in the global fight for gender equality is CEDAW. This is one of the most widely ratified human rights treaties in the world. CEDAW was adopted by the UN General Assembly in 1979 and full implementation in 1981 marked a significant milestone in the international struggle for women's human rights. The treaty has helped to improve women's rights in Africa through constitutional and legislative reform. For example, the women's rights groups in Uganda rely on CEDAW as a tool in their effort to protect gender equality in the 1995 constitution (Bouta et al., 2005). Likewise in Kenya, the constitutional reform reflects CEDAW stance in the constitutional process.

The 1995 Beijing Women's Conference—The UN organised four world conferences on women, out of which is the Beijing women conference, 1995. Others are women conferences in Mexico City in 1975, Copenhagen in 1980 and Nairobi in 1985. The last conference was followed by a series of five-year reviews. The Beijing conference calls for a 30% affirmative quota for women in the economy.

Women Economic Empowerment (WEE)—The women's economic empowerment programme (WEE) was established by United Nations Women Regional Office for Eastern and Southern Africa, to provide medium for women and youth in the region to promote their rights by effectively participating in gainful economic activities and provide opportunities for wealth creation and asset building. The UN Women's global and regional (for Eastern and Southern Africa) strategic plans (2014–2017) lay more premium on women's economic empowerment, as a critical prerequisite for the achievement of gender equality and the empowerment of women. The goals of the programme are to: (i) increase women's access to economic empowerment and opportunities, (ii) build the entrepreneurial capacities of women as leaders in business and agricultural innovation, (iii) bring women to the forefront in the process of agricultural transformation and commercialisation across specific value chains by linking them to innovative business models and the formal sector.

The long-term goal of the WEE programme is to reach a minimum of 2 million women and youth in three years through an accelerated economic development approach that draws on a combination of proven successful gender inclusion models; strategic partnerships at all levels; and innovative interventions that address systemic bottlenecks and policy reform, institutional arrangements, and service delivery systems to realise women's economic empowerment.

Ending Violence against Women (EVAW)—Ending Violence against Women (EVAW) is a UN women's mandate support brought about to make a catalytic and innovative programme that can promote human rights, gender equality and women's empowerment. It is formed as a legal framework to address violence against women and girls towards the progress of the Beijing platform for action. Violence against women can take various forms such as domestic or intimate partner violence, sexual harassment and assault, female genital mutilation (FGM), trafficking and gender-related killings. These, in any setting, are a barrier to lasting peace, a burden on national economies, and an impediment to achieving sustainable development. In Africa, generic inequalities, poverty, humanitarian crisis and negative cultural norms on women could lead to permanent/ short-term damage or even death of women. The EVAW programme thus seeks to prevent and address all manners of violence by improving knowledge and awareness, creating safer public and private places for women, focusing on prevention by supporting innovative approaches to ending violence, and advocate for women. For instance, the UNiTE Campaign to end violence against women (United Nations Women, 2015).

In 2007, the Danish Prime Minister, Anders Fogh Rasmussen, introduced the Africa commission to bring to life how to meet the obvious challenges of Africa with specific focus on women and empowerment (Statsministeriet, 2008). By 2008, the commission held a conference on 'Women and Employment in Africa' in Maputo, Mozambique (Africa Commission, 2008). There are three major recommendations from the conference which are summarised as follows:

1. Since women are over-represented in the informal sector, which is featured by poor wages, insecure working conditions, etc. Therefore, improving the working conditions in the informal sector will go a long way to better the lives of women and thereby bridging the gender gap.
2. Support capacity development of non-governmental agencies and organisations, employers' associations and trade unions in advocating for women's economic empowerment and train women in organising themselves in economic organisation.
3. Provision of enabling environment, which include both legal and regulatory framework as well as financial services.

There is also the United Nations Security Council Resolution (UNSCR) on Women, Peace and Security (WPS). The resolution is guided by a series of commitments to women's rights that calls for national action and reporting on women in conflict prevention, conflict, and post-conflict situations. This resolution was first made on the Security

Council's agenda and adopted in October 2000 as Security Council Resolution (SCR) 1325 on Women, Peace and Security. The four (4) pillars of SCR 1325 revolve around women in the following ways:

i. Participation in peacemaking and peacebuilding.
ii. Rights protection during and after conflict.
iii. Role in conflict prevention.
iv. Specific needs during repatriation, rehabilitation, resettlement, reintegration, and post-conflict recovery (UN, Department of Political and Peacebuilding Affair, 2019).

Subsequently, the Council adopted nine additional resolutions on women, peace and security. These 10 resolutions are grouped into two: the first focuses on promoting women's active and effective participation in peacemaking and peacebuilding processes, and the second aims to prevent and address conflict-related sexual violence.

These resolutions are to ensure women participation in peacebuilding, protection from human rights violations, and importantly, women are empowered to access justice and services to eliminate discrimination. Also, there are country-specific legal provisions and policies to enhance female economic empowerment.

Legislations and Policies and the State of African Women

In Africa, women constitute a great spring of manpower for sustainable development and are therefore a powerful but untapped economic resource. However, socio-economic, cultural and other factors inhibit women's economic performance. To understand the state of African women in the face of numerous women-friendly legislations and policies, this chapter chose one country from the following regions in Africa Northern, Western, Eastern, Central and Southern Africa. Intuitively, high population translates to a high female population proportion, hence countries with highest population were chosen, using the 2019 World Population Data Sheet. These countries were Egypt, Nigeria, Ethiopia, Democratic Republic of Congo and South Africa. Even though a country has been chosen for Eastern Africa based on the population and as revealed in the Figure 7.1, Rwanda was added to make the sixth country,

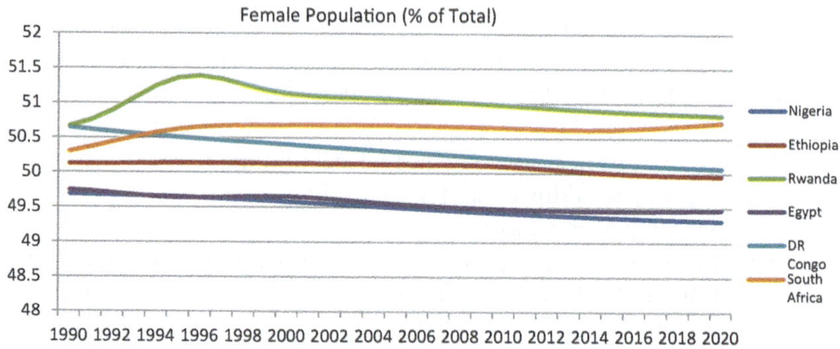

Fig. 7.1 Female population in selected African countries (*Source* It was constructed by the author in 2022 based on the data that was retrieved from World Development Indicators and World Bank Data Bank)

especially as a yardstick. This study presents empirical and theoretical explanations of the states of these chosen countries after most of these laws have been in place.

This chapter collects data from World Development Indicators (WDI) of the World Bank data bank and constructs a chart on the female population as the percentage of total population from 1990 to 2020 as presented in the above figure. Though with different population estimates, all the countries (Nigeria, Ethiopia, Rwanda, Egypt, Congo and South Africa) have female representing about 50% of its population. Nigeria remains the most populous and populated country in Africa, particularly in West Africa, with estimated population of over 206 million in 2020, and 49.3% of women population.

Ordinarily, this rapid population growth in the country particularly for female should be an advantage, but this is not true due to several factors like patriarchal ideology of gender roles, legal structure, religious values and norms, poverty, poor economy among others. This is followed by Ethiopia and Democratic Republic of Congo with estimated population of over 114 million and 102 million, respectively, in 2020. On the other hand, Rwanda has the least population among the chosen countries with over 12 million people but with remarkable women economic participation.

Economic Empowerment Indicators

There are different indicators for women economic empowerment ranging from female participation in labour, education attainment, employment rate to political involvement. These indicators were compared from the time when these legislations were made, reasonably choosing the important and widely accepted legislations such as CEDAW of 1981 and the Beijing conference of 1995.

Descriptive Statistics of Women Economic Empowerment Indicators in Africa

This section presents the descriptive statistics of the indicators of women economic empowerment in Africa, and due to data availability and to allow for some time frame for these legislations to be effective, the scope of this descriptive statistics was limited to 1990–2020.

a. **Labour Force Participation Rate**

The labour force participation rate is the total amount of labour force divided by the total working-age population (Organisation for Economic Cooperation and Development, 2022). Usually, the working population age refers to people between the ages 15 and 64 years. This indicator is useful in determining the size and composition of a country's human resources, policy formulation and understanding labour market behaviour for different segments of the population. Female labour force participation is the proportion of female population of ages 15 years and above that are economically active, all women who render their labour supply to produce goods and services for the period under study. In studying the relationship between female labour force participation and fertility, a country can predict the evolution of fertility rates from the current pattern of female participation in economic activity (ILO, 2003, 2022).

Table 7.1 presents female labour force participation in all the regions of Africa between 1990 and 2020 with an interval of 10 years. As shown in Table 7.1, in 1990 out of 132.61 million of female ages 15–64, 62.943% participated actively in the labour market of sub-Saharan Africa. By the year 2020, it declined to 59.663% of the female population with a percentage change of −5.211 from 1990 to 2020. Middle East and

Table 7.1 Female labour force participation

			Female labour Participation				
			1990	*2000*	*2010*	*2020*	*% change*
		Sub-Saharan	62.943	63.665	62.874	59.663	−5.211
		MENA	17.569	18.963	19.897	18.490	5.242
Africa Region							
N. Africa	Egypt		22.273	20.534	23.233	15.423	−30.755
E. Africa	Ethiopia		66.594	71.105	74.393	71.029	6.660
W. Africa	Nigeria		56.391	56.993	56.784	47.593	−15.602
C. Africa	DR. Congo		71.487	71.321	65.075	60.870	−14.852
S. Africa	South Africa		44.166	46.327	44.514	44.044	−0.276
	Rwanda		83.573	84.722	84.008	82.291	−1.534

Source It was constructed by the author based on the data that was retrieved from World Development Indicators and World Bank Data Bank

North Africa, on the other hand, experienced a positive change of 5.242 in female labour force participation between 1990 and 2020.

Apart from North Africa with evidence from Egypt that has a negative change of 30.755%, Southern Africa has the least female labour force participation of about 44% throughout these periods, with a percentage change of −0.276. This means that South Africa, which was chosen in Southern Africa, has no considerable change in female labour force participation from 1990 to 2020. This shows that the increase in female labour participation over the years has not been able to match up with an increase in job creation in South Africa. Coupled with the feminisation of poverty and occupational segregation, women are largely in low-paid occupations in South Africa.

In addition, Table 6.1 shows that the Democratic Republic of Congo, except for Rwanda from East Africa, has the highest female labour force participation in the region, with 71.487 in 1990 but drastically declined to 60.870 in 2020, leaving Ethiopia with the highest participation of 71.029 in 2020. However, all the regions and with the inclusion of Rwanda experienced a decrease in female labour participation for the period under study. The reasons for this may be linked to the ripple effects of Great Recession, changes in social norms that are offset by changing industrial structure and the segregation of employment in the labour market, household formation and unpaid care work, and the effect of the coronavirus.

b. **Female Education**

Education for women or female education is all forms of education which aims at improving knowledge and skills for women or girls. It encompasses both formal education and non-formal education. In every sense, female education is one of the rudiments of the growth and development of a country. It can potentially transform lives, ensure economic growth, and achieve gender equality. Formal education provides women the impetus to command decent wages and to make their own decisions. Table 7.2 shows the percentage change in female secondary school enrolment between 1990 and 2020. This represents the percentage of total enrolment in secondary schools that comprises female students. Secondary education is fundamental in establishing the groundwork for lifelong learning and development. There is a tremendous positive change in female education in Africa. In sub-Saharan Africa, women constitute 19.951% of total secondary school enrolment. By 2000, it rose to 23.038% and in 2020 it was 40.722%. The percentage change of female secondary school enrolment in sub-Saharan Africa is 104.110% from 1990 to 2020.

In Table 7.2, the percentage change in female secondary school enrolment for these periods (1990–2020) is 62.901 in the Middle East and

Table 7.2 Percentage change in female secondary school enrolment

		Education				
		1990	*2000*	*2010*	*2020*	*% change*
	Sub-Saharan	19.951	23.038	35.7833	40.722	104.110
	MENA	48.363	65.020	72.7431	78.784	62.901
Africa Region						
N. Africa	Egypt	64.280	79.151	67.941	86.679	34.847
E. Africa	Ethiopia	10.742	10.879	31.589	–	194.095
W. Africa	Nigeria	21.496	22.447	41.191	42.635	98.335
C. Africa	DR. Congo	15.806	–	30.131	–	90.630
S. Africa	South Africa	74.595	85.497	96.564	107.690	44.367
	Rwanda	14.410	10.800	31.618	42.613	195.729

Source It was constructed by the author based on the Data that was retrieved from World Development Indicators and World Bank Data Bank

North Africa (MENA). The amount of growth experienced in sub-Saharan Africa is greater than what is observed in MENA. At the regional level, all regions had growth in their female secondary school enrolment between 1990 and 2020. However, there was tremendous growth in East Africa with evidence from Ethiopia (194.095) and Rwanda (195.729) percentage change. The least growths of 34.847% were seen in Northern Africa and 44.367 percentage change in Southern Africa. Studies show that reduction in fertility is linked to improvement in education. Over the years, there is considerably decrease in fertility and this has given more opportunities for girls' schooling.

c. **Political Participation**

Political participation involves taking part in the decision-making process and making public policies. Women political participation deals with women's understanding of their fundamental human rights to participate and have a voice at every stage of decision making and in ensuring better accountability to women. Increasing the number of women political participation, particularly in parliament is giving stronger attention to women's issues. Women political participation is important in attaining gender equality and genuine democracy.

In absolute term the proportion of women in national parliament in sub-Saharan is greater than that of MENA, but there was good improvement in MENA with about 335.681% change between 1990 and 2020. As of 2000, 11.585 and 4.207 proportion of national parliaments seats were occupied in sub-Saharan and MENA, respectively. By 2020 the proportion increased to 24.869% in sub-Saharan Africa, and 18.329 proportion in MENA. Regionally, Northern Africa with evidence from Egypt experienced greater change in the proportion of women in national parliament with about 1282.728 percentage change, from 1.982 proportion of women in parliament in 1990 to 27.411 in 2020 (Table 7.3).

This was followed by Eastern Africa (Ethiopia) from 7.692% of total national parliament seats to 38.757 in 2020, representing a 403.840 percentage change. While all regions experienced improvement in women political participation, in absolute terms, Nigeria has the least proportion of women in its national parliament as of 2020. 7.222% of the national parliament seat was occupied by women. Women in Central

Table 7.3 Percentage change in the proportion of women in national parliament

		Proportion of Women in National Parliament				
		1990	*2000*	*2010*	*2020*	*% change*
	Sub-Saharan	–	11.585	18.737	24.869	114.655
	MENA	–	4.207	10.426	18.329	335.681
Africa Region						
N. Africa	Egypt	–	1.982	12.695	27.411	1282.728
E. Africa	Ethiopia	–	7.692	27.788	38.757	403.840
W. Africa	Nigeria	–	3.419	6.983	7.222	111.250
C. Africa	DR. Congo	–	–	8.400	12.800	52.381
S. Africa	South Africa	–	29.825	44.500	46.750	56.750
	Rwanda	–	25.714	56.250	61.250	138.194

Source It was constructed by the author based on the data that was retrieved from World Development Indicators and World Bank Data Bank

Africa (Democratic Republic of Congo) and Southern Africa (South Africa) have the least percentage change in national parliament from 1990 to 2020. Rwanda had started on a good note in 2000; thus, women occupied 61.250% of seats in the Rwandan national parliament.

d. **Female Employment**

Employment is another form of economic empowerment. Female employment is any form of work for pay or profit that females or women are engaged in. Female employment is a lever for all social change (Idowu & Owoeye, 2019). According to ILO (2022), female employment is the percentage of women of working-age out of the total working-age population (from ages 15 upward), who were engaged in any activity to produce goods or provide services for pay or profit. This is employee employment of women. In Table 7.4, sub-Saharan Africa and MENA had negative percentage changes of 6.909% and 4.858%, respectively, of the percentage of women who are employed by women's population between 2000 and 2020. This means the percentage of women who were employed decreased from 59.289% in 2000 to 55.193% in 2020 for sub-Saharan Africa, despite the advocacy for female empowerment.

Table 7.4 Percentage change in female employment

		Employment				
		1990	*2000*	*2010*	*2020*	*% change*
Sub-Saharan			59.289	58.805	55.193	−6.909
MENA		–	15.672	16.495	14.946	−4.858
Africa Region						
N. Africa	Egypt	–	15.879	18.145	11.78	−25.814
E. Africa	Ethiopia	–	67.763	72.113	68.157	0.006
W. Africa	Nigeria	–	54.719	54.677	43.509	−20.487
C. Africa	DR. Congo	–	69.652	62.993	58.122	−16.554
S. Africa	South Africa	–	29.673	32.486	30.375	2.366
	Rwanda	–	84.249	83.128	80.976	−3.885

Source It was constructed by the author based on the data that was retrieved from World Development Indicators and World Bank Data Bank

In 2000, the regions with the least female employment in proportion to their population were North Africa (Egypt) with 15.879%, and Southern Africa (South Africa) with 29.673%. On the other hand, while all the regions experienced negative changes, Ethiopia and South Africa had positive changes. Northern Africa (Egypt), Western Africa (Nigeria) and Central Africa (DR. Congo) had negative changes of 25.814%, 20.487% and 16.544%, respectively.

In summary, Rwanda is relatively a good representation of women empowerment in all the indicators except in female secondary education. Notwithstanding the country experienced negative growth between 1990 and 2020 in its female employment and female labour force participation. In proportion to population, Nigeria has the least share of women representation in national parliament (7.2%), even though women constitute about 49.32% of Nigeria's estimated population of 206,139,587 (ILO, 2022). This was a gradual increase, from 15 out of 454 seats in 1999, to 29 seats out of 440 seats in 2019. Though there is improvement in all the regions, a lot must be done to fill the huge gaps.

Rwanda: A Case Study

Rwanda gained independence in 1962. Its post-colonial period was marred with ethnic violence that resulted in the 1994 genocide. The Tutsis faced persecution from the militia Hutu groups, such as the 'Interahamwe', as well as from civilians, soldiers of the Rwandan armed forces, including the presidential guard. The administrative, military and political leaders, at both national and local levels, were also involved in these targeted actions (Human Rights Watch, 1996). They were perceived to be associated with Rwandan Patriotic Front (a group that was allegedly planning another invasion), which necessitated a self-defence.

Extremist propaganda during the genocide, and encouraged by the Hutus who were spreading a false belief that the sexuality of Tutsi women, was a means through which the Tutsi society aimed to infiltrate and dominate the Hutus (Hogg, 2010). The propaganda claimed that Tutsi women were working for the interest of their ethnic group and threatening to steal the jobs and the husbands of Hutu. They directed and encouraged both the killings and sexual violence to further their political goal (i.e. ethnic cleansing). Hutu women hated and became jealous of the Tutsi women, who were adjudged beautiful and arrogant, and their wealth. Hence, sexual violence was committed against the Tutsi women as a means of dehumanising and subjugating the ethnic group. Some Hutu women were also targeted because of their affiliation with the 'enemy', either as a spouse or by protecting the Tutsis.

Rwanda progress in female empowerment was a consequence of the country 1994 genocide, which out-rightly disrupts its demographic configuration. In support of this is the launching of societal reformation process emphasising that no one should be left behind. Women constituted about 70% of the country and as a result, gender equality became the central policy reform in Rwanda. According to the World Economic Forum (2021), Rwanda is among the first 10 countries that are closing the gender gap in the world. The Rwandan 2003 constitution implemented the principle of equality between men and women, and it emphasises that women should occupy at least 30% of parliament positions. It is quite interesting that women occupy 61.2% of parliamentary seats in Rwanda (World Development Indicators, 2022).

This further creates the opportunity to successfully push for major legal frameworks that can empower or strengthen women participation and gender equality in Rwanda. Thus, it is imperative to reflect on what works in Rwanda, particularly in relation to laws, institutions and policies. In terms of law, the country has passed some laws to ensure inclusive governance and gender equality. Some of which are:

Property Law—First, law No 27/2016 of 08/07/2016 provides equal inheritance, succession, and land rights and prohibits gender discrimination on property possession and ownership among married couples. Second, there are also equal rights for both men and women on land access, ownership and utilisation in law No 43/2013 of 16/06/2013. This provision has been implemented in Rwanda as against other African countries where laws do not see the light of the day.

Labour Law—There is legislation on labour matters to institute equal wage and working conditions for both sexes and protection against gender-based violence or harassment of any kind in the workplace in law No 13/2009 of 27/05/2009. Furthermore, there are specific rights and benefits on issues related childbearing, such as childcare supporting system for pregnant and breastfeeding working mothers. Also, Section 3 of 2016 law contains the provision of three months of paid maternity leave (Abbott & Malunda, 2016), which makes it much easier for women to stay in labour market once they started having family. It further helps in protecting the child. All these are responsible for the country's higher rate of 82.291% in female labour force participation, as against what is obtained in sub-Saharan Africa (59.663%) and the global average of 49.922% (World Development Indicators, 2022).

In South Africa, women labour rights include right for collective bargaining, access to the dispute resolution processes, and be protected from dismissal. Other considerations for women include the minimum conditions of employment such as maternity leave, sick leave and overtime pay, prevention of discrimination, affirmative action and access to skills development. Also, minimum wages were legislated through sectoral determinations for domestic and agricultural workers, particularly for vulnerable workers, where collective bargaining forums are not in place. (Chen, 2008). Ghana Act contains special provisions relating to casual and temporary workers that allow them to benefit from the provisions of collective agreements, which include access to the same medical provisions available to permanent workers, equal pay for work of equal value, full minimum wage for all days in and public holidays (Asamoah, 2018).

Tax Law—Introducing gender into budgeting is about being gender sensitive in the preparation and in the execution process of a budget. Gender related principles are adopted in Rwandan budgetary system. It is required that a gender budget statement that shows how gender is mainstreamed is provided with Rwandan budget. Also, all public entities are mandated to submit an individual audit report of how programmes for gender equality have been implemented. Implying that, beyond legislating gender equality, there must be political will from the top public office holders and policymakers to ensure its success. While property and tax laws relate with economic empowerment, there are other laws, such as:

1. Laws that are institutionalised to finance gender equality across all government expenditures.
2. Laws to prevent and to punish gender-based violence offences on cases such as child defilement, forced marriage, marital rape, human trafficking, and spouse harassment.
3. Laws for the protection of children against child abuse, and
4. Laws for the promotion of gender equality principle through persons and family as well as relation between persons.

In Rwanda, the government enshrined gender consideration in its major programmes. These are institutions with specific and complementary roles, set up to ensure and the realisation of gender equality and women empowerment under the umbrella of the National Gender Machinery (NGM). The following offices support the NGM for effective performance of its goals: Ministry in charge of Gender and Family Promotion (MIGEPROF); Rwandan Forum for Women Parliamentarians (RFWP); National Women's Council (NWC); and Gender Monitoring Office (GMO).

In addition, there are policies developed by the government to ensure that the principle of equality between men and women is mainstreamed in all sectors of the economy. Examples of these policies are: National Gender Policy; National Family Promotion and Protection Policy; National Policy Against Gender-Based Violence; and the National Strategy for Transformation, which is a seven-year national strategy underpinned by sectoral strategies on achieving the sustainable development goals, ensuring equal opportunities and fostering cultural solidarity with vulnerable groups.

Other areas of women empowerment can be seen in Information and Communication Technology (ICT), and in the field of Science, Technology, Engineering and Mathematics (STEM). Rwanda government has driven initiative for other African countries in support of ICT for their school-age girls, including those in rural areas, this is popularly called Miss Geek. There is the establishment of the Carnegie Mellon University, Africa campus and funding from banks. In line with this, the University of Rwanda College of Science and Technology has for some years produced women leaders in ICT both in Rwanda and globally. In addition, there is a gender-free recruitment policy by the African Institute of Mathematics (AIMS). The country has further adopted an e-governance platform (Irembo) to improve public services and facilitating closer relationship between the people and government. Other areas of achievements are decline in maternal mortality rates due to adequate access to quality and affordable health services.

Conclusion: Lessons to be Learned from Rwanda

This chapter has reflected on the place of women's economic empowerment in Africa. It looked at theories of women's empowerment as it relates to economic development. It also examined some measures adopted to enhance gender equality and women's empowerment in Africa. Additionally, this chapter investigated the state of women amidst various legislations by country-specific case study from five regions in Africa. It explores the place of African women in labour participation, education enrolment, political participation and employment. It went further to highlight Rwanda's approach to women empowerment and suggested policy recommendations.

African countries ought to enhance their appeals to international investors in order to enrich their knowledge reservoir and foster innovation. The key to fostering growth and development in Africa lies in harnessing the full potential of its human capital and talents, with a crucial emphasis on enabling women to actively engage in social, political, and economic spheres. Sustainable development is dependent on consistent efforts to eliminate discrimination and promote gender equality in countries where progress has been seen, and intensified in countries that are lagging behind. It thus becomes important for the government to provide essential services to the people through technology and other forms of innovation as being demonstrated in Rwanda. A replica of the Rwandan e-governance ('Irembo') platform can be adopted by other AU member-states to reach people in the rural areas. This is required to bridge the gender gaps in education, employment, access government services and for inclusive governance.

There is a need to reform countries' legal framework. Indeed, maternity leave and paid maternity leave should be adopted in other Africa countries to retain women at work. In line with these childcare facilities should be encouraged in workplaces. While government promotes women in ICT and innovation sector to dispel the myth of women incapability in ICT, there should be a kind of dis-orientation against occupational segregation and patriarchal ideology of the kinds of jobs women can do.

Rwanda has a statutory order of at least 50% of women in the parliament as against the Beijing conference of 1995 that calls for a 30% affirmative quota for women in the economy and Women Economic Empowerment (WEE). It is commendable that the country achieved 61% of women representation in parliamentary seats in 2020. This has further increased women's political participation and involvement in matters that affect them, thereby bridging the gender gap in Rwanda. Thus, women organisations, activists and policymakers in African countries should ensure strict compliance with enacted laws as it relates to gender equality. African countries that have not yet enacted gender-parity laws or put in place policies or programmes to ensure gender equity in leadership positions, education, employment and other economic opportunities, should be encouraged or empowered to do so.

Furthermore, the link between political commitments and operational implementation should be significantly strengthened. Also, there is a need to increase the capability of girls to actualise their rights, determine life outcomes and influence decision making to have access to safe, quality education programmes and services. In line with this, there should be mentorship and scholarship programmes for the girls' child.

References

Abbott, P., & Malunda, D. (2016). The Promise and the Reality: Women's Right in Rwanda. *African Journal of International and Comparative Law, 24*(4), 561–581.

Adler, F. (1975). *Sisters in Crime: The Rise of the New Female Criminal.* McGraw-Hill.

Africa Commission. (2008). *Africa Commission Fact Sheet, Commission on Effective Development Cooperation with Africa.* https://www.ft.dk/samling/20072/lovforslag/l188/pgf/6/spm/1/svar/570287/594322.pdf

Asamoah, S. (2018). Historical Overview of Development of Communal Labour from Pre-colonial to Post Independent Ghana. *International Journal of Scientific and Research Publications, 8*(4), 10–16.

Bayeh, E. (2016). The Role of Empowering Women in Achieving Gender Equality to the Sustainable Development of Ethiopia. *Pacific Science Review b: Humanities and Social Sciences, 2*, 37–42.

Booth, K. (2007). *Theory of World Security*. Cambridge University Press.

Bouta, T., Frerks, G., & Bannon, I. (2005). *Gender, Conflict, and Development*. The World Bank.

Chen, M. (2008). Women and Employment in Africa: A Framework for Action. *Second Conference of the Africa Commission*. http://wiego.org/sites/wiego.org/files/publications/files/Chen-Women-Employment

Ernst and Young. (2011). *Women of Africa, a Powerful Untapped Economic Force for the Continent*.http://www.ey.com/Publication/vwLUAssets/WomenofAfrica/$FILE/Women%20of%20Africa%20final.pdf

Gate Foundation. (2022). *Women Economic Empowerment*. https://www.gatesfoundation.org/equal-is-greater/

Goldin, C. (1994). *The 'U' Shaped Female Labour Force Function in Economic Development and Economic History* (NBER Working Paper Series [WP 4707]).

Gonzale, C., Jain-Chandra, S., Kochhar, K., & Newiak, M. (2015). *Fair Play: More Equal Laws Boost Female Labor Force Participation* (IMF Staff Discussion Note SDN/15/02). International Monetary Fund.

Hogg, N. (2010). Women's Participation in the Rwanda Genocide: Mothers or Monsters. *International Review of the Red Cross, 12*, 69–102.

Human Rights Watch. (1996). Human Rights Watch World Report. Retrieved from https://www.hrw.org/reports/pdfs/worldreports/world.96/intro.pdf

Idowu, O. (2019). Demand Drivers of Female Labour Force Participation: Evidence from Selected African Countries. *Economics, 17*(1), 81–94.

Idowu, O. O., & Taiwo, O. (2019). Female Labour Force Participation in African Countries: An Empirical Analysis. *Indian Journal of Human Development, 13*(1), 278–293.

Inglehart, R., & Welzel, C. (2005). *Modernization, Cultural Change and Democracy*. Cambridge University Press. https://doi.org/10.1017/CBO9780511790881

International Labour Organization. (2003). Female Labour Force Participation Rate and Fertility. *Key Indicators of the Labour Market* (3rd ed.). Chapter 1 (Geneva).

International Labour Organization. (2022). *ILO STAT Database Description* (LFS, STLFS, RURBAN). https://ilostat.ilo.org/resources/concepts-and-definitions/description-labour-force-statistics/. Accessed on 13 September, 2022.

International Monetary Fund. (2022). *Tackling Legal Impediments to Women's Economic Empowerment* (Working paper 22/37: 1–74).

Kolasi, K. (2019). Emancipation. In *The Palgrave Encyclopedia of Global Security Studies* (pp. 1–4). Springer International Publishing. https://doi.org/10.1007/978-3-319-74336-3_197-1

Madgavkar, A., Ellingrud, K., & Krishnan, M. (2016). The Economic Benefits of Gender Parity. *Stanford Social Innovation Review.* https://www.mckinsey.com/mgi/overview/in-the-news/the-economic-benefits-of-gender-parity. Retrieved on 20 September 2022.

Organization for Economic Cooperation and Development. (2011). Women Economic Empowerment (Issues Paper). Ac Network on Gender Equality (GENDERNET). https://ww.oecd.org/dac/genderdevelopment/47561694.pdf. Retrieved 16 September 2022.

Organization for Economic Cooperation and Development. (2022). *Labour Force Participation Rate* (Indicator). https://doi.org/10.1787/8a801325-en. Accessed on 13 September 2022.

Rau, W., & Wazienski, R. (1999). Industrialization, Female Labour Force Participation and the Modern Division of Labour by Sex. *Industrial Relations, 38*(4), 459–617.

Reyes, G. E. (2001). *Four Main Theories of Development: Modernization, Dependency, Word-system and Globalization.* Euro Mediterranean University Institute, Universidad Complutense de Madrid.

Robinson, J. (2005). Female Labour Force Participation in the East and North Africa. *Wharton Research Scholars Journal.* Penn Libraries, University of Pennsylvania.

Rostow, W. W. (1959). The Stages of Economic Growth. *The Economic History Review* (New Series), *12*(1), 1–16.

Statsministeriet. (2008). *Intervention by Ander Fogh Rasmussen, Prime Minister of Denmark, at the MDG High-Level Event.* https://www.un.org/millenniumgoals/2008highlevel/rt/1/Denmark.pdf

Tsani, S., Paroussos, L., Fragiadakis, C., Charalambidis, I., & Capros, P. (2012). Female Labour Force Participation and Economic Development in Southern Mediterranean Countries: What Scenarios for 2030? *Mediterranean Prospects, Thinking Ahead for the Mediterranean. Working Paper 7—Human Capital, Social Protection, Inequality and Migration* (pp. 1–18). http://www.medpro-foresight.eu

United Nations Women. (2015). Prevent Violence Against Women. In *commemoration of the International Women's day.* Retrieved from https://www.unwomen.org/en/news/in-focus/end-violence-against-women/2015

United Nations. (2014). *Women's Rights Are Human Rights.* United Nations Human Rights.

United Nations. (2019). *Department of Political and Peacebuilding Affairs (DPPA) Women Peace and Security Policy*. https://dppa.un.org/sites/default/files/190604_dppa_wps_policy_-_final.pdf

World Bank. (2019). *World Development Report 2019: The Changing Nature of Work*. World Bank. https://doi.org/10.1596/978-1-4648-1328-3.

World Bank. (2023). *Female Population (Percentage of total population)*. World Development Indicators, World Bank Data Bank. Retrieved from https://data.worldbank.org/indicator/SP.POP.TOTL.FE.ZS?locations=ZG

World Economic Forum. (2021). *Global Gender Gap Report 2021*. https://www.weforum.org/publications/global-gender-gap-report-2021/

World Economic Forum. (2022) *Global Gender Gap Report: Insight Report*. http://reports.weforum.org/global-gender-gap-report-2022

CHAPTER 8

SADC Peacekeeping Missions and the Quest for Regional Security: From Congo to Mozambique

Naledi Ramontja and Adeoye O. Akinola

Introduction

Since its establishment in August 1992, the Southern African Development Community (SADC) has been mandated to address regional issues such as peace, security, and stability. The regional body also aimed at enhancing regional integration, democratisation, and economic development. Stakeholders are quick to realise that SADC's success depends on the peace and security of the region. Thus, while acknowledging the wider scope of SADC, this chapter focuses particularly on its peace and security mandate, as the organisation enters 30 years of existence. The complex character of conflict in the Southern African region and its protracted nature have inevitably attracted the attention of the regional body. From the Congo to Mozambique, divergent conflicts have led to

N. Ramontja · A. O. Akinola (✉)
Institute for Pan-African Thought and Conversation, University of Johannesburg, Johannesburg, South Africa
e-mail: aoakinola@uj.ac.za

A. O. Akinola and E. A. Liaga (eds.), *Development and Regional Stability in Africa*, https://doi.org/10.1007/978-3-031-56695-0_8

the destruction of lives and property, including massive displacement of a cross-section of the citizens and their impoverishment. As reported by the United Nations High Commissioner for Refugees (UNHCR, 2022), about 8.4 million are categorised as forcibly displaced and stateless people in the region, due to devastating conflict and internal displacement in Mozambique and the Democratic Republic of the Congo (DRC).

Zimbabwe has been associated with dictatorship and human displacements, despite the exit of President Robert Mugabe in 2017. The incumbent President Emmerson Mnangagwa continued in a similar fashion by ruthlessly cracking down on the opposition and perpetuating "electoral autocracy" during the 2018 election that consolidated his hold on power (Feldstein, 2018). In continuation of the long-standing separatist struggle in Angola, in 2016 armed insurgents attacked the army in the Cabinda province, noted for oil resources, and disrupted the extraction of crude oil in the area (Aeby, 2018). While the nature of the conflicts in the region differs, their effect on regional peace, security, and development has been devastating. The SADC, through its peacekeeping force, has attempted to combat violent conflicts through military intervention.

The chapter thus reflects on the root causes of regional insecurity, contends with the SADC's peace and security architecture, and examines the role of the SADC's peacekeeping mission in enforcing peace and order in the region, through the cases of Mozambique and Congo DRC. Over the past decades, the SADC region had enjoyed peace and stability and is considered one of the most peaceful regions in Africa, but the eruption of terrorism in Mozambique's resource community and resurgence of armed conflict in the DRC has forced SADC to mobilise regional military forces to secure peace in the troubled zone. The chapter offers an overview of the challenges to regional peace and security and explores the necessity of peacekeeping missions in the region. The last section delves into the case studies with a particular focus on the ongoing conflict in the DRC and the escalating insurgents in the Cabo Delgado province of Mozambique.

Political Instability and Insecurity in SADC

The SADC has been established to promote regional peace and stability and to "prevent, contain and resolve inter and intra state conflicts in the region through peaceful means" (Kgosi, 2021: 38). The outbreak of conflicts in the region and the need for SADC reform necessitated hosting of an Extra-ordinary Summit in Windhoek, Namibia, on 9 March 2001, which led to the adoption of the SADC Treaty Amendment (2001). The regional organisation is mandated to facilitate the creation and strengthening of a regional institutional framework that promotes the peaceful resolution of conflicts and promotes a sense of shared responsibility and interests in the SADC region (Mbuende, 2001). Its main goal is the adoption of robust strategies for effective peacebuilding and reconstruction of Southern Africa. The Organ for Politics, Defense and Security Cooperation (OPDS), one of the eight (8) institutions established under Article 9 of the Treaty Amendment (2001) remains the main institution within SADC responsible for the implementation of peace and security in the region (SADC, 2022c). The institution, which is responsible for the enforcement of action under international law, is therefore mandated to provide member states with a plan and direction to approach matters that threaten peace, security, and stability in the region (Kgosi, 2021).

The regional bloc is also committed to the maintenance of peace in the region through the SADC Standby Force established in 2007 to support peace operations and missions in the region (Deleglise, 2021). The SADC Standby Force has mediation and election-monitoring capacities, these activities are fulfilled in collaboration with a panel of SADC Elder Mediators and the Mediation Support Unit (Albuquerque & Wiklund, 2015). All these structures deal with different aspects of integration and contribute to promoting peace and security in the region (Kgosi, 2021). The Protocol on Peace and Security Cooperation and the Mutual Defence Pact are the main documents that guide SADC's interventions (Albuquerque & Wiklund, 2015). Other structural support systems include the Strategic Indicative Plan for the Organ on Defense, Politics, and Security (SIPO), which focuses on the socio-economic factors that influence the intervention of the regional body as well as regional security. The main objective of SIPO is to create a friendly environment in which the region can achieve economic growth, appreciable standards of living, peace, security, and poverty alleviation (Kgosi, 2021).

The vision of SADC is to position itself consistently and strategically as the first respondent to conflicts in the region. While it has struggled to achieve this due to several impediments including institutional weaknesses and lack of political will by regional political elites, it has not hesitated to contain and resolve inter- and intra-state conflicts in the region. These have been achieved through military interventions and conflict prevention mechanisms, which take the form of military response, negotiations, mediation, preventive diplomacy, and arbitrations (Kgosi, 2021). These mechanisms have been implemented in various conflicts in the region, such as the intervention in the DRC (1979), Zimbabwe's post-election conflict (2008), Lesotho (1998), and the Madagascar coup (2009). These interventions are characterised by controversies, failures, and limitations.

The SADC has been rocked by several limitations and challenges, which are typical of its quest to become a supranational institution. In some cases, the regional body has failed to exercise its mandate; two notable cases were its inability to intervene in the political crisis in both Zimbabwe and Madagascar (Albuquerque & Wiklund, 2015). The Zimbabwean political crisis could be traced back to politics of exclusion promoted by the ruling political party, Zimbabwe African National Union-Patriotic Front (ZANU-PF), and its autocratic posture. While the establishment of the Movement for Democratic Change (MDC), and a considerable loss of constitutional referendum for ZANU-PF strongman, former President Robert Mugabe continue to run the country like a one-party state (See Cawthra, 2010). The country experienced a period of political standoffs leading to increased state repression, pre-election violence, political oppression, and to a larger extent hyperinflation (Cawthra, 2010). In March 2008, Zimbabwe held elections, which led to the assault and wrongful arrests of some members of the opposition parties (Kgosi, 2021). This drew negative attention within the international communities, including its regional partners, leading to calls for the imposition of sanctions against the country, including a call for SADC to intervene in the growing autocracy of both Mugabe and his successor, President Mnangagwa.

Despite the mounting pressures on the regional body, SADC was very reluctant to intervene in the political crisis in Zimbabwe, instead the regional body agreed to some extent that the crisis in Zimbabwe was caused by foreign powers, including Western sanctions and the pressures to reverse the radicalisation of the county's land redistribution policy (Cawthra, 2010). Aside from the 'aloofness' of SADC, one of the regional powers, South Africa, also failed to live up to its responsibility as a regional peacemaker and act against the high-handedness of the Zimbabwean ruling elite, led by its close ally, Robert Mugabe. This silence has been categorised as a display of 'quiet diplomacy' (Alden, 2002). Not only did SADC fail to intervene timelessly in the crisis, but Pretoria also has 'refused' to condemn the electoral processes and the violations of human rights, political repression, and the breach of the rule of law that have become the norm in Zimbabwe (Cawthra, 2010). The PSC Report

(2020) provides more context to the silence of SADC and South Africa to the protracted Zimbabwean political crisis,

> Ruling parties such as the ANC in South Africa, ZANU PF in Zimbabwe, Frelimo in Mozambique, SWAPO in Namibia, and the MPLA in Angola tend to shield one another from interference or criticism. This well-known 'brotherhood' – as African heads of state like to describe it – allows some regimes to get away with murder. This is also where SADC differs from ECOWAS, where the memories of the struggle against colonialism are not as fresh in everyone's minds as in Southern Africa. Here the links between former liberation movements remain strong. SADC is also hamstrung by a number of institutional obstacles.

However, the regional organisation eventually implemented mediation efforts alongside the African Union (AU), which led to the signing of the Global Political Agreement (GPA) (Albuquerque & Wiklund, 2015). The GPA aimed to create the required electoral framework to ensure that elections were free and fair (Albuquerque & Wiklund, 2015). In the case of the Mozambican conflict, it took about two and a half years for SADC to respond to the crisis. This shows SADC's lackadaisical disposition toward the maintenance of laws and order within the region. Its lack of cohesion and consensus on the reign of terror in Mozambique has led to major backlash on the regional body as well as the intervention of non-SADC African countries, such as Rwanda, as one of the first external actors to respond to the conflict in Cabo Delgado region of the country (Peace & Security Report, 2020).

Despite the efforts of the regional body, several SADC countries had less interest in the political instability in Madagascar and only a few of the member states have diplomatic representations in the country (Cawthra, 2010). SADC managed to intervene in the early stages of the conflict through different approaches, including meditations. The regional institution later suspended Madagascar from membership due to unconstitutional changes of government imposed by President Andry Rajoelina (Cawthra, 2010). The repressions of President Andry Nirina Rajoelina offer compelling evidence for the insinuation that SADC could not end the political turmoil in the country.

On the other hand, in 2014, a fallout between Lesotho's Prime Minister Thomas Thabane, and the Deputy Prime Minister, led to political instability that threatened the peace and security of the 'small' state.

Thabane raised alarm over a purported military coup that aimed at unseating him, thereby suspending the parliament in the bid for political stability. Thabane reached out to the regional body, which rejected his plea for the immediate deployment of peacekeepers to assist restore peace and order to the troubled country (BBC, 2014). SADC maintained that the regional body would only dispatch a 'facilitator' to help in mending the political fences and restoring peace to the country (BBC, 2014). An agreement was subsequently reached after the coup leader, Tlali Kamoni, was exiled (Albuquerque & Wiklund, 2015). Thus, South Africa was a decisive actor in restoring order to the country.

The principle of non-interference poses a challenge to the operationalisation of the SADC in conflict prevention and resolution (Albuquerque & Wiklund, 2015). As noted by these authors, when the conflict is centred on internal socio-economic realities like poverty, unemployment, elections and party politics, resource mismanagement and corruption, political fractions, and ethnic hostilities, it becomes very difficult for SADC to effectively intervene. For instance, Mozambique was rated one of the most unequal societies in the world, "with a Gini Co-efficient Index of 54%, and also ranked 180 out of 189 countries in the world in terms of human development" (Vhumbunu, 2021).

Apart from its inability to douse political tensions in Zimbabwe, the regional organisation has been unable to restore order in Mozambique's troubled zone. Since 2017 the Cabo Delgado region has been confronted by terrorism that has threatened the territorial integrity of the country. The terrorist attacks started in October 2017 when armed and unknown young militias attacked government institutions in Mocimboa da Praia town, situated in Cabo Delgado area (Matsinhe, 2021). The government was initially overprotective of its sovereignty and concealed vital information from media organisations and the international community (Amnesty International, 2020b). Years of neglect of the resource community and the complicit character of the foreign companies, operating in the area, accounted for the evolution and destructive nature of the Islamic terrorist group—al-Shabaab otherwise called Al-Sunna wa Jama'a (ASWJ)—with links to an international terrorist network (Islamic States), operating in the resource zone. Media practitioners that were first to cover the conflict have been subjected to either intimidation or arrests (Amnesty International, 2020b). The sudden rise of terror in the zone and its highly destructive nature was a dent in the effectiveness of regional early warning systems (EWS).

Violent Conflict in the SADC Region: Cases of Congo DRC and Mozambique

The DRC Congo epitomes poverty, disorder, and insecurity in Africa. It exemplifies the contradictions of resource wealth and validates the 'resource curse' hypothesis. Since the early 1960s, the country has experienced a surge of violence that shattered post-independence optimism and threatened the continued existence of the country as a governing entity (Scarnecchia, 2011). Congo gained independence in 1960 from Belgium and its symbolic independence was followed by a civil and constitutional crisis, sparked by hostility between the former colonial power (Belgium), France, the United States, and the United States of Soviet Republic (USSR), using the Congo DRC as a battlefield (Scarnecchia, 2011). Primarily, the Congo government's inability to retain full political and economic control after its independence led to the outbreak of violent conflict. Foreign powers, who seek to control Congo's mineral resources after its independence, became key actors in the ensuing conflict. As a result of the conflict, the resource-rich province of Katanga succeeded from Congo with intentions to become a sovereign entity, the secessionists were funded by Belgium and its foreign ally, with the aim to control the resources and other economic opportunities fully.

The mining area of Katanga became a battlefield and mineral resources played a central role in the dynamics of the violence. Congo was a main source of gold, copper, tin, and Uranium for most of the Western countries; thus, they have stakes in the protracted conflict. As this conflict was winding up, a self-inflicted conflict broke out due to the quest for political power and control by President Laurent-Désiré Kabila in 1998, a year after he brought the government of Sese Mobutu to an end. After local militia circled around the seat of power in Kinshasha, Kabila rallied neighbouring countries for protection, and countries such as Angola, Namibia, and Zimbabwe responded militarily by sending troops (Masuku, 2022). This led to what is usually referred to as the Second Congo War or 'Africa's First World War.' The 1996 mass killings of the Hutus in the northeast of the country triggered increased violence (Mutusi, 2016). The decade-long conflict involved "nine African countries…and 25 armed groups. By its end, in 2003, an estimated 350, 000 people had been killed in the fighting, and more than five million had died in resulting humanitarian crises" (Masuku, 2022). It was a very devastating violent conflict.

Since the end of the conflict in 2003, Congo has not enjoyed enduring peace. The situation in the country continued to remain unstable and very fragile, particularly in the eastern part of the country and in the Katanga province, threatening to extend into Kinshasha's regional headquarter, Goma, due to the violent activities of the March 23 Movement (M23) group (Masuku, 2022; Mutusi, 2016). As of 2016, several armed groups continued to operate in the restive country, and the most dominant conflict was the uprising in the central Kasai province, tagged the Kamwina Nsapu rebellion. About 3000 civilians were killed and 20,000 citizens sought refuge in neighbouring countries. The United Nations High Commissioner for Refugees (UNCHR) reported about 27,400 documented human rights violations and abuses in eastern Congo. The conflict is multifaceted (UNCHR, 2022).

Apart from misgovernance and state fragility, security, socio-economic, and political factors aggravated the conflict in the country and dominated by poor governance and a lack of political will (Mutusi, 2016). Between 1996 and 1997, the multi-dimensional conflict in the DRC was so rife to the point that it was referred to as 'Africa's first World War,' due to the number of countries involved and the destabilisation of the country, underscoring the depth of the violence, including the extent of the destruction of human lives and property (Mutusi, 2016). The conflict in the DRC has been characterised by communal violence, high-intensive destruction of lives and property, scramble over resources, and lust for political power. Like in any other violent conflict, civilians are usually paying hefty prices. In Congo, women and young girls were subjected to abusive behaviours like rape, forced marriages and other forms of violence, and other forms of sexual exploitation (Mutusi, 2016).

Since 2022, several African countries have been involved in the aggravated conflict in the country. The M23, which had been quiet for a time, suddenly became a formidable terror around Kinshasha. The resource-diplomacy by neighbouring countries and the battle for the soul of the country have aggravated terror in Congo. Rwanda has been heavily linked with the conflict and has allegedly backed the M23 with financial support in the quest to gain access to Congo's "untapped reserves are worth an estimated $24 trillion" (Masuku, 2022). The United Nations peacekeeping forces, the United Nations Organisation Stabilisation Mission in the Democratic Republic of the Congo (MONUSCO), and the Congolese military could only offer a feeble resistance against the might of the invading M23 forces (Masuku, 2022). The Tutsi-led militant group, who have taken over Kibumba (a town very close to Goma) in eastern DRC, have caused mayhem in the restive North Kivu province, leading to the displacement of hundreds of thousands of Congolese. By late 2022, both Kenya and Burundi have sent troops to support the Congolese army, while a truce has been negotiated between the DRC and Rwanda, leading to the decision of the M23 to lay down their arms (Aljazeera, 2022). It remained to be seen if the ceasefire would be sustained.

Since its independence in 1975 and a civil war between the Mozambican National Resistance (RENAMO) and the Front for the Liberation of Mozambique (FRELIMO) that jeopardise its post-independence gains, Mozambique has recently been confronted with Islamic terrorism in the resource-rich Cabo Delgado. The reign of terror started in 2017 by al-Shabaab's supported militant group, and it held the Cabo Delgado area and the central government into a spellbound. The group, established in the early 2000s by some young men within the Islam Council of Mozambique and financed through the illicit trafficking of products through Cabo Delgado, aimed to turn the gas-rich region of Cabo Delgado into a caliphate (Kgosi, 2021). The ultimate idea, backed by the Islamic State of Iraq and Syria (ISIS) and its regional affiliates in other African countries such as Somalia and DRC, is to turn the Cabo Delgado province into the Islamic State's Central African Province (ISCAP) (Kgosi, 2021). The mobilisation of forces and resources from other countries was designed by al-Shabaab to enhance its capacity to conquer the SADC forces present in Cabo Delgado.

As reported by the UNHCR, about 800,000 people had been internally displaced persons (IDPs) as of 2021. Of these figures, children made up about 48% of the IDP. The figure increased dramatically in March 2021, following the gruesome attack on Palma town that led to the displacement of more than 88,000 people (Human Rights Watch, 2022). On 12 January 2022, Aljazeera (2023) reported that since the outbreak of the conflict in 2017, more than 4,500 people have been killed, while more than a million people have been displaced. Broadly, the root and remote causes of the conflict include both internal factors such as impoverishment and dislocation of the resource community, growing inequalities and poverty, and external factors that could be linked with global Islamic radicalism and complicity of the foreign companies operating in the resource region (Kgosi, 2021). The Mozambican conflict, perpetuated by religious overtones, coincided with global terrorism threatening several Western countries and the United States. Like most cases of terrorism, while the reasons could be coloured under religious affiliations, the ulterior motives for conflict in countries like Iraq and Somalia, and Nigeria, have been the quest to have control of political and resource power.

The growing illegal exploitation of natural resources and illicit trade of rubies, narcotics, ivory, and timber in the northern region fuels the conflict and has serious repercussions on the already fragile economy of the country (Kgosi, 2021). While the maginalisation of the youth and the rising unemployment rates became unbearable, there was no genuine attempt by both the government and the multinational companies operating in the area to alleviate the suffering of the community, including the youth. This provides the motivation for the youth to resent public institutions. Across the region, young boys have been recruited and some have been coerced into becoming child soldiers to fight against the government forces (Human Rights Watch, 2022). The discovery of gas and oil reserves in Cabo Delgado generated high expectations for the community, and the disappointment led to acute resentment and the rise of armed militias that evolved into foreign-backed terrorist groups (Kgosi, 2021).

Historically, the coastal Northern part of the Cabo Delgado province is home to communities, noted for long centuries of fishing income and absolute reliance on the sea for their livelihood (Matsinhe, 2021). As noted by Matsinhe, the discovery and extraction of the gas deposits resulted in the relocation of the communities, which has been adjudged to be unfair, inequitable, and poorly managed by the government, and the loss of their source of livelihood and income. The effect on the youth was particularly negative, as they became unproductive, idle, hungry, and helpless; thus, they became easy targets for recruitment into hardened insurgent groups. The region witnessed several cases of kidnapping and ransom-taking. For instance, a ransom of US$600,000 was demanded for the kidnapping of a businessman in June 2021 (Human Rights Watch, 2022). The tension in Cabo Delgado escalated rapidly in March 2021 leading to the killing of over 5000 civilians and 700,000 displacements by April 2022 (Deleglise, 2021; Kgosi, 2021). The number of people who are in dire need of humanitarian assistance has increased to 1,300 000 and necessities such as food, shelter, and water remain the top need for IDPs (Kgosi, 2021).

While the country boasts enormous crude oil and gas deposits, including Total's $20bn gas liquefaction plant—the largest foreign investment in Africa—that stood high in the oil-producing community, the government and its citizens have been unable to reap the dividends of the resource wealth. Indeed, the conflict has also led to dire economic losses. The country's main business association revealed that small- and medium-sized firms had lost about $90 (£64m) to the conflict and insecurity in the war-torn region (BBC, 2021). For instance, in 2021, the religious militants attacked the resource location in Palma town, leading to the death of more than 12 people and the destruction of property, including the suspension of the exploration of Liquefied Natural Gas (LNG) in the area (BBC, 2021).

Military hubs and government facilities have been destroyed creating further political and economic instabilities in the country (Kgosi, 2021). The anger of the gun-wielding armed group has also been meted out to the innocent civilian population in the region. The Islamic insurgents have deliberately attacked them through hideous killings and burning of victims and, in many instances, through decapitations (Vhumbunu, 2021). Women and young girls are abducted, raped, and forced into marriages; houses, businesses, and properties are looted and destroyed at will (Kgosi, 2021). The economic impact of the crisis cannot be measured merely by the damage caused by insurgents to businesses and government properties but also by the action taken by several multilateral companies such as Total to halt resource extraction and other operations in the area due to rising security concerns (Kgosi, 2021). Despite the growth of the Mozambique economy by 3.6% year-on-year in the third quarter of 2022, the country's GDP growth slows to a one-year low (Trading Economics, 2022).

Governance deficit and rising corruption also play a big part in fuelling the crisis. As of 2020, Mozambique ranked 149 in 180 countries in terms of corruption, this places it in the top 20 most corrupt countries in the world (Amnesty International, 2020a). The conflict in Cabo Delgado has serious economic implications, not only for the government of Mozambique but also for other neighbouring African countries such as South Africa, Malawi, and Zimbabwe, which depend on Mozambique as a gateway for global markets (Deleglise, 2021). The conflict threatens the investment projects and resource extraction in Cabo Delgado, while individuals' property (including farms and houses), has been destroyed. A rise in military spending would also curtail investment in public infrastructure and social policies.

SADC Peacekeeping Missions in Congo DRC and Mozambique

The major motivations for a regional approach to security have been the impact of conflict in a member state on regional political stability and development, and the fear of the spillover effect of conflict on neighbouring countries. The DRC joined the SADC in 1998 after the opposition led by Laurent Kabila overthrow Mobutu Sese Seko's government and upon the attack on Congo by Uganda and Rwanda (Mutusi, 2016; Wilén, 2012). The two countries joined forces with a rebel group to overrun the Kabila-led new government and its Alliance of Democratic Forces for the Liberation of Congo (AFDL). Since then, SADC has been the main regional organisation with a heavy presence in the DRC (Mutusi, 2016). It seems more strategic to join the regional body for regime consolidation and internal security concerns; thus, the DRC joined SADC in 1998. Its intervention in the DRC involves mediation, signing peace agreements, implementing ceasefires, mobilising peacekeeping and stabilising missions, and partnering with member states such as South Africa through the South African National Defense Force (SANDF) (Mutusi, 2016). SADC's first mission in the DRC began in 1998 through both military intervention and mediation efforts. The operation, named 'Operation Sovereignty Legitimacy' (OSLEG) under the auspices of the Politics, Defense and Security Cooperation organ of the SADC, embarked on a four-year mission to dislodge the rebel groups operating in the eastern part of the country, protect the civilian population, and maintain the territorial integrity of the Congo (Mutusi, 2016).

Apart from military intervention and deployment of peacekeeping missions to the DRC, SADC also assisted the Congolese government through mediation and preventive diplomacy. Three SADC members (Zimbabwe, Namibia and Angola) strongly supported the Congolese government in wadding off attacks from the pro-Mobutu alliance. Zambia was tasked with leading the mediation aspect of the intervention (Ngoma, 2004). As the war raged on, Zambian President Frederick Chiluba and Ugandan President Yoweri Museveni became deeply involved in facilitating a ceasefire in the DRC (Naidoo, 1999). SADC's difficulty in breaking a truce was partly due to Kabila's refusal to engage in diplomatic talks with the warring faction, including leaders of the countries that were complicit in the conflict (Naidoo, 1999). SADC-led mediation efforts led to the Inter-Congolese Dialogue, under the leadership of Thabo Mbeki of South Africa and Ketumile Quett Masire of Botswana (Mutusi, 2016). By 2001, SADC facilitated the Declaration of Fundamental Principles by the Congolese Parties and the inter-Congolese Dialogue, which reflected the commitment of the regional organisation to the breakdown of law and order in Congo (Ngoma, 2004).

As SADC and other actors were making concerted efforts to restore normalcy to Congo, the DRC was rocked by a fresh attack by M23. The Congolese government approached the SADC for military assistance, leading to the dispatching of about 3000 troops from Malawi, South Africa, and Tanzania, under the leadership of the SADC Standby Force (Albuquerque & Wiklund, 2015). The SADC-led military might overpower the M23 forces and agreed on two peace accords between the rebel group and the Congolese government (Mutusi, 2016). Under the peace agreements, Rwanda and Uganda were to withdraw their troops from the eastern DRC, leading to the 2006 post-conflict democratic elections, and the strengthening of public trust and the legitimacy of state institutions (Mutusi, 2016). While conflict broke about two years after the peace accords and conduct of the election, SADC and other partners were to intervene again, giving way to the 2011 electioneering process.

SADC remains involved with the security situation in Congo through the deployment of the Force Intervention Brigade, largely supported by Malawi, Tanzania, and South Africa, to assist the United Nations Organisation Stabilisation Mission in the DRC (MONUSCO) since 2013 (SADC, 2018, 2022a). This was initiated through the recommendations of Secretary-General Ban Ki-moon and in response to the call of Governments in Africa's Great Lakes region under a UN "Resolution 2098 (2013) Enables 'Offensive' Combat Force To 'Neutralize and Disarm' Congolese Rebels, Foreign Armed Groups" (UN, 2013). As the M23 escalates its attack on the Congolese government and its people in 2022, regional actors continue to reiterate their commitments to partner with the UN in resolving the conflict in Congo, as part of its efforts toward the attainment of sustainable peace and security of Southern Africa (SADC, 2022b).

Prior to the attacks in the northern part of Mozambique, which hosts Cabo Delgado province, the hostility between the ruling party, Frente de Libertação de Moçambique/Mozambique Liberation Front

(FRELIMO) and the main opposition, Resistência Nacional Moçambicana/Mozambique National Resistance (RENAMO), played out during the 2014 general election (Sousa, 2014). The government of Mozambique had initiated different mediation efforts, led by different religious groups such as the Catholic Church of Mozambique. This led to the August 2014 ceasefire, signed by the leaders of both FRELIMO and RENAMO to end hostilities that lasted almost half a century, and ensure the successful conduct of the legislative and presidential elections (Peace & Security Report, 2020).

Despite the government's promise to ensure free and fair elections, the 2014 general elections sparked yet another tension between RENAMO and FRELIMO, before and after the declaration of FRELIMO's candidate, President Filipe Nyusi, as the newly elected president of Mozambique. RENAMO rejected the election results and demanded some concessions from the government (Peace & Security Report, 2020). Not just in Mozambique, but in other countries like Zimbabwe, the opposition parties have always alleged the ruling parties of election irregularities, which threaten the political stabilities of its member states. SADC is responsible for ensuring that its member states comply with the Guidelines for Governing Democratic Elections as contained in Article 5 of the SADC principles to implement the required interventions that promote democratic values (Peace & Security Report, 2020).

The SADC Lawyers' Association (SADC LA) which acted as an election-monitoring group, noted few incidences of disturbances during the election. Though this dented the credibility and transparency of the voting process, SADC LA maintained that "the elections occurred peacefully and to a large extent within the existing legal framework" (Sousa, 2014: 14). SADC also declared the election to be 'generally peaceful, transparent, free, fair and credible.' Indeed, SADC supported the FRELIMO-led government, while pushing for lasting peace between the two parties. By 2017, SADC's intervention in the affairs of Mozambique had to dramatically shift from the FRELIMO-RENAMO conflict to combating fierce attacks from the al-Shabaab-supported terrorist group in Cabo Delgado region.

SADC's intervention in Mozambique started in July 2021, upon Mozambique's official request for SADC's intervention at the SADC Extra-Ordinary Organ Troika summit of Heads of State in Harare in May 2020 (Vhumbunu, 2021). The nature of the conflict in Cabo Delgado province exposed the government's weakness to combat the rising insecurity and lawlessness, requiring SADC's intervention. The involvement of the regional institution would not necessarily be a peace support intervention, but more of a counterterrorism and counter-insurgency mission (Deleglise, 2021). Therefore, through the auspices of the Organ for Politics, Defense, and Security (OPDS), the SADC mission in Mozambique (SAMIM) was established to end violence and counterterrorism in the Cabo Delgado province of Mozambique (Peace & Security Report, 2020). While finance has been a challenge for regional peacekeeping missions, SADC member states, with support from the AU and the UN, have been able to fund the operations (Deleglise, 2021).

SADC's initial lack of cohesion and consensus on the conflict in Mozambique accounted for a major backlash on the regional body and accounted for the intervention of non-SADC African countries such as Rwanda, which acted as one of the first actors to respond to the conflict in Cabo Delgado (Peace & Security Report, 2020). The Rwandan Defence Force (RDF) deployed 1,000 soldiers and police officers to northern Mozambique to strengthen the government's effort to maintain law and order in the troubled country (Peace & Security Report, 2020).

On 23 June, after months of discussions and prevarication, SADC's sixteen member states agreed to deploy troops under its Standby Force to "combat terrorism and acts of violent extremism in Cabo Delgado" (Demuynck & Weijenberg, 2021), under the leadership of South Africa (Carvalho, 2021). South Africa has always favoured a military approach to SADC's intervention in Mozambique, which had been resisted by some member states, including President Filipe Nyusi-led Mozambican government (Carvalho, 2021). SADC members had previously struggled to agree on the most effective approach to eradicating the insurgency movement in the region.

In a sharp turn of events, SADC eventually endorsed the recommendations of the technical team deployed in Mozambique, following the summit held in Maputo in April 2021 and supported by the 16 members of the organisation. The committee advised SADC to mobilise and send a 3,000-strong joint military force, comprising land, air, and naval capabilities, under the framework of the SADC Mutual Defence Pact (Demuynck & Weijenberg, 2021). The protracted and complex nature of the conflict, the destructive character of the armed group, and the inability of SADC to rid the country of terrorism led to the indefinite extension of the SADC Mission in Mozambique (SAMIM) in

October 2021. Just like other military operations on the continent, the mission, which SADC launched in July for an initial three-month term, has become an indefinite peacekeeping mission. The mission's troop-contributing countries include South Africa, Botswana, Tanzania, and Angola (Human Rights Watch, 2022).

The organisation has made some positive strides, while also recording losses in their interventionist roles. Since the deployment of SAMIM to the terrorist zone, SADC forces have been able to resist the expansionist tactics of the terrorist. The forces have also seen improvement in humanitarian and security situations in the volatile region, resulting in the return of IDPs to their areas of origin (SADC, 2022b). On a contrary note, on 29 November 2022, the regional peacekeeping troops (SAMIM) lost two of its members, while another was also seriously wounded during a gun battle with the terrorist group in Namgade district (SADC, 2022b). The regional body confirmed the killing of 30 members of the terrorist sect and the seizure of several lights and small weapons during this attack. The peacekeeping forces are lacking in resource capacity and the required experience in counterterrorism and very diverse conflicts as the one raging in the resource community of Ceba Degaldo (Deleglise, 2021). The insurgents are driven by religious agendas and engaged in acts of international organised crime and terrorism, which the SADC has never experienced or dealt with before (Kgosi, 2021).

SADC continued to struggle with the efforts to resolve and manage the armed insurgency, protect trade routes and borders, and minimise the possible spillover effects of the conflict to other neighbouring countries (Deleglise, 2021). The failure to address the chronic problems of government legitimacy, neglect of the resource community and human development problems, and the government's sensitivity over its sovereignty limit SADCs intervention in the conflict (Deleglise, 2021). For instance, the government has tried to conceal information about the threat of the insurgencies in its territories and the amorphous nature of the armed group (Deleglise, 2021).

The deteriorating security concerns and increasing loss of lives and property, human rights violations, and displacements in both the DRC and Mozambique call for concerns within SADC peace and security architecture. Over the years, the efficacy of SADC as a regional body has been questioned. Some scholars regard SADC's response to Cabo Delgado as slow and devoid of effective strategy and decisive actions, which have strengthened the hold of the insurgent group on the country (Kgosi,

2021). It is argued that the government of both the DRC and the Mozambican governments prioritised military response; sorely because they believe that military response will end the conflict, but civilians are neglected in the process, and they are not offered enough humanitarian response to the affected and displaced persons (Kgosi, 2021).

Conclusion

As demonstrated in the chapter, from the DRC to Mozambique, divergent conflicts have led to the destruction of lives and property, including massive displacement of the citizens. While the nature of the conflicts in the region differs, their effects on regional peace, security, and development have been very devastating. The SADC, through its peacekeeping force, has attempted to combat violent conflicts through military intervention. The chapter has attempted to present an overview of the conflict and SADC's quest to intervene through its peacekeeping forces in Congo and Mozambique.

The involvement of SADC in these two countries reflects a political will and commitment by its leaders to end restore peace and security to its most troubled member states. The intervention in both countries yielded different results; however, it helped to douse tension and reduce the depth of the destruction of lives and property, including the reduction and return of IDPs. SADC's role in regional peace and security cannot be measured in terms of its ability to enforce peace and coerce warring parties to lay down their arms and ammunitions, but by its preventive mechanism, through its early warning systems, capacity to promote effective governance as well as the protection of innocent civilians and vulnerable groups from human right abuses.

The deteriorating crisis in both the DRC and Mozambique calls for renewed commitments by national and regional actors, strong political will in the deployment of effective peacekeeping operations, timely adoption of mediation, and the utility of other conflict prevention mechanisms. SADC should be more serious about its early warning signs and create more space for the effectiveness of its Panel of Elders. SADC should also be wary of all potential political, environmental, and economic challenges, and be pragmatic in its responses to such threats to peace and security.

While the militarisation of SADC's intervention seems the perfect response to the conflict in both countries, a deeper understanding of Mozambique's conflict in the northern part of the country requires an understanding of the political economy of the country, including that of its oil wealth. As reflected by Demuynck and Weijenberg (2021), it is very important to understand the factors that made Cabo Delgado a fertile ground for violent and Islamic extremism. While there are several reasons, as discussed in this chapter, the two most decisive reasons are poverty and neglect. Indeed, both Mozambique and DRC, despite their resource wealth, lead the chart for the poorest countries in the world.

SADC intervention, as moderate as its achievements might have been, is a deterrent to armed insurrection in the Southern African region. The multilateral approach to restoring order and combating violent conflict and religious extremism in the region should be commendable while noting its struggles. A notable scepticism has been SADC's history of not recording 'perfect success' in its interventionist roles. As shown in Congo, despite its decades-long intervention, the regional body has failed to rid the Congo of armed insurrection and resource-based and communal conflicts. While the nature and trend of the conflicts could have been different, its contemporary, ECOWAS, has been able to restore lasting peace and security to the hitherto troubled West African countries like Liberia, Sierra Leone, and Côte d'Ivoire—countries that were once devastated by highly intensive violent conflicts.

References

Aeby, M. (2018). *Peace and Security Challenges in Southern Africa: Governance Deficits and Lacklustre Regional Conflict Management* (Policy Note no 4). https://reliefweb.int/report/democratic-republic-congo/peace-and-security-challenges-southern-africa-governance-deficits

Albuquerque, A. L., & Wiklund, C. H. (2015). Challenges to Peace and Security in Southern Africa: The Role of SADC. *Studies in African Security*. Project number A15104. https://www.foi.se/download/18.7fd35d7f166c56ebe0bb390/1542369060270/Challenges-to-Peace-and-Security-in-S-Africa_The-Role-of-SADC_FOI-Memo-5594.pdf

Alden, C. (2002). *South Africa's 'Quiet Diplomacy' and the Crisis in Zimbabwe* (pp. 187–211). https://journals.openedition.org/cea/1341

Aljazeera. (2022, December 23). *M23 Rebels Pledge to Retreat from Key Position in Eastern DRC*. https://www.aljazeera.com/news/2022/12/23/dr-congos-m23-rebels-pledge-to-retreat-from-key-position

Aljazeera. (2023, January 12). *Mozambique*. https://www.aljazeera.com/where/mozambique/

Amnesty International. (2020a). *Corruption Perceptions Index*. https://www.transparency.org/en/cpi/2020

Amnesty International. (2020b, August 31). *Mozambique: Unprecedented Arson Attack on Canal Media Must be Promptly Investigated*. https://www.amnesty.org/en/latest/news/2020/08/mozambique-unprecedented-arson-attack-on-canal-media/

BBC. (2014, September 1). *'Lesotho Coup': Sadc Rejects Thabane's Troop Request*. https://www.bbc.com/news/world-africa-29010132

BBC. (2021, April 26). *Mozambique Gas Project: Total Halts Work After Palma Attacks*. https://www.bbc.com/news/world-africa-56886085

Carvalho, R. (2021, June 24). *SADC Members Approve Deployment of Military Forces to Mozambique*. Further Africa. https://furtherafrica.com/2021/06/24/sadc-members-approve-deployment-of-military-forces-to-mozambique/

Cawthra, G. (2010). The Role of SADC in Managing Political Crisis and Conflict The Cases of Madagascar and Zimbabwe. *Peace and Security Series*. Friedrich-Ebert-Stiftung Mozambique

Deleglise, D. (2021). *Issues and Options for the SADC Standby Force Mission in Mozambique*. https://www.accord.org.za/analysis/issues-and-options-for-the-sadc-standby-force-mission-in-mozambique/

Demuynck, M., & Weijenberg, G. (2021). *The Upcoming SADC Intervention: A New Way Ahead to Combat Terrorism in Mozambique*? International Centre for Counter-Terrorism. https://icct.nl/publication/the-upcoming-sadc-intervention-a-new-way-ahead-to-combat-terrorism-in-mozambique/

de Sousa, C. (2014, December 13). Election in Mozambique. *De Rebus*. https://doi.org/10.10520/EJC162311

Feldstein, S. (2018, August 16). *Zimbabwe's Coup Did Not Create Democracy from Dictatorship*. Carnegie Endowment for International Peace. https://carnegieendowment.org/2018/08/16/zimbabwe-s-coup-did-not-create-democracy-from-dictatorship-pub-77069

Human Rights Watch. (2022). *Mozambique Events of 2021*. https://www.hrw.org/world-report/2022/country-chapters/mozambique#:~:text=The%20human%20rights%20situation%20in,displacement%20of%20over%20800%2C000%20people

Kgosi, S. (2021). Could SADC's Institutional Framework and Instruments for Peacekeeping Have Been Effective in Preventing the Insurgency in Northern Mozambique. *African Journal of Terrorism and Insurgency Research, 2*(2), 37–76.

Masuku, D. (2022, December 10) In the DRC, an Ugly History of War Risks Repeating Itself. *Mail & Guardian*. https://mg.co.za/africa/2022-12-10-in-the-drc-an-ugly-history-of-war-risks-repeating-itself/

Matsinhe, S. F. (2021, April 29). *An Overview of the Conflict in Cabo Delgado: Narratives, Causes and Strategies on the Way Forward*. https://www.accord.org.za/analysis/an-overview-of-the-conflict-in-cabo-delgado-narratives-causes-and-strategies-on-the-way-forward/

Mbuende, K. M. (2001). Conflict Prevention and Resolution in the South African Development Community (SADC). Executive Secretary, South African Development Community. *International Journal on Minority and Group Rights, 8*, 45–49.

Mutusi, M. (2016). *SADC Intervention in the Democratic Republic of the Congo*. https://www.accord.org.za/conflict-trends/sadc-interventions-democratic-republic-congo/

Naidoo, S. (1999). Rebels Without a Pause: Diplomacy in the DRC Conflict. *South African Journal of International Affairs, 6*(2), 155–162.

Ngoma, N. (2004). *Hawks, Doves or Penguins? A Critical Review of the SADC Military Intervention in the DRC* (Institute for Security Studies Occasional Paper 88). Pretoria.

Peace and Security Report. (2020). *Mozambique Conflict Insight*. Institute for Peace and Security Studies. Addis Ababa.

PSC Report. (2020, August 26). *Why Is SADC Slow to Intervene in Political Crises?* https://issafrica.org/pscreport/psc-insights/why-is-sadc-slow-to-intervene-in-political-crises

SADC. (2018). *UN and SADC Conduct a Follow-up Engagement Regarding Strengthening Support to the SADC Force Intervention Brigade in the DRC*. https://www.sadc.int/news-events/news/un-and-sadc-conduct-follow-engagement-regarding-strenghtning-support-sadc-force-intervention-brigade-drc/

SADC. (2020). *SADC Reiterates Its Position for a Stable and Peaceful DRC*. https://www.sadc.int/news-events/news/sadc-reiterates-its-position-stable-and-peaceful-drc/

SADC. (2021). *SADC Has Responsibility to Help Member State Under Terrorist Threat*. https://www.sadc.int/news-events/news/sadc-has-responsibility-help-member-state-under-terrorist-threat/

SADC. (2022a, December 1). *SADC Ministerial Committee of the Organ Calls for Concerted Efforts to Consolidate Peace and Security for a Prosperous Africa*. https://www.sadc.int/latest-news/sadc-ministerial-committee-organ-calls-concerted-efforts-consolidate-peace-and-security

SADC. (2022b, November 30). *Two SAMIM Force Members and One Member Suffers Minor Injuries During Contact with Terrorists in Cabo Delgado Province in the Republic of Mozambique*. https://www.sadc.int/document/two-samim-force-members-and-one-member-suffers-minor-injuries-during-contact-terrorists

SADC. (2022c). *History and Treaty*. https://www.sadc.int/pages/history-and-treaty

Scarnecchia, T. (2011). *The Congo Crisis, the United Nations, and Zimbabwean Nationalism*. https://www.accord.org.za/ajcr-issues/the-congo-crisis-the-united-nations-and-zimbabwean-nationalism/

Trading Economics. (2022). *Mozambique GDP Annual Growth Rate*. https://tradingeconomics.com/mozambique/gdp-growth-annual

UN. (2013, March 28). *'Intervention Brigade' Authorized as Security Council Grants Mandate Renewal for United Nations Mission in Democratic Republic of Congo*. https://press.un.org/en/2013/sc10964.doc.htm

UNHCR. (2022). *Southern Africa*. https://reporting.unhcr.org/globalreport2021/southern-africa

Vhumbunu, C. H. (2021). *Insurgency in Mozambique: The Role of the Southern African Development Community*. https://www.accord.org.za/conflict-trends/insurgency-in-mozambique-the-role-of-the-southern-african-development-community/

Wilén, N. (2012). Intervention, Justifications and Interpretations: The Case of the SADC in the Congo. *Justifying Interventions in Africa* (pp. 92–115). Palgrave Macmillan.

CHAPTER 9

African Union and the Consequences of Coup d'états in West Africa

Arushi Singh

Introduction

Time and time again, it has been reiterated that democracy is not the best of governance for the African continent (Mclure, 2010). Interestingly, "democracy in Africa is like a flashlight without batteries" (Wentling, 2022). Additionally, democracy is being valued in some African countries as retaining only its "instrumentalist value" in the context of what it can provide to citizens as opposed to being the best form of governance (Kotze, 2022). Furthermore, there have been multiple coups on the continent, which have resulted in unconstitutional governments and military rule (Cowan, 1966). This pattern has continued contemporaneously with coups in Burkina Faso, Chad, Guinea, Sudan, and Mali, while attempts have been allegedly made to topple civilian administrations in the Central African Republic (CAR) and Guinea-Bissau.

Military regimes are a particularly troubling development as they not only partake in human rights violations but contribute to economic

A. Singh (✉)
Consortium of Indo-Pacific Researchers, New Delhi, India
e-mail: arushi4525@gmail.com

A. O. Akinola and E. A. Liaga (eds.), *Development and Regional Stability in Africa*, https://doi.org/10.1007/978-3-031-56695-0_9

decline in the affected countries. They also can contribute to instability in the region due to an increase in aggression and military spending. However, in Guinea-Bissau and Mali, democratically elected leaders had chosen non-democratic ways such as illegitimate constitutional changes to hold on to office, election rigging, and corruption to maintain power that had resulted in the coups to remove them from power. In Sudan, there were protests in opposition to the coup that removed Omar al-Bashir, which was motivated by a military power grab that stood opposed to the peaceful transition of power. The events further showcased and emphasised the desire of the populace for democratic norms and practices (Cheeseman, 2022).

In recent years, coup d'états have been witnessed in West African countries, which have compelled the intervention of the Peace and Security Council (PSC) of the African Union (AU). The AU has considered suspension or individual sanctions for countries where the coups have occurred. Thereafter, in the case of Chad, a fact-finding mission to N'djamena was sent by the PSC, as its intercession was slated to set a precedent for future unconstitutional acts. However, in Chad, the Transitional Military Council (TMC) was provided with an 18-month mandate to restore constitutional order. This was despite the actions of TMC that were against the content and the spirit of the AU Constitutive Act, the African Charter on Democracy, Elections and Governance, and the Lomé Declaration.

The AU has, in the case of Burkina Faso, consented to suspend the country's membership, a decision that came in the aftermath of the Economic Community of West African States (ECOWAS) suspension of the country. Notwithstanding, the AU took a stringent position due to the concurrent military intervention in four West African countries in a single calendar year. This has subsequently altered the regional security architecture. Experts have posited that AU has endeavoured to disincentivise coups, yet it has not prioritised its focus on the best approach for effectively addressing the root causes of coups in Africa (Kuwali, 2022).

The chapter attempts to highlight the organisational prerogatives of the AU with particular reference to coup d'états, explore the current geopolitical context of coups in West Africa, assess the response of AU and its organs to the coups in West Africa, and critically evaluate the challenges and prospects for future AU actions regarding coups in Africa.

Coup D'États: The Organisational Prerogatives of the AU

Recently in Burkina Faso, Paul-Henri Sandaogo Damiba offered his resignation to avert altercations that were likely to lead to "serious human and material consequences." It was the second coup in the country in a year (Aljazeera, 2022). It has been insinuated that West Africa has become the "predominant centre of coup activity," while all regions on the African continents have been subject to coup attempts (McGowan, 2003). Nevertheless, Africa is extremely diverse and many countries have operated based on multiparty democracies. Authoritarianism is the basis of military rule and in the African context, militaries on the continent have vastly diverse organisational structures with cliques of armed camps owing "primary clientelist allegiance" to some officers of different ranks that are themselves in competition with each other due to "a variety of corporate, ethnic and personal grievances" (Lee, 2008).

Additionally, many times militaries are neither able to offer sustainable models for development nor stability. During military rule, the ruling elites from the armed forces set up monopolies in various sectors that may limit the prospects for development of the country as opposed to democratic rule that opens development opportunities for all citizens. Notably, Thyne and Powell (2019) have opined that coups can pre-empt revolution or steer towards it. They can be used to bring a civilian or military government to power but "violence is the ultimate determinant" (First, 1970). The scope can be limited as well with only the leader being removed, the removal of the ruling officials, or changes in prevailing constitutional associations. There are wide-ranging reasons for coups (Collier, 1978).

The AU has constructed a normative framework in terms of handling coup d'états that have their genesis in the Organisation of African Unity's (OAU) Lomé Declaration or "Declaration on the Framework for an OAU Response to Unconstitutional Changes of Government," which demarcated four circumstances of unconstitutional alteration that result in a military coup d'état (Ikome, 2007). These encompass an intercession by mercenaries; a commandeering of power by armed dissident factions as well as rebel movements; and a rejection by a sitting government of peaceful transfer of power after democratic elections. Article 23(5) of the OAU Charter also includes a fifth situation that declares that "any amendment or revision of the constitution or legal instruments, which is an infringement on the principles of democratic change of government" (Elias, 1965).

The Declaration and the OAU Charter recognise several considerations that might decrease the possibility of military coups through strict adherence to the tenets of good governance, transparency, and human rights (African Union, 1965). The Charter likewise states that "the perpetrators of unconstitutional change of government shall not be allowed to participate in elections held to restore the democratic order or to hold any position of responsibility in political institutions of their State" (Souaré, 2009).

Notably, the OAU took a path that consisted of sanctions and suspensions, of a country wherein the coup occurred, from the continental body. This course of action was codified in the Constitutive Act of the AU (Article 30) thus, "Governments which shall come to power through unconstitutional means shall not be allowed to participate in the activities of the Union." Subsequently, the PSC in 2003 took the helm to assist with unconstitutional vicissitudes of government. PSC was ratified by 51 countries at the time and focused on the sanction clause as stipulated in the Lomé Declaration. Another legacy document that highlights sanctions is the African Charter on Democracy, Elections and Governance (ACDEG) which aims to "deepen and consolidate the rule of law, peace, security and development." However, it has not been ratified by all member states of the AU (Wiebusch, 2019).

Nevertheless, the PSC has been criticised due to its stance in Chad, where due to geopolitical reasons, it endorsed the Transitional Military Council (TMC) with an 18-month plan to reinstate constitutional order, instead of castigating and taking a stern stance on the coup plotters. The reasons included the location of Chad as a stopgap against the spillover effect of the conflict in Libya on Central and Western Africa, as well as the importance of the country in counterterrorism operations. Thus, the PSC decided against suspending Chad from the AU or imposing individual sanctions (Anon, 2021).

These actions have in turn levied assertions of unresponsive of the AU in addressing the deeper issues that appear to plague countries and give rise to coups. There are also limitations facing the AU, particularly on the definition of unconstitutional changes of government, which does not cover vital undemocratic acts, such as election tampering and illegitimate constitutional amendments to retain power. The AU's response has been "reactive despite extensive early warning signs, particularly mass protests agitating for change" (Anon, 2022).

The AU Assembly also reserves the right to impose sanctions on a country state that encourages or promotes a constitution. However, the AU still faces a quandary in executing its policy as it is extremely challenging to differentiate between genuine popular uprisings in opposition to authoritarian leaders and unconstitutional government alterations against democratically elected administrations. There also remain inadequate rules regarding the participation of coup leaders in the next elections. Furthermore, the AU has been accused of double standards and preferential treatment for some erring countries, thereby jeopardising its continental leverage. However, the AU has been involved in mediation in some conflicts that ultimately some resolution through the involvement of other actors such as the Economic Community of West African States (ECOWAS) or countries with colonial legacy on the continent, actions that undermine the authority of the AU (Anon, 2017).

Coups also appear to be triggered through factors such as factionalism and governmental stalemates in multiparty systems that might enable provoking military interventions (Kposowa, 1992). The AU's ability to effectively deal with these issues was hindered by the appointments of authoritarian leaders to sensitive positions within the continental organisation. For instance, Malian President Ibrahim Keita, who was appointed as the AU's champion of Arts, Culture, and Heritage, was later removed through a military coup. A coup remains a prompt and surprise strike that poses a much more immediate and unforeseeable threat to individuals and the polity. This threat can lead leaders to implement coup-proofing that might further jeopardise democratic reforms (Roessler, 2011).

There are varied reasons for a coup that might range from a reaction to revolution and other reasons. Several degrees of violence might be encountered during a coup, which may transform a supposedly bloodless coup into a distinctly violent coup. There appears to be debate and deliberations regarding what constitutes a "successful" coup, with various experts highlighting one week of the dislocations of government personnel or constitutional relationships as a basic requirement of a coup. Meanwhile, others believe that a "mere" attempted assassinations and seizures of some government representatives and the mobilisation of the armed forces are not necessarily counted as coups (Ikome, 2007).

Notably, factors such as civilian control over the military, factionalism with the armed forces, and institutionalisation affect the rate of recurrence and site of a coup. However, the Economist Intelligence Unit's Democracy Index has highlighted some indicators as the remote or immediate cause of military coups, such as the deteriorating conditions in Burkina Faso, Guinea, and Mali, including the high rate of poverty. Furthermore, coups in the aforementioned countries also received support from the civilians, who also opposed any external interventions, while censuring colonial countries of interference and complicity.

A cross-section of citizens of countries under military dictatorships has condemned the West African regional body, ECOWAS, for mobilising against the military and making concerted efforts to reinstate the deposed civilian leaders or ensure the democratic transition of power and restoration of constitutional governance. A cascading lack of faith that seems to be impacting the whole region. However, the actions of ECOWAS and AU appear to be increasingly focused on the military as opposed to understanding the primary reasons that saw the civilian populace supporting the coups and conferring legitimacy on coup leaders (Nyei, 2022).

The Current Geopolitical Context of Coups in West Africa

Coups have led to the emergence of the "military-opposition alliances", and a configuration of similar preferences between military elites and popular protestors (Albrecht, 2019). This development has been linked to the concept of "democratic coups d'etat and disputed by many others" (Varol, 2012: 292). Nonetheless, three widely acknowledged categories of coups, encompassing grievances, opportunities, and organisational features, are accepted by major perspectives (Kuehn, 2017). These categories have manifested in West Africa and the Sahel region. West Africa has been home to some of the most stable countries, such as Ghana, and has witnessed several transitions to peace after intense periods of violent conflicts in countries like Côte d'Ivoire, Liberia, and Sierra Leone.

The turn of the century seemed to be marked by transformation, signifying a shift in established rule systems, patterns, behavioural norms, and expectations. During transitions, these systems also contribute to conflict as individuals become part of "conflicting rules systems" (Weijer, 2011). Guinea-Bissau witnessed numerous coups attempts between 1974 and 2012, reflecting the establishment of various systems during that period. This has resulted in a "fragility trap" where Guinea-Bissau has been trapped in a slow-growth and poor governance imbalance that is formed by weak institutions and impotent policies (Collier, 2019).

There has also been a spillover effect of the war in Libya, Charles Taylor's activities in the Mano River Basin, and Foday Sankoh's Revolutionary United Front (RUF) (Rashid, 2016). Other conflict systems, like the southern Senegambia conflict system involving Senegal, the Gambia, and Guinea-Bissau, along with the Mali and Niger conflict systems, served as motivating factors for the coup plotters. Furthermore, the evolution and activities of various terror groups, such as al-Qaeda in the Islamic Maghreb (AQIM) and Boko Haram, in these countries have raised the profile of the military along with garnering the interest of extra-regional powers.

Notably, the Islamic insurgency has led to the interrogation of the "military, political and economic influence of the former colonial power, France", which has been a force behind Operation Barkhane. Furthermore, the US has been deeply involved in the region with its trained officers having been involved in several coups in West Africa. Leaders of coups have engaged in military exercises, including Flintlock—an organised counterterrorism training course in the US—as well as the Africa Contingency Operations Training and Assistance course. Additionally, they have participated in a US-sponsored Military Intelligence training engagement for African officers while collaborating with the U.S. Defense Department Civil Military Support Element.

A Malian military officer, Amadou Sanogo, who toppled a civilian government in 2012, "learned English in Texas, received intelligence training in Arizona, and underwent infantry officer basic training in the State of Georgia, took matters into his own hands. He overthrew his government's democratically elected government" (Sayid, 2022). Furthermore, countries, such as Burkina Faso and Chad, are also beneficiaries of the African Growth and Opportunity Act (AGOA), even though the country has been hijacked by coupists, without being subjected to any consternation (Blanchard, 2022). AGOA is a Trade Act, enacted and passed by the US Congress on 18 May 2000, to strengthen the country's trade relations with African countries. The continued engagement of the US with these countries appears to be in response to China's rise and expansion in the region, thereby supporting "coups to stop Beijing's march in the region" (Isilow, 2022).

The Response of AU and Its Organs to Coups in West Africa

The AU suspended Mali when Colonel Assimi Goita who orchestrated a coup against President Ibrahim Boubacar Keita opposed the head of the Transitional Government, Bah Ndaw, and Prime Minister Moctar Ouane. Ndah's "sin" was his move to institute a new cabinet, without requesting for the input and approval of the Goita-led military. The country thus witnessed two coups within eight months. This would exacerbate the country's poverty and insurgency and the development of democratic norms.

Meanwhile in Chad, after the death of President Idriss Deby, the military swiftly grabbed power and proclaimed a de facto government, referred to as the Transitional Military Council (TMC), which was headed by the late President's son, Mahamat Idriss Déby. He subsequently proclaimed an 18-month plan for the establishment of civilian rule. The AU's PSC, after starting a fact-finding mission to N'djamena, essentially supported the plan, which contrasts with the bloc's enduring tradition of handling unconstitutional seizures of power. Notably, the army had violated Article 81 of the Constitution, which stipulates that the head of the National Assembly is to act as interim President, in case of a vacuum in leadership.

In Burkina Faso, the military with the withdrawal of Blaise Compaore overthrew the interim President Michel Kafando that resulted in the country's suspension by the AU (Kato, 2021). In Guinea, a military officer, Mamady Doumbouya, captured and overthrew President Alpha Conde and subsequently, dissolved the apparatus of the civilian government, and suspended the Constitution. Interestingly in Guinea, President Lansana Conte had sought tenure extension, which was "in the form of a coup, which could also be seen as a rebellion against the former President's unconstitutional actions" (Bennett, 2022).

The AU suspended Guinea after the military arrested and overthrew Alpha Conde. The AU had also condemned the military takeover and asked for the release of Conde, who is Guinea's first democratically elected leader. The continental body "decides to suspend the Republic of Guinea from all AU activities and decision-making bodies" (Anon, 2021). The PSC thus asked the AU Commission to "engage with stakeholders in the region" on the crisis (Anon, 2021).

AU Stance on Coups: Challenges and Prospects for the Future

Coup-proofing

To prevent coups, leaders and stakeholders in the democratisation project should be focused on coup-proofing. The expansion and institutionalisation of armed forces contribute to the strengthening of the hierarchical chain of command, task cohesion, and functional separation among various units within coercive forces, encompassing armies, praetorian guards, domestic security forces, and intelligence services, which could unintentionally ensure better coordination for a successful and sustainable coup. While coup-proofing may prevent coups, it could also increase the capacity of leaders to plan and lead a coup (Powell, 2012). Leaders might also implement counterbalancing wherein additional branches of the armed forces may be created to decrease the control of one officer and increase the ineffectiveness of communication to mount a coup (Bruin, 2017). However, these actions can increase grievances that can directly result in coups. Indeed, "the anticipation of the costs" by incumbent leaders can also affect coup attempts (Escribà-Folch, 2013).

Perception

ECOWAS is viewed as being subservient to the AU. Any effort to increase collaboration, especially in preventing coups, might reinforce this perception; hence, the AU must take proactive measures to address and alleviate this concern (Cascais, 2022). Additionally, there is also a perception there is inconsistency in AU electoral monitoring initiatives, and the question of illegitimate constitutional changes as experienced in Guinea and Côte d'Ivoire, without any meaningful actions from the AU. These perceptions have discredited the AU to a significant extent. This results in the absence of a reprimanding mechanism to address such grievances and hold the leaders who threaten the legitimacy of their government accountable.

Emphasis on the Structural Concerns

The AU should prioritise addressing structural issues like poverty and limited opportunities for youth outside the defence forces, which contribute to coups in West Africa. There should be a heightened focus on AU policies aimed at resolving these problems. Economic crises can also challenge the legitimacy of the state, creating conditions conducive to coups. Additionally, the political systems are overly restrictive with high entry costs. Political systems in Africa have been referred to as winner-takes-all systems that are an obstacle to democracy in Africa's highly ethnicised political terrain. The continent hosts "partial" democracies, plagued by factionalism, thus, increasing the risk of coups in countries like Guinea and Benin (Marc, 2015). There is an understanding that "once the structures of civilian authority and constitutional procedures are torn down, many years are required to rebuild them" (Böhmelt, 2011).

There remain similarities in structural problems in Mali, Chad, Burkina Faso, and Guinea where young military officers, aged between 38 and 41, dethroned aged leaders who were democratically elected. As West Africa grappled with severe conflict in latter the twenty-first century, the AU must also commit to the building of institutions that solve structural problems, through explicit support and financial backing, to reduce the possibility of coups and prevent "constitutional coup d'etats" (Akinwotu, 2022). The AU can promote greater inclusion and decrease coup attempts by ensuring the active participation of marginalised groups, including ethnic minorities, women, youth, and grassroots organisations in the political process (Sany, 2022).

Effective Coordination

The AU should be more active in its "proactive role" and should aim to coordinate with multiple regional organisations like ECOWAS. Intelligence sharing and increased awareness could be an important component of coordination that might assist in the preemption of potential democratic interruptions and cessations. AU can also construct accountability mechanisms in tandem with regional organisations that can then be monitored jointly at the regional level. This collaboration can also increase the leverage available to the AU (Bennett, 2022).

Multilateral Collaboration

There has already been some success when regional bodies such as ECOWAS have been supported both by the AU and international actors in such areas as elections management, norm-setting, and establishment of policy instruments such as the Praia Declaration on Elections and Stability.

Other players are the Kofi Annan International Peacekeeping Training Centre (KAIPTC) in Accra, Ghana; the National Defense College in Abuja, Nigeria; the Peacekeeping School of Bamako, Mali; and the Finnish-funded Africa Civil-Military Coordination (ACMC) programme, hosted by the African Centre for the Constructive Resolution of Disputes (ACCORD) in Durban, South Africa. The three institutions have also played an important role in fostering civil-military ties. Therefore, to prevent coups, the AU has nurtured multilateral interactions. In the 1990s, external donors were instrumental in the "reform and restructure of the security forces in West Africa." A re-engagement on the same lines facilitated by the AU could lessen the frequency of coups (Marc, 2015).

Conclusion

Over the past years, Africa has experienced a resurgence of coups and the emergence of a "dynastic coup" (Anon, 2021). In most cases, coup leaders almost consistently disavow their actions as a coup, seeking to present a façade of legitimacy. While the frequency of coups per year between 1960 and 2000 was estimated at four annually, there has been a recent increase in frequency and a coup is a harbinger of more coups. Furthermore, international cooperation encounters challenges as significant power competition intensifies, leading to heightened impunity and increased attempts by leaders to orchestrate coups (Mwai, 2022).

Consequently, to deter coups, the AU can also lean towards an action wherein "a more sustainable response to coups is to eliminate the adverse socio-economic and political conditions in national and international politics that allow immediate causes of political instability to hide behind a democratic façade" (Onapajo, 2022). Due to the inaction by the AU and other regional organisations regarding constitutional changes and undemocratic acts by regional leaders, a view has emerged that sees the organisations as coup enablers. The AU has struggled to effectively contribute towards easing the structural problems that account for coups in the affected African countries (Nyei, 2022). Some strategic analysts and experts have also highlighted the need to reform AU's institutions and agencies to effectively deter coups (Taibe, 2022).

References

African Union, A. (1965, May 25). *OAU Charter. Addis Ababa.* 25 May 1963. https://au.int/en/treaties/oau-charter-addis-ababa-25-may-1963

Akinwotu, E. (2022). *Contagious Coups: What Is Fuelling Military Takeovers Across West Africa?* [Online]. https://www.theguardian.com/world/2022/feb/07/contagious-coups-what-is-fuelling-military-takeovers-across-west-africa

Albrecht, K. K. H. (2019). *Revolutions and the Military: Endgame Coups, Instability, and Prospects for Democracy*. Armed Forces & Society.

Aljazeera, A. (2022). *Burkina Faso Coup: Ousted Military Leader Damiba 'Resigns'*. https://www.aljazeera.com/news/2022/10/2/ousted-leader-damiba-agrees-to-resign-after-burkina-faso-coup

Anon. (2017). *Actions of the African Union Against coups d'état.* European Parliament.

Anon. (2021). *Chad President's Death: Rivals condemn 'Dynastic Coup'.* https://www.bbc.com/news/world-africa-56830510

Anon. (2022). *What Is Behind the Spate of Coups in West Africa?* https://newafricanmagazine.com/28086/

Bennett, L. M. (2022). *Coups in West Africa—A Critical Analysis of AU and ECOWAS Responses.* https://gga.org/coups-in-west-africa-a-critical-analysis-of-au-and-ecowas-responses/

Blanchard, A. A. (2022). *"An Epidemic of Coups" in Africa? Issues for Congress.* https://crsreports.congress.gov/product/pdf/IN/IN11854

Böhmelt, U. P. (2011). Coup-Proofing and Military Effectiveness in Interstate Wars, 1967–99. *Conflict Management and Peace Science.*

Bruin, E. D. (2017). Preventing Coups d'etat: How Counterbalancing Works. *Journal of Conflict Resolution, 62*(7), 1433–1458.

Cascais, A. (2022). *ECOWAS Criticized Over West African Coups.* https://www.dw.com/en/ecowas-criticized-over-west-african-coups/a-61685721

Cheeseman, L. M. (2022). *Coups in Africa: Why They Don't Spell the End of Democracy.* https://www.bbc.com/news/world-africa-60289571

Collier, P. (2019). *A New Approach to State Fragility.* https://www.brookings.edu/research/a-new-approach-to-state-fragility/

Collier, R. B. (1978). Parties, Coups, and Authoritarian Rule: Patterns of Political Change in Tropical Africa. *Comparative Political Studies, 11*(1), 62–93.

Cowan, L. G. (1966). Military Rule in Africa. *Survival, 9*(1), 9–13.

Elias, T. O. (1965). The Charter of the Organization of African Unity. *The American Journal of International Law, 59*(2), 243–267.

Escribà-Folch, A. (2013). Accountable for What? Regime Types, Performance, and the Fate of Outgoing Dictators, 1946–2004. *Democratization* (pp. 160–185). Routledge.

First, R. (1970). *The Barrel of a Gun: Political Power in Africa and the Coup d'État*. Allen Lane.

Ikome, F. N. (2007). *The Lomé Declaration: Context, Content, and Interpretation*. https://www.jstor.org/stable/resrep07759.8

Isilow, H. (2022). *Why Are Military Coups on the Rise in Africa?* https://www.aa.com.tr/en/africa/why-are-military-coups-on-the-rise-in-africa/2500953

Kato, R. L. (2021). *Coups: Why the AU Acted Tough on Mali But Ignored Chad*. https://www.africanews.com/2021/06/02/coups-why-the-au-acted-tough-on-mali-but-ignored-chad/

Kposowa, J. C. (1992). The Political Origins of African Military Coups: Ethnic Competition, Military Centrality, and the Struggle over the Postcolonial State. *International Studies Quarterly*, 271–291.

Kuehn, D. (2017). Midwives or Gravediggers of Democracy? The Military's Impact on Democratic Development. *Democratization, 24*, 783–800.

Kotze, J. S. (2022). *Democracy Loses Its Glow for South Africans Amid Persistent Inequality*. https://theconversation.com/democracy-loses-its-glow-for-south-africans-amid-persistent-inequality-181489

Kuwali, D. (2022). *Countering Coups: Strengthening Social Contracts in Africa*. https://rwi.lu.se/blog/countering-coups-strengthening-social-contracts-in-africa/

Lee, T. (2008). The Military's Corporate Interests. *Armed Forces & Society, 34*(3), 491–502.

Marc, A. (2015). *The Challenge of Stability and Security in West Africa*. Agence Française de Développement and the World Bank.

McGowan, P. J. (2003). African Military coups d'état, 1956–2001: Frequency, Trends and Distribution. *The Journal of Modern African Studies, 41*(3), 339–370.

Mclure, J. (2010). *Why Democracy Doesn't Work in Africa*. https://www.newsweek.com/why-democracy-doesnt-work-africa-73203

Mwai, P. (2022). *Are Military Takeovers on the Rise in Africa?* https://www.bbc.com/news/world-africa-46783600

Nyei, F. A.-b. (2022, February 11). *Why have civilians welcomed the recent coups in West Africa?* Retrieved from https://www.aljazeera.com/opinions/2022/2/11/why-have-civilians-welcomed-the-recent-coups-in-west-africa

Onapajo, H. (2022). *Africa's "Coup Contagion": What Is Driving the Rise in Military Intervention?* https://www.institutmontaigne.org/en/analysis/africas-coup-contagion-what-driving-rise-military-intervention

Powell, J. (2012). Determinants of the Attempting and Outcome of Coups d'état. *Journal of Conflict Resolution, 56*(6), 1017–1040.

Rashid, I. (2016). *Sierra Leone: The Revolutionary United Front*. https://cco.ndu.edu/news/article/780201/chapter-8-sierra-leone-the-revolutionary-united-front/

Roessler, P. (2011). The Enemy Within Personal Rule, Coups, and Civil War in Africa. *World Politics, 63*(2), 300–346.
Sany, J. (2022). *A Sixth Coup in Africa? The West Needs to Up Its Game*. https://www.usip.org/publications/2022/02/sixth-coup-africa-west-needs-its-game
Sayid, A. M. (2022). *The Recent Wave of Military Coups in West Africa*. https://www.dailysabah.com/opinion/op-ed/the-recent-wave-of-military-coups-in-west-africa
Souaré, I. K. (2009). *The AU and the Challenge of Unconstitutional Changes of Government in Africa*. https://www.files.ethz.ch/isn/105906/P197.pdf
Taibe, D. T. (2022). *African Union Reform in the Face of Military Coups in Africa*. https://onpolicy.org/african-union-reform-in-the-face-of-military-coups-in-africa/
Thyne, C. L., & Powell, J. (2019). *Coup Research*. https://doi.org/10.1093/acrefore/9780190846626.013.369
Varol, O. O. (2012). The Democratic Coup d'Etat. *Harvard International Law Journal,* 53(2), 66.
Weijer, L. P. (2011). *Fragile States: Stuck In A Capability Trap?* World Development Report.
Wiebusch, M. C. C. (2019). The African Charter on Democracy, Elections and Governance: Past, Present and Future. *Journal of African Law,* 9–38.
Wentling, M. G. (2022). *Democracy in Africa Is Like a Flashlight Without Batteries*. https://americandiplomacy.web.unc.edu/2022/05/democracy-in-africa-is-like-a-flashlight-without-batteries/

CHAPTER 10

Regionalism, Trade, and the Development of Member States: A Perspective of ECOWAS Trade Liberalization Scheme in Nigeria

Ganiyu Lai Ejalonibu

Introduction

Regional integration is complex and multifaceted but can generally involve a collection of economies cooperating in socio-economic and political spheres to pursue shared goals (Lee et al., 2022).The economic sphere, situations like dwindling resources, increased population, and fierce competition for control of the limited resources, has made regional cooperation and agreements more attractive in solving regional economic difficulties and international trade distortions (Lee et al., 2022; Shaw, 2003). Indeed, regional integration is geographical, and in some cases, political, linking together geographically and ideologically related States

G. L. Ejalonibu (✉)
National Institute for Legislative and Democratic Studies, National Assembly, Abuja, Nigeria
e-mail: ejalonibuganiyu@yahoo.com

A. O. Akinola and E. A. Liaga (eds.), *Development and Regional Stability in Africa*, https://doi.org/10.1007/978-3-031-56695-0_10

since the end of the Second World War has been impressive (ADB, 2013; Imobighe, 2003).

Africa's pre-independence history of regionalism and economic integration dates to the early twentieth century, when the South African Customs Union (SACU) was formed (Asante, 2000: 234). However, the post-independence period saw many African leaders embracing the concept of regionalism and economic integration as an important element of their development agenda. Thus, following political independence in Africa, the call for regionalism and economic integration was renewed during the dispensation of Kwame Nkrumah, the first President of Ghana. Nkrumah and many other leaders in Africa agreed that political independence in Ghana was meaningless unless it was linked with the total liberation of Africa and that Ghana's independence was only the first step toward a united and integrated Africa (Sakyi & Opoku, 2014).

On 28 May 1975, Economic Community of West African States (ECOWAS), a regional group of 15 of countries was founded with the signing of the treaty of Lagos with a long list of laudable economic goals for the region. The mission and the main goal of ECOWAS is to promote economic cooperation among member states for collective development (ECOWAS, 2018). These 15 members States are Benin, Burkina Faso, Cabo Verde, Cote d'Ivoire, The Gambia, Ghana, Guinea, Guinea-Bissau, Liberia, Mali, Niger, Nigeria, Senegal, Sierra Leone, and Togo.

ECOWAS also aimed to address some security issues by developing a peacekeeping force for regional conflicts. Nigeria, as a country, has been an active participant in championing the course of regional integration arrangements among African states (Akinkugbe, 2017). In 1979, the ECOWAS Trade Liberalization Scheme (ETLS) was initially set up to cover farm products and high-quality artworks and in 1990, it was expanded to include industrial items. The scheme intended to offer unhindered market access to the fifteen member Countries and promotes economic relations within the sub-region. Countries covered by this Scheme are: Nigeria, Ghana, Benin, Côte d'Ivoire, Gambia, Guinea, Guinea-Bissau, Liberia, Mali, Niger, Senegal, Sierra Leone, Togo, Burkina Faso, and Cape Verde (NEPC, 2024; Shortridge, 2020).

ECOWAS has, for over three decades, dedicated its efforts toward promoting the economic integration of the region using, among other things, ETLS, but the gains are quite small considering the efforts made so far to achieve economic development. According to Article 3 of the Revised ECOWAS Treaty, one of the principal targets of the ETLS is to create a free trade area (FTA) (Chikodiri et al., 2019). The ETLS guarantees the free transportation of products without customs obligations and charges of comparable impact on importation into ECOWAS member states. The scheme thus has three main benefits: it guarantees free movement of goods and persons between member countries; unprocessed goods and traditional handicraft products circulate within the region free of quantitative restrictions; there is total exemption from import duties and taxes; and lastly, there is no compensation for loss of revenue resulting from the importation of these products from a third country into a member state (see Article 36, paragraph 2 of The ETLS Protocols and Regulations). The main qualification requirement for admission into the ETLS products is that it must originate from the ECOWAS region with at least 60% local content; 30% value addition for products; and change of tariff headings (NEPC, 2024).

However, despite Nigeria's cooperation with other member states for nurturing the ETLS initiative since 1979, the country is still facing economic or development crisis. The research problem, then, is whether ECOWAS, through the instrumentality of ETLS, has accomplished its specific developmental agenda of removing the technical and physical barriers to trade, establishing a free trade area, along with the ultimate goal of developing the West African States. Despite the effort toward achieving development generally in the West African region and particularly in Nigeria, very few empirical studies have been conducted to assess the level of development through the influence of ETLS among member states.

Through desktop research, this chapter seeks to explore how successful the ETLS has performed in relation to the development of local product content in Nigeria. Thus, it focuses on the examination of the impact of ETLS on Nigeria's economic development as a member state within the West African region. The chapter specifically seeks to verify whether ETLS has really contributed anything toward the development of local content of product in Nigeria. This is crucial, if appropriate policy measures toward promotion, development, and diversification of the Nigerian economy is to be achieved.

The rest of the chapter is structured as follows. The next section is dedicated to the literature review of the effect of regional integration and economic growth development of member states. Section three lays out the methodological approach of the study and the data used. The fourth section presents the main results and their policy implications. The fifth and the last section concludes.

Regionalism: A Review of Literature

Existing literature on structures of regional cooperation has used different concepts of regionalism. Thus, in conceptualizing some variables that are relevant to this chapter, it is important to note that regionalism and economic integration are not necessarily the same concept. To Hurrell (1995), the idea of regionalism can be seen and explained "under five different headings: regionalization, regional awareness and identity, regional interstate cooperation, state promoted regional integration, and regional cohesion." Furthermore, he describes regionalization as the development of cultural integration inside a region and to the regularly undirected cycles of social and economic interaction, commenting that "this is an informal integration of countries, a non-government initiative that emerges from the actions of private individuals." Within this context, regionalization can be seen as an interaction of regional incorporation driven by the impact of market sectors through the drives of corporate or economic agents of the member nations and not really an administration started provincial exchanging arrangement. This suggests that regionalization, which might be affected by regionalism, may in any case happen if regionalism is employable. Regional awareness and identity have to do with the sort of regionalism exuding from nations inside a region that share social, historical, traditional, religious, or prudent attributes and belief systems. With this, nations are incorporated dependent on their identities.

Regional integration is the sort of regionalism that various nations or governments incorporate for economic welfare, tackling internal or external challenges, and enhancing common values. Whereas state-promoted regional integration includes a purposeful and express arrangement by the nations' governments to take out trade obstacles and boost the development of capital and individuals. Regional cooperation involves cooperation among distinct countries with a shared interest in a particular issue. According to Lee (2002: 3), regional cooperation may include "the execution of joint projects, technical sector cooperation, normal running of services and strategy harmonization, and joint advancement of common natural resources." ·Regional integration is "an interaction whereby political entertainers in a few unmistakable public settings are convinced to move their loyalties, expectations, and political exercises toward another center, whose establishments have or request ward over the preexisting national states" (Haas, 1958: 16).

Development integration, then again, includes cooperation by various particular nations whose principal objective or plan is their locale's financial and social improvement. This requires more state intercession, as it was viewed as a reaction to the issues made by economic integration, although it has demonstrated harder to execute. Regional cohesion, the best type of regionalism, happens through the blend of all the above regionalism measures. With this, there is the arrangement of a bound together and joined territorial element.

According to Lee (2002), regionalism refers to the efforts by a group of countries to enhance their economic, political, social, or cultural interactions. He groups regionalism under four major headings: economic (market) integration, regional cooperation, regional integration, and development integration. Salvatore (2010) observes that economic integration is the commercial policy of discriminatively reducing or eliminating protectionist policies only among participating countries. It centers around broadening the market of the nation's joining together.

While extensive empirical literature exists examining the determinants of intra-ECOWAS trade and its linkages to investment flows, studies explicitly dealing with the relationship between regional integration and economic development through trade liberalization is scanty. It is thus important to review some relevant literature that examines regionalism as a development strategy in post-Independence Africa.

Asante (1997) produced a comprehensive and a masterpiece on the role of regionalism in African economic development by providing a rich critical review of the process of regionalism, highlighting Africa's strategies and problems in the global world. His main idea is that a continent with fifty fragmented, balkanized, and patchy but sovereign entities cannot be taken seriously as an important and effective partner in the global economy if there are many development issues which transcend national boundaries are not treated at the regional level (Asante, 1997). He further argues that for African countries, integration constitutes an important tool that can help them to overcome constraints associated with the small size of individual economies, low per capita incomes, narrow resource bases, and limited diversity of production. In this respect, economic cooperation among African countries is the "sine qua non for the achievement of national social-economic goals, and not an 'extra' to be given thought to after the process of development is well advanced" (Asante, 1997: 17).

Exploring the issue of regional integration in the context of "development" theory and the neo-patrimonial state system in Africa, a central contention of Gibb's work is that Western, Eurocentric conceptions of regionalism, particularly those centered on the market integration approach, have promoted a very biased understanding of regional integration in many parts of the developing world. Gibb (2009) therefore argues that the various meta-theories focused on explaining the political economy of regionalism, often closely allied to a development theory paradigm, fail to account for the nature, character and evolution of regional integration. Conversely, in a comparative context, Paul Brenton and Barak Hoffmann argue that regional integration in sub-Saharan Africa is more successful than one would expect given the difficult setting in which it takes place. The vocal point of that study is that regional integration in sub-Saharan Africa (SSA) is crucial for increasing trade within Africa, building more competitive African economies, and creating larger markets for goods and services produced in the region. They also question perceptions that regional integration in SSA is doomed to be less successful than in other parts of the world (Brenton & Hoffmann, 2016).

Becker (2006) observes that moderately liberal scholars such as Friedrich List favored a more development-centered approach to regionalism. From this perspective, List advocates that states should actively promote their industrial development in the regional bloc—on the single country level and jointly. However, for (semi-) peripheral countries, scholars like Sloan developed, based on List's legacy, the concept of "developmental regionalism" for economic catch-up (Sloan, 1971). It has been argued that "development-centred regionalism would serve not only to expand trade but also to encourage the emergence of new industries, to help diversify national economies, and to increase the region's bargaining power with developed nations" (Eder, 2021: 334). Thus, the concept aspires to shift the accumulation of a particular (sub-) region toward more productive, intensive, and at least partially, introverted accumulation (in order to decrease external dependence). The idea in Sloan's work is that regional economic prosperity depends upon realizing the full economic potential of all sub-regions.

Seck et al. (2020) examine the relationship between market integration and African economic growth spillovers. Using a spatial dynamic panel data approach, the authors analyze the extent to which Africa and its major regional groupings have been able to generate shared growth. The chapter indicates that the continent as a whole is indeed a spatially integrated economic zone. They discover that market integration is often associated with economic growth spillovers, to the extent that strengthened trade linkages would make economic growth in one country an opportunity for growth to its partners. They further argue that, compared to advanced economies, Africa's contemporary spatial growth effect is associated with strong growth convergence and a large rate of return to physical capital.

Studies that examine some challenges or barriers to intra-regional trade in ECOWAS include Meyer et al. which opine that "technical barriers" to trade are not important in regional trade agreements in sub-Saharan Africa (Meyer et al., 2010). Zannou (2010) finds that exchange rate depreciation and openness are determinants of intra-ECOWAS trade. Study of Olayiwola et al. (2011) show that trade facilitation in ECOWAS is below the world average.

In summary, while it is evident that regional integration has one key strategy for West African development, the various scholars seem not to emphasize the ETLS as development strategy in the ECOWAS region. At the same time, few have identified challenges of implementing ETLS and how to surmount these challenges in West Africa. The empirical literature review also indicates that although several studies have examined the effects of regional cooperation and economic integration in the ECOWAS region, none of the recent studies have focused specifically on the specific case of ETLS and the development of member states. Besides, the few studies that have been carried out on the effects of regional economic cooperation in the ECOWAS sub-region were not done in such a way to reveal the effects of ETLS on development of member states. This study, therefore, aims to fill this gap in the literature. This is significant given that the implementation of ETLS across the region is to facilitate the development of the member states in all fields of economic activity. Evidence is needed to show whether the scheme has achieved its set goals and if not, what can be done to ameliorate the situation?

Theoretical Framework

Using post-neo-functionalism theory, this research draws on the work of Aniche (2014), "Problematising Neofunctionalism in the Search for a New Theory of African Integration: The Case of the Proposed Tripartite Free Trade Area (T-FTA) in Africa," to appraise the performance of the ETLS in relation to Nigeria's economic development. A post-neo-functionalism is a conceptual and theoretical instrument that helps understand the current crisis and the future consequences of regional integration. It is an analytical framework of regional integration, especially in Africa, which combines or synthesizes neo-nationalism and post-nationalism, rejects neo-functionalist, one-size-fits-all, state-centric or inter-governmental approach to integration in the region, and rather accepts bottom-top, humanistic, people-centric, or private sector-driven approach to integration, or people-to-people integration (Aniche, 2014).

The analysis would not be complete without understanding neo-functionalism and its three major principles. Neo-functionalism endorses regionalism. Thus, while functionalism implies free trade and global liberalism with individuals and groups conducting trade and interacting with little interference from governments, neo-functionalism, on the other hand, would seem to suggest that such liberalism be limited to a region (Zormelo, 1994). The three major principles of neo-functionalism are: the principle of positive spillover effects; the mechanism of a transfer in domestic allegiance; and principle of "technocratic automaticity" which states that as integration hastens the supranational institution(s) will take the lead in fostering further integration as they become more and more autonomous of the member states (Aniche & Ukaegbu, 2014).

The above principles of neo-functionalism embody John Galtung's Staircase Hypothesis, which involves the process of beginning with limited domain (or memberships) and limited scope (or area of cooperation) and gradually deepening the scope before extending the domain. But neo-functionalism has many defects and while assuming that regional integration may be a gradual process, its conception of integration as a linear process makes explanation of setbacks or shortcomings impossible. Another of its defects is that neo-functionalism assumes that integration of states is an integration of interdependence. Therefore, it is not adequate for explaining the incidence of dependence of African economies to Western economies and integration of dependence of the African state to a different (Aniche, 2014). This made the protagonists of post-neo-functionalism to begin to think that neo-functionalism is Eurocentric, and thus, parochial. Consequently, they saw need for a paradigm shift in Africa, that is, a theory which will be appropriate or adequate in explaining the African predicament (Okafor & Aniche, 2017).

The neo-functionalism of Ernst Hass, unlike the functionalism of David Mitrany, is non-normative and thus describes or explains the process of regional integration based on empirical data (Aniche, 2014). Again, while classical functionalism of David Mitrany advocates for global supra-nationalism, neo-functionalism of Ernst Haas advocates for regional supra-nationalism. The point of departure of post-neo-functionalism, therefore, is national integration, nation-building, and nationalism as a necessary step or start line or begin point toward achieving stable and sustainable regional integration and ultimately global integration (Aniche, 2009). Thus, the need for a theory that transcends neo-functionalism—post-neo-functionalism theory—which enables Africans to tell their stories by themselves. Neo-functionalism is a foreign theory, which was propounded by the West to facilitate regional integration in Europe and was intrinsically tailored to suit Europe (Aniche, 2009). Therefore, the post-neo-functionalism is versatile and can be deployed in addressing issues relating to technical cooperation, economic underdevelopment, insecurity, diseases, instability, etc., in the region. Therefore, to understand the impact of ETLS in relation to Nigeria's economic development, the study assesses the success of the implementation of ETLS in Nigeria in the light of post-neo-functionalism.

ETLS and the Development of Local Contents in Nigeria

The significance of trade openness within the economic development of countries has long been documented within the literature. Of paramount importance is the concept of comparative advantages, which a country must be ready to identify (Olayiwola, 2020). With ETLS, tariffs on traded goods of member states are eliminated in accordance with relevant Agreements/Protocols. Within ETLS, free movement of goods would require zero tariffs and eliminating non-tariff barriers (NTBs). Another major component is the Inter-State Road Transit Convention (ISRT): and integrated customs procedures. Others are the enhancement of the ECOWAS "Rules of Origin" including its certification procedures;

and harmonizing standards and conformance procedures. Agricultural products and handicrafts enjoyed zero tariffs, and this was subsequently extended to include manufactured products of origin in 1990. Taxes and levies were also eliminated. The phased liberalization of trade in industrial products comprised of two phases: consolidation of customs duties and NTBs and total trade liberalization (Elumaro & Olayiwola, 2020).

The ETLS scheme covers three groups of products namely, unprocessed goods which include fish, plant, or minerals that have not undergone industrial transformation; traditional handicraft products including those made by hand with or without the use of tools or machineries such as wood, articles of wood, basket works, carpet mats, lace embroidery, etc., and industrial products. It stipulated the scheme for industrial products originating from member states as well as the timetable for the elimination of tariffs on the said products by the groups of member states. The Article created three country groups and two sets of industrial products: priority and nonpriority industrial products. The groups for industrial products and timetable for the elimination of tariffs on the identified products are documented in Table 10.1.

The ETLS makes provision for institutional architecture of the Enterprise and the National Approvals Committee (NAC) for the processing of the Country of Origin (CoO). The approval for ETLS products is not made at the regional level alone but also at the national level (Karaki & Verhaeghe, 2016). Regional economic integration is a pan-African development agenda for attaining an eventual continental community. One of the instruments to achieve this agenda is the ETLS. As we noted earlier,

Table 10.1 ETLS, product grouping, and tariff reduction obligations

Group	*Countries*	*Tariffs eliminated*	*Rate of reduction of Customs duties and taxes*
Group I	Cape Verde, The Gambia, Guinea-Bissau, Burkina Faso, Mali, Mauritania, and Niger	10 years	10% reduction each year
Group II	Benin, Guinea, Liberia, Sierra Leone, and Togo	8 years	12.5% reduction each year
Group III	Côte d'Ivoire, Ghana, Nigeria, and Senegal	6 years	16.6% reduction each year

Source Decision A/DEC.6/7/92, ECOWAS

ETLS is meant to be an instrument of regional economic development among the West African countries; and as African Development Bank (ADB) had rightly observed, ECOWAS seeks to drive economic transformation by deepening integration through the ETLS (ADB, 2019).

According to the Community Computer Centre (CCC, 2016), the total ECOWAS trade for a while now has been dominated by mining commodities (oil resources, iron, bauxite, manganese, gold, etc.) but some agricultural commodities (coffee, cocoa, cotton, rubber and other products rather marketed within the region such as dry cereals, roots, tubers, and livestock products, etc.) are contributing very significant to the regional trade. Apart from mining commodities (oil-related trade), cocoa beans is one of the agricultural commodities in which Nigeria has a comparative advantage in producing rather than processing. However, UNECA (2012) and Ogunleye (2014) emphasize the importance of paying attention to the entire value chain to deliver the income and other welfare gains to all actors rather than laying emphasis on only increases in production.

Nigeria accounts for more than 60% of the GDP of West Africa (Ukaoha & Aniekan, 2013). It must be emphasized, however, that non-oil exports provide abysmal 4% of the country's total export; this means that oil-related trade still account for 56% of the country's GDP. Therefore, the country's overriding priority in the ETLS is two-pronged, namely: securing greater regional market access and promoting industrialization through an export-led growth. Nevertheless, to export, a country must produce locally. Thus, local content development becomes a strategic management issue with significant efficiency and profitability implications for many countries, Nigeria inclusive. Table 10.2 summarizes the situation before and after the introduction of the Local Content Policy.

Nigerian Content Measurement may be categorized into two: Partial Nigerian Content and Real Nigerian Content. Partial Nigerian Content is based on proportion of value of contracts awarded to Nigerian Companies and it can be between 70 and 80%; while Real Nigerian Content is based on proportion of contract sums spent on Nigerian made goods and this can be between 12 and 18%.[1] It is instructive to note that local content of product in the area of manufacturing is not doing much, as only 10% has

[1] Nigerian Content Development and Monitoring Board (NCDMB), "Local content implementation—10 key lessons".

Table 10.2 Nigerian local content policy—preliminary results

Policy direction	*Before the local content policy*	*After the local content policy*
Average annual industry spending	US$ 8 billion	US$ 20 billion (US$ 4 billion locally)
Contribution to national Revenue	71%	80%
Contribution to export earnings	>90%	96.60%
Contribution to GDP	12%	25%
Local value addition (local content)	10–15%	>40%
Local refining capacity	445,000 bpd	445,000 bpd
Workforce use	Increased use of expatriate workforce	Increased use of local workforce

Source African Development Bank (AfDB) and the Bill and Melinda Gates Foundation (BMGF), 2015

been recorded in the sector (Iruoma, 2021). However, there is a growing need to firmly diversify within the context of the economic challenges confronting Nigeria today.

In fact, as Leena Koni Hoffmann and Paul Melly opine that given the country's current sobering economic outlook, this critical perspective is even more urgent (Hoffmann & Melly, 2015). They argued that the reduced revenues from crude oil, Nigeria's major export and the source of 80–90% of its foreign-exchange earnings, have once again put the country under pressure to insulate itself better from the perennial cycles of oil-market boom and bust and improve the socio-economic stability of the country. It is therefore logical and reasonable to understand that non-oil-related trade of the country is key to national development process and can offer Nigerian government a critical opportunity to pursue a path of economic growth that is less volatile and more sustainable.

Therefore, in the bid to transform the agricultural sector (being a very crucial sector to the economy of Nigeria) and use it to foster its economic growth, Nigeria embarked on an Agricultural Transformation Agenda (ATA) in 2010. One of the products that were earmarked as priority commodities in order to achieve the objectives of the ATA was cocoa beans. The Agricultural Transformation Agenda noted cocoa beans value chain as a strategic commodity value chain that is expected to generate over 350,000 jobs in primary production, plantation establishment, and across its value chain in 2015 (Obasaju et al., 2016).

In the context of a regional economic community, cocoa beans value chain would imply that the production processes are fragmented across national borders within the region. For example, within ECOWAS, production of cocoa beans is done in Nigeria, processing done in Togo and marketing and selling to final consumers done in Benin Republic. Though, Nigeria is one of the leading exporters of this commodity after Cote d'Ivoire, Indonesia and Ghana respectively, notwithstanding the huge potentials of this commodity, it is characterized by low value addition and productivity which retard the gains of actors along its value chain (Ajetomobi, 2011).

The platform created by ECOWAS, ETLS, is meant to allow for free movement of goods, people and services, and removal of trade barriers within this region and the ECOWAS Agricultural Policy (ECOWAP) meant to improve productivity and competitiveness of the agricultural sector of member states (Obasaju et al., 2016). It is important to note that despite the immense potential for regional value chain development, West African exports tend to be biased toward advanced economies, with more than 70% of goods for further export directed to Europe and North America. ECOWAS member countries tend to be mainly suppliers of primary inputs without significant value addition to penetrate export markets. In fact, the ADB argues that "the proportion of intra-ECOWAS exports in total ECOWAS exports was still just 11.9 percent in 2017—below the proportion of intra-Africa exports in total African exports (16 percent)" (ADB, 2019: 36).

The ECOWAS regional industrialization objective had three elements: information sharing on major national industrial projects; harmonization of industrial incentives and industrial development plans; and training, joint ventures, and personnel exchange. The next major step in regional integration was in 2010: the West African Common Industrial Policy, based on the WAEMU Common Industrial Policy. The policy aims to "accelerate the industrialisation of West Africa through the promotion of endogenous industrial transformation of local raw materials, development and diversification of industrial productive capacity, and strengthening regional integration and export of manufactures."[2] It sets out four objectives, to be achieved by 2030, these are: to raise the local raw material processing rate from 15–20% to an average of 30%, to increase manufacturing's contribution to regional GDP from 6–7% to over 20%, to increase intra-ECOWAS trade in manufactured goods from less than 12% to 40%, and to increase the volume of exports of goods manufactured in West Africa to the global market from 0.1% to 1% (ADB 2019, p. 31).

The policy was revised and updated in 2015 with four key focus areas: (1) reinforcing national industry policies and advancing harmonization and regional cooperation, (2) promoting regional and international market opportunities, (3) supporting industrial quality and competitiveness, and (4) mobilizing resources (ADB, 2019). Again, the revised policy also identified four priority sectors to include: food and agroindustry, pharmaceuticals, construction materials, and automotive and machinery assembly (ADB, 2019). Choosing regional integration as the vehicle to deliver growth and development in ECOWAS suggests that the inherent tradeoffs were fully understood and considered. Regional integration typically involves trade liberalization within the defined space and trade protection outside it. And it often involves both trade creation and trade diversion, which means that benefits and costs may not be equally distributed. In principle, appropriate compensation arrangements can address the tensions caused by these inherent features of regional integration.

This section evaluates how and the extent to which regional integration in West Africa has enhanced intra-ECOWAS trade flows. It seeks to eliminate trade barriers, including taxes and levies, and aimed to improve trade links; facilitate free movement of certain goods; progressively eliminate customs duties and taxes with equivalent effects on industrial products on a schedule that factors in countries' different levels of development; and gradually eliminate customs duties and non-tariff barriers to totally liberalize trade. The ETLS initially focused on two groups of products:

i. Unprocessed goods, including fish, plants, and minerals that have not undergone industrial transformation.

[2] ECOWAS (Economic Community of West African States). 2010. "West African Common Industrial Policy." Abuja.

ii. Traditional handicraft products made with or without tools or machinery, such as wood, articles of wood, basket works, carpet mats, lace embroidery, and the like.

Industrial products were incorporated in May 1983.[3] These were divided into two groups: priority and nonpriority. Also, countries were divided into three groups based on their level of development and capacity to meet the obligations; each group had a different timetable for eliminating tariffs on industrial products; ranging from 6 to 8 and 10 years, respectively. Under the ETLS, Nigeria is among the countries under product groupings that were expected to have achieved the tariff elimination obligations in 6 years. It must be noted that at the beginning, implementation of ETLS has been very difficult and for this reason, ECOWAS, in 1992, attempted to address the difficulties encountered in implementing the ETLS through the introduction of the following three main strategies: rules of origin, national participation in the equity capital of production enterprises, and the categorization of priority and nonpriority industrial products.[4]

The goal was to simplify the scheme to speed implementation. The psychology behind this is that since country and product groups were created to benefit from the ETLS, intra-regional trade needs be strongly correlated with the liberalization schedule. Countries were expected to liberalize at different rates, so the ETLS contribution to intra-regional trade performance should also vary by country. In January 2003, the ETLS was harmonized with the WAEMU preferential tariff to facilitate the free movement of originating products of the community and simplify application of the ETLS. The main issues considered here are how and the extent to which Nigeria and product in the ETLS has performed relative to other countries and products and whether ETLS implementation has affected the Nigeria's national economic development.

Rules of origin can significantly impact trade creation and trade diversion. It has been argued that the main objectives of and economic justification for preferential rules of origin are to prevent trade deflection and transhipment. Yet "rules of origin" have also been used to attain other objectives as a development tool. Cadot et al. (2008) state that

[3] Decision A/DEC.1/5/83.

[4] Decision A/DEC.6/7/92.

in the context of preferential trade agreements between developed and developing countries, rules of origin have been justified as promoting manufacturing activities in developing economy members. The United Nations (UN) also argues that since trade preferences granted to eligible goods increase the price competitiveness of domestic products and of products from the preferential trade agreement region, the use of rules of origin can help retain and promote production capacities in the region (United Nations, 2019). This can stimulate regional value chains and promote economic development.

Ojo identifies six key elements contained in the ETLS for promoting trade and economic integration within the trade area. These are:

i. The Rule of Origin; this implies that goods to be traded under the ETLS must be produced or sourced from any of the 15 member states in the community;
ii. Goods must appear on the lists of goods annexed to the Decisions of the Authority of ECOWAS Heads of State and Government liberalizing trade in those goods;
iii. Goods must be accompanied by a Certificate of Origin and an ECOWAS Export Declaration Form issued by relevant Customs Authority of the member states;
iv. Goods must be subjected to necessary Customs formalities at the importing country;
v. Goods must satisfy all Sanitary and Phytosanitary Standards (SPS) of the country of origin;
vi. Beneficiary of the scheme must be resident within the ECOWAS sub-region (Ojo, 2019).

Ojo (2019) further observes that the Rule of Origin (RoO) needs to be strictly adhered to as a key condition for the ETLS. He opines that to satisfy the RoO, goods must:

a. Be produced from materials of community origin which value is equal to or higher than 40% of the total cost of raw materials employed;

b. Be produced from materials of foreign or indeterminate origin which CIF value does not exceed 60% of the total cost of materials employed or which quantity is equal to or higher than 40% of the total quantity of all raw materials employed in its manufacture;
c. Have received a value added through processing or at least 35% of the ex-factory price before tax (Ojo, 2019).

The country of origin for goods imported into Nigeria is deemed to be the country in which they were wholly produced or where at least 75% of the production cost was incurred, either in the form of value-added during production or from materials and components used in production.[5] In addition, as a member of ECOWAS, Nigeria applies ECOWAS rules of origin, under which a finished product is deemed to come from within the region, if at least 60% of the raw materials used in its production come from member states or if the value added is 35% of the ex-works cost price (excluding taxes). In case of dispute, appeals are made in first instance to the customs authorities in the country of importation, and if unresolved, it is referred to the ECOWAS Commission (Ajetomobi, 2011).

Import prohibitions, restrictions, and licensing are some of the measures under Nigeria's current customs legislation, import prohibitions may be imposed to protect domestic industries; reduce balance-of-payments deficits, as contingency measures, or on moral or safety grounds. Nigeria has two lists of prohibited goods: the Import Prohibition List and the Absolute Import Prohibition List. The Import Prohibition List is used mainly to protect domestic industry.[6]

Conclusively, ETLS was designed to create immense opportunities for member states (including Nigeria) through trade liberalization and free trade arrangements. Considering her status in the community, with the scheme, Nigeria is in a position in such a strategic way that it can benefit from export opportunities outside the community such as to organized markets of Europe, America, and Asia. Specifically, the private sector in Nigeria have benefited in no small means from the implementation of ETLS. These opportunities are summarized by Ojo (2019) as follows:

[5] WT/TPR/S/247, Trade Policy Review, Page 30.

[6] "Import Prohibition List." Available at http://www.customs.gov.ng/ProhibitionList/Import.php.

i. Nigerians are opening new markets for goods and services across the community, e.g., banks, telecoms, etc.
ii. Increasing investment opportunities from both domestic and foreign sources;
iii. Making trade cheaper by eliminating all tariffs and non-tariff barriers;
iv. Making trade faster by facilitating goods transit through customs and setting common rules on technical and sanitary standards (Ojo, 2019).

Furthermore, the private sector from Nigeria and across the member states have benefited the following by registering their products for the ETLS:

i. Huge Market: registering and admittance of products for the ETLS by manufacturers in the region open such products to the huge markets of ECOWAS compared to individual member state's markets.
ii. Price Competitiveness: reduction and elimination of duties and taxes as well as waivers, where applicable, has offered price competitive advantage to products in the community market; and
iii. The free movement of goods and services in the region has offered access to local sourcing of raw materials, labor, and investment capital within ECOWAS market. This has provided a broad base for local content in production activities across the region (Ojo, 2019).

Aside the private sector benefits, in terms of political benefits to Nigeria and other member states, the realization of the need to have common stability in political system across the region has promoted increased level of cooperation, diplomacy, and security management. Nigeria is also enjoying support from member states in terms of fight against terrorism, especially from Niger and Chard.

Factors Influencing Successful Implementation of ETLS in Nigeria

The implementation ETLS is still facing a myriad of socio-economic and development issues that threaten to shake the region's relative stability and economic progress. The challenges range from ubiquitous red tape and poor infrastructure to the entrenched protectionism of some of its members, excessive border bureaucracy, tariff and non-tariff issues, political unrest, fears of losing out to more competitive neighbors, lack of monetary union, intra-regional migration issues, poor road and rail links or petty corruption. These and other economic development-related issues are hardly limited to one country alone but tend to lead to the spillover of instability across the region (Joe, 2021).

The implementation of ETLS however has suffered severe setbacks and the scheme has been unable to deliver on its full potentials. Implementation of the ECOWAS trade agenda is linked to the level of inclusion and participation in negotiations. Some of the challenges facing ETLS implementation are discussed here. Like other regional economic communities (RECs), ECOWAS has limited authority over member governments and lacks active dispute and sanction mechanisms on economic integration issues (unlike governance and security issues). Hence, the organization must rely on persuasion and continual dialogue with member states to garner ownership and effective implementation. Further, the needs and interests of private sector actors are often poorly articulated and presented at regional levels and therefore difficult to address. Consequently, private sector forces tend to ignore regional policies or seek to block implementation. Examples include resistance to the ETLS and CET schemes in Nigeria, where operators seek waivers and other protective measures against cheap extra-regional imports.

Different levels of success of the ETLS and CET reflect different degrees of inclusiveness and involvement. The ETLS was not based on extensive discussions and dialogues, often overlooking both the interests of member states and the interests of private sector actors. After more than 30 years, the implementation of ETLS remains limited with most small- and medium-sized enterprises and the informal sector (a major share of intra-regional trade) not even aware of such a scheme. The CET, on the contrary, resulted from a more inclusive process, with over eight years of extensive consultations with the private sector, civil society, and public sector, especially customs officers. In five years, the CET has been better implemented than the ETLS, with 10 out of 15 ECOWAS countries reportedly implementing it.

The ECOWAS Commission has also launched a series of trade facilitation measures, particularly in the road transport sector. The Axle Road Harmonization Policy (2012) and the Joint Border Posts programme (2003) particularly stand out. Yet, both initiatives face challenges. Initially, Ghana was the only country to implement the Axle Road Harmonization policy, with only a handful of Joint Border Posts completed and with many unresolved issues within those operational border posts. Trade facilitation measures also depend on the backing by both member states and private sector actors. Incentives to comply with regional axle load regulations are limited, while corruption related to officials "looking the other way" is hard to address. Additionally, the policy requires coordinated implementation across countries to avoid losses to first movers such as Ghana—as it initially was the only country to implement this policy, Ghana arguably put its truckers at a disadvantage by having to comply with more stringent axle load regulation vis-a-vis its neighbors in Côte d'Ivoire and Togo serving the same hinterland. This led to protests and increased prices by Ghanaian truckers to maintain profit margins.

External actors also influence the ECOWAS trade agenda. The Economic Partnership Agreement (EPA) process with the European Union (EU) was instrumental in renewing regional dynamics, including convergence between UEMOA and ECOWAS. Adoption of the ECOWAS CET paved the way to adoption of the ECOWAS liberalization schedule in the EPA and successful conclusion of negotiations with the EU. But this was not sufficient to overcome different interests and incentives among West African states. Côte d'Ivoire and Ghana needed to sign an EPA to maintain their duty-free, quota-free access to the EU market while Nigeria, on the other hand, has so far preferred not to do so, fearing competition from EU imports that it argues could undermine its industrialization process. As a result, the EPA process now threatens to undermine and disrupt economic integration in West Africa.

Formal intra-regional trade flows are also low because of weak trade complementarity among West African countries. Higher flows revealed comparative advantage of foreign countries in the products imported into West Africa, and the higher trade costs within than outside the region. These factors reduce the competitiveness of local West African products, while weak institutional and physical infrastructure also drive-up costs. Non-tariff barriers and import bans further limit intra-regional trade.

Several challenges must be addressed to strengthen regional integration and engender structural transformation that enhances growth, creates jobs, and tackles poverty and other social ills in West Africa.

The first task is to increase the share of intra-regional exports in total exports, which should enhance structural transformation, and the second is to expand structural transformation beyond the service sector to the manufacturing sector. The third is to strengthen the primary links between regional integration and structural transformation by developing a dynamic industrial base with manufactured exports. Specific challenges of ETLS implementation have been identified as follows:

a. ***The Non-Tariff Barriers***—Several non-tariff barriers have been lined up by member states to stand on the way of the ETLS, and these are as follows:

    (i) The non-recognition of quality certificates issued by national structures, sometimes owing to non-harmonization of sanitary, phytosanitary, and technical standards at the regional level.
    (ii) The non-acceptance of approvals issued by the National Approval Committees (NACs) of member states.
    (iii) The prohibition on the importation of some goods despite being on the list and originating from the domestic/regional economy.
    (iv) The road harassment and malpractices.

b. ***Corruption among Law Enforcement Agents***—Extortions, intimidation, and harassment carried out by the police, gendarmerie, customs, and immigration officers on duties at the various borders have contributed negatively to the implementation of the ETLS in West Africa. Such corrupt practices among these law enforcement agencies have sometimes provided excuses for some unscrupulous traders who engage in smuggling of goods under the pretext of ETLS goods. This is often the case with goods coming into Nigeria from neighboring West African countries. Added to this, is that there is need for proper control in check of substandard goods which is statutorily enforced by the Nigerian Customs and the Standards Organisation of Nigeria (SON).
c. ***Poor Trade Infrastructure***—The epileptic nature and complete absence of trade infrastructure especially at the regional level (e.g., regional rail) provide a platform for failure of the trade scheme. For

instance, most times, goods leaving under the ETLS have to travel to EU countries before returning to the targeted West African countries. This is due to the government's failure to put functional local shipping lines in place.

d. ***Reliance on Manual Processes***—Some of the official operators at the borders across West Africa still rely on manual processes to conduct government business such as the calculation of taxes/duties payable by the business sector. An illustration is the use of calculator or other manual means to calculate levies or other taxes at ports of entries/ exits while ECOWAS has emphasized the need for a computerized system as a way of speeding up transactions under the ETLS.
e. ***Tariff Barriers***—Some of the tariff barriers plaguing the ETLS as impediment include: levying of illegal taxes at the borders and on the roads (such as transit fee, parking fee, conveyance tax, municipality taxes).
f. ***Ignorance on the Part of Operators***—Many importers/ exporters are ignorant of the rules which are unfortunately not simplified enough to guarantee their appreciable level of understanding. Some traders operating under the ETLS sometimes fail to submit complete documentation, a situation that normally leads to delay at the border points. The poor understanding among regional farmers/traders regarding the movements of agro produce as well as animals across member states also constitutes a significant challenge. Ignorance here is not limited to the private sector but also found on the part of the public sector practitioners who neither know the contents of the rules nor the interpretation of the ETLS procedure.
g. ***Nigeria's recent closure of border chokes regional trade***—In August 2019, Nigeria's total closure of its borders to prevent movement of all goods has been met with harsh criticism from neighbors and regional integration advocates. Export trade is a catalyst for sustainable economic development. Through export trade, Nigeria earns vital foreign exchange, increases its revenue base, and may avoid trade deficits. It also helps to consolidate economic diversification. Nigeria's closure of the Benin border has blocked the vital Abidjan-Lagos trade artery and is chipping away regional integration. Nigeria's closure of the Benin border, to curb the smuggling of illicit goods, has blocked a vital West African trade artery and is chipping away regional integration (Davis, 2021)

The economic relationship between the two countries, both members of the ECOWAS, is already asymmetric, with Nigeria exerting much more influence on Benin than vice versa. Given Nigeria's larger population, economy, and natural resource wealth, Benin has adopted a strategy centered on being "entrepôt state," i.e., serving as a trading hub, importing goods and re-exporting them legally but most often illegally to Nigeria. Thus. Benin profited from distortions in Nigeria's economy. Benin's dependence on Nigeria is not apparent from official trade statistics, as Benin's reported trade with Nigeria accounted for only about 6% of Benin's exports and 2% of Benin's imports in 2015–2017. These official statistics are very misleading, however, as they do not reflect the vast informal trade along the border (Davis, 2021)

h. ***Nigeria's Trade Policies Create Distortions That Incentivize Smuggling***—Nigeria's heavy dependence on oil and many dysfunctional economic policies have created an environment for Informal Cross-Border Trade (ICBT) between it and its neighbors, mainly Benin and Togo, to flourish. The wide gap between the official and black-market rates of the naira; Nigeria's subsidized fuel prices; import barriers; poor trade facilitation; and Benin Republic's business climate have incentivized local traders to turn to the Informal Cross-Border Trade. The following are some of the technical issues limiting the full implementation of ETLS in Nigeria and among member states:
i. ***Bureaucratic bottlenecks***—there are several internal and external constraints from country to country in the trade community and the lack of harmonized platforms for implementation constitute a major constraint.
j. ***Weakness of Compensation Mechanism***—in the past, there used to be financial compensation for member states that are net intra-ECOWAS importers with fewer exports than others. At a time, this was suspended to implement a broader based one which is yet to be finalized. This has led to discouragement for countries in this category. The intention was to create ECOWAS Solidarity Fund that will be used to finance capital projects in countries that have fewer exports than imports within the trade community, but the fund is yet to be concluded upon.
k. ***Lack of Commitment at National Levels***—some countries in the community have not fully directed their respective agencies of trade

administration to fully implement the ETLS. This writer sees this constraint more from the perspective of external influences on the trade community through a kind of "divide and rule" mechanism by organized markets of Asia, America, and Europe.

l. ***Other challenges such as the lack of common currency—high cost of transportation and communications infrastructure, language barriers,*** and other logistics problems such as improper or inadequate packaging of goods, etc., also constitute delays or obstacles in the implementation of the ETLS.

Conclusion: Improving the Implementation of the ETLS in Nigeria

Following from the various obstacles identified as militating against the successful implementation of the ETLS in Nigeria, the following actions are recommended in fulfillment of the second objective of the chapter—to recommend ways to solve the problem. There must be an acceleration and localization of public education on the ETLS and its benefits to the socio-economic development of ECOWAS member countries. This will enhance public awareness on the ETLS and further educate the individuals who already know about the ETLS on how to benefit more from the scheme. The more people and businesses know about the scheme, the further the increased utilization of the scheme will lead to deeper and greater chances for the country in intra-ECOWAS trade and development.

The must be the deepening of bilateral relations between member states in the region. Nigeria has institutionalized bilateral relations with some ECOWAS member states including Benin, Niger, and Ghana under the Permanent Joint Council on Cooperation (PJCC). Further deepening of relations between ECOWAS member states can increase the areas of cooperation between them and improve trade, while eliminating the propensity for conflict or dispute among West African states in trading with each other.

Nigeria can contribute to the increase in trade and improve its gains from the ETLS, while further aiding ECOWAS as it has finally signed the free trade area agreement within West Africa. This was achieved by improving local production through policies and programs and the provision of financial and technical support to local production industries. Provision of fertilizers and other incentives to local cocoa farmers are some of the practical ways Nigerian government can support its private production base to boost production in the country. This can increase exports of the country to other countries in the regions. Without goods to trade, the scheme will fail.

The rules of origin within the ETLS are very strict, and it eliminates a lot of free trade opportunities between ECOWAS countries. Currently, the rules of origin cover goods that are wholly produced in member states; produced in member states, but with raw materials from other states provided that such materials have undergone processes that confer community origin status; and goods whose production requires the use of materials which have received a value-added of, at least, 30% of ex-factory price. Lowering these rules of origin by, for instance, reducing the ex-factory price to, at least, 20% can open up the region to a lot more products to be traded among each other.

ECOWAS should establish research centers in the various universities across the region, fully funded, to conduct research into how to improve the implementation of ECOWAS protocols and programs including the ETLS. Research can even be conducted to determine what kind of regulations would be more favorable for the region, putting the West African unique situation into focus. Some of the very successful regional trade agreements like the EU, identifies as a customs union, have research centers all over Europe that helps to identify problems and makes recommendations to solving them. Such an initiative will enable the ETLS to improve its implementation mechanisms and help it achieve its goals of establishing a free trade area and a customs union in West Africa.

Other recommendations include expanding the scope of the ETLS to include services, investment, and intellectual property. This will significantly increase the volume of trade between ECOWAS countries. Finally, the private sector and civil society organizations should be involved in the decision-making and the implementation process of ECOWAS protocols, for a fair representation of their interests.

References

African Development Bank. (2013). *Regional Cooperation and Integration in a Changing World.* Asian Development Bank. https://www.adb.org/sites/default/files/publication/30224/regional-cooperation-changing-world.pdf

African Development Bank. (2019). *West Africa Economic Outlook. Macroeconomic Performance and Prospects*. https://www.afdb.org/fileadmin/uploads/afdb/Documents/Publications/2019AEO/REO_2019_-_West_africa.pdf

Ajetomobi, J. O. (2011). *Market Power in Nigerian Domestic Cocoa Supply Chains*. www.csae.ox.ac.uk/conferences/2011-edia/papers/417-ajetomobi.pdf

Akinkugbe, O. D. (2017) Revisiting the Economic Community of West African States: A Socio-Legal Analysis. *Thesis submitted to the Faculty of Graduate and Postdoctoral Studies in partial fulfillment of the requirements for the Doctorate in Philosophy (PhD) degree in Law*. Graduate Studies in Law, University of Ottawa.

Aniche, E. T. (2009). *A Modern Introduction to Political Science*. Desvic Publishers.

Aniche, E. T. (2014). Problematising Neo-functionalism in the Search for a New Theory of African Integration: The Case of the Proposed Tripartite Free Trade Area (T-FTA) in Africa. *Developing Country Studies, 4*(20), 128–142.

Aniche, E. T., & Ukaegbu, V. E. (2014). Vertical integration, economic dependence and African regionalism: A comparative study of ECOWAS and SADC. *ANSU Journal of Peace and Development Studies, 2*(1), 58–76.

Asante, S. K. B. (1996). *The Strategy of Regional Integration in Africa*. United Nations Economic Commission for Africa. https://hdl.handle.net/10855/4409

Asante, S. K. B. (1997). Regionalism as a Key Element of African Development Strategy. In *Regionalism and Africa's Development*. Palgrave Macmillan.

Asante, S. K. B. (2000). *The Political Economy of Regionalism in Africa: A Decade of the Economic Community of West African States (ECOWAS)*. Praeger Special Studies, p. 234.

Becker, J. (2006). Metamorphosen der regionalen Integration. *Austrian Journal of Development Studies, 22*(2), 11–44.

Brenton, P., & Hoffmann, B. (2016). Cautious Optimism for Regional Integration in Sub-Saharan Africa. *GREAT Insights Magazine, 5*(4), July/August.

Cadot, O., Djiofack, C., & de Melo, J. (2008). Trade Preferences and Rules of Origin: The Economic Partnership Agreements' Prospects for West and Central Africa. *De Boeck Supérieur, 5*(16), 93–135.

Chikodiri, N., Chukwuemeka, E., et al. (2019). Regionalism in World Politics; Interrogating the Relevance of ECOWAS in Global Political Economy. *Central European Journal of International and Security Studies, 13*(2), 111–132.

Davis, B. (2021). *What Are the Barriers to International Trade in Nigeria?* https://www.mvorganizing.org/what-are-the-barriers-to-international-trade-in-nigeria/

ECOWAS. (2016). *The Community Computer Centre (CCC) in Collaboration with the Directorate of Communication, "Trade"*. https://www.ecowas.int/ecowas-sectors/trade/

ECOWAS. (2018). *Final Communiqué: Fifth Meeting of the Task Force on the ECOWAS Single Currency Programme*. https://ecowas.int/fifth-meeting-of-the-task-force-on-the-ecowas-single-currency-programme/

Eder, J. (2021). Moving Towards Developmental Regionalism? Industrial Cooperation in the Eurasian Economic Union from an Armenian and Belarusian Perspective. *Post-Communist Economies, 33*(2–3), 331–358.

Elumaro, A., & Olayiwola, W. (2020). ECOWAS Integration Agenda: Status of Existing Regional Trade Agreements and Prospects of Custom Union and Common Market. In W. Olayiwola (Ed.), *Contemporary Issues on Regional Trade Agreements. A Book in Honour of Gbenga Obideyi*. Abbi Books.

Gibb, R. (2009). Regional Integration and Africa's Development Trajectory: Meta theories, expectations and reality. *Third World Quarterly, 30*(4), 701–721.

Haas, E. B. (1958). *The Uniting of Europe: Political, Social, and Economic Forces 1950–1957*. Stanford University Press.

Hurrell, A. (1995). Regionalism in Theoretical Perspective. In L. Fawcett & A. Hurrell (Eds.), *Regionalism in World Politics: Regional Organization and International Order*. Oxford University Press.

Imobighe, T. (2003). *The OAU (AU) and OAS in Regional Conflict Management: A Comparative Assessment*. Spectrum Books Limited.

Joe, B. (2021). *African Free Trade Bloc Opens for Business, but Challenges Remain*. https://www.weforum.org/agenda/2021/01/african-free-trade-bloc-business-challenges/

Okafor, J., & Aniche, E. (2017). Deconstructing Neo-Functionalism. *Journal of Humanities and Social Science, 22*(2), 60–72.

Karaki, K., & Verhaeghe, E. (2016). *Understanding ECOWAS Trade Policy and Trade Facilitation: Advancing Economic Integration One Hurdle at a Time*. http://www.ecdpm.org/pedro

Iruoma, K. (2021). *Nigeria's Long-Awaited Petroleum Industry Act Targets Oil Industry Overhaul*. https://african.business/2021/09/energy-resources/nigerias-long-awaited-pia-targets-oil-industry-overhaul/

Lee, M. (2002) Regionalism in Africa: A Part of Problem or a Part of Solution. *Polis/R.C.S.P./C.P.S.R.* 9, Numéro Spécia.

Lee, Y., Anukoonwattaka, W., Taylor-Strauss, H., & Duval, Y. (2022, March). Trade, Investment and Innovation. *The Economic and Social Commission for Asia and the Pacific (ESCAP)* (Working Paper Series, No. 01).

Hoffmann, L. K., & Melly, P. (2015). *Nigeria's Booming Borders the Drivers and Consequences of Unrecorded Trade*. Chatham House, the Royal Institute of International Affairs.

Meyer, N., Fenyes, T., Breitenbach, M., & Idsardi, E. (2010). *Bilateral and Regional Trade Agreements and Technical Barriers to Trade: An African Perspective* (OECD Trade Policy Working Paper, No. 96.)

NEPC. (2024). *Ecowas Trade Liberalization Scheme (ETLS)*. https://nepc.gov.ng/blog/trade-agreement/ecowas/

Obasaju, B. O., Olayiwola, K. W., & Okodua, H. (2016). The Role of ECOWAS in Fostering Nigeria's Cocoa Beans Value Chain, 3rd International Conference on African. *Development Issues (CU-ICADI 2016)*.

Ogunleye, E. K. (2014). Global Value Chain Development and Structural Transformation in Nigeria. *Africa Economic Brief, 5*(2), 1–12.

Ojo, O (2019, April 21). *Trade Liberalisation in West Africa: A Case Study of Ecowas Trade Liberalisation Scheme (ETLS)*.

Okoroafor, J (2013). Is the Economic Community of West African States (ECOWAS) Really Working? *Democracy & Governance*. https://www.opinionnigeria.com/is-the-economic-community-of-west-african-states-ecowas-really-working/

Olayiwola, W. (2020, November 2). *Governing the Interface between the African Continental Free Trade Area and Regional Economic Communities Free Trade Areas: Issues, Opportunities and Challenges* (A Final Revised Draft Report of UNECA).

Olayiwola, W., Osabuohien, E., & Okodua, H. (2011). *Economic Policy Analysis Unit (EPAU) ECOWAS Commission* (EPAU Monograph Series, No. 1). Abuja: ECOWAS.

Sakyi, D., & Opoku, E. E. O. (2014). *Regionalism and Economic Integration in Africa: A Conceptual and Theoretical Perspective* (The African Capacity Building Foundation, Occasional Paper 22).

Salvatore, D. (2010). *International economics*. John Wiley & Sons, Inc.

Seck, A., Fall, F. A., & Aidara, K. (2020). Regional Integration and Growth Spillovers: Is Africa an Economic Space? *Journal of African Trade, 7*(1–2), 1–8. https://doi.org/10.2991/jat.k.200724.001

Shaw, M. N. (2003). *International Law* (5th ed.). Cambridge University Press.

Shortridge, T. (2020). *West Africa—A Novel Approach to Regionalism*. https://www.internationalaffairs.org.au/resource/west-africa-a-novel-approach-to-regionalism/

Sloan, J. W. (1971). The Strategy of Developmental Regionalism: Benefits, Distribution, Obstacles, and Capabilities. *Journal of Common Market Studies, 10*(2), 138–162.

Ukaoha, K., & Aniekan, U. (2013). The ECOWAS Trade Liberalisation Scheme: Genesis, Conditions and Appraisal. *NANTS Regional Trade Advocacy Series, 2*(3), 1–12.

UNECA. (2012). Regional Integration: Agricultural Value Chains to Integrate and Transform Agriculture in West Africa. *A Publication of the United Nations Economic Commission for Africa*—ECAWA/ADHOC/2012/02

United Nations. (2019). *Economic Development in Africa Report 2019, Made in Africa—Rules of Origin for Enhanced Intra-African Trade*. https://unctad.org/system/files/official-document/edar2019_en_ch2.pdf

Zannou, A. (2010). Determinants of Intra-ECOWAS Trade Flows. *African Journal of Business Management, 4*(5), 678–686.

Zormelo, D. K. (1994). Integration Theories and Economic Development: "A Case Study of the Political and Social Dynamics of ECOWAS." PhD Thesis Presented at the University of London. The London School of Economics and Political Science. https://core.ac.uk/download/pdf/46518152.pdf

CHAPTER 11

The Role of RECs in Mitigating the Impact of Natural Disasters in Africa: The Case of SADC

Siphumelele Duma and Rich Mashimbye

Introduction

Natural disasters are not new in the African continent in general and southern Africa in particular. However, the frequency with which they have occurred since the turn of the twenty-first century is alarming. The affected countries, such as Mozambique, Malawi, and Zimbabwe have had to find measures to mitigate the devastating impacts of these natural disasters. These impacts are transboundary and have necessitated effective measures beyond national boundaries. While the continent's Regional Economic Communities (RECs) were established for what may be described as economic purpose, as stipulated in the Abuja Treaty, the scope of their functions has expanded over the years to deal with issues beyond economic integration. For instance, over the years, the continent's

S. Duma (✉) · R. Mashimbye
Institute for Pan-African Thought and Conversation, University of Johannesburg, Johannesburg, South Africa
e-mail: dumasphume@gmail.com

A. O. Akinola and E. A. Liaga (eds.), *Development and Regional Stability in Africa*, https://doi.org/10.1007/978-3-031-56695-0_11

eight RECs, as recognised by the African Union (AU), have taken up the task of formulating response initiatives to climate change-related disasters. This chapter focuses on one of these RECs, the Southern African Development Community (SADC).

In the last five years, the southern African region has been hit by the worst and most devastating cyclones in the region's history, leaving millions of people either displaced, dead, or without shelter. For instance, Mozambique, Botswana, Madagascar, Malawi, Zimbabwe, and South Africa are recent victims of these cyclone-motivated floods. These recurring incidents have become a security threat in the region. They have not just damaged infrastructure and property but have claimed human lives and accounted for a catastrophic increase in food and water insecurity. In 2022, 51.3 million people in the SADC region reportedly struggled with the food insecurity crisis (CCARDESA, 2022). While it is also true that socio-economic and socio-political factors have a role to play in these crises, the natural disasters-related environmental challenges are a significant factor.

Droughts destroy crops and livestock, curtailing harvest, which usually lasts for several years. When the food supply becomes unstable due to the scarcity generated by drought, food prices skyrocket, causing food security issues. Thus, these natural disasters have the propensity to wreak havoc across borders when they strike in the region and with wide-ranging catastrophes. This calls for strengthening of the mechanisms for disaster mitigation at a regional level, especially for climate change. Thus, every country in the region needs a clear-cut climate change impact mitigation framework or strategy in line with the regional and continental response measures: as stipulated in the SADC Climate Change Strategy and Action Plan (2020–2030) and the African Union Climate Change and Resilient Development Strategy and Action Plan (2022–2032).

Against this backdrop, this chapter analyses the frequency and severity of ecological and climate change-related disasters in southern Africa since 2000 and the role of SADC in mitigating their impact. The chapter deploys a qualitative research approach and uses secondary sources for data collection, including journal articles, books, SADC's official organisational reports, and other relevant documentation available to the public domain. There are several initiatives that SADC has established supposedly to deal with the devastating effects of climate change-related disasters, with the latest being the SADC Humanitarian and Emergency Operation Centre (SHOC). However, as the results will show, they have been dysfunctional. Understandably, cooperation on climate change and natural disasters is a recent phenomenon in SADC (Compagnon et al., 2011). This is because, for a long time after independence, the primary objective has been to do away with the colonial economic and political legacy through pan-African approaches to development, like intra-continental trade and industrialisation. However, if the region is to sustain its development gains, it must step up climate change-related disaster mitigation efforts.

The chapter is structured as follows: it starts with the introduction and proceeds with the second section, which provides an understanding of natural disasters, while the third section explores the cases of natural disaster occurrences in the SADC region. The fourth part examines the regional initiatives by SADC to mitigate the devastating impact of natural disasters, and the fifth analyses the effectiveness of these initiatives, followed by a conclusion.

Understanding Natural Disasters

A series of devastating natural disasters across the world in the 2000s raised the global alarm and a renewed academic and policy interest in understanding the causes and consequences of climate change-induced natural disasters and how to mitigate the impacts. These events included most notably the 2004 Tsunami in Asia, believed to be the deadliest in history as it killed over 230,000 people in over ten countries (Mater Christi College, 2022); the 2005 Hurricane Katrina in the United States, and the early 2010s Tsunami in Japan, 2011 (Guha-Sapir & Santos, 2013). According to the Centre for Research on the Epidemiology of Natural Disasters (CRED), the global annual average number of natural disasters increased from 357 between 2001 and 2020 to 432 in 2021. This led to the killing of 10 492 people, affecting 101.8 million people, and causing economic damage estimated at USD 252 billion in the latter year (CRED, 2022). However, these disasters have not been occurring at similar rates across the continents, as Asia and Africa have witnessed a rapid increase of these phenomena over the years relative to other continents (CRED, 2022; Debarati Guha-Sapir et al., 2013).

Countries that are categorised as developing countries are distributed across Africa and Asia. Inevitably, the devastating impact of natural disasters has the potential to set back their development process for decades, as they can affect not only the rates but also the pattern of this process

(Benson & Clay, 2004: 3; Hallegatte et al., 2020; Naqvi & Monasterolo, 2021). While the general assessment of the impact of disasters has predominantly been on the direct losses, like physical damage to properties and the financial costs for the repairs, there is a need to consider the accumulative impacts on the long-term development process (Benson & Clay, 2004: 3; Naqvi & Monasterolo, 2021), especially in developing countries. Natural disasters are the "occurrence of an abnormal or infrequent hazard that affects vulnerable communities or geographic areas, causing substantial damage, disruption and death. These would generally leave the affected communities unable to function normally" (Benson & Clay, 2004: 5).

The heavy and prolonged rain that battered Nigeria in October 2022 was an example of natural disasters emanating from climate change. A sustained period of heavy rain resulted in flooding in 27 of Nigeria's 36 states, uprooting houses and industrial establishments and killing over 600 people (BBC, 2022). In addition, about 1.3 million people were displaced, while an estimated 2400 people sustained injuries due to the floods (BBC, 2022). This was the severest flooding in Nigeria for about a decade. Nigeria is presently occupied with rebuilding the homes and businesses that were wiped out by the flooding. The United States Agency for International Development allocated 1 million U.S. dollars to humanitarian relief (Development Diaries, 2022). Similarly, the European Union (EU) provided €500 000 in aid to combat the cholera epidemic that has intensified in the wake of the floods (Reliefweb, 2022). However, the role of the Economic Community of West African States (ECOWAS) in assisting Nigeria to rebuild is unclear; but this may be a case of absent transparency than the organisation did not assist the country.

As a cause of natural disasters, climate change primarily emanates from the destruction or disruption of the climate, mainly by industrial activities through which countries attempt to develop economically (Lin et al., 2015: 1228–1231). More pointedly, countries mainly located in Europe, Asia, and North America engaged and continue to engage in large-scale industrialisation driven by carbon-intensive energy sources like oil and coal, resulting in enormous emissions of carbon into the atmosphere (Meyer & Roser, 2006). The negative impact on the climatic ecosystem is significant: the climatic processes that produce weather patterns become affected, resulting in spells of either drought or flooding becoming frequent and devastating in effect (Bryant et al., 2009). In response to the challenge of climate deterioration, countries and intergovernmental organisations alike have been calling for a shift from carbon-intensive energy sources to wind and solar-based energy as well as renewables.

While natural disasters have the most direct impacts in developed countries, in terms of property losses, developing countries suffer the most casualties (Botzen et al., 2019). This is because these poor communities are often ill-prepared to deal with these events (Guha-Sapir & Santos, 2013: 5). As a result of the lack of institutional mechanisms to respond to disasters in developing countries, which are present in advanced economies, these communities often help each other in the immediate aftermath of disasters. This assistance involves immediate search and rescue and evacuations (Guha-Sapir & Lechat, 1986; Guha-Sapir & Santos, 2013; Hallegatte et al., 2020). The African continent is more vulnerable to climate change-related disasters because many of its economies rely on climate-sensitive sectors for livelihoods, growth, and development (African Union, 2022); these include the services industry, rain-fed agriculture and natural resources.

Furthermore, poor people are more likely to find themselves living in disaster-prone areas, as these places sometimes offer them good economic opportunities (Hallegatte et al., 2020). This becomes a nightmare in the aftermath of a disastrous event, as it induces a series of shocks, such as losses of livelihoods, the disruption of the productive base, and loss of assets and crops (Guha-Sapir & Santos, 2013; Naqvi & Monasterolo, 2021). These communities are then exposed to food insecurities, as they cannot rely on productive supplies from other areas (Hallegatte et al., 2020). It is these impacts on the poor that Hallegatte et al. (2020) have noted that the traditional metrics for measuring the impact of natural disasters do not account for, which end up underestimating the real impact on the poor people who have few assets to lose. That is to say, the replacement value of assets measure cannot account for severe vulnerabilities in poorer communities within developing countries (Dartanto, 2022; Hallegatte et al., 2020).

It is important to note that the frequency of disasters does not determine the vulnerability of a particular country and community. The socio-economic status of households determines how likely they are to suffer from these events (Chakraborty et al., 2013; Dartanto, 2022; Zhang et al., 2022). It is also noted that while having effective measures to deal with the impact in the immediate aftermath of disasters, like rescues and evacuation, is essential, poverty remains the main factor determining the long-term consequences of these events

(Guha-Sapir & Santos, 2013; Naqvi & Monasterolo, 2021). These socio-economic vulnerabilities have made natural disasters a security threat in developing regions, with skyrocketing poverty rates and food insecurity crises.

Naqvi and Monasterolo (2021) have argued that while the direct impact of natural disasters has been well understood for some time, research still needs to be conducted on how shocks spread to non-affected regions. They note that in some instances, these impacts spread far beyond the epicentre, more so in the agricultural and low-income regions. In these cases, they disrupt the supply networks and the demand side through income losses and migration, which triggers the cascading impact into other regions (Dartanto, 2022; Naqvi & Monasterolo, 2021). On the other hand, advanced economies can circumvent adverse production shocks, as opposed to less diversified economies (Botzen et al., 2019). For this reason, it is crucial for the post-disaster responses to also pay attention to the state of readiness and preparedness for future events to avoid being caught off guard each time a devastating event occurs. This further rationalises planning and dealing with these issues at regional and global levels, then cascading down to the national for implementation.

Climate change has long been regarded as a serious threat to humanity by institutions like the United Nations Environment Programme (UNDP), the AU, and the EU, as it has a direct impact on people's livelihoods and health (African Union Commission, 2015; European Union, 2014; UNEP, 2002). It further threatens the economic development of the most vulnerable countries as it sets back gains with years, which makes capacity building to mitigate these impacts a significant undertaking in these regions and countries. However, for the poor regions, building these capacities often means redirecting the limited financial and non-financial resources from other strategic national programmes, making it even more challenging.

Cases of Natural Disasters in the SADC Region

In order to understand the extent to which natural disasters resulting from climate change have caused destruction and anguish in southern Africa, it is important to examine a number of cases of these incidents in the region. Any discourse on natural disasters in the SADC region is bound to reference the catastrophic cyclone Idai that has recently hit the region.

Cyclone Idai was an intense tropical cyclone that made landfall in Mozambique on 4 March 2019, spread to several countries in southern Africa, including Malawi and Zimbabwe and lasted until 21 March 2019 (Oxfam, 2020). It was recorded as the deadliest tropical cyclone to ever form in the South-West Indian Ocean basin and hit southern Africa (Nature, 2019). Over 1300 people perished because of cyclone Idai, and many more were recorded as missing as a direct consequence of the storms and floods associated with the cyclone. It was the most devastating natural disaster to strike Africa in history.

As cyclone Idai swept across the SADC region and intensified, people flee from their homes, infrastructure was destroyed, and economic activities abruptly halted (Reliefweb, 2019). Governments of the affected countries were clearly overwhelmed and lacked strong natural disaster response mechanisms to adequately respond to Idai and, more crucially, provide much-needed relief to communities that were battered by the floods and storms. The regional organisation, SADC, responded to the crisis primarily by offering relief aid in the form of a grant of 500 000 USD to the affected countries (The Economist, 2019). While essential and appreciable, this contribution and the involvement of SADC in response to Idai did not necessarily result in significant alleviation of the crisis, as the situation remained dire. Confronted with ineffective and insufficient assistance from their governments and SADC, the affected people sought assistance from international organisations, such as the United Nations International Children's Emergency Fund (UNICEF). However, given the magnitude of the cyclone and its damage, this intervention did not make a serious dent in mitigating the impact of Idai. Equally, domestic civil society organisations also came to aid the affected people.

A more recent natural disaster that struck the region and resulted in widespread destruction was the flooding that occurred in South Africa, KwaZulu-Natal (KZN) in April 2022. The floods happened after a prolonged spell of heavy rains in the province in the early to middle of April. The floods had both social and economic impacts. As floods swept across the province, people's homes were swept away, and in the process, many people (about 400) died (Aljazeera, 2022). In certain instances, some people were swept by the rising water tides and remained declared missing persons. The KZN province is crucial to South Africa's economy, being second in terms of its contribution to the country's gross domestic product (GDP) (Statistics South Africa, 2021).

The indiscriminate nature of the flooding meant that the industrial areas of the province would not be spared. The eThekwini, iLembe, and the Ugu industrial areas were the most affected in terms of the disruption and destruction that the floods caused to economic activities in the province. The industrial damage caused by the floods in the province is estimated at R7 billion, and the three aforementioned areas account for roughly 80% of this amount. Given the KZN's significant share of the national economy, this is problematic for the province's economy and the country. In summary, the floods in KZN claimed lives, inflicted damage to both residential and commercial property, and resulted in the pervasive internal displacement of people in the province.

As pointed out in the foregoing, the flooding in the KZN created a humanitarian crisis of significant proportions, and a humanitarian relief intervention became necessary. Being a member of SADC, the regional body was expected to take the lead in the disaster relief efforts. However, this was not the case, as the organisation limited its involvement to expressing sympathy to and solidarity with the affected people and South African government. This is despite the existence of natural disaster mechanisms within the organisation. This is more problematic because the organisation has always contended that the region is vulnerable to climate change-inspired disasters and must build the capacity to respond to them. Besides SADC, the South African government approached its humanitarian relief efforts in KZN in a manner that lacks urgency. The government set aside funds to resettle and feed people displaced by floods and rebuild infrastructures. But these resources have been exceedingly slow to get to the affected people. Albeit with limited resources, civil society organisations, like the 'Gift of Givers' have been able to provide relief aid, mainly in the form of basic needs like foodstuffs and clothing, to people who were affected by the floods.

Given their geographic location, Madagascar and Mozambique are countries in southern Africa that are exceedingly vulnerable to cyclones, floods, and storms. Madagascar is an island country patched on a strip of land in the Indian Ocean, while Mozambique is almost entirely a coastal country. Considering that cyclones form in the ocean through a climatic process that occurs within the sea basin, the proximity of these two countries to the ocean may mean that they are hugely exposed to potential flooding and storms emanating from cyclones. Indeed, as previously pointed out, cyclone Idai first made landfall in Mozambique and had the most devastating impact there. Given this fact, and considering the natural disaster examples outlined above, SADC needs to recognise the region's vulnerability to climate change-related disasters and develop systems that would allow the organisation to respond effectively.

Regional Initiatives to Mitigate the Impacts of Disasters

Over the years, it has become apparent that many ecosystems in the African continent, particularly southern Africa, move beyond national borders. This necessitates a transboundary management and coordination approach in terms of policy planning and implementation dealing with associated challenges (African Union, 2016; SADC, 2017). Given that climate change-related natural disasters are global phenomena with local consequences (Denton et al., 2016), planning and coordination over multiple governance levels further offer ideal conditions and a conducive environment. This is because the environmental challenges have no regard for political and national borders, particularly climate change; thus, its impacts are affecting the whole of humanity (African Compagnon et al., 2011; Union, 2016). When the unexpected flooding hit the SADC region in 2007, member states were caught off guard without effective response measures. These mid-2000s events displaced 1.5 million people in Zambia and more across the region while killing six people in Zimbabwe and Mozambique (SADC, 2022a; Shacinda, 2008).

Against this backdrop, the officials of SADC began to meet and consult annually to prepare for future disasters. The region created a disaster risk reduction unit tasked with coordinating regional preparedness and response programmes for transboundary disasters; the culmination was the inauguration of the SADC Regional Platform for Disaster Risk Reduction (RPDRR) in 2011 (SADC, 2022a). Moreover, the SADC region is a party to several global disaster risk reduction initiatives while having devised several of its own to cope with and mitigate the devastating impacts of natural disasters and enhance resilience. These include the Sendai Framework for Disaster Risk Reduction, 2015–2030 (SFDRR), adopted by the United Nations at its 3rd World Conference for Disaster Risk Reduction in Sendai, Japan, 2015 (United Nations, 2015). The AU Heads of State and Governments expressed overwhelming support for the framework, which was then to be implemented at the regional level by the RECs (African Union, 2016).

The SFDRR's mandate was to "reduce disaster risks and losses of lives, livelihoods and health and in the economic, physical, social, cultural and environmental assets of persons, businesses, communities and countries" (United Nations, 2015). Within the SADC region, this framework was adopted not only to reduce the existing disaster risks but also to increase the region's preparedness for response to and recovery from these events, as emphasised in the SADC Disaster Preparedness and Response Strategy and Fund (DPRSF), 2015–2030 (SADC, 2017).DPRSF serves as SADC's mechanism for preparedness and response, aiming to enhance resilience to disasters in accordance with SFDRR. Its goal is to cultivate a culture of safety and resilience by implementing an efficient response system in the region by the year 2030 (SADC, 2017). It outlines three priority actions as the means to achieve its goals and desired outcomes. These include understanding risk and disaster management, strengthening disaster preparedness and response planning, and establishing the preparedness and response fund (SADC, 2017: 16).

The Regional Disaster Preparedness and Response Fund was established and adopted by the region's Council of Ministers in 2015. This was after noting that at the regional level, SADC lacked adequate funds for a coordinated response to disaster events. Its mandate would be to provide immediate financial support to the member states overwhelmed by the disasters in the region to save and sustain lives effectively. The size would depend on the principle of affordability by the organisation's member states (SADC, 2017). Thus, every country in the region needs a clear-cut climate change impact mitigation framework or strategy in line with the regional and continental response measures, as stipulated in the SADC Climate Change Strategy and Action Plan (2020–2030) and the African Union Climate Change and Resilient Development Strategy and Action Plan (2022–2032).

The most recent of these initiatives is SHOC, having been established and adopted by the region's council of ministers in 2021 (SADC, 2022b), albeit it has been on the cards since 2016, as its creation was pronounced in the DPRSF. SHOC's responsibility is to facilitate enhanced disaster risk preparedness, rapid response, and recovery to support the member states affected and overwhelmed by natural disaster events (SADC, 2017, 2022b). The region's Council of Ministers responsible for disaster risk management have noted that the recurrence of these catastrophes necessitated a shift in approach to risk reduction. They have emphasised that reacting after the fact is insufficient; there ought to be vigilance and proactiveness (SADC, 2022b),which the establishment of SHOC would address.

The Council of Ministers noted that SHOC would enable the SADC Secretariat, with the support of the international cooperating partners, to coordinate a regional response, including the deployment of staff in the event of disaster events in the region (SADC, 2022b).SHOC will have a direct link to all member states' emergency operation centres. However, it can only be activated under specific circumstances. The initiative has provided three levels. According to Level 1, SHOC will be activated when the disaster is deemed to be overwhelming for the affected member state, without adequate resources to manage it. Under Level 2, SHOC will not be activated unless the event seriously overwhelms the national capacity of the affected member state. In the case of Level 3, the disaster must overwhelm the affected member state, and its activation will include the provision of communication systems and coordination to guide a timely response through accurate messaging (SADC, 2017, 2022b).

The SADC region has also underscored the significance of prepositioning relief items in disaster-prone areas, as this would reduce the required time in response to an emergency disaster. It is noted that this would reduce higher facilitation costs as ad hoc decisions result in delayed responses and high costs as opposed to when there are stored emergency supplies (SADC, 2017, 2018, 2022a). There is no shortage of disaster risk reduction programmes in the SADC region. However, to what extent have they effectively dealt with disasters in member states since the turn of the century? This question is crucial because it is well understood that adopting an initiative to address a particular issue is not a success in and of itself. However, it is the practical implementation that allows for a discernible impact. Thus, given the SADC region's projects, protocols, and programme implementation record, one wonders if these promising initiatives to circumvent the devastating impact of natural disasters have been effectively deployed.

The Effectiveness of Regional Initiatives: Analysis

Natural disasters have become more frequent in the African continent since the early 2000s. This shows that the sometimes-divisive phenomenon of climate change is indeed real and is drastically changing weather patterns. As a region located in the Southern part of the African continent, SADC has not been spared from the devastating consequences of climate change, as cyclones, heavy floods, storms, and droughts are the present realities of the region (Brookings, 2021). Specifically, the fact that natural disasters are increasing in frequency and also becoming damaging in impact indicates that they are linked to climate change. This is more so considering that while natural disasters have always been a feature of nature in Africa and, indeed, the rest of the world, they did not occur often and were less devastating in their effect.

As already highlighted in the section that delved into some of the cases of natural disasters in the SADC region, aside from the destruction of industrial and residential infrastructure, cyclones and floods like Idai and those that hit South Africa in 2022 also resulted in displacement and death of people (Climate Change Knowledge Portal, 2022). One of the lessons that can be derived from cyclone Idai is the spread and spillover effect of natural disasters to neighbouring countries that did not initially experience the disaster. Therefore, SADC initiatives that would coordinate collective and region-wide responses to natural disasters become even more crucial.

As indicated earlier, most of the SADC's regional integration agenda has been predominantly oriented towards economic growth and development since its establishment. Only after the earlier mentioned disaster hit the region in 2007 did the organisation institutionalise efforts to mitigate the impact of these disasters in the event of reoccurrence. This left a gap in addressing climate change-related issues within the region and the continent in general. While SADC began to establish committees in the mid-2000s that would look at measures to mitigate the impacts of natural disasters following the flooding in 2007 that affected millions across the region, more so in Zambia, Zimbabwe, and Mozambique (SADC, 2022a), the region was not prepared when cyclone Idai hit, over ten years later. While it is impossible to stop natural disasters, the idea behind establishing committees was to put in place measures that would mitigate their impact when they strike (SADC, 2022a). This would involve giving warnings to hotspot areas prior to the occurrence and quick emergency services to the people in the affected areas after.

However, SADC's initiatives, discussed in the previous section, were inadequate to execute this assignment. It is not because they were poorly formulated, but because there was compelling evidences of lack of effective implementation. The African RECs, including SADC, have been criticised for lacking linkages between their institutions and people in communities on the ground (Denton et al., 2016). This poor linkage may also partly be blamed for the ineffectiveness of the response measures following a disaster. The implementation record of SADC's initiatives, especially in economic growth and development areas, suggests this phenomenon is not new. There has only been a proliferation of initiatives without implementation to improve the living standard of the region's citizenry. This is the main challenge in the region, lack of well-established and functional implementation of what, at times, appear to be comprehensive strategies. However, this must be addressed, especially when dealing with natural disasters, which pose security threats to the lives and livelihoods of the region's citizenry. There is an urgent need to transcend political rhetoric and take action to ensure no loss of lives and livelihoods that could have been prevented.

There is an urgent need to institutionalise civil society organisations (CSOs) and other relevant non-state actors within the region's integration agenda, especially within disaster mitigation mechanisms. Their proximity to the people and communities at the grassroots levels has proven efficient. A case in point was the significant life-saving roles played by the 'Gift of the Givers' and other CSOs in the aftermath of the KZN floods in South Africa in early 2022. This is not to say there is a magic bullet to dealing with these issues, but that CSOs are strategically positioned in society to see that no lives are lost unnecessarily to the devastating impact of natural disasters. This is unlike the SADC region's emergency response services which take days or weeks to intervene in times of need, where in many cases, lives that could have been saved have already been lost. Thus, close cooperation between the CSOs and relevant regional institutions to deploy these measures before and in the aftermath of disaster occurrences might benefit the concerned communities.

Conclusion

This chapter has examined the mitigation mechanisms of natural disasters by the RECs through the case of SADC. It has analysed the frequency and severity of natural disasters in the SADC since the turn of the twenty-first century and the role of the SADC in mitigating their devastating impact. It was established that natural disasters have multiplied in the recent past in the SADC region. Furthermore, the magnitude and impact of these disasters have also increased significantly. They have tended to cover vast areas or multiple regions and produce wide-scale destruction in terms of displacements, deaths, and damage to infrastructure.

While the chapter recognises that the SADC organisation has been preoccupied with matters of economic growth and development for most of its existence, it notes that it could have done better in mitigating the recent disasters in the region. Of note was the cyclone Idai in 2019 and other disasters that followed. Despite the establishment of committees and initiatives that would mitigate the impacts of disasters in the past 10 years, its impacts and effectiveness have been frequently questioned. Indeed, CSOs and other relevant non-state actors have a central role to play in the region's natural disaster mitigation mechanisms, given their proximity to the people on the ground. Their effectiveness was seen during the April 2022 floods in the South African province of KwaZulu-Natal, where the 'Gift of the Givers' and other grassroots organisations played heroic roles in the aftermath. Action on this matter is urgent, given that it is a security threat to the citizens. In the case of disasters management and government's responsiveness, political rhetoric would be counterproductive.

References

African Union. (2022). *African Union Climate Change and Resilient Development Strategy and Action Plan (2022–2032)*. https://au.int/sites/default/files/documents/42276-doc-CC_Strategy_and_Action_Plan_2022-2032_23_06_22_ENGLISH-compressed.pdf

African Union. (2016). *Programme of Action for the Implementation of the Sendai Framework for Disaster Risk Reduction 2015–2030 in Africa: In line with the Africa Regional Strategy for Disaster Risk Reduction*. https://www.unisdr.org/files/49455_poaforsendaiimplementationinafrica.pdf

African Union Commission. (2015). *Agenda 2063: The Africa We Want*. https://doi.org/10.2345/0899-8205-44.1.49

ALJAZEERA. (2022). *'Catastrophic' Durban Floods Leave Trail of Death and Destruction*. https://www.aljazeera.com/news/2022/4/15/s-africa-durban-residents-count-their-losses-in-intense-floods

Benson, C., & Clay, E. J. (2004). Understanding the Economic and Financial Impacts of natural Disasters. In *World Bank Disaster Risk Management Series* (Issue 4). The World Bank. https://doi.org/10.1596/0-8213-5685-2

Botzen, W. J. W., Deschenes, O., & Sanders, M. (2019). The Economic Impacts of natural Disasters: A Review of Models and Empirical Studies. *Review of Environmental Economics and Policy, 13*(2), 167–188.

British Broadcasting Corporation (BBC). (2022). *Nigeria Floods: 'Overwhelming' Disaster Leaves More Than 600 People Dead*. https://www.bbc.com/news/world-africa-63280518

Brookings. (2021). *Increasing Droughts and Floods on the African Continent*. https://www.brookings.edu/blog/africa-in-focus/2021/10/08/increasing-droughts-and-floods-on-the-african-continent/

Bryant, L., Carver, L., Butler, C., & Anage, A. (2009). Climate Change and Family Planning: Least-Developed Countries. *Bulletin of the World Health Organization, 87*, 852–857.

CCARDESA. (2022). *Food Security Challenges in the SADC Region*. https://www.ccardesa.org/about-ccardesa

Chakraborty, D., Bandyopadhyay, S., Gupta, I., Das, Sen, S., & Mitra, D. (2013). Natural Disaster Mitigation in West Bengal. In Debarati Guha-Sapir & Indhira Santos (Eds.), *The Economic Impacts of Natural Disasters* (pp. 199–225). Oxford University Press.

Climate Change Knowledge Portal. (2022). *Country: South Africa*. World Bank. https://climateknowledgeportal.worldbank.org/country/south-africa/vulnerability

Compagnon, D., Florémont, F., & Lamaud, I. (2011). Sub-Saharan Africa: Fragmented Environmental Governance Without Regional Integration. *Comparative Environmental Regionalism*, pp. 92–112.

CRED. (2022). 2021 Disasters in Numbers. In *Cred Crunch* (Issue 66). https://doi.org/10.1038/s41598

Denton, F., Kituyi, E., Lo, H., & Wouapi, H. (2016). *Regional Economic Communities and Climate Change Adaptation in Africa* (No. 4; CARIAA Working Paper, Issue November). https://www.researchgate.net/publication/337155607_Regional_Economic_Communities_and_Climate_Change_Adaptation_in_Africa_Background_Paper_on_Lessons_Learned_from_CCAA

Dartanto, T. (2022). Natural Disasters, Mitigation and Household Welfare in Indonesia: Evidence from a Large-Scale Longitudinal Survey Natural Disasters, Mitigation and Household Welfare in Indonesia: Evidence from a Large-Scale Longitudinal Survey. *Cogent Economics & Finance, 10*, 1–31.

Guha-Sapir, D., D'Aoust, O., Vos, F., & Hoyois, P. (2013). The Frequency and Impact of Natural Disasters. In D. Guha-Sapir & I. Santos (Eds.), *The Economic Impacts of Natural Disasters* (pp. 7–27). Oxford University Press.

Development Diaries. (2022). *Flooding: Nigeria Secures USAID Funds for Response*. https://www.developmentdiaries.com/2022/10/flooding-nigeria-secures-usaid-funds-for-response/

Economist. (2019). *SADC to Avail US$500,000 to Countries Ravaged by Cyclone Idai*. https://economist.com.na/42902/general-news/sadc-to-avail-us500000-to-countries-ravaged-by-cyclone-idai/

European Union. (2014). *EU Climate Finance in the Context of External Aid.* https://www.eca.europa.eu/Lists/ECADocuments/SR13_17/SR13_17_EN.pdf

Guha-Sapir, D., & Lechat, M. F. (1986). The Impact of Natural Disasters: A Brief Analysis of Characteristics and Trends. *Prehospital and Disaster Medicine, 2*(1–4), 221–223.

Guha-Sapir, D., & Santos, I. (2013). Introduction. In Debarati Guha-Sapir & Indhira Santos (Eds.), *The Economic Impacts of Natural Disasters.* Oxford University Press.

Hallegatte, S., Vogt-Schilb, A., Rozenberg, J., Bangalore, M., & Beaudet, C. (2020). From Poverty to Disaster and Back: A Review of Literature. *Economics of Disasters and Climate Change*, 223–247.

Lin, B., Omoju, O., & Okonkwo, J. (2015). Impact of Industrialisation on CO2 Emissions in Nigeria. *Renewable and Sustainable Energy Reviews, 52*, 1228–1239.

Mater Christi College. (2022, May 12). *Natural Diasters of the Asia Pacific Region.* LibGuides at Mater Christi College. https://materchristi.libguides.com/natural_disasters/2004_Indian_Ocean_Tsunami

Meyer, L., & Roser, D. (2006). Distributive Justice and Climate Change: The Allocation of Emission Rights. *Analyse and Kritic, 28*(2), 223–249.

Naqvi, A., & Monasterolo, I. (2021). Assessing the Cascading Impacts of Natural Disasters in a Multi-Layer Behavioural Network Framework. *Scientific Reports, 11*, 1–14.

Nature. (2019). *Why Cyclone Idai Is One of the Southern Hemisphere's Most Devastating Storms.* https://www.nature.com/articles/d41586-019-00981-6

Oxfam. (2020). *After the Storm: One Year on from Cyclone Idai.* https://www.oxfam.org/en/after-storm-one-year-cyclone-idai

Reliefweb. (2022). *EU Allocates Fresh €500,000 to Nigeria to Contain Cholera Epidemic.* https://reliefweb.int/report/nigeria/eu-allocates-fresh-eu500000-nigeria-contain-cholera-epidemic

Reliefweb. (2019). *Infrastructure Worth Over a Billion Dollars Lost to Cyclone Idai, says ECA Chief.* https://reliefweb.int/report/mozambique/infrastructure-worth-over-billion-dollars-lost-cyclone-idai-says-eca-chief

SADC. (2017). *SADC Disaster Preparedness and Response Strategy and Fund 2016–2030: Enhancing Coordination for Effective Disaster Preparedness, Response and Resilience.* www.sadc.int

SADC. (2018). *Report on Disaster Risk Reduction 2015–2018. Southern African Development Community an Addendum to the Biennial Report on the Programme of Action for the Implementation of the Sendai Framework for Disaster Risk Reduction 2015–2030 in Africa.* https://www.preventionweb.net/publication/report-disaster-risk-reduction-2015-2018-southern-african-development-community

SADC. (2022a). *Disaster Risk Management|SADC*. SADC: Towards a Common Future. https://doi.org/10.1007/978-1-4020-4399-4_300

SADC. (2022b, August 1). *SADC Ministers Responsible for Disaster Risk Management Call for Acceleration of Disaster Risk Mitigation Programmes*. Southern African Development Community: Towards a Common Future. https://www.sadc.int/latest-news/sadc-ministers-responsible-disaster-risk-management-call-acceleration-disaster-risk

Shacinda, S. (2008). *Floods Hit Southern Africa, More Than 1 mln at Risk*. Reuters. https://www.reuters.com/article/idUSL07195770

Statistics South Africa. (2021). *Four Facts About Our Provincial Economies*. https://www.statssa.gov.za/?p=12056

UNEP. (2002). Global Environment Outlook 3. In *United Nations Environment Programme*. http://www.unep.org/geo/GEO3/english/pdf.htm

United Nations. (2015). *Sendai Framework for Disaster Risk Reduction 2015–2030*. https://www.preventionweb.net/files/43291_sendaiframeworkfordrren.pdf

Zhang, R., Zhang, Y., & Dai, Z. (2022). Impact of Natural Disasters on Mental Health: A Cross-Sectional Study Based on the 2014 China Family Panel Survey. *International Journal of Environmental Research and Public Health, 19*(2511), 1–17.

CHAPTER 12

The Global Gateway Africa-Europe Investment Package and the Future of EU-AU Relations

Gabriele Casano and Eleonora Panizza

The contribution was jointly conceived by the authors. The final draft is also the result of joint work, within which, however, the following attributions can be distinguished: to Gabriele Casano sections "Introduction" and "General Allocation of SDRs and the Transfer of European Quotas Towards Africa"; to Eleonora Panizza sections "The Global Gateway Africa—Europe Investment Package" and "Challenges and Opportunities"; to both of the authors section "Conclusion".

G. Casano · E. Panizza (✉)
Department of Political and International Sciences, University of Genoa, Genoa, Italy
e-mail: eleonora.panizza@edu.unige.it; eleonora.panizza@cimafoundation.org

CIMA Research Foundation, Centro Internazionale in Monitoraggio Ambientale, Savona, Italy

G. Casano
e-mail: gabriele.casano@edu.unige.it

A. O. Akinola and E. A. Liaga (eds.), *Development and Regional Stability in Africa*, https://doi.org/10.1007/978-3-031-56695-0_12

Introduction

Recent events underline, once again, the importance and the potential opportunities for a stronger partnership between the European Union (EU) and the African Union (AU). To reinforce the importance of this relation, an interesting article on Project Syndicate underlines that "to tackle the climate crisis in Africa and put the continent on a new sustainable growth trajectory requires concerted efforts across national governments, the private sector, and the international community" (Georgieva & Tshisekedi, 2021).[1] Thus, it is evident that a strengthening of cooperation between Africa and Europe could go in the right direction. The last major event involving the EU, the AU and many of their member states during the 6th EU-AU Summit that took place on 17–18 February 2022 in Brussels. The Summit falls in the wake of what was outlined in the document, *Towards a Comprehensive Strategy with Africa*, and drafted by the Von der Leyen Commission and contained in the Agenda 2063 adopted by the AU in 2013. These documents already delineated some of the fundamental principles and objectives reaffirmed during the last EU-AU Summit and presented in the *Joint Vision for 2030*.

In recent years, there has been a strengthening of African and European awareness of the opportunities that greater cooperation at the continental level could represent (Fontana, 2022; Majocchi, 2020). On the one hand, the strategic priority of a strengthened partnership between the EU and Africa in both the economic and geopolitical spheres was highlighted, as well as the need to establish a real relationship between equals based on common values and interests that will make it possible to respond concretely to the challenges of the coming decades, such as climate change, migration and security. In the long term, the perspective of both parties after the Summit has been to work towards "the progressive and mutually beneficial integration of the respective continental markets" (EU-AU, 2022). The establishment of the African Continental Free Trade Area (AfCFTA) remains a welcome development.

[1] Kristalina Georgieva is Managing Director of the International Monetary Fund; Félix Antoine Tshilombo Tshisekedi is the President of the Democratic Republic of the Congo, and was the Chairman of the African Union in between February 6th 2021 to February 5th 2022.

Alongside these considerations, the different demographic trajectories of the two continents constitute a challenge and an opportunity at the same time, especially if we consider that "by 2030, 42 percent of the world's young people will live in Africa, making the continent home to the largest supply of affordable labour on the planet in the coming decades" (Tanchum, 2022). According to G20 estimates, infrastructure investments needed in Africa to reach the standards of the most advanced countries will amount to USD 6 trillion in the period up to 2040, representing a shortfall compared to current investments of USD 1.7 trillion (Global Infrastructure Outlook, 2022). These last statements highlight, once again, the importance and the potential opportunities for a stronger partnership between the EU and the AU.

Considering the current economic and political situation, it seems more than ever necessary to address the issue of deepening European investments in/for the African continent for four main reasons. First, the strategic priority of strengthening the already existent partnership between the two continents in both the economic and geopolitical spheres. This priority will make it possible to respond concretely to the challenges of the next decades, such as climate change, migration, and security. Second, the chronic lack of sufficient economic, infrastructural and technological resources in almost the entire African continent reduces its capacity for development and political control, conditions that consequently facilitate interference by imperialist powers and the operations of unscrupulous multinationals to the detriment of the African population. The third is the vast availability of resources in Europe following the implementation of the Next Generation and the 2021 General Allocation of Special Drawing Rights (SDRs) of the International Monetary Fund (IMF). The last is the targeted implementation of The Global Gateway Africa-Europe Investment Package presented after the 6th EU-AU Summit.

This chapter engages the debates on how to strengthen the Euro-African continental partnership and how to use the resources provided by the IMF through a "General Allocation" of $650bn in Special Drawing Rights to the 190 countries belonging to the organisation (Aryeetey, 2004; Guillaumont et al., 2021; Jensen, 2021; Masini, 2022). It is fundamental to remember that the use of this instrument depends on country-specific decisions and strategies. This General Allocation is a great opportunity for shaping the future of the relationship between the European and African continents. The main idea is to build a sustainable system that could reallocate a fraction of the EU Members' SDRs to the African continent and sustain the Global Gateway Africa-Europe Investment Package. Several criticisms could be raised, but it is necessary to underline that it will be neither a new expression of neo-colonialism nor a form of Western paternalism. The purpose of this chapter is to explain how it could be possible to allocate already available resources from Europe to Africa according to the shared pathway of development presented in the Joint Vision for 2030 without neglecting the specific challenges that the two continents will face in the near future, and bearing in mind that the African vulnerabilities and strengths could become European ones and vice versa.

Most of the ideas here presented are based on the findings of the project "For a European Union - African Union Plan on the New Allocation of the IMF's SDRs", coordinated by the Centre Studies on Federalism (CSF) with the Robert Triffin International Foundation (RTI) and the Centre Studies on European and Global Governance (CesUE), and co-financed by the Italian Ministry of Foreign Affairs and International Cooperation. This chapter proposes, according to the most recent events, particularly the conclusions of the 6th EU-AU Summit.

The Global Gateway Africa–Europe Investment Package

After the 6th EU-AU Summit, although general satisfaction among the parties involved, several doubts remain about how the most important proposal, the Global Gateway Africa-Europe Investment Package, would be implemented. In fact, it is an extremely ambitious investment scheme that exceeds all previous development aid plans between Europe and Africa. There was a resource mobilisation amounting to EUR 150 billion, which was meant to support Africa mainly through the acceleration of green and digital transitions, the expansion of sustainable growth combined with decent jobs creation, the strengthening of health and transportation systems and the improvement of education and training facilities.

One of the most positive improvements on this cooperation facility, in comparison with past ones, is that the financing instruments of the Global Gateway Africa-Europe Investment Package will include EU and the EU member states' bilateral aid, grants and loans, and also private funding. Furthermore, the EU will help mobilise investment by sharing risks involved in investing through blended finance and guarantees (European Commission, 2022). Nevertheless, it seems not sufficient. The main challenge of the Investment Package appears to be the definition and realisation of adequate tools for its implementation able to mobilise, manage and monitor such a huge amount of resources and ambitious development plan. The final statement does not clearly illustrate what tools and resources need to be introduced to ensure the success of the development plan. The Joint Vision aims to consolidate a renewed partnership for solidarity, security, peace and sustainable and sustained economic development and prosperity for European and African citizens of today and future generations, bringing together individuals, regions and organisations (EU-AU, 2022).[2]

The complexity of the Africa-Europe Investment Package can be detected in the presentation documents available on the EU and AU institutional websites. The objective is to mobilise at least EUR 150 billion for three separate packages: Investment, Health and Education. This development plan aims to boost public and private investment, starting from existing initiatives and partnerships, with the possibility of mobilising innovative financing instruments.[3] These last statements are the most relevant according to our understanding. Furthermore, the two continental institutions want to promote "accountable, transparent, inclusive and responsive governance" and improve "investment and the business climate" (EU-AU, 2022: 4). Another crucial aspect is the commitment to boosting "regional and continental economic integration, particularly through the African Continental Free Trade Area"

[2] This includes inter alia: the security and prosperity of African and European citizens, the protection of human rights for all, gender equality and women's empowerment in all spheres of life, respect for democratic principles, good governance and the rule of law, actions to preserve the climate, environment and biodiversity, sustainable and inclusive economic growth, the fight against inequalities, support for children's rights and the inclusion of women, young people and the most disadvantaged (EU-AU, 2022).

[3] As noted, "*We will use all means of implementation, including Official Development Assistance and financial tools such as infrastructure trusts and capital market instruments, to ensure support to African entrepreneurship in engaging in strong and vibrant economies. International and national financing development institutions, including the European Investment Bank, and the African Development Bank, and public/private partnerships will be mobilised to this effect*" (EU-AU, 2022: 4).

working "gradually towards the progressive and mutually beneficial integration of our respective continental markets" (European Commission, 2022). This perspective represents an innovative target that is, in some respect, consistent with some potential uses of SDRs at the international level (Flor, 2019).

Reconsidering the Global Gateway Africa-Europe Investment Package more generally, the goals of each of the individual packages are outlined below according to the descriptions provided on the EU and AU websites. The Investment individual package will boost large-scale sustainable investments in different areas: (1) energy, transport and digital infrastructure; (2) fair, just and equitable energy transition; (3) green transition under the Paris Agreement to enhance mitigation and adaptation; (4) digital transformation considering investments in infrastructures and an affordable and enhanced access to the digital and data economy while boosting digital entrepreneurship and skills; (5) sustainable growth and decent job creation, youth-owned businesses; (6) transport facilitation and efficiency of connected transport networks; (7) human development, notably through scaling up mobility and employability of students, young graduates and skilled workers (EU-AU, 2022).

For the health sector, the partners intend to "support initiatives for pandemic preparedness, health security and equitable access to quality essential health services, in line with the Rome Declaration adopted at the Global Health Summit" (EU-AU, 2022: 4). The education package will be focused on the investment,

> In inclusive and equitable quality education by improving policy and legal frameworks, access and teacher training, to contribute to safe delivery of education services and ensure learning gaps resulting from the pandemic are addressed" the parties want to "promote opportunity oriented technical and professional Vocational Education and Training, including at regional level. (European Commission, 2022)

Challenges and Opportunities

As underlined by Macky Sall, President of the AU in 2022, at the opening of the 35th Ordinary Session of the Conference of Heads of State and Government of the African Union:

> Africa continues to lag behind in development despite its enormous potential: 30 million km2; more than 1.3 billion inhabitants; large water and hydrocarbon reserves; 60% of the world's undeveloped arable land; 40% of gold reserves; 85-95% of chromium and platinum group metal reserves; 85% of phosphate reserves; more than 50% of cobalt reserves; and one-third of bauxite reserves. (Sall, 2022)

These are fundamental factors that need to be reflected upon to understand the opportunities and the obstacles in the realisation of the Global Gateway. The widening gaps between different African countries have been accompanied by divergences within countries, aggravated by the impact of COVID-19 pandemic, while the consequences of the Russian-Ukraine conflict are being felt on the continent. These have negatively affected the quest to combat poverty over the past two decades, and the prospects for development in a broader sense. It would therefore be of primary importance to be able to discuss a common strategy, particularly with the availability of resources at this point in time.

The European strategy towards Africa aims at "substantially increase environmentally, socially and financially sustainable investments that are resilient to the impacts of climate change; to promote investment opportunities by scaling up the use of innovative financing mechanisms; and to boost regional and continental economic integration" (European Commission, 2020: 8). This is in addition to providing for incisive interventions in the areas of digital transformation, education and health, strengthening the international rules-based order and the multilateral system, integrating good governance, democracy, human rights, the rule of law and gender equality and a more effective management of the problem of migration and internal and external mobility. If the Global Gateway Africa-Europe Investment Package is considered as the evolution of the document presented by the Commission in 2020, it emerges as a concrete foreign policy and sustainable transition strategy. In this regard, it would be opportune for the EU to unequivocally recognise the great contribution that Africa can make if a phase of green economic development can be secured already in the short term (Majocchi, 2022).

General Allocation of SDRs and the Transfer of European Quotas Towards Africa[4]

Starting from the draft schedule that can already be glimpsed in the Joint Vision for 2030, the idea of utilising SDRs to respond to African countries' challenges seems to be partly mooted. In fact, we read in the document that member states of both organisations "call for ambitious voluntary contributions, by channelling part of the recently allocated Special Drawing Rights, in order to achieve the total global ambition of at least USD 100 billion liquidity support to countries most in need, of which a major part should benefit Africa" (EU-AU, 2022). Thus, this cannot be defined as a sustainable strategy that would guarantee the degree of co-definition and mutual support that the two partners would like to establish, precisely because the primary role of the IMF would prevent it from being managed jointly at the continental level. It would make much more sense to try to match the exploitation of the SDR resources already available with the implementation of the Global Gateway Investment Package.

The EU's quotas of SDRs could be devoted to meeting African strategic goals of long-term and sustainable endogenous growth strengthening the continent's integration process and institutions coupled with EU external action strategies including access to new markets, energy and resources (Masini, 2022). Despite the European intent of a "substantial re-channelling of part of the EU's Special Drawing Rights (SDR) to Africa", it remains that "SDR will be mostly channelled by EU Member States on a voluntary basis as loans through two IMF trust funds: the Poverty Reduction and Growth Trust Fund and the new Resilience and Sustainability Trust Fund" (European Commission, 2022).

Considering that the use of SDRs quotas depends on country-specific decisions and strategies, the IMF General Allocation of $650bn in SDRs to the 190 countries belonging to the organisation could be considered an exceptional opportunity not to be missed for shaping both today's Euro-African and next generations' future (Masini, 2022). Nevertheless, political factors, countries' debt conditions, conflict and pandemic uncertainties may act as crucial obstacles. Furthermore, it cannot be overlooked

[4] This chapter echoes what has already been presented in the research paper: Casano (2022: 6–12).

that technical problems are a major issue when considering the possibilities of an SDR's reallocation, especially if this activity requires changes in the statute of the IMF or an 85% majority in the IMF Executive Board (Flor, 2019). Considering the above-mentioned possible impediments, if there is a strong conviction and willingness on the part of even a small group of developed states, the SDRs reallocation for the Global Gateway Africa-Europe Investment Package may take shape.

Accordingly, it is important to avoid the necessity of changes in the Articles of Agreement of the IMF and to strengthen the multilateralism in the Euro-African cooperation, bearing in mind the need to maintain strict monitoring on the utilisation of the resources towards agreed priorities, preferably through a supranational approach. Several studies have underlined the technicalities of the reallocations of SDRs. One of the main issues at stake is maintening reserve asset status. In the case of EU members states, the apparent obstacle concerns "the direct financing of multilateral development banks by national central banks through SDR channelling [because it] is not compatible with the monetary financing prohibition" (Lagarde, 2021).[5] For present purposes, the first step is to define which actors may play a decisive role in the realisation of the Global Gateway Africa-Europe Investment Package through the SDRs quotas reallocation.

There are two main areas of action in which selected actors operate: (1) in structuring and managing the mechanism of SDRs reallocation from Europe to Africa; (2) in ensuring the monitoring of the utilisation of the resources. Each actor involved should play the role it is best designed for, some of them may operate in one or both action areas. Based on this perspective, we identify three main categories of institutions: (a) Governmental International Organisations with their operational arms; (b) Multilateral Development Banks and multinational banks with a strong development vocation; (c) Governments and National Central Banks.[6]

[5] As Masini has pointed out, Lagarde's statement refers to Euro area central banks, their activity of SDRs channelling towards MDBs will not be allowed. Nevertheless, it seems possible that a joint, ad hoc fund, agreement or institution may perform this task (Masini, 2022).

[6] African sub-regional organisations were deliberately left out of the analysis as their contribution was considered somewhat superfluous at an early design stage. Nevertheless, there is no doubt that also these actors could play a major role in the implementation of the Global Gateway Africa-Europe Investment Package, but to a less extent in the

(a) *Governmental International Organisations with their operational arms*

In the first category of institutions, we consider the pivotal role of the IMF in this project. This is because, in the frame of the 1st area of action, it will be probably necessary to request the status of SDRs prescribed holder[7] for at least one Europe-based Multilateral Development Bank in order to channel resources from Europe to Africa. At the same time, obtaining IMF support and expertise competencies for the 2nd area of action could be useful. In addition to setting the rules on the use of SDRs, the IMF has acquired a great deal of experience over time in managing economic policy, supervising the overall macroeconomic performance of member countries, particular in negotiating conditions on lending and loans under the policy of conditionality and consequently in ensuring their monitoring. This knowledge and expertise are key sources of information for large-scale investment management.

The already widely developed systems of guidelines for the dissemination of standards and "good practices" of the IMF—particularly in complex and fragile contexts—provide crucial knowledge. It was decided not to use the instruments provided by the IMF such as the Poverty Reduction and Growth Trust and the upcoming Resilience and Sustainability Trust, for two reasons. On the one hand, to overcome the obstacles represented by the conditionalities. In fact, these two instruments are still too closely linked to the Washington Consensus (the effectiveness of which is widely criticised), thus alternative parameters for the new instrument must be defined. On the other hand, a new instrument is necessary to allow a specific focus on the African continent, ensuring the strengthening of the EU-AU partnership and responding to the needs defined in the African context and, in particular, in that of deepening African continental integration.

definition of the instruments of SDRs reallocation. Further analysis in this sense must be considered.

[7] According to the IMF, "*a prescribed holder may acquire and use SDRs in exchange for an equivalent amount of a monetary asset, other than gold, in transactions and operations with any other prescribed holder and with any of the IMF's members. However, a prescribed holder may not be allocated SDRs issued by the IMF, nor may it be required by the IMF to receive SDRs in exchange for currency*" (International Monetary Fund, 2021).

The second institution involved in the project and part of the first category is the EU, with its European Central Bank (ECB). The institutions are ultimately responsible for the allocation/destination of SDRs reserve assets from euro area member states, play a key role in the process of rechannelling part of the European quotas towards Africa. As the ECB does not foresee alternative uses for SDRs, a political change is needed, a common will to modify current rules. The European Commission and the European Council may be able to put pressure on the ECB to make the necessary change. As the IMF, the main area of activity for the ECB will be the 1st; thus, the primary challenge in this context is to obtain the ECB's recognition that such investment funds do not violate the monetary financing prohibition.

The European Union's role will be strictly related to its member states' political will. Suppose the creation of this system of reallocating SDR quotas for the benefit of Africa were to be promoted by a substantial number of willing and strategically relevant states. In that case, the ECB positions in this regard might also be less assertive and allow a satisfactory solution—for the creation of the rechannelling mechanism—to be found within the existing treaties and, consequently, motivate the IMF to accept the request to make prescribed holders one or more European multilateral banks. Furthermore, the ECB's role will also be relevant for the 3rd area of action. We consider the role of the EU to be crucial, especially in light of the results of the 6th EU-AU Summit.

The third institution, related to the 1st category, is the AU, which is crucial in both the areas of action above presented. In structuring and managing the mechanism of SDRs reallocation from Europe to Africa, the AU must provide information and support in the advocacy phase, especially when dealing with the IMF constraints and ECB hesitations. The Global Gateway Africa-Europe Investment Package is a co-produced project with a strong recipient involvement and shared responsibilities, thus the legitimacy of the European countries' request for the definition of an ad hoc instrument devoted to the reallocation of SDRs quotas will be reinforced by the support of the 54 member states of the AU. The support of the AU in this project fits in the strategic plan for the strengthening of the EU-AU relations and may represent a deepening in continental integration, especially in view of the recent establishment of the AfCFTA.[8] The Investment Package, the AfCFTA and the Agenda 2063 will benefit each other and potentially ensure the sustainable development of the African continent. Financing is needed in regional integration and sustainable development. Thus, Agenda 2063 promotes a financing strategy that includes: domestic resource mobilisation, intermediation of resources into investments and access to finance. According to several studies,[9] the AU has inadequate financial resources to implement most of the Agenda 2063 programmes concretely. The Global Gateway Africa-Europe Investment Package—funded through the European SDRs quotas reallocation—would allow overcoming this limitation on the condition that a cooperative, non-paternalistic approach is guaranteed to ensure African ownership.

(b) *Multilateral Development Banks and Multinational Banks with a strong development vocation*

Multilateral Development Banks (MDBs) core aim is to raise capital; moreover, they are involved actively in managing and directing the implementation of the projects financed. For the purposes of this analysis, a primary role will be played by the European Investment Bank (EIB) and European Bank for Reconstruction and Development (EBRD) multilateral development banks. As already presented, the main difficulty is to find a technical solution allowing these MDBs to hold SDRs and channelling these resources to the African continent counterpart; but the option of applying for the status of SDR prescribed holder could significantly reduce the present technical limits. Leaving aside this technical issue closely related to the implementation of the reallocation mechanism, the most important role in the implementation of the Global Gateway Africa-Europe Investment Package funded through European SDRs quotas is reserved for MDBs.

Focusing on the EIB, its core priorities in Africa are vital infrastructure and private sector development, the main purpose of the EIB is to deliver investments to implement EU policies and standards in Africa. The EIB

[8] As clearly stated, "*The AfCFTA aims to boost intra-African trade by providing a comprehensive and mutually beneficial trade agreement among the member states, covering trade in goods, services, investment, intellectual property rights and competition policy*" (African Continental Free Trade Area, 2021).

[9] For a general overview of these studies, see: Ndizera et al. (2018: 142–154).

has been playing a key role in African development since the very first and it offers a wide set of supporting activities (European Investment Bank, 2021). Although the EIB has so far never managed a portfolio similar to that which a possible reallocation of European SDRs would generate, there is no doubt about its proven ability to manage medium- to long-term investments on the African continent, precisely in those areas we have selected as primary for development. Furthermore, the strengthened partnership with the African Development Bank Group (AfDB)[10] is a further element that motivated for the consideration of EIB as the ideal actor for the implementation of the Global Gateway Africa-Europe Investment Package, especially given the specific competencies in both the areas of action defined above (European Investment Bank, 2022)

Although its range of action in Africa is limited to Egypt, Tunisia and Morocco, a similar role could be played by the EBRD. The possibility of implementing the Global Gateway Africa-Europe Investment Package on a sub-regional basis and exploiting already operational and local-based tools should not be excluded in advance. The EBRD offers a wide range of financial instruments, its principal forms of direct financing offered are loans, equity and guarantees; furthermore, it provides business advisory services. The main sectors in which it is involved are agribusiness, infrastructure and transport (European Bank for Reconstruction and Development, 2021). While in the case of the EIB the activities are presented as a direct "emanation" of the EU policies, in the case of the EBRD there would be no such exclusivity since non-European states are members of this MDB, too. On the one hand, this could be a limitation in terms of freedom of action, but on the other hand, it could be an advantage in terms of further mobilisation of resources.

As the EIB, the EBRD has already defined a detailed set of priorities and strategies for Africa, largely attributable to those defined both in Europe and Africa to enhance resilience and development in Africa (European Bank for Reconstruction and Development, 2020). Another relevant aspect is the recent Memorandum of Understanding (MoU) between the EBRD and the African Development Bank Group (AfDB), which intends to promote and reinforce the partnership between these institutions in the geographic and sectorial areas where both operate in order to unlock

[10] The AfDB Group is an Africa-based Multilateral Development Bank. As we will see later, the AfDB Group is a key player in this analysis and its relationships with Europe-based MDBs are fundamental.

investment opportunities and promote sustainable private sector development (Zgheib, 2021). As for the EIB, the EBRD may be considered a primary player thanks to its potentially crucial role in all three areas of action above-mentioned.

The strengthening of the partnerships between EIB and EBRD with the AfDB demonstrates the strategic role played by MDBs in Africa. Thus, with regard to the African MDB on which to focus on the realisation of both the SDRs reallocation mechanism and the implementation of the Global Gateway Africa-Europe Investment Package, the profile of the AfDB appears to be the most suitable in light of what has already been said about its consolidated collaboration with the EIB and EBRD, but also given its strong regional character and its proximity to the African Union, its continental relevance and its status of Prescribed Holder. The AfDB includes three entities: the African Development Bank (ADB), the African Development Fund (ADF) and the Nigeria Trust Fund (NTF). In this analysis, the focus will be on the first two entities.

Given the specific competencies of ADB and ADF, the former would potentially be able to deal with the management of loans and the latter with grants coming from the identified SDR reallocation facility. As already prescribed holders, the technical obstacles in the management of SDR resources appear to be less decisive than for the European MDBs mentioned above. Even if many criticisms[11] have been levelled against the AfDB, both in terms of the effectiveness of its actions and its organisation, the AfDB enjoys a good reputation among African countries and regional institutions, and this is a decisive factor.

The AfDB is one of the main catalysts for convening and connecting the right players in the African development context, enhancing regional cooperation and integration, and even guaranteeing public-private partnerships. It presents itself as "the voice for Africa in the development community" (African Development Bank, 2013). It has embraced the objective of scaling-up its activities by leveraging and crowding in financial resources and moving from "billions to trillions" (African Development Bank Group, 2021). Thus, the opportunity presented by the Global Gateway Africa-Europe Investment Package could fit the bill. As for the two European MDBs above presented, the AfDB Group must be considered a prime actor in all three areas of action above-mentioned.

[11] See for example: Humphrey (2014) and Birdsall (2018).

Its contribution to the lobbying activities for the implementation of the SDRs reallocation tool is fundamental. As an MDB, its operational and organisational vocation in the African context is an essential aspect of implementing and monitoring the investment plan. The AfDB Group will undoubtedly be under watch as the institution that will have to put itself to the test and exploit its potential to the best of its ability.

The fourth element included in the second category is multinational banks with a strong development vocation. The role of these banks could be in some ways parallel and complementary to the previous project that wants to channel resources through MDBs. The idea is that European States can directly finance multinational banks through additional loans and capital allocations denominated in SDRs. The ideal vehicle for this alternative opportunity could be the African Export-Import Bank[12] which is already involved in the design of the Pan-African Payment and Settlement System (PAPSS),[13] in collaboration with the AfCFTA Secretariat. Indeed, the idea of integrating among the actors potentially involved multinational banks with a strong development vocation responds to the strategic necessity of financing inter-African trade and, in particular, to use SDRs to finance the probably negative balance of the relevant transactions; it could be a repeat of the process that led to the union of payments in Europe.

More specifically, European countries first and foremost (and if wished, African countries as well) could use part of their SDR quotas to strengthen the capital of the African Export-Import Bank, which could acquire the status of Third Party Holder as provided for in the IMF guidelines. By doing this, it would be possible to create the conditions to constitute a first nucleus of African countries whose financial transactions determined by the intra-African trade are compensated in SDR, without having to have recourse to the balance in convertible currencies,

[12] According to the Bank, "*Our Vision: To be the Trade Finance Bank for Africa. Mission Statement: To stimulate a consistent expansion, diversification and development of African trade, while operating as a first class, profit-oriented, socially responsible financial institution and a center of excellence in African trade matters*" (African Export-Import Bank's, 2021).

[13] It is a "*Financial Market Infrastructure to enable instant, cross-border payments in local currencies between African markets. By simplifying cross-border transactions and reducing the dependency on hard currencies for these transactions, PAPSS is set to boost intra-African trade significantly and underpin the implementation of the African Continental Free Trade Area (AfCFTA)*" (African Export-Import's Bank, 2021).

such as the euro, dollar, renminbi, pound. This would be a process like what European countries did after the Second World War with the Union of Payments that made it possible to deal with the dollar shortage at least for intra-European trade.

It should be emphasised that in this process, other multinational banks could join the African Export-Import Bank, strengthening the plan and its chances of its success. This would be especially likely if African states were to import knowledge and technology from Europe. Even in this case, there are technical difficulties that would have to be resolved both within the IMF and within the ECB. Multinational banks with a strong development vocation, particularly the African Export-Import Bank, may play a decisive role in managing and ensuring the monitoring of the utilisation of the resources.

As indicated earlier, the heart of the action for the implementation of a Global Gateway Africa-Europe Investment Package funded thanks to SDRs quotas lies in the second category of institutions, in particular through the involvement of the MDBs. There is no doubt that the intrinsic characteristics of these institutions make them ideal partners for the implementation of development projects and that, to date, their potential is highly unexpressed. For this very reason, it seems very necessary to exploit the opportunity represented by the recent and very large allocation of SDRs to increase the legitimacy of these institutions and ensure their optimal operability, especially in the context of a vulnerable continent such as Africa. It is evident—given the structures of the institutions presented in the first two categories—that states, their Governments and Central Banks play a major role, both highly political and strategic in nature.

(c) *Governments and National Central Banks*

Governments and National Central Banks will primarily participate in structuring and managing the mechanism of SDRs reallocation from Europe to Africa because they will ensure the availability of the SDRs resources according to their financial needs and dispositions with respect to national, international and notably European Law. Furthermore, European Governments should put pressure on the supranational institutions of reference through lobbying, declarations of intent, requests for evaluations and proposals for reform that would allow the concrete realisation of an instrument that would channel quotas of SDRs from Europe to Africa in one of the various ways presented so far. As repeatedly pointed out, the technical obstacles are basically surmountable through a strong and concrete political will. Governments will have a fundamental role in the phases of negotiation, and definition of conditionalities; a secondary role could also be played in the field of monitoring.

Governments will have to rely on the cooperation structures they already have (Ministries and Development Agencies), as well as act as intermediaries between the potential national providers of goods and services that could benefit from the establishment of such a bold development project for the African continent and that would certainly also benefit a vast number of national actors, both public and private. European states must realise the strategic nature of a long-term development project for the African continent; with this awareness and a clear agenda for action, it is highly likely that the technical limits will be overcome. The structure of the international organisations (IMF and EU) to which governments—in this case both European and African—must turn their attention does not guarantee democratic decision-making but is based on more or less institutionalised systems of veto. This peculiarity calls for strong cooperation between the various members involved in the project and a strong and unequivocal position to generate change.

Synthetically, we can say that SDRs are promissory notes issued by the IMF to member states on the basis of quotas associated with their relative strength in the world economy. According to Triffin, SDRs were conceived as a tool to make the rich even richer (Triffin, 1968). Members that receive these notes may either hold them or exchange a part of them over time for hard currency, through the IMF itself and central banks. SDRs General Allocation aims to supplement existing official reserve assets of member countries and the decision of its implementation is based on the finding that there is a long-term global need to supplement existing reserve assets. Participating members and prescribed holders can buy and sell SDRs in the voluntary market. To date, 15 organisations obtained the status of "prescribed holders". IMF members and the IMF itself may use SDRs in accordance with the Articles of Agreement and decisions adopted by the Executive Board and Board of Governors (IMF, 2022b). Specifically for smaller countries that may find it complex to gain access to foreign currency on the regular market, SDRs trading provides a crucial opportunity, especially in times of crisis.

As presented by several authors, technical problems are a major issue when considering the possibilities of an SDR's reallocation from the most developed States to the most in-need ones, especially if this process requires changes in the statute of the IMF or an 85 per cent majority in the IMF Executive Board (Andrews, 2021; Flor, 2019; Li Gislén & Kangas, 2020; Plant, 2021; Viterbo, 2021). Despite these technical challenges, the main difficulty the funding and management of the ad hoc fund may face is the political will of the main stakeholders involved: the IMF and its most powerful members, MDBs, national/regional Central Banks and other relevant financial, economic and political actors. As said before, States' availability—to invest part of their SDRs quotas for a climate-related action which would benefit most developed countries not immediately but over a longer period—should not be taken for granted.

The realisation of the Global Gateway Africa-Europe Investment Package through the SDRs reallocation would, require an ad hoc fund/institution that could be the expression of the common will of the EU (or part of its member states) and the AU. This would be a body that would be responsible for the management of the mobilised resources (both in terms of grants and loans), coming from the European countries as a portion of their respective shares of SDRs deriving from the last IMF General Allocation, and that would guarantee the implementation of the Global Gateway Africa-Europe Investment Package. This instrument would operate directly on the African continent through the MDBs (EIB, EBRD and AfDB Group)—without excluding the possibility of using other instruments and institutions already operating in the context—to implement the Investment Package and ensure its monitoring. This instrument may enhance the realisation of the co-produced strategy presented at the 6th EU-AU Summit. The institutionalisation of this ad hoc fund/institution should take the form of a treaty that unequivocally commits the EU, the AU and the main actors identified here to achieve well-defined objectives and implement projects. This would create a form of international cooperation that goes beyond the limits of a blind conditionality approach and focuses on a truly long-term perspective.

Conclusions

The chapter has been able to show the importance and the potential opportunities for a stronger partnership between the EU and AU. Furthermore, it provides innovative insight into how to access resources from the recent General Allocation of Special Drawing Rights of the IMF, through the creation of an ad hoc instrument that would allow for their rechannelling from the EU to Africa. This chapter contains relevant suggestions about an alternative use of SDRs aimed at supporting development, rather than being hoarded in central banks accounts. It has examined which actors may play a decisive role in the realisation of the Global Gateway Africa-Europe Investment Package through the SDRs quotas reallocation (i.e. IGOs with their operational arms; MDBs and multinational banks; governments and National Central Banks). These constitute the main areas of action in which selected actors operate by structuring and managing the mechanism of SDRs reallocation from Europe to Africa, and/or ensuring the monitoring of the utilisation of the resources. To reach meaningful results in realising the Global Gateway Africa-Europe Investment Package, it is important to employ an ad hoc fund/institution that could be the expression of the common will of the EU or part of its member states, and the AU.

Despite the undeniable opportunity that Global Gateway Africa-Europe Investment Package represents, there remains difficulties and obstacles in its implementation, which should not be underestimated. First, the question of obtaining the status of Prescribed Holder by the EIB and EBRD, and maintaining the reserve assets character of the SDRs resources committed to the Global Gateway Africa-Europe Investment Package. Many studies have pointed out that bad leadership, corruption, poor infrastructure, unemployment, lack of access to healthcare and conflicts constitute major obstacles to the realisation of the development process in Africa. Nevertheless, such an ambitious project of investment for development would also entail strengthening the organisational and management capacities of many of the actors concerned. It remains a question of political will, if the instruments for implementation do not yet exist, they can always be created.

References

African Continental Free Trade Area. (2021). https://afcfta.au.int/en

African Development Bank. (2013). *At the Center of Africa's Transformation—Strategy for 2013–2022*. African Development Bank Group.

African Development Bank Group. (2021). https://www.afdb.org/en.

African Export-Import's Bank. (2021). https://www.afreximbank.com/

Andrews, D. (2021, October). *Reallocating SDRs to Multilateral Development Banks or other Prescribed Holders of SDRs* (pp. 1–8). Center for Global Development. CGD Note.

Aryeetey, E. (2004). A Development-Focused Allocation of the Special Drawing Rights. *WIDER* (Discussion Paper No. 2003/3, pp. 1–21).

Birdsall, N. (2018). *The Dilemma of the African Development Bank: Does Governance Matter for the Long-Run Financing of the MDBs?* (Center for Global Development, Working Paper 498).

Casano, G. (2022). Next Generation Africa: Which Opportunities and Challenges in the Definition of a New Instrument Reallocating European SDRs to the African Continent. *Perspectives on Federalism, 14*(1), 44–63.

European Bank for Reconstruction and Development. (2020). *EBRD Strategic Capital Framework 2021–2025.*

European Bank for Reconstruction and Development. (2021). https://www.ebrd.com/home

European Commission. (2020). *Joint Communication to the European Parliament and the Council—Towards a Comprehensive Strategy with Africa.* High Representative of the Union for Foreign Affairs and Security Policy.

European Commission. (2022). *EU-Africa: Global Gateway Investment Package.* https://ec.europa.eu/info/strategy/priorities-2019-2024/stronger-europe-world/global-gateway/eu-africa-global-gateway-investment-package_en#investing-in-education-and-training.

European Investment Bank. (2021). *A Partnership with Africa.* Luxembourg.

European Investment Bank. (2022). https://www.eib.org/en/index.htm

European Union and African Union (EU-AU). (2022). *6th European Union—African Union Summit: A Joint Vision for 2030.* https://au.int/sites/default/files/pressreleases/41509-pr-PR-_6th_European_Union_-_African_Union_Summit_-_A_Joint_Vision_for_2030.pdf

Flor, E. (2019). *SDR: From Bretton Woods to a World Currency.* Peter Lang.

Fontana, O. (2022). Next Generation Africa: Economic Impact and Mutual Benefits from a Strategic EU-Africa Partnership. *Perspectives on Federalism, 14*(1), 13–35.

Georgieva, K., & Tshisekedi, F. (2021). Africa Cannot Confront Climate Change Alone. *Project Syndicate.* https://www.project-syndicate.org/commentary/supporting-climate-adaptation-in-africa-by-kristalina-georgieva-and-felix-tshisekedi-2021-12

Global Infrastructure Outlook. (2022). *Forecasting Infrastructure Investment Needs and Gaps.* https://outlook.gihub.org/

Guillaumont, P., et al. (2021). *How to Allocate New External Financing to African Countries? The Vulnerability Challenge. A Briefing in Response to the Paris Summit on Financing African Economies* (FERDI Notes brèves / Policy Briefs, Working Paper 498).

Humphrey, C. (2014). *The African Development Bank: Ready to Face the Challenges of a Changing Africa?* (Expertgruppen för biståndsanalys (EBA), Report 04).

IMF. (2022a). *Factsheet—Special Drawing Rights (SDR).* https://www.imf.org/en/About/Factsheets/Sheets/2016/08/01/14/51/Special-Drawing-Right-SDR

IMF. (2022b). *Special Drawing Rights (SDRs).* https://www.imf.org/en/Topics/special-drawing-right

Jensen, L. (2021). *An Unprecedented Opportunity to Boost Finance for Development—The Upcoming Special Drawing Rights Allocation* (UNDP Global Policy Network Brief).

Lagarde, C. (2021). *Statement—Forty-Fourth Meeting of the International Monetary and Financial Committee.*

Li Gislén, M., & Kangas, M. (2020). *Special Drawing Rights—The Role as a Global Reserve Asset, the Riksbank's Experience and the Way Forward* (Economic Commentary—Sveriges Riksbank, 7).

Majocchi, A. (2020). *Africa and Europe: A Shared Future.* Peter Lang.

Majocchi, A. (2022). *Europa-Africa: una partnership per lo sviluppo sostenibile* (Centro Studi sul Federalismo, Policy Paper, 50).

Masini, F. (2022). Time for a Next Generation Africa. *Perspectives on Federalism, 14*(1), 1–12.

Ndizera, V., & Muzee, H. (2018). A Critical Review of Agenda 2063: Business as Usual? *African Journal of Political Science and International Relations, 12*(8), 142–154.

Plant, M. (2021). *The Challenge of Reallocating SDRs: A Primer.* Center for Global Development. https://www.cgdev.org/publication/challenge-reallocating-sdrs-primer

Sall, M. (2022). *Discours de SEM Macky Sall, Président en exercice de l'Union lors de la 35e Session ordinaire de la Conférence des Chefs d'État et de Gouvernement de l'Union Africaine.* https://au.int/en/node/41445

Tanchum, M. (2022). *Gateway to Growth: How the European Green Deal Can Strengthen Africa's and Europe's Economies* (European Council on Foreign Relation—Policy Brief).

Triffin, R. (1968). *Our International Monetary System; Yesterday, Today, and Tomorrow.* Random House.

Viterbo, A. (2021). The 2021 IMF Allocation of Special Drawing Rights: Too Little, Too Late and Too Unequal. *Osservatorio sulle attività delle organizzazioni internazionali e sovranazionali, universali e regionali, sui temi di interesse della politica estera italiana.*

Zgheib, N. (2021). *AfDB and EBRD Partner to Unlock Sustainable Investment Opportunities in Africa.* https://www.ebrd.com/news/2021/afdb-and-ebrd-partner-to-unlock-sustainable-investment-opportunities-in-africa.html

CHAPTER 13

Peace and Security: The Question of "Reunification" or "Unification" of Cameroon

Gallous Atabongwoung

Introduction

Geographically, Cameroon is border to the West by Nigeria, to the North by Chad, to the East by Central African Republic and to the South by Equatorial Guinea, Gabon and Congo-Brazzaville (CIA, 2018; Awasom, 2000). Before the Europeans arrived in Cameroon in the fifteenth century, the Bantu-speaking people occupied the region (Awasom, 2000). The Bantu-speaking people evolved historically as independent indigenous polities varying in size and administrative system (Chem-Langhëë, 1995).

Contemporary Cameroon is ironically referred to as a former French colony. This is probably because of Cameroon's geographic location in the central part of Africa, where previous French colonisation had

G. Atabongwoung (✉)
Department of Development Studies, University of Pretoria, Pretoria, South Africa
e-mail: u15402071@tuks.co.za

A. O. Akinola and E. A. Liaga (eds.), *Development and Regional Stability in Africa*, https://doi.org/10.1007/978-3-031-56695-0_13

a stronghold (Fichter, 2019; Lekane & Lucky, 2017). It could also be because majority of Cameroon's population speak French (Fonlon, 1969). However, misconstruing Cameroon as a former French colony ignores the burden of the country's triple legacy of colonial encounters with the Germans, French and British (Oyono, 2005). The triple colonial encounters were responsible for shaping the country's historical, socio-economic and political destiny hitherto (Oyono, 2005).

Before the European colonisers arrived present-day Cameroon, the territory and people evolved as sovereign ethnic entities. Between 1884 and early 1914, the Germans colonised and administered "Kamerun" as a single polity (Agwanda et al., 2020). The German rule lasted for 30 years during which the Germans negotiated and established Kamerun's international boundaries and set up institutions of administration. However, the outbreak of the First World War changed the course of Kamerun after the Germans were defeated in the war. Cameroon was partitioned between the British and French in an agreement that saw the former and the latter receiving one-quarter and three-quarters of the territory respectively. The French ruled French Cameroon until January 1, 1960, when it gained independence to become "*La Republic du Cameroun*". On the other hand, the British ruled British Southern Cameroons until October 1, 1961, when the British Southern Cameroon gained independence through reunification with *La Republic du Cameroun* to form a two-state federation. The federation lasted until May 20, 1972, when a constitutional referendum was held to unify the two Cameroons (Eluke, 2020; Stark, 1976).

Furthermore, the name Cameroon was given by a Portuguese sailor by the name of Fernando Po who arrived the region in 1472 (Bifuh-Ambe, 2020). When Fernando Po sailed across the river Wouri in Douala—Cameroon, he saw a lot of shrimp/prawns in the river and named the river "*Rio dos Camarões*" ("river of prawns") (Atabongwoung, 2021; Bifuh-Ambe, 2020). From then, the territory was called *Camarões* until it became "*Kamerun*" after the Germans annexed the territory and signed the Germano-Duala treaty in July 1884 (Elango, 1985). The name "Kamerun" was later changed to French East Cameroun and British Southern Cameroons by the French and British respectively, after the territory was partitioned between the French and the British, and after Germany lost the First World War between 1914 and 1918 (Dupraz, 2019; Elango, 1985: 658–660). The war was described a world war because fighting took place across several continents which shaped European interest across the world (Strachan, 2010).

The then German Kamerun was partitioned at the aftermath of the war, and one-fifth of the territory was allocated to the British, who named it British Southern Cameroons, and four-fifth was given to the French, who named it French East Cameroun (Elango, 1985: 658–660). This occurred under the supervision of the League of Nations, and later the United Nations (UN) Trust Territories in 1946 (Ngoh, 1979: 28). The entire history of Cameroon should be understood in the context whereby the Germans, French and British took stock of their activities in the territory (Fanso, 1975). This means that to comprehend the history of Cameroon, it is important to look at Cameroon under the German colonial rule and the partition of Cameroon to the French and British colonial rule.

This chapter argues that the unification of Cameroon has created marginalisation and agitation among the Anglophones (citizens of former British Southern Cameroons), which has led to a deadly civil war that has created a lot of insecurity since 2016. The chapter therefore recommends a return to the two-state federation as solution to the ongoing crisis in Cameroon.

Kamerun Under German Colonial Rule 1884 to 1916

The Germans under Gustav Nachtigal arrived in Cameroon on the 17 of August 1884, and raised the German flag at a fishing port town called Bimbia (Stoecker, 1960). The Germans proceeded to "Duala" now Douala where they signed the Germano-Douala treaty that granted the Germans full legitimacy to administer Cameroon as a German protectorate. This lasted until March 1916, when Germany was defeated in the First World War (1914–1918) and dispossessed of most of its African colonies (Diduk, 1993). The Germans made efforts to expropriate the urban landholdings belonging to the people of Duala (Austen, 1977). This led to a protracted struggle which, in 1914, led to the execution of Duala Manga Bell, the paramount chief of the people of Duala (Austen, 1977).

The people of Duala, however, overestimated the willingness of the Germans to prevent a racist colonial policy in Cameroon (Austen, 1977). The German colonial administration misconstrued the resistance of the people of Duala even though the people of Duala made a lot of compromise to accommodate the Germans (Austen, 1977). However, after crushing all forms of colonial resistance, the Germans controlled Cameroon's indigenous labour which helped them to have access to the country's interior (Diduk, 1993). Notwithstanding, memories of German colonial rule in Cameroon are envisaged through tangible artefacts that reminded the French and British of the economic and infrastructure success of German colonial rule in the country (Amaazee, 1994).

The accomplishment of the German colonial rule in Cameroon included harbour facilities in Douala, Kribi, Campo, Tiko and Limber (previously Victoria); the "*Nordbahn and Mittelbahn*" rail lines; the Victoria plantation narrow-gauge railway and many bridges, roads, paths and well-constructed government and private buildings (Amaazee, 1994). These facilities and more have survived history (Amaazee, 1994). Indeed, the German colonial plantations formed the foundation for a productive agricultural economy in Cameroon. The plantations where latter taken over by the French and British administration after the partitioned of Cameroon (Amaazee, 1994).

The Partition of Kamerun

During the outbreak of the First World War in 1914, initiated by Germany and spread across Europe, "allied powers" such as the Britain and France extended the war towards previous German colonies in Africa; Togoland, Tanganyika, South-West Africa (present-day Namibia) and Kamerun (present-day Cameroon) (Osuntokun, 1974). Arguably, the British and French extended the war to these territories due to territorial covetousness, rather than a mere attempt to weaken the Germans from their African sphere (Osuntokun, 1974). For example, Osuntokun (1974) argued the British and French were envious of territories Germans took by default of the Berlin Conference of 1884–1885 (Craven, 2015). The German territories in Africa were perceived to contain the richest soil among the world's most productive areas, having the potential for economic development (Calvert, 1917).

However, on the part of the French, long before the war and during the partition of Africa, the French considered Duala the most strategic port of entry for their previous colonies of Central African Republic and Chad. Therefore, the French extended the war to previous German colonies such as Cameroon with the intention of reclaiming the strategic port of Duala (Dze-Ngwa, 2015). General Dobell (a Briton) therefore commanded a joint Anglo-French expeditionary Force of 7000 men to launch an attack against the Germans (Fanso, 1989). While General Aymerich (French) commanded a joint Franco-Belgian forces to launch similar attacks against the Germans (Fanso, 1989). Other French forces under General Largeau and Colonel Brisset in Chad constantly come to fortify the allied troops in Cameroon (Fanso, 1989).

In Nigeria, General Cunliffe commanded a strong Nigerian regiment which operated along the Cameroon-Nigeria border (Fanso, 1989). Even Indian forces were deployed to support Britain during the war (Fanso, 1989). The Germans had a strong army, including well-trained troops, policemen and paramilitary, under the command of Lt. Colonel Zimmermann. However, the Germans could not win the war because they fought at multiple fronts against allied forces (Fanso, 1989). Even though the German forces received support from Cameroon ethnic groups such as the Ewondo under Chief Charles Atangana; and assistance from the Spanish subjects in Rio Muni and Fernando Po, they could not repel the allied forces out of Cameroon (Ngoh, 1987).

By September 27, 1916, the British forces under General Charles M. Dobell captured Douala the German economic capital. Under General Joseph George Aymerich, the French attacked the Germans from French Congo, while General Cunliffe attacked the Germans from northern Cameroon (Ngoh, 1987). After Douala fell into the hands of the allied powers, the forces moved on to the German political capital of Buea (Kale, 1969). However, to avoid the destruction of German artefacts in Buea, the Germans withdrew their troops into the interior and left the keys of the Government residence with the German District Officer who handed the keys to the English and French joint forces (Kale, 1969).

Buea therefore bowed to the allied forces without any resistance (Kale, 1969). The next target of the allied forces was the seaport town of Kribi, followed by Edea towards Yaoundé (Kale, 1969). While the other forces who were attacking the Germans from the North and East of Cameroon kept advancing and posing threats to the Germans. The last German stronghold of Mora had no strength of resistance and fell into the hands of the Allied forces on February 20, 1916 (Fanso, 1989). The date marked the end of German rule in Cameroon.

The Complexity and Compromise of the Partition

With the ousting of the Germans from Cameroon, the Anglo-French forces established an Anglo-French Condominium in Duala from 1914 to 1916. The Condominium however, disagreed on how to jointly administer Cameroon. The disagreement led to a series of talks. The last of such talks was held on 6 March 1919, in London to decide on the future of Cameroon. Lord Milner, (the British Colonial Secretary) who led the talks on behalf of the British, and M. Henri Simon, (the French Colonial Secretary) who negotiated on behalf of the French came to a consensus (Osuntokun, 1979: 283). The French colonial Secretary accepted the provisional partition of Cameroon in 1916, with a bit of moderation that suggested that the British cede a portion of their territory close Dschang to the French. As the portion was needed for railway extension to Garoua (Osuntokun, 1979: 283).

The British on their part, requested a readjustment of the borders towards the south in order to have access to the Mungo River, so that they could sail across the Bimbia flats (Osuntokun, 1979: 283). The British argued that since the Picot Line was hastily drawn, there was a need to make some adjustments on the borders. There was therefore a need to create a task team to revise the initial borders (Osuntokun, 1979: 283). Therefore, a task team comprising French and British experts was set up. Nonetheless, while the task team was busy working, the British insisted that they needed the entire German Bornu (a strip left under French sphere by the Picot Line) and the Mandara Emirate (Osuntokun, 1979: 283).

The British also requested parts of the Emirates of Kontscha, Lere and Dodo, which the Picot Line had cut off from the rest of the districts and left in the French sphere. The British were therefore willing to trade off the whole Emirate of Banyo which was under the British sphere in exchange for their request (Osuntokun, 1979: 283). The French agreed to cede the whole of German Bornu to the British, but rejected the British request for Mandara Emirate on grounds that the road from the south to Mora goes via the Mandara Emirate, thereby cutting the area into two parts (Osuntokun, 1979: 283). The French therefore agreed to concede the part of the Emirate that include areas such as Zumu and Malau to the British. But rejected the British demand for the former Adamawa possessions of the Lamido of Yola.

The situation was different in the South, where after much persuasion, the French handed the Mungo River, the most valuable transportation channel between the coast and the plantations in hinterlands (Osuntokun, 1979: 283). The negotiations officially ended on July 10, 1919, when the two colonial Secretaries (Milner of Britain and Simon of France) signed the Milner-Simon Accord, which adopted the revised borders that were mapped out by the experts of the two colonial governments (Osuntokun, 1979: 283). The adoption of the Agreement containing the revised borders gave birth to the unequal partition of Kamerun into British West and French East Cameroon on March 4, 1916 (Elango, 1987). The two territories were administered under direct and indirect rules.

Cameroon Under the French (Direct) and British (Indirect) Rules

The French ruled East Cameroon from 1916 until January 1960, while the British ruled West Cameroon from 1916 until February 1961 (Ngoh, 1987). During that period the French and British adopted distinct colonial administrative systems in their respective territories.

French Direct Rule in East Cameroon

The French administered French East Cameroon under direct rule. Direct rule was a system of governance whereby the state maintained and administered a monopoly of law, policy and administration to the population without any form of intermediaries, but through bureaucrats without independent means of coercion (Weber, 1991). Mamdani (1999) claims under direct rule, the relationship of individuals vis-à-vis the colonial state is that under direct rule individuals are related by the colonial state as citizens. Hence, the French direct rule in East Cameroon focused on developing closer ties between French colonies and metropoles (LeVine, 1964). The mechanism to achieve close ties between France and its colonies was through the policy of assimilation, by which Cameroonians or French-speaking Africans in general, who received "western education" were granted access to French citizenship and legal rights of Frenchmen (LeVine, 1964). The rights include the possibility to participate in all forms of elections of urban councils and French parliament members (Rubin, 1971: 49–50). However, Geschiere (1995) argues that the policy of assimilation in French Cameroon led to fewer and less active local associations.

Nonetheless, when the French took over East Cameroon, it was difficult to immediately get rid of the services of the local chiefs who the Germans appointed because under French direct rule of assimilation, East Cameroonians were supposed to be assimilated into the socio-political structure of the region (LeVine, 1964: 92–98). Nonetheless, the French decided to slowly reduce the autonomy and authority that the Germans had granted to the local chiefs to get rid of their services (LeVine, 1964: 92–98; Rubin, 1971: 49–50).

In addition, under the French direct rule, the French adopted the French civil law system to govern East Cameroon (Anyangwe, 1987: 251–260). The decisions of the French civil law were based on codified legal text from France. The French civil law system however gave less autonomy to judges, but granted more autonomy to prosecutors and investigating magistrates to prosecute individuals who break the law (Anyangwe, 1987: 251–260). In a nutshell, the French administrative system in East Cameroon was in practice "quasi-direct" (LeVine, 1964: 98).

Furthermore, the French re-imposed the labour tax disguised as the pre-station, which was mostly for railway construction. East Cameroon workers were often left without salary under French rule and were also unfairly treated at work. This caused the death rate to be high averaging about 60 per thousand workers (LeVine, 1964: 104–110). Some local chiefs and colonial task masters (officials) often used kidnapping and corporal punishment to fulfil labour obligations and were often able to divert workers for work on private farms and plantations (Rubin, 1971: 57).

Nonetheless, the French administrators played a marginally larger social role in East Cameroon (Johnson, 1970: 84). For example, the French government policy consciously favoured the Roman Catholic Church over the Protestants and others. This assisted the Catholics to develop a large and successful network of secondary schools, while the Protestants focused on the primary level (Johnson, 1970: 82–88). The French continued to rule East Cameroon until the territory was granted independence in 1960 to become "*La Republic du Cameroun*" with Ahmadou Ahidjo as the President. It is also important to note that the independence of *La Republic du Cameroun* did not occur with any form of resistance against French colonial rule.

During the first wave of decolonisation in Africa, there was a popular nationalist movement, called "*Union des Populations du Cameroun*" (*UPC*), in East Cameroon in the mid-1950s (Terretta, 2010). Some of the nationalists went into exile, most to Accra, where they received the support of Kwame Nkrumah's Pan-African Bureau for African Affairs to conduct underground resistance camps in East Cameroon (Terretta, 2010). The Cameroonian nationalist movement even continued to fight for the total liberation of Cameroon even after East and West Cameroon gained their independence (Terretta, 2010). The nationalists aimed to eradicate any form of colonial attachment with Cameroon. They continued to fight against colonial influence in the country even after East and West Cameroons gained independence through reunification.

However, the nationalists failed to eradicate colonial attachment in Cameroon because post the reunification of Cameroon. The postcolonial government of Cameroon prioritised "territorial sovereignty" in the mid-1960s (Terretta, 2010) over the "political unification of Africa" (Gumede, 2019). This added complexity in the fight against colonial influence in the country as the new postcolonial government waged war against the dominant nationalist movement of Cameroon—Cameroonian Peoples Union (UPC) which fought for the eradication of colonial influence and the political unity of Africa (Gumede, 2019).

Notwithstanding, Ghana's support to the dominant nationalist movement in Cameroon was no longer sustainable because of the negative impact of the "cold war" (Terretta, 2010). Therefore, the long-term programme for the development and modernisation of Cameroon which saw the emergence of vital financial and economic relationship between France and Cameroon (Rechniewski, 2017). Led to the gradual disintegration of nationalist movement and the unsuccessful eradication of colonial influence in Cameroon. However, to have a deep understanding of the present security question in Cameroon, it is important to look at British West and French East Cameroons under colonial rule.

British Indirect Rule in West Cameroon

The British on the other hand adopted a colonial policy of indirect rule in British West Cameroon. Indirect rule is perceived as a form of political governance in which state agents delegate day-to-day control to local power-holders in areas considered beyond the state's direct authority (Furnivall, 2014). The local power-holders often hold "traditional or customary" authority and can represent and enforce political authority on behalf of official rulers (Furnivall, 2014). Mamdani (1999) claims, the colonial state relates to individuals under indirect rule as subjects who are under hierarchies of power.

However, some scholars believed that "the British indirect rule led to a greater vitality of local political institutions" in West Cameroon (Babou, 2010; Gerring et al., 2011; Lee & Schultz, 2011). Fonchingon and Fonjong (2002: 85) posit that the traditional authorities, for example, that were put in place under the British indirect rule had the capacity to rally the local population to be interested in local development, thereby leading to greater community-level participation. The British indirect rule was already a standard practice in the British colony of Nigeria where native chiefs were performing most executive and judicial functions (Fonchingon & Fonjong, 2002). This system appealed to the British because it appeared to be cost-effective by involving native traditional rulers in the affairs of the state which reduces the administrative budget and the need to bring more manpower from Britain (Rubin, 1971: 74).

However, in the British West Cameroon or Southern Cameroons the question of indirect rule was a little bit tricky because the wide variety of ethnic groups in the region did not have a form of centralised political institutions before the British took over (Chiabi, 1997: 15–18). The British however were still able to administer West Cameroon through "headmen" who often had no traditional political status (Chiabi, 1997). But, as a native-educated elite emerged, the British integrated the elites into the existing governance structure by creating elected advisory councils. And after 1945, the British decided to strengthen the native authorities by amalgamating them into larger units and granting them higher level of autonomy (Chiabi, 1997: 18–19). Therefore, the high level of autonomy gave them a relatively high degree of legitimacy (Geschiere, 1993). The British indirect rule also adopted the British common law system to administer justice in West Cameroon (Anyangwe, 1987: 251–260). The British common law attributed legal standing to judicial opinions and traditions (Anyangwe, 1987: 251–260). The British therefore rule West Cameroon until 1961, when West Cameroon was granted independence through reunification with French East Cameroon.

The Reunification of French East and British West Cameroons

On 11 February 1961, the UN organised a plebiscite to determine the future of British West or Southern Cameroons (Percival, 2008). The plebiscite was the most significant event in the history of Cameroon's southern and northern parts of the British-administered trust territory. Mr. John Percival was sent by the then Colonial Office as part of the team to oversee the process of the plebiscite (Percival, 2008). And on the 12 of February 1961, the results of plebiscite held in Southern Cameroons were announced (Percival, 2008). The result showed that Southern Cameroons had voted in favour of reunification with *La Republic du Cameroun* (the already independent Republic of Cameroon) in 1961 (LeVine, 1961). The reunification of the British Southern Cameroons and the Republic of Cameroon was assumed to be an extraordinary political move as communities of different colonial linguistic backgrounds decided to collapse their entity to form a federal state (LeVine, 1961). It is worth mentioning that the British and French had administered the two Cameroons separately since 1916. Therefore, the reunification of the two Cameroons came against the expectations of most people.

Notwithstanding, when the debate of the reunification was at the apogee in the 1960s, LeVine (1961) allegorically gave a comprehensive analysis and warned against the power balance of the two previous colonies. LeVine (1961) described the British West Cameroon as the "bride" and the Republic of Cameroon as the "bridegroom" in an effort to portray marital relationship between a woman (who is considered weaker) and a man (who is considered stronger). LeVine (1961) contends the marriage between the East and West Cameroons was inappropriate when considering the fact that the Republic of Cameroon (French Cameroon) was ten times the area of the British West Cameroon, had four times its population, and immeasurably greater resources and a much higher level of social and economic development than British West Cameroon.

Conversely, many African scholars and politicians naïvely saw the reunification of French East and British West Cameroons as an example of political expediency. Considering the fact that these were two previous colonies with distinct socio-political experiences; the British "indirect rule" and the French "direct rule through the policy of assimilation", with two distinct sociolinguistic backgrounds; French and English (the two distinct official languages) have decided to form a federal union (LeVine, 1964: 273). After more than four decades of separate colonial rules which promoted separate political ideologies, and the cultures and lifestyles of the French and the British.

But scholars such as Bernard Fonlon did not resist in idealising the glories of the reunification as "the crucible of African unity" (Fonlon, 1963: 4). LeVine (1964: 273) claims the reunification of British West and French East Cameroons was a symptom of "imperial design" as it undermined the distinct socio-political realities of the two previous colonies which in reality was an attempt to compromise the future of peace in the region. LeVine (1964) in a metaphorical writing depicted an imbalance union as a result of gross incompatibilities between a subjected in-group (West Cameroon) versus a dominant out-group (East Cameroon).

LeVine (1976) therefore foresaw the emergence of a marginalised minority in such relationship and raised the possibility of French East Cameroon perceiving British West Cameroon as a minority collective in terms of the smaller size of the population of West Cameroon as a consequence of the complexity and compromise of the partition of German Kamerun. He further highlighted the chances of French East Cameroon marginalising British West Cameroon and stressed the inevitable tension in majority–minority relationship at any given time across any socio-political landscape. Indeed, political leaders in Africa still hailed the reunification of Cameroons as appropriate and inconceivable because it was the process that was without bloodshed (LeVine, 1976: 273). The plebiscite of the 11 February 1961 therefore gave birth to the Federal Republic of Cameroon.

The Federal Republic of Cameroon: From Federation to Unification of Cameroon

The political structure in East and West Cameroons were collapsed into a new federation. However, the new federation was given the responsibility to manage the two federal states into a peaceful union (Kale, 1967: 70). Hence, the first constitution of the Federal Republic of Cameroon was drafted in October 1961. The provisions of the constitution were supposed to guarantee the future of the new Federal Republic, by maintaining the legitimacy of the organic nature of the previous colonies in the context of upholding and ensuring their continuity as two autonomous federal states, in consideration of their bi-jural, bicultural and bilingual nature as inherited from the British and French (Kale, 1967: 70). Conversely, the new federation without wasting time quickly switched to a "Unitary State" in 1972 (Kale, 1967).

In 1972, a referendum was conducted in French East Cameroon national assembly to decide on the future of Cameroon. The highly dominated numbers of French East Cameroon deputies voted in favour of the creation of a "unitary state" (Kale, 1967: 70). Even when the vote violated Article 47 of the first Constitution of the Federal Republic of Cameroon that was enforced into law in 1961 (Kale, 1967: 70), the vote was upheld. The result of the vote therefore dismantled the federal structure that advocated for evolution of Cameroon as two autonomous states.

Therefore, on 2 June 1972, the United Republic of Cameroon came into existence. The United Republic of Cameroon was perceived as a product of unification of the two federal states. However, it was stated that the new United Republic of Cameroon would continue to maintain the status quo of French East Cameroon (Ngoh, 1987: 257). While the British West Cameroon would be collapsed into two new administrative regions (previously provinces) under a single Central government based in Yaoundé that would also be led by the President of French East Cameroon (Ngoh, 1987: 257). However, in order not to create an immediate political eruption, it was stated that English would remain the official language of the two new regions/provinces which were previously British West Cameroon (Ngoh, 1987: 257).

Ahmadou Ahidjo (the President of French East Cameroon, which has now become the United Republic of Cameroon) stated in one of his speeches that, "[…] the federal structure was collapsed to a unitary state in order to promote national development because to administer Cameroon as two federal states was very costly, and a hindrance to national development efforts as the federal system was cumbersome" (Chem-Langhëë, 1995: 23). Ahmadou Ahidjo further argued that the difficulty of harmonising public and town planning services in the two federal states were hindering agricultural productivity and urban development policies which were oriented towards separate colonial experiences (Chem-Langhëë, 1995: 23).

However, John Ngu Foncha refuted the argument of President Ahidjo (then Prime Minister of British West Cameroon). President Ahidjo therefore decided to replace Foncha with S. T. Muna, because President Ahidjo and Foncha were constantly at loggerheads (Chem-Langhëë, 1995). The replacement of Foncha was only possible after President Ahidjo through consultation with his French Cameroon cabinet realised that Muna agreed to Ahidjo's argument on the collapse of the federation and the Unification of Cameroon (Chem-Langhëë, 1995). However, on 6 November 1982, President Ahidjo resigned from power, and Paul Biya was sworn into office as the President of the United Republic of Cameroon (Eboua, 1996).

President Biya, within a short period of time, also decided to transform Cameroon from the United Republic of Cameroon to the Republic of Cameroon[1] (Eboua, 1996). The collapse of the United Republic of Cameroon forced the citizens of former British West Cameroon to lose their identity (Eboua, 1996). Paul Biya deliberately intended to collapse the United Republic of Cameroon because he was determined to deconstruct the Anglophone identity by forcing the Anglophones to negotiate belonging within the broader Francophone society. This tendency has fostered the marginalisation of Anglophone Cameroonians which has led to agitation and violent conflict that began in 2016 (Atabongwoung, 2021).

Anglophone Marginalisation, Agitation and Violent Conflict in Cameroon

The Anglophone marginalisation dominated the territorial landscape of former British West Cameroonians for more than three decades that Paul Biya has been in power. Not only that the Anglophone marginalisation has posed insurmountable challenges to efforts aim at maintaining peace and stability in postcolonial Cameroon (Konings & Nyamnjoh, 2019). The Anglophone marginalisation remains the root cause of agitation among citizens of former British West Cameroon, leading to a bloody civil war in 2016 (Konings & Nyamnjoh, 2019). Arguably, there was no precise indication as to the actual nature and involvement of the "two-state federation that was born in 1961. This was because the then Federal Republic of Cameroon did not provide effective institutions that could preserve

[1] The name, Republic of Cameroon, refers to the name of French East Cameroon after independence.

the equal partnership of the two previous colonies as envisaged in the first federal constitution of 1961" (Kale, 1967: 70).

Consequently, there was dependency of the former British West Cameroon on former French East Cameroon. As Rodney (Rodney, 1975) rightly argued, "when two societies of the unequal level of socio-political and economic development interact which each other at any level, the more advanced one would exert total influence on the less advanced one". It was obvious from the onset that French East Cameroon would dominate British West Cameroon in all aspects of the society, thereby leading to sentiment of marginalisation.

The increasing consciousness of marginalisation in the context of a failed attempt to forcefully assimilate the Anglophone population into a Francophone-dominated state according to Lazar (2019: 1–2) is the cause of the bloody war in Cameroon. Notwithstanding, the complexity of Anglophone marginalisation and agitation are not stand-alone facts. The duality of Cameroon's colonial and postcolonial history severely impacts how Cameroonians generally negotiate belonging. The latter also presents an interesting feature in terms of why Anglophones increasingly don't feel that they are a part of the Republic of Cameroon, and therefore are determined to secede from Cameroon (Konings & Nyamnjoh, 2019). The war of secession, part of the reason of the insecurity in that region, that began in 2016 has hitherto killed more than 30,000 civilians and military personnel (Atabongwoung, 2021).

Conclusion: Towards the Security of the Former British West Cameroon

The chapter has attempted to provide historical contexts to the quest for peace and security in Cameroon. It has argued that from the onset, the reunification of Cameroon (formation of the Federal Republic of Cameroon) did not pose serious insecurity challenges in Cameroon. This is because the reunification gained momentum through the first constitution of 1961 that advocated that Cameroon should be governed as a federation (precisely a two-state federation), owing to the country's distinct sociolinguistic and political heritage from the British and French.

However, at the post-reunification period, a Francophone-dominated parliament voted in a referendum in 1972 in favour of the creation of a unitary state (United Republic of Cameroon) without due consultation with the Anglophones. The unitary state lasted for less than twelve years as it collapsed to form the "Republic of Cameroon (which maintains the status quo of former French East Cameroon after independence)". The Republic of Cameroon maintained a highly centralised government dominated by Francophone Cameroonians. This created agitation among Anglophone who felt excluded because most of their socio-economic and political institutions were collapsed alongside the collapse of the federal state. This paved the way for the rise of the sentiment of marginalisation among Anglophones Cameroonian who perceived that their sociolinguistic and political heritage from the British was endangered because of the dominance of Francophone Cameroonians in terms of language, population size and political power.

The sentiment of marginalisation among Anglophones has created a huge political divide between them and their Francophone counterparts. The government of Cameroon since the collapse of the unitary state until now, has failed to reconcile the political and linguistic divide that existed in Cameroon because of colonisation. The government of Cameroon has instead enforced more unfavourable policies towards the Anglophone regions of Cameroon. This has added "more salt into the injury". For example, after several failed attempts by students of the Anglophone regions to get answer to the queries that they had addressed to the central government in Yaoundé regarding the issue of late registration and unpaid scholarship, they decided to organise a peaceful protest in order to create more public awareness on their plight. Instead, they were violently suppressed by excessive force and experienced a lot of human rights violation from members of the state security. Several students were severely beaten and arrested.

A similar peaceful protest was also organised by Anglophone lawyers in the same year to protest the presence of Francophone civil law magistrates presiding in Anglophone common law courts. During the peaceful protest, Anglophone lawyers were also severely beaten by the state security agents. More than 100 Anglophone lawyers and journalists who were covering the protest were arrested. The government passed a new anti-terrorism law which allowed Anglophone students, lawyers and journalists who were arrested during the protest to be judged by a military court under the provisions of the Anti-Terrorism Act. This was followed by targeted killings of Anglophones and the arbitrary arrest of prominent Anglophone personalities. The government use of excessive force against the Anglophone population paved the way for the rise of separatists' movements across the Anglophone regions. The separatist movements are at the heart of the conflict in Cameroon because they have also killed more than one thousand state security personnel.

Notwithstanding, while the conflict in Cameroon threatens to split the country, it has received little attention from scholars and peace advocates. The slow response of the international community to resolve the conflict in Cameroon has prolonged the war and encouraged arm trafficking which has increased the level of insecurity in Cameroon. Therefore, in order to address the issue of insecurity in Cameroon. There is a need of an inclusive dialogue between members of the government of Cameroon, political leaders from various opposition parties and credible members of Anglophone secessionist movements. Even though the Anglophone separatist/secessionist movements do not represent the views of all Anglophone Cameroonians. The majority of Anglophone Cameroonians who have experienced marginalisation as a result of the unification of Cameroon certainly, have grievances against the Central government in Yaoundé.

Obviously, the war in Cameroon has significantly increased opposing political movements within the Anglophone and Francophone collective. Among the two broad collectives, some individuals seek outright decentralisation of the central power in Yaoundé. This chapter, therefore, concludes that the way out of the conflict may not necessarily be the cessation of former British West Cameroons or the return to a two-state federation, but the strengthening of democratic institutions in Cameroon to ensure accountability from government officials.

Furthermore, Cameroon should remain a single political entity that can compete effectively in the global stage. And Cameroonians should live together in harmony and tolerance within the colonially constructed space they have found themselves. The government should be committed to devolution or decentralisation power. The power of the executive should be reduced to the appointment of cabinet members, while other political positions such as governors and country leaders should be done through universal suffrage. This would reduce the political divide that overtime is heightened by injustice and high level of corruption. The attainment of sustainable political stability and security depends on the establishment of ethical governance.

References

Agwanda, B., Nyadera, I. N., & Asal, U. Y. (2020). Cameroon and the Anglophone Crisis. In O. Richmond & O. Visoka (Eds.), *The Palgrave Encyclopedia of Peace and Conflict Studies*. Palgrave Macmillan.

Amaazee, V. B. (1994). The Role of the French Cameroonians in the Unification of Cameroon, 1916–1961. *Transafrican Journal of History, 23*, 195–234.

Anyangwe, C. (1987). *The Cameroonian Judicial System* (pp. 1–11). CEPER.

Atabongwoung, G. (2021). History Never Dies, How Silent Past Returns: Southern Cameroons/"Ambazonia." *Africana Studia, 33*, 95–109.

Austen, R. (1977). Duala Versus Germans in Cameroon: Dimensions of a Political Conflict. *Outre-Mers. Revue d'histoire, 64*(237), 477–497.

Awasom, N. F. (2000). The Reunification Question in Cameroon History: Was the Bride an Enthusiastic or a Reluctant One? *Africa Today*, pp. 91–119.

Babou, C. A. (2010). Decolonization or National Liberation: Debating the End of British Colonial Rule in Africa. *The Annals of the American Academy of Political and Social Science, 632*(1), 41–54.

Bifuh-Ambe, E. (2020). Harnessing the Transformational Potential of Education to Meet National and Global Developmental Needs of Southern Cameroons: Re-Thinking Theory and Practice. *Theory & Event, 23*(2), 445–463.

Calvert, A. F. (1917). *The Cameroons*. T Werner Laurie Ltd.

Central Intelligence Agency (CIA). (2018). *The World Factbook*. https://www.cia.gov/library/publications/the-world-factbook/geos/print_cm.html

Chem-Langhëë, B. (1995). The Road to the Unitary State of Cameroon 1959–1972. *Paideuma, 41*, 17–25.

Chiabi, E. (1997). *The Making of Modern Cameroon* (Vol. 1). University Press of America.

Craven, M. (2015). Between Law and History: The Berlin Conference of 1884–1885 and the Logic of Free Trade. *London Review of International Law, 3*(1), 31–59.

Diduk, S. (1993). European Alcohol, History, and the State in Cameroon. *African Studies Review, 36*(1), 1–42.

Dupraz, Y. (2019). French and British Colonial legacies in Education: Evidence from the Partition of Cameroon. *The Journal of Economic History, 79*(3), 628–668.

Dze-Ngwa, W. (2015). The First World War and Its Aftermath in Cameroon: A Historical Evaluation of a Centenary, 1914–2014. *International Journal of Liberal Arts and Social Science, 3*(2), 78–90.

Eboua, S. (1996). *D'Ahidjo a Biya: Le changement au Cameroun - Collection of Points of Views*. Harmattan.

Elango, L. Z. (1985). The Anglo-French Condominium in Cameroon: The Myth and the Reality. *International Journal of African Historical Studies, 184*, 658–671.

Elango, L. Z. (1987). *The Anglo-French Condominium in Cameroon, 1914–1916: History of a Misunderstanding*. Navi-Group Publications.
Eluke, E. J. (2020). The Role of the Us in Finding a Solution to the Current Anglophone Crisis in Cameroon. *Philosophy and Political Science in the Context of Modern Culture, 12*(1), 189–194.
Fanso, V. G. (1975). Background to the Annexation of Cameroon, 1875–1885. *Abbia: revue culturelle camerounaise, 29*(30), 231–280.
Fanso, V. G. (1989). *Cameroon History for Secondary Schools and Colleges* (Vol. 1). Macmillan Education Limited.
Fichter, J. R. (Ed.). (2019). *British and French Colonialism in Africa, Asia, and the Middle East: Connected Empires Across the Eighteenth to the Twentieth Centuries*. Springer.
Fonchingong, C. C., & Fonjong, L. N. (2002). The Concept of Self-Reliance in Community Development Initiatives in the Cameroon Grassfields. *GeoJournal, 57*(1), 83–94.
Fonlon, B. (1963). A case for early bilingualism. *Abbia, 4*, 56–94.
Fonlon, B. (1969). *The Language Problem in Cameroon: An Historical Perspective*. http://www.jstor.org/view/03050068/sp030013/03x0446d/0
Furnivall, J. S. (2014). *Colonial Policy and Practice*. Cambridge University Press.
Gerring, J., Ziblatt, D., Van Gorp, J., & Arévalo, J. (2011). An Institutional Theory of Direct and Indirect Rule. *World Politics, 63*(3), 377–433.
Geschiere, P. (1993). Chiefs and Colonial Rule in Cameroon: Inventing Chieftaincy, French and British Style. *Journal of the International African Institute, 63*(2), 151–175.
Geschiere, P. (1995). Working Groups or Wage Labour? Cash-Crops, Reciprocity, and Money Among the Maka of South-Eastern Cameroon. *Development and Change, 26*(3), 503–523.
Gumede, V. (2019). Revisiting Regional Integration in Africa-Towards a Pan-African Developmental Regional Integration. *Africa Insight, 49*(1), 97–111.
Johnson, W. R. (1970). *The Cameroon Federation: Political Integration in a Fragmentary Society*. Princeton University Press.
Kale, P. (1967). *Political Evolution in the Cameroons*. Government Printer.
Kale, P. M. (1969). *Political Evolution in the Cameroons*. Government Printers.
Konings, P., & Nyamnjoh, F. (2019). Anglophone Secessionist Movements in Cameroon. In P. Konings & F. B. Nyamnjoh (Eds.), *Secessionism in African Politics: Aspiration, Grievance, Performance, Disenchantment* (pp. 59–89). Palgrave Macmillan.
Lazar, M. (2019). Cameroon's Linguistic Divide Deepens to Rift on Questions of Democracy,Trust, National Identity. http://afrobarometer.org/sites/default/files/publications/Dispatches/ab_r7_dispatchno283_anglo_francophone_divisions_deepen_in_cameroon.pdf

Lee, A., & Schultz, K. A. (2011). *Comparing British and French Colonial Legacies: A Discontinuity Analysis of Cameroon* (APSA 2011 Annual Meeting Paper).

Lekane, G. M., & Lucky, A. (2017). One Country, Three Colonial Legacies: The Politics of Colonialism, Capitalism, and Development in the Pre-and Post-colonial Cameroon. *Journal for Contemporary History, 42*(1), 134–153.

LeVine, V. T. (1961). The Cameroons: From mandate to independence. University of California Press.

LeVine, V. T. (1964). *The Cameroons: From Mandate to Independence*. University of California Press.

LeVine, V. T. (1976). Political Integration and the United Republic of Cameroon. In D. R. Smock & B. E. Kwamena (Eds.), *The Search for National Integration in Africa*. Macmillan.

Mamdani, M. (1999). Historicizing Power and Responses to Power: Indirect Rule and Its Reform. *Social Research, 66*, 859–886.

Ngoh, V. J. (1979). *The Political Evolution of Cameroon 1884–1961*. Navi-Group Publications.

Ngoh, V. J. (1987). *Cameroon 1884–1985: A Hundred Years of History*. Navi-Group Publications.

Osuntokun, A. (1974). *Administration and Franco-British Rivalry in the Cameroons, Sept. 1914, to March 1916*. Paper Presented at a seminar, University of Ibadan.

Osuntokun, A. (1979). *Nigeria in the First World War*. Longman.

Oyono, P. R. (2005). The Foundations of Language Conflict over Land and Forests in Southern Cameroon. *African Study Monographs, 26*(3), 115–144.

Percival, J. (2008). *The 1961 Cameroon Plebiscite. Choice or Betrayal: Choice or Betrayal*. African Books Collective.

Rechniewski, E. (2017). 1947 Decolonisation in the Shadow of the Cold War: The Case of French Cameroon. *Australian and New Zealand Journal of European Studies, 9*(3), 52–67.

Rodney, W. (1975). *How Europe Underdeveloped Africa*. Verso Trade.

Rubin, N. (1971). *Cameroun: An African Federation*. Praeger.

Stark, F. M. (1976). Federalism in Cameroon: The Shadow and the Reality. *Canadian Journal of African Studies, 10*(3), 423–442.

Stoecker, H. (1960). *Cameroon Under German Colonial Rule: Studies* (Vol. 2). Rütten and Loening.

Strachan, H. (2010). The First World War as a Global War. *First World War Studies, 1*(1), 3–14.

Terretta, M. (2010). Cameroonian Nationalists Go Global: From Forest Maquis to a Pan-African Accra. *The Journal of African History, 51*(2), 189–212.

Weber, M. (1991). Politics as a Vocation. In H. Gerth & C. Wright Mills (Eds.), *From Max Weber*. Routledge.

CHAPTER 14

MNCs, Conflict and the Contradictions of Resource Extraction in the DRC

Divine K. Yamulamba and Adeoye O. Akinola

Introduction

Since the partitioning of Africa, its subjugation by European imperial powers between 1884 and 1885, and establishment of Belgium's reign over the Democratic Republic of Congo (DRC) through the leadership of King Leopold II, the DRC has struggled to convert its enormous resources to the sustainable development of the society, thereby engendering a "resource curse"[1] for decades. Nigeria and the DRC, are rich in several mineral resources such as oil, gas, and diamond. The two countries produce more than 250 million people living in extreme poverty,

[1] According to the Natural Resource Governance Institute, the "resource curse", which is also synonymous with *the paradox of plenty*, refers to resource-rich countries, such as the DRC, whose wealth in non-renewable resources has contrarily resulted in poor development outcomes and a higher propensity for violent conflict, rather than improved levels of living to its people and better prospects for economic and political development.

D. K. Yamulamba · A. O. Akinola (✉)
Institute for Pan-African Thought and Conversation, University of Johannesburg, Johannesburg, South Africa
e-mail: aoakinola@uj.ac.za

A. O. Akinola and E. A. Liaga (eds.), *Development and Regional Stability in Africa*, https://doi.org/10.1007/978-3-031-56695-0_14

which constitute more than one-quarter of the total poverty in Africa. According to the 2022 Global Multidimensional Poverty Index (MPI), the 2016–2021 survey estimates a total of 46.4% of Nigerians living in multidimensional poverty and 64.5% of Congolese in the DRC.[2] Furthermore, while Nigeria's unemployment rate for 2021 was at 9.8%, in the DRC, it stood at 23% (The World Bank, 2022).

The DRC remains the continent's biggest producer of copper and cobalt, which are important components used for mobile phone batteries (BBC, 2013). Furthermore, the mining sector boast of wealth in important resources like diamond, tantalum, tin, and gold, which constitute the country's major sources of income. For instance, the DRC provides more than 60% of the global supply of cobalt (BBC, 2013).

Despite its political independence from Belgium, Congo continues to groan under the weight of colonialism and suffer the illicit extraction of its resources without adequate compensation to improve the country's economic performance and increase the standards of living of its citizens. In 1900, the extraction of diamonds in the Congo Belge (now known as the DRC) commenced, when Belgium approved the Tanganyika Concessions Limited's (TCL) rights over 155,000 km in the country (de Wit & Jelsma, 2014: 361–369). The pattern of the exploration of resources, including environmental degradation has deepened poverty and accounted for protracted violent conflicts and political instability. Thus, the nation's richness in minerals has had an impact on the domains of development in three interrelated levels: social, economic, and political.

Over the last century, state governments, states security apparatus and public officials, non-state actors such as civil society organisations (CSOs), rebel groups and resource militants, and Multinational Corporations (MNCs), have played a significant role in the way these natural resources are extracted, managed, as well as in the control of armed conflicts. Among the actors involved in exploring and managing states' resources, MNCs have become the most complicit in the violent conflict that has bedevilled the country. The discoveries of diamonds in the Kasai region in 1907 and large kimberlite field on the Kundelungu plateau

[2] The World Bank's Multidimensional Poverty Measure (MPM) measures poverty by three non-monetary dimensions: the population's deprived access to basic health, education, and living standard indicators which to name a few include infrastructure/housing, electricity, and water (see Onyeiwu, 2022).

the following year "motivated Forminie're to continue its exploration programme that in 1918 led to the discovery of diamonds near Bakwanga (Mbuji Mayi) Town" (de Wit & Jelsma, 2014: 361). The long years of MNCs' operation in the DRC have not resulted in beneficial outcomes, rather, they have been associated with conflict, capital flight, corruption, and human rights violation. In 2021, more than 500 civilians were killed in North Kivu and South Kivu's resource communities (Tasamba, 2021).

As the issue of human rights and insecurity dominate the discourse on MNCs' engagement in Africa, the impact of the corporations' investment in the socio-economic space of the host country is of paramount importance. China's investment in DRC has called to question its readiness to take its companies' social responsibilities more seriously. There is also a concern that "China's primary crude oil suppliers are in conflict zones such as Angola, Sudan, and the DRC. More than 90 percent of oil from the DRC's resource-rich Katanga Province is reportedly exported to China" (Bu, 2018). Due to its "go global" project, the past decades have seen the rise of China as a formidable exporter of MNCs across Africa.

Beijing has been making concerted efforts to dominate African markets and its industrial initiation through its investments in several sectors. For instance, China National Petroleum Corporation (CNPC) operates in Sudan and Chad, and China National Offshore Oil Corporation (CNOOC) conducts business in Morocco, Gabon, and Nigeria. Apart from the dominant posture of China's MNCs in the mineral resources sectors, the corporations have increasingly invested in roads, railways, dams, pipelines, and ports in Africa, thereby enhancing China's presence in Africa (Bu, 2018: 37). Despite the link between foreign direct investment and sustainable development, the case of Congo, just like in several African countries, represents a contradiction. Indeed, as the conflict intensifies, MNCs activities are expanding across the conflict zones, which are the country's resource communities.

Against this background and through the desktop research methodology, this chapter explores the place of the MNCs in the protracted resource conflict that has threatened the corporate existence of the DRC as a national entity. While it delves into the political economy of the mining activities in North and South Kivu, it adopts an Afrocentric approach to understanding the resource conflict and the role of the MNCs.

After the background to the chapter, the study conceptualises MNCs in relation to the Afrocentric approach to resource governance in the DRC, drawing case studies from a few African countries. It generally reveals the nature and character of MNCs on the continent and focuses specifically on those in the DRC. This is followed by a section on the historical background of MNCs' activities and delves into the complicit activities of MNCs in the country's protracted conflict in the DRC. The next section focuses on the importance of Congo's mineral wealth to global value chains. Due to its strategic importance to the world, this part locates Kivu within the discourse of "the scramble for Africa" and highlights the factors that make the zones attractive to foreign direct investment. Shortly afterwards, the causes of conflict in the Kivu region are listed and expanded, and the response of MNCs towards this conflict is analysed. The last section explains the Afrocentric approach and why it is an important lens to wear when dealing with conflict resolution and transformation in developing countries such as the DRC. Also included in this same section, is a list of a few recommendations beyond the norm of strengthening the MNCs' Corporate Social Responsibility (CSR).

Understanding MNCs and the Afrocentric Approach to Resource Governance

Ataman (2003: 42) observes that one of the most visible effects of globalisation is the declining relevance of the state and the proliferation of effective non-state actors. This includes civil society organisations (CSOs) and non-governmental organisations (NGOs) such as MNCs, NGOs, religious institutions, and terrorist groups. Of these groups, MNCs have influenced global politics the most (Ataman, 2003: 47). They are one of the most visible agents of globalisation, cutting through both emerging and established societies, including peaceful and conflict zones.

The MNCs, also regarded as transnational corporations, are business firms or corporations with established headquarters in one country, usually the country of origin, and their subsidiaries in another, better known as the host countries (Irogbe, 2013: 223–247). In general terms, MNCs engage in business and operate in several countries, including the country of their origins. This means that they produce and distribute products and facilitate services in various sectors across the globe, such as transportation, mining, oil, and banking. MNC is "a corporation that invests in other countries for a variety of reasons, to have access to a foreign market, to secure foreign sources of supply, or to have the benefit of lower-cost production or lower taxes" (Udofia, 1984: 356).

The study of MNCs under the international political economy clearly reinforces the convergence of state and politics, economy, and society. As noted by Frieden and Lake (2000: 1), the activities of MNCs also expose the interplay between state policies and market operations because of their heavy involvement in the market through international trade and Foreign Direct Investment (FDI), and cross-border resource exploration and service delivery.

The nature and character of MNCs in developed countries are starkly different from their engagements in Africa. In developing countries, the role of MNCs is conceived in two ways: as agents of employment through industrialisation and skills transfer, as instruments of development and a clean environment, while the contrasting perspective regarded them as agents of imperialism and capitalism for profit maximisation, instruments of underdevelopment, misery, unemployment, and environmental degradation (Amusan, 2018: 42; Irogbe, 2013: 223).

Therefore, through a body of evidence gathered from the case study of the DRC, the chapter expands these arguments to locate the role of MNCs in resource exploration and protracted conflict. While international actors such as multinational corporations are organised under some sort of international rules and regulations, "MNCs are not formally the bearers of the legally binding obligations under international human rights law" (Bu, 2018: 50). While many of them are not directly involved in conflicts, they usually create conditions for the outbreak and perpetuation of conflict (Bennett, 2002). This accounts for their infamous complicity in conflict situations in Africa and the difficulty in bringing erring companies to justice. MNCs have also been noted for aiding the growth of corruption in host countries (Zhu, 2017). They have taken advantage of the political corruption rocking African countries and engaged in bribery to push through their businesses in these societies.

The African Union (AU) attempted to lead the implementation of Afrocentric policies to guide the activities of MNCs' operation on the continent through the Multinational Enterprises, Development and Decent Work (MEDDW) initiative (ILO, 2015). Indeed, a commitment to the Afrocentric approach is needed to govern and regulate MNCs' activities within the continent. The MEDDW raises concerns about the rather restricted opportunities for developing the local economy and expanding the labour force (ILO, 2015: 13). It has not also led to a dramatic increase in workers' welfare. States such as the DRC have also not shown commitment to their adherence within their national borders.

While the AU's regulations on the role of MNCs in Africa's conflicted regions have recorded a moderate improvement in CSR, the absence of a regional treaty regulating MNCs' practices has weakened its stance (Ekhator, 2018).

"Afrocentric" in this case refers to an approach that displaces and challenges the adoption of the European worldview as absolute knowledge and only regards it as one of the many others (Mazama, 2001: 387–405). An Afrocentric approach examines the African experience—its ideas, culture, economies, politics, and society—from the standpoint of regarding Africans as the main players, and not the victims of resource exploration. Afrocentricity represents African-driven win-win solutions that would address the political and economic effects of conflict where MNC operations are hosted and mitigate their remote or root causes. States should understand the character of these MNCs and respond effectively to their excesses.

Historicising MNCs in the DRC

The activities of MNCs in Africa date back to the nineteenth century. Pre-colonial Africa had played hosts to several MNCs, such as the Standard Bank in South Africa in 1862, ONA/SNL in Morocco by 1919, the United African Company of Nigeria in 1931, Orascom Construction in Egypt by 1950, and the Bamburi Cement in Kenya in 1951 (Amungo, 2020: 84). These corporations were among the earliest to directly benefit from the wealth of Africa. In Nigeria, apart from the decades of the operation of the Royal Niger Company in the country, by the 1950s, the United Africa Company (AUC), one of the British MNCs that UNILEVER owned, made a sum of £15 million in Nigerian industrial projects (Amungo, 2020: 82).

American and European companies such as Shell-British Petroleum (BP), the Standard Oil of New Jersey, Ford Motors, and General Motors, began to penetrate African countries in search of lucrative businesses (Udofia, 1984: 355). In Liberia, the Swedish-American-Liberian Mining Company (LAMCO) and Republic Steel immensely benefited from the country's mining deposit (Udofia, 1984: 357). In oil-rich countries like Algeria, Standard Oil and Gulf Oil firms dominated the sector, while Shell-BP (jointly controlled by the Dutch and British) and Agip-Phillips (Italy) held sway in Nigeria. At the height of the resource conflict in the Niger Delta area of Nigeria in 1995, Shell became infamous due to its record of environmental degradation and its alleged involvement in the killing of the environmental activist, Ken Saro Wiwa, by the military junta led by General Sani Abacha. This led to the militarisation of the oil communities and the proliferation of oil militancy and criminality in the Nigerian Niger Delta.

Indeed, discussions around MNC activities in Africa have appeared in academic literature since the 1970s (Amusan, 2018: 41). The subject re-emerged in the 1990s, mostly because of an unprecedented rise in technological advancements and market deregulation within the continent (Ferdausy & Rahman, 2009: 111–112). Since the early evolution of globalisation, MNCs' access to a "world without borders" has resulted in the search for new and strategic markets outside the sphere of Western states. As noted by Akinola,

> The direct convergence between globalization and the continued expansion of MNCs into developing countries cannot be overstated. Globalization has physically allowed state-borders to be flattened, and encouraged free finance and capital inflows across the world as part of a deliberate attempt to create markets for MNCs. (Akinola, 2018: 190)

Furthermore, the influence of one of the agencies of globalisation, the World Trade Organisation (WTO), on trade openness has been very significant. It has favoured the expansion of MNCs and disadvantaged developing economies such as the DRC.

Africa's wealth in mineral resources such as gold, diamond, crude oil, and gas deposit, would make the continent a destination for MNCs, while competition among the global powers would usually be a reoccurring phenomenon. In other words, Africa's extractive industry has over decades been an important source of capital in the supply chains of foreign MNCs. While the MNCs have been adjudged to be a vehicle of development, this has not been so in the DRC, where the manipulative strategies of MNCs in Africa have become more evident. In contrast to the developed economies, although cases differ from country to country, MNCs in developing economies operate under heterogeneous environments that are often characterised by conflict and economic crisis (Ghauri et al., 2012: 3–4).

Conflict in Africa is conceived as "organised physical force, resulting from grievances between two or more parties" (Oetzel & Getz, 2007: 331–358), leading to unfortunate repercussions such as the damage of goods or harm to individuals. The major causes of conflict on the continent are rooted in poverty and the unequal distribution of wealth between different groups of societies. Other factors are linked to identity formation or the politicization of ethnic groups, including the exploitation of resource communities by the government and MNCs operating in such areas.

As located in the literature, while these corporations could contribute to pre-conflict and conflict prevention strategies in higher-risk societies (Berneth, 2002: 37), they have perpetrated human rights abuses and engaged in environmental degradation, without any regard for the well-being of the resource communities (Amusan, 2018: 52). In Angola, for instance, the political elites colluded with the MNCs to exploit the resource communities during the proxy cold World War in the country. The MNCs became a law unto themselves as they took advantage of the disorder, fuelled the conflict, and assumed the provocative role hitherto played by the South African apartheid regime in the conflict.

As stated by the Organisation for Economic Cooperation and Development (OECD) (2002: 10), multinational enterprises are sometimes directly or indirectly involved in conflictual situations and are as a result, conscious of the urgency to protect their investment, infrastructures and ensure access to the mineral resources that are being extracted. MNCs' involvement in conflict or their continued operation in conflict has made them infamous in Africa. Some MNCs have tried to be involved in peace-building efforts to diffuse the backlashes coming from both political tensions and economic harshness in their host countries, but their utterances betrayed their ulterior motives, which are usually to take advantage of "resource wars" and generate more wealth.

There are several multinational enterprises that van Dorp (2014) identifies as "corporate criminals" and accomplices to internal conflicts in countries such as Angola, Sudan, and Sierra Leone. In 1970, for instance, a few years before the Angolan Independence, Gulf Oil, a former US-owned company now acquired by Chevron, with the help of its accomplices in the Portuguese colonial government, was involved in the exploitation of the Cabinda territory (Le Billon, 2001: 55–80).

Even after the independence of Angola from the Portuguese regime in 1975, this pattern persisted as the structural ruins of the former colonial system were translated into the new administration. The influence of MNCs in politics left the country in a vulnerable state of a power struggle between the country's most dominant liberation movements: the People's

Movement for the Liberation of Angola (MPLA), The National Liberation Front of Angola (FNLA), and the National Union for the Total Independence of Angola (UNITA) (Rosie, 2020). During the subsequent civil war, Angola's extractive industry—particularly the mining and petroleum sectors became a target or means to financially sustain each movement's agenda, while maintaining political control within the country and diplomatic influence outside.

In his contribution, Le Billon (2001: 77) goes on to explain how the leading diamond company, De Beer, which at the time had controlled 70% of the world's trade in rough diamonds, suffered much scepticism concerning its subsidiary, the De Beers Central Selling Organisation (CSO). This company purchased diamonds from "UNITA-marked" areas. Additionally, the continuation of the Angolan Civil War, which coincided with UNITA's sanctioning of non-CSO diamond suppliers, as well as Angola's neighbouring conflict with the DRC, served De Beer well with the rise in the sale of its diamonds and the profitability of its corporation (Saunders, 2000: 1–77). Strangely, De Beers was never held accountable for its role in the conflictual diamond trade.

Congo's Strategic Assets, MNCs, and Conflict

As reported by BBC News (2013), what makes the DRC so unique from many other African countries, goes beyond its European-sized geography, and lies more within the composition of its natural resources. According to the International Trade Administration of the US (2021), there are numerous economic reasons why the DRC is a strategic location for investment. For instance, the DRC's extractive industry provides a positive prospect to investors who want to earn high profit margins in a few economic hubs. The Haut-Katanga Province, which together with the Lualaba Province forms the DRC's southern economic sphere, is home to Lubumbashi, the country's largest city after Kinshasa. This economic hub is vital for its countless domestic and international mines due to the rich copper deposits found in the land.

The connected North and South Kivu along with Haut-Vele, Bas-Uele, and Tshopo Province are recognised for their constant political clashes, mostly between the Congolese government and non-state armed factions. The main cause of this tension lies in the search for control over the hub's supply of precious stones such as diamonds and gold and a productive agricultural sector. Therefore, aside from the agricultural opportunities for generating income, there is artisanal mining, known as small-scale mining, which should also be considered.[3]

The production of about $2 billion worth of gold in the DRC per annul holds great promises for job creation (Radley & Geenen, 2021). This was especially the case for South Kivu's largest city, Kamituga, which for decades has attracted mining markets that have been a source of livelihood for the resource community. The community are usually digging pits as deep as a hundred metres, to earn a "salary" for survival. The probing question remains: if the DRC owns the richest soil in the world, how do those who live on it still suffer? Since 1996, there have been several causes of the protracted conflict within the mining sector of the Kivu Province (both North and South included). It is important to reflect on de Brier's (2021) findings and how he categorised some of the main causes as the state's brutality, political corruption, and MNCs high-handedness. The armed forces, otherwise regarded as an undisciplined national army, such as the Land Forces of the DRC/Forces d'Armées de la République Démocratique du Congo (FARDC), have interfered with MNCs exploration system, through systemic and institutional corruption. The tension between MNCs and unregulated artisanal miners has also been decisive in the conflict discourse.

Interference by the Armed Forces

In the DRC's troubled zone, the military has been infused with politics and the MNCs to restore peace and wade off attacks from foreign armed groups operating in resource areas, particularly in the Kivu Province. According to the findings of the Congo Study Group (Groupe d'étude Sur le Congo), there were 125 non-state armed factions—both foreign and local—in the Kivu Province alone in 2019. The more prominent among them are—the Maï-Maï—the DRC's self-proclaimed defenders of local communities; Uganda's Allied Democratic Force (ADF); and Rwanda's Democratic Forces for the Liberation of Rwanda (FDLR) (Barry, 2019). These ruthless groups are known in the region for extorting money by imposing taxes on road users through several roadblocks and extortion of money in mining sites. These ongoing patterns of inflicting

[3] Artisanal mining is an informal method of digging, mostly conducted by local labourers who use their own resources to extract and resell vital substances from the earth (Rosie, 2020).

terror upon the Kivu population have not only endangered human rights from a political point of view but have tarnished the transparency of the artisanal and foreign-owned mining sectors from an economic standpoint.

Foreign armed groups, such as the ADF and the FDLR, led by former genocidaires, have been particularly more notorious, with its 3,000–4,000 troops. Despite the relatively low number of its members, the 60,000-Congolese soldiers deployed in the Kivus have been unable to overpower the armed groups (Vircoulon, 2010). They have continued to create fear in the region, to repossess the territory or reclaim the economic power that the state elites have relinquished to the MNCs. Foreign countries such as China, the US, Belgium, and South Africa, whose MNCs are operating in the country, have joined forces with state security to enforce peace and stability in the troubled area without success (Vircoulon, 2010).

Locally based groups such as the Maï-Maï have had to defend themselves from both state's security apparatus and these foreign armed groups, which have launched attacks to drive out the "outsiders" from the country. However, each rebel and armed group interpret the rhetoric of "outsiders" differently. For instance, while some believe that international MNCs are "outsiders", others like the Yakutumba group have extended this hostility to other ethnic groups, by treating them as "outsiders". Prominent among these groups is the Banyamulenge people who identify as Tutsis from neighbouring Rwanda.

Corruption

As listed by de Brier (2021: 16–17), there are four main routes to attaining moderate financial advancement within the Kivu region, namely: working in the agricultural industry, becoming an artisanal miner, joining forces with armed rebels, or getting employed by the government which translates to becoming a civil servant or member of the FARDC national army. The first three are mostly occupied by men and women whose level of household poverty does not permit them to further their education beyond the elementary level, and the last one is mostly associated with those who managed to get as far as finishing a degree in higher education. And even though that may be the case, the civil service is still counted among the three as the one that remunerates its employers the least. Apart from the ridiculously low salaries paid to this group of labour, they are not usually paid at all for long periods. In a society that has been militarized and where poverty remains endemic, they resort to illegal means of earning an income.

The illegal means of economic survival include making regular "visits" to mining sites to collect tax from miners themselves or their traders, usually called the "middlemen". The amount may vary from 500 to 1500 Congolese Francs and sometimes depends on how big or small the mining site is. In most cases, these agents work together with armed factions and divide the fraudulent profit among themselves. For instance, they purposely shut down mines for frivolous reasons and may insinuate that the mines are not owned by certain proprietors. These mines would later be reopened at a fee of several thousand of US dollars.

The proliferation of mining spots, privatisation of mining, and the affinity of foreign direct investment by the government have engendered conflict with the miners, many of whom have experienced displacement and marginalisation (Tasamba, 2021). This massive displacement is often orchestrated and financed by MNCs and implemented by the government through what Tasamba tagged as the brutal military-led "sweeps" of the resource areas. This scramble for diamonds and gold in the mines at all costs has also faced resistance from the foreign armed groups operating in the resource communities.

This dynamism and complications have made the country unsecured and susceptible to devastating conflict, high levels of bribery, and corruption, including illicit arms deals. Apart from the conflict, the high level of corruption in the area and the country generally has led to a low degree of industrialisation and productivity. The country boasted about 10,000 production units at independence from Belgium in 1960 and was categorised as one of the most industrial countries in Africa (Tasamba, 2021). As documented by Tasamba, just about 500 industries are servicing the 105 million Congolese population by 2021.

MNCs Versus Artisanal Miners

Despite the devastating conflict, Radley and Geenen (2021) have argued that the country's economic advantages and wealth in minerals have made the DRC the dwelling place of MNC giants the Anglo American, Glencore, and Barrick Gold. However, Radley and Geenen also claimed that the presence of MNCs have caused much controversy with the country's small-scale miners in South Kivu—those from whom the world receives about a quarter of its gold, coltan, and tantalum. Thousands of miners who work in the resource communities have been very productive. In 2020, the market value of the gold that was extracted from the mines in the Kivu region was about $265 million, out of the countrywide estimated total gold production of $2 billion per year (Radley & Geenen, 2021). Apart from mining, the region also hosts a very productive agricultural sector, which remains an attraction to agro-allied MNCs. Indeed, artisanal mining is the most important source of livelihood after agriculture in South Kivu and other parts of the country.

Despite the presence of rebel militia activity in the region, Kamituga has continued to attract all kinds of MNCs since the discovery of its gold in the 1920s. Among them, is Banro Corporation—a Canadian-owned company which has held most of South Kivu's gold under its control. Its control of the resource was made possible through the support of the Congolese state and its security apparatus. The company has succeeded to marginalise the artisanal miners, replacing their rudimentary or traditional tools and techniques. The sophistication that comes because of the DRC's radical shift towards FDI and privatisation of resource exploration in the country has isolated the artisanal miners, rending their skills of little relevance. Thus, the MNCs have succeeded to tamper with the country's home-grown "processes of adopting technology and forming capital" (Radley & Geenen, 2021).

In 2018, the DRC's mining code was even revised to restrict all artisanal miners from land ownership or mineral rights. While it also contradicts existing agreements with foreign firms and increases government royalties from the companies, it makes it only possible for officially recognised MNCs to gain mineral concessions from the state (Zeuner, 2018: 1–6). Due to this economic privilege extended to MNCs, artisanal miners are considered trespassers. In most cases, if not evicted or deprived of their own land, they are subjected to exploitative conditions because they are not bound to any regulatory framework. And while there is overwhelming literature on how these small-scale miners and MNCs clash, forcing them into displacement, there is a dearth of studies about the depth of the exploitation of resources in the country and the main beneficiaries of the resource revenue in a systematic manner.

MNCs and the Resource War in Kivu

The reaction of the MNCs to the conflict in Eastern Congo has generated a mixture of both positive and negative outcomes. For example, taking into consideration the fragility of the DRC's government, in terms of corruption and a lack of transparency and accountability, as well as the aggressive posture of the profit-seeking armed groups, Global Witness (2016) reported that Kun Hou Mining, a Chinese extractive enterprise, strengthened its relations with the armed group Rai Mutomboki in the Shabunda territory, to extract gold from South Kivu's Ulindi River, in exchange for rifles and money. About $17 million worth of gold production was smuggled out of the country to its subsidiary Alfa Gold Corp DMCC, in Dubai, through the involvement of several local authorities who supported the repatriation of funds.

Despite the pessimism around the complicated involvement of MNCs in conflict and misgovernance, there are still a few MNCs whose activities are very admirable with an acceptable pattern of operation in the Kivu Province. For instance, the Emerging Markets Private Equity Association (2011) demonstrates that while many multinational mining companies in Congo fall into widespread scepticism—because of their corporate practices in conflict zones—Banro Corporation, the Canadian-based gold enterprise with a mine located near the city of Bukavu, is one of the few with outstanding Corporate Social Responsibility (CSR).

Through the Banro Corporation Foundation in the DRC, financial investments have facilitated the development of the region's education and health sectors, including an improvement in social infrastructures. This has increased employment opportunities. Through the Foundation, there has also been concerted support for constructing and rehabilitating roads in Bukavu. The corporation has been able to combine making a profit with the initiation of developmental programmes in the resource communities.

Conclusion

The chapter has reinforced the complicit roles of foreign MNCs in Africa and the convergence between resource extraction in Africa and the impoverishment of the resource communities. Despite the huge natural resources in the DRC, the lack of industrialisation and failures to convert the resources into developmental projects are evident. The quest to mitigate against these calls for a regional instrument that mirrors the AU's agenda for sustainable development and clearly sets out what measures are required to ensure that MNCs standardise a pattern of corporate behaviour that does not lead to illicit transactions by the investors.

It is important for MNCs to take cognisance of the unique context of each country's history with conflict, its vulnerability, and the state's fragility. Instead of acting like instruments of development and social stability, MNCs in the DRC have aggravated social divisions and instigated conflict. While the AU continues to push for sustainable policy to guide the management of FDI in member states, all the stakeholders discussed in the chapter—the state, artisanal miners, MNCs—should demonstrate great responsibility and accountability. This remains a germane condition for the effectiveness of any governance of natural resources and the implementation of effective policies in the mining sector.

National and other levels of government should be alive to their responsibilities. For instance, local authorities need to address the ethnic conflict in their respective regions for peace in resource communities and in ensuring national and regional stability. The spillover effects of insecurity in neighbouring countries have the tendency to affect the stability of resource zone and the disposition of the companies operating in such spaces. Where there is regional stability, security will be guaranteed around the DRC's Eastern Provinces. Furthermore, to reduce all levels of extortion, the country's government should prohibit any form of taxing or customary payments and royalties (i.e. other than those of legal exports) paid by artisanal miners to civil servants, rebel groups, or FARDC.

Artisanal miners should be monitored based on mining licences that confirm their ownership of a plot, rather than paying fixed royalties. This is why the DRC government's pragmatic policy option would be to fully formalise the country's small-scale mining industry and employ creative means of making the extraction of minerals sustainable and safe for everyone. Additionally, these royalties received from exports, as mentioned previously, should be utilised for the development of local infrastructural projects or any other development-related projects that would improve the economic situation of civilians. Where impoverishment is rampant, peace and stability become a mirage.

On the other hand, decision-makers (local authorities) within these affected communities need to create a bridge between the MNCs in their region, which have paid mineral concessions for natural resources right, and the hand-mined operations of artisanal miners who "share" a similar block. For instance, by working together with groups such as the Réseau pour l'Autonomisation des femmes des Communautés Minières

(REAFCOM), which specialises in the monitoring of mine conflicts, local authorities would be able to strengthen conflict resolution between disputing actors. Ultimately, the state has the responsibility to defend the rights of its citizens to enjoy the dividends of natural resources.

References

Akinola, A. O. (2018). *Globalisation, Democracy and Oil Sector Reform in Nigeria*. Palgrave Macmillan.

Amungo, E. (2020). *The Rise of the African Multinational Enterprise (AMNE): The Lions Accelerating the Development of Africa*. Springer Nature.

Amusan, L. (2018). Multinational Corporation's (MNCs) Engagement in Africa: Messiahs or Hypocrites? *Journal of African Foreign Affairs, 5*(1), 41–62.

Ataman, M. (2003). The Impact of Non-state Actors on World Politics: A Challenge to Nation-States. *Turkish Journal of International Relations, 2*(1), 42–66.

Barry, B. (2019). *A Hundred Armed Groups Active in Eastern DRC*. https://www.dw.com/fr/une-centaine-de-groupes-arm%C3%A9s-actifs-dans-lest-de-la-rdc/a-51664664#:~:text=Selon%20les%20chiffres%20

BBC News. (2013). *DR Congo: Cursed by Its Natural Wealth*. https://www.bbc.com/news/magazine-24396390

Bennett, J. (2002). Multinational Corporations, Social Responsibility and Conflict. *Journal of International Affairs, 55*(2), 393–410.

Bu, Q. (2018). Chinese Multinational Companies in Africa: The Human Rights Discourse. *African Journal of Legal Studies, 8*, 33–86.

De Brier, G. (2021). *Conflict Analysis and Stakeholder Mapping in South Kivu and Ituri*. International Peace Information Services (IPIS). Antwerp.

De Wit, M., & Jelsma, H. A. (2014). A Review of the Kimberlites of the Democratic Republic of Congo. In M. de Wit, F. Guillocheau, & M. de Wit (Eds.), *Geology and Resource Potential of the Congo Basin* (pp. 361–369). Springer.

Ekhator, E. O. (2018). Regulating the Activities of Multinational Corporations in Nigeria: A Case for the African Union? *International Community Law Review, 20*(1), 30–68.

EMPEA. (2011). *Case Study: Banro (DR Congo)*. https://www.globalprivatecapital.org/app/uploads/2017/03/cordiant_case_study_banro_web.pdf

Ferdausy, S., & Rahman, S. (2009). Impact of Multinational Corporations on Developing Countries. *The Chittagong University Journal of Business Administration, 24*, 111–137.

Frieden, J. A., & Lake, D. A. (2000). *International Political Economy: Perspectives on Global Power and Wealth*. Routledge.

Ghauri, P., Hadjikhani, A., & Ulf, E. (2012). The Three Pillars: Business, State and Society: MNCs in Emerging Markets. *International Business and Management, 28*, 3–16.

Global Witness. (2016). *Mining Company Funds Armed Men in Eastern Congo Gold Rush While State Loses Tax Windfall*. https://www.globalwitness.org/en/press-releases/mining-company-funds-armed-men-eastern-congo-gold-rush-en/

International Labour Organisation (ILO). (2015). *Multinational Enterprises, Development and Decent Work*. ILO.

Irogbe, K. (2013). Global Political Economy and the Power of Multinational Corporations. *Journal of Third World Studies, 30*(2), 223–247.

Le Billon, P. (2001). Angola's Political Economy of War: The Role of Oil and Diamonds, 1975–2000. *African Affairs, 100*(398), 55–80.

Mazama, A. (2001). The Afrocentric Paradigm: Contours and Definitions. *Journal of Black Studies, 31*(4), 387–405.

OECD. (2002). *Multinational Enterprises in Situations of Violent Conflict and Widespread Human Rights Abuses* (OECD Working Papers on International Investment). https://doi.org/10.1787/410036718701. Accessed on April 10, 2022.

Oetzel, J., & Getz, K. A. (2007). The Role of Multinational Enterprises in Responding to Violent Conflict: A Conceptual Model and Framework for Research. *American Business Law Journal, 44*(2), 331–358.

Onyeiwu, S. (2022). *Nigeria's Poverty Profile Is Grim. It's Time to Move Beyond Handouts*. https://theconversation.com/nigerias-poverty-profile-is-grim-its-time-to-move-beyond-handouts-163302

Radley, B., & Geenen, S. (2021). *How Large Miners and States Stifle Local Capital and Innovation in DR Congo*. https://theconversation.com/how-large-miners-and-states-stifle-local-capital-and-innovation-in-dr-congo-157529

Rosie, B. (2020). *The Angolan Civil War: Conflict Economics or the Divine Right of Kings*. https://www.e-ir.info/2020/12/02/the-angolan-civil-war-conflict-economics-or-the-divine-right-of-kings/

Saunders, L. (2000). Rich and Rare Are the Gems They War: Holding De Beers Accountable for Trading Conflict Diamonds. *Fordham International Law Journal, 24*(4), 1–77.

Tasamba, J. (2021, September 11). *Conflict, Corruption Result in Deindustrialization of Congo*. https://www.aa.com.tr/en/africa/conflict-corruption-result-in-deindustrialization-of-congo/2362024

The World Bank. (2022). *Unemployment, Total (% of Total Labor Force) (Modelled ILO Estimate)*. https://data.worldbank.org/indicator/SL.UEM.TOTL.ZS?locations=CG

Udofia, O. E. (1984). Imperialism in Africa: A Case of Multinational Corporations. *Journal of Black Studies, 14*(3), 353–368.
United Nations Development Programme and Oxford Poverty and Human Development Initiative. (2022). *Global Multidimensional Poverty Index: Unpacking Deprivation Bundles to Reduce Multidimensional Poverty.* https://hdr.undp.org/system/files/documents/hdp-document/2022mpireportenpdf.pdf
US International Trade Administration. (2021). *Democratic Republic of the Congo—Country Commercial Guide.* https://www.trade.gov/country-commercial-guides/democratic-republic-congo-market-overview
van Dorp, M. (2014). *Multinationals and Conflict: International Principles and Guidelines for Corporate Responsibility in Conflict-Affected Areas.* SOMO, Centre for Research on Multinational Corporations.
Vircoulon, T. (2010, November 23). *DR Congo: Why Is There Still a Kivu Problem?* International Crisis Group. https://www.crisisgroup.org/africa/central-africa/democratic-republic-congo/dr-congo-why-there-still-kivu-problem
Zeuner, B. (2018). An Obsolescing Bargain in Rentier Estate: Multinationals, Artisanal Miners, and Cobalt in the Democratic Republic of Congo. *Frontiers in Energy Research, 6*(123), 1–6.
Zhu, B. (2017). MNCs, Rents, and Corruption: Evidence from China. *American Journal of Political Science, 61*(1), 84–99.

CHAPTER 15

Pan-African Integration: Afrophobia Conundrum and Migration Politicking in South Africa

Farai Joseph Chidhume, Olawale Akinrinde, and Mandiedza Parachi

Introduction

Since the attainment of political independence by South Africa in 1994, the country has experienced a serious migration conundrum as the number of document and undocumented migrants has risen to an alarming state in recent times. The rise in immigration from other African countries to South Africa has led to the escalation of tensions between

F. J. Chidhume (✉) · M. Parachi
Midlands State University, Gweru, Zimbabwe
e-mail: chidhumef@staff.msu.ac.zw

M. Parachi
e-mail: Parichim@staff.msu.ac.zw

O. Akinrinde
Osun State University, Osogbo, Nigeria
e-mail: olawale.akinrinde@uniosun.edu.ng

A. O. Akinola and E. A. Liaga (eds.), *Development and Regional Stability in Africa*, https://doi.org/10.1007/978-3-031-56695-0_15

black South Africans and African migrants from other countries. This has engendered anti-migration sentiments and Afrophobic violence—an attack by the local population against foreigners from other African countries. The victims of Afrophobic violence have largely been individuals and groups of African descent, which include asylum seekers, stateless peoples, refugees, and African migrants in South Africa (legally or illegally) in the hopes of accessing greener pastures. Afrophobic violence has marred and threatened to erase the Pan-Africanist ethos of brotherhood and co-existence.

Afrophobic violence has consistently unfolded in post-apartheid South Africa, undermining the African Union's (AU) quest for African Unity. Episodes of Afrophobic violence have severed South Africa's diplomatic relations with its neighbouring countries and some African countries. Landau (2012) postulates that the establishment of subjection and politics of "us and them" is now being witnessed. The migration issues have also been used to scapegoat administrative failures of the government to address the socio-economic deprivation of the economically languishing black community in South Africa, which has necessitated the Afrophobic conflict of the in-group and the out-group jostling for the limited social and economic resources. Mhlanga (2008) pontificates that the political setting coupled with deprivation has escalated the recurrence of Afrophobic attacks on migrants. Fellow African countries namely Nigeria, Zimbabwe, Burundi, Malawi, and Mozambique, among others, have had citizens that encountered Afrophobic violence and mayhem in South Africa.

Since the first massive xenophobic attacks in 2008, the various episodes of Afrophobic violence have attracted varying diplomatic reactions on the African continent, threatening the goals and ideals of Pan-Africanism and the AU's founding principles of an integrated and united Africa. Expectedly, the banning of music artists, deliberate boycotts, issuing of travel alerts, looting corporate stores that are South African-owned, protests at consular buildings and Nigerian Ambassador recall were a few of the retaliatory actions that greeted the Afrophobic violence in South Africa from affected African states (Punch, September 2019).

The conundrum of Afrophobia has been catalysed by push factors namely failed political transitions and governance in much of Africa that have resulted in the migration of citizens legally and illegally to South Africa. It has been stated by Akinrinde and Tar (2021) that challenges bedevilling the continent have also prompted a national security risk for South Africa as the rise in undocumented migrants has escalated underhand dealings of rampant corruption to gain entry. A significant portion of the South African population experiences deprivation, lacking the essentials for a dignified life. As a result, there is a tendency to target the most vulnerable members of society—African migrants in their communities—accusing them of being responsible for social problems and widespread crime. Ncube (2018) has argued that the various public officials have been involved in the scapegoating of African migrants.

Many South African government officials have also indirectly influenced their citizens to believe that the out-group of African migrant sare responsible for unemployment and crimes. Community action groups have also enacted several operations to which they feel deprived by the government and its failures to deliver empowerment and fulfilment of electoral promises on employment and service delivery. One notable group is *Operation Dudula* and its attempt to target and push out foreign migrants and destroy their entrepreneurial trades in Soweto and other communities across the country.

Mbeki (2017) commended the South African government for its hands-off approach in not playing a central role in supporting the socio-economic development of other African states. Despite acknowledging the prevalent culture of violence within South Africa and the government's shortcomings in delivering crucial services and enhancing the well-being of the majority of black South Africans, Mbeki argued that directing violence against foreigners is misplaced. Mbeki (2017) alludes that migration is a big political and diplomatic issue, which the South African government must pragmatically addressed by engaging fellow African states on how to address issues of poverty instead of quiet diplomacy, which has prompted the migration influx threatening Pan-Africanism.

Through desktop research, this chapter examines Afrophobic violence and explores the diplomatic implications for South Africa and African Union member states. This study argues that economic and governance deficits prevalent among South African blacks, and continued neglect of the economic and social needs of the black South Africans by the post-apartheid South African government relatively deprives indigenous black South Africans of socio-economic capital.

Conceptual and Theoretical Frameworks

This section provides a brief, but concise understanding and interpretations of concepts used in this chapter by the researchers. Afrophobia, also known as anti-Black racism or anti-African sentiment, refers to the fear, hatred, prejudice, and discrimination against people of African descent or Black people. Afrophobia can take many forms, including verbal abuse, hate speech, physical violence, exclusion from social and economic opportunities, and systemic racism. Afrophobia, also known as xenophobia or anti-foreigner sentiment, has been a long-standing issue in South Africa. The violent outbreaks against foreign nationals, particularly from African countries, have become a recurring theme in South Africa. Tshaka (n.d.) alludes that while xenophobia is the fear for other races, Afrophobia is the fear of the specific other "black African Migrant".

Relative Deprivation

Afrophobic attacks have occurred as a result of frustration and aggression resulting from relative deprivation. Indeed, there is a huge existence of socio-economic inequality gap in South Africa. While the locals suffer, migrants have taken advantage of the economic environment to establish their entrepreneurial skills and business in the formal and informal sectors (Akinrinde & Tar, 2021). Failure to bring socio-economic change and employment creation to improve the lives of ordinary South African citizens has catalysed the recurrence of Afrophobic attacks in South Africa. Similarly, Tella (2016) alludes that the local South African populace feels threatened by the influx of migrants on the labour market as some of them offer low rates just to make a living and save enough to remit back home.

In addition, several pull factors have facilitated migration from host countries, namely, governance and instability issues rocking the African continent. Thus, migrants have resorted to migrating to countries with better pulling conditions such as South Africa (Campbell, 2009). With the ANC dispensation failing to meet their obligated electoral campaign targets, foreign migrants are paying the steep price for the state's incompetence and maladministration through other means: Afrophobic attacks. Administrative failures by the central government to tackle the high inequality issues have prompted the deprived South African blacks to become aggressive and belligerent towards foreigners, who are the scapegoats for the failures of the government (Soyombo, 2008).

The State is arguably the main provider of economic, political, and social resources in any society. It is also the body that determines who gets entitlements and who does not. It is also "a definite social space, fairly well demarcated and bounded territory, with which members identify and to which they feel they belong" (Smith, 1991). Communities (bound together by ethnicity, race, culture, or language) within the boundaries of a nation-state also have their sense of what they are entitled to. A community gets its identity from itself, other communities (that it compares itself with), and the State. To access resources, communities need to have an identity that gives them legitimate access to these resources. Hence, the presence of another community (with their own set of organising principles) is perceived as a threat to their access and full enjoyment of entitlements" (Smith, 1991).

Further to the foregoing, in forging a nation out of a multicultural and multi-ethnic society, South Africa could not rely on a common culture or ethnicity to create its desired community (Peberdy, 2001). As such, it focused on citizenship as the unifying force. The concept of citizenship is a sense of belonging and ownership that provides and guarantees access to state resources. In creating this notion of inclusiveness, those who do not meet the criteria are effectively excluded. The South African nation became an imagined community of solidarity whereby the people own the State in a sense. Smith (1991) argues that the idea of citizenship creates a sense of minimal reciprocal rights and obligations among members and the correlative exclusion of outsiders from those rights and duties. Thus, in defining itself, South Africa had to define who or what was to be excluded from the nation. Citizenship, therefore, forms the grounds for exclusion by drawing boundaries between "insiders" (South Africans) and "outsiders" (foreigners from other African countries).

Based on the above, the principle of national identity in the new democratic South Africa was then anchored on citizenship. Access and entitlement to the State or public resources are determined by citizenship and protected by legal instruments. For this reason, the Constitution through the Bill of Rights differentiates between the rights of citizens and non-citizens, just like any democratic country in the world with the freedom of rights. While some rights are held by all regardless of nationality others are for citizens only. Therefore, according to the politics of access, only citizens have the legitimate right to access the fruits of this newly founded democracy.

Of all the racial groups, black South Africans can now enjoy full citizenship with all its rights and obligations, a position not previously experienced owing to their exclusion under apartheid legislation which stripped them of their citizenship due to the Bantustan principle (Peberdy, 2001). However, the majority of South Africans realised the inability to translate their constitutional rights to material improvement in the livelihood of citizens. The economic policies embraced by the South African government through the Redistribution and Development Program (RDP) from 1994 to 1996 and the Growth, Employment, and Redistribution Strategy (GEAR) from 1996 onwards did not build houses fast enough, nor alleviate unemployment which is currently at 40% (CORMSA, 2008).

Xenophobia became an obvious expression of disillusionment and dissatisfaction with the government's inability to deliver. Khosa and Muthein (2008) highlighted the challenges South Africa faces when they stated that the country had a formidable task of building a unified nation from the fragments of a divided society and apartheid regime. Therefore, a sense of national unity and affiliation needed to be forged among South African citizens to promote an all-inclusive identity that would spread across both citizens and foreigners.

The state is arguably the main provider of economic, political, and social resources in any society. It is also the body that determines who gets entitlements and who does not. It is also "a definite social space, fairly well demarcated and bounded territory, with which members identify and to which they feel they belong" (Smith, 1991: 3). Communities—bound together by ethnicity, race, culture, or language—within the boundaries of a nation-state also have their sense of what they are entitled to. A community gets its identity from itself, other communities (that it compares itself with) as well as the State. To access resources, communities need to have an identity that gives them legitimate access to these resources. "Hence, the presence of another community (with their own set of organising principles) is perceived as a threat to their access and full enjoyment of entitlements" (Smith, 1991).

Further to the foregoing, in forging a nation out of a multicultural and multi-ethnic society, South Africa could not rely on a common culture or ethnicity to create its desired community (Peberdy, 2001). As such, it focused on citizenship as the unifying force. The concept of citizenship is a sense of belonging and ownership that provides and guarantees access to state resources. In creating this notion of inclusiveness, those who do not meet the criteria are effectively excluded. Although relative deprivation is one key framework of analysis to describe the catalyst for Afrophobic attacks, it does not however sufficiently account for the choice of targets.

The struggle for resources, through discrimination and prejudice, in South Africa has also led to the increase in Afrophobic attacks. Oksana (2008) alludes that the struggle between groups for limited resources makes conflict and stereotyping highly inevitable. Sniderman et al. (2004) assert that group competition for opportunities and resources will resultantly become violent, such as has been the case in post-apartheid South Africa, in which migrants have been blamed for almost every societal and governmental failures.

In the diplomatic community, most South African neighbouring countries are somehow reliant on South Africa economically as it is an industrial and economic power hub. The outbreak of Afrophobic attacks have, at times, affected diplomatic relations between South Africa and these countries, as these countries whose citizens have been victimised took a tough diplomatic stance in protesting Afrophobia. Bordeau (2009) concurs that foreigners are easy to blame for the deprivation and poverty prevailing in South Africa. Though, the scapegoat theory fails to explain the rationale and nature of frustration to catalyse the Afrophobic attacks are complemented by the relative deprivation thesis. Hence, the appropriateness of the relative deprivation theory as the analytical medium for the understanding of the Afrophobic politics in South Africa.

The Recurrence Triggers of Afrophobic Attacks in South Africa

South Africa since the end of Apartheid has been termed a "Rainbow" nation due to its diverse ethnic groups coupled with eleven officially recognised languages. Violence has become another language for the oppressed, and disenfranchised natives to speak out. Fundamental observations have attributed administrative incompetence, scapegoating, and migrant politicking related to Afrophobia violence triggers. The systematic use of violence has been a common reality in South Africa both for the state and the subjects. The post-apartheid era missed the vital sustainable conflict resolution moment to build and strengthen local societies and communities around the country.

The requirement arose for the implementation of peacebuilding strategies that involve both the reconstruction and strengthening of effective governance structures. This necessitates the cultivation of local democratic relationships and capabilities within communities to ensure the success of peacebuilding efforts, aiming to eliminate the language of hostility, violence, and animosity. These shortcomings were observed during the independent and top-down transitional justice initiative, specifically the Truth and Reconciliation Commission led by Desmond Tutu. South Africa has mainly focused on the political reconstruction process rather than institutional building. This yielded patronage and not participation. The ramifications are haunting South Africa with the frustration and despair resented by migrants of African dissent. Gumede (2015) notes that violence, and not peace, has a way of unifying South Africans for a "common" goals—anti-migration sentiments, rhetoric, and acts.

The failure to deliver electoral campaign promises of job creation, economic emancipation, and effective service delivery to the electorate has precipitated the escalation of Afrophobic attacks in South Africa. Former Democratic Alliance (DA) leader, Mmusi Maimane alluded that the failures of the administration to readdress the economic discrepancy and steer economic growth have been the major stumbling block for natives (Mail & Guardian, 2022). Employment competition between the locals and migrants has created a disparity that has seen the undocumented migrants competing with the local population for jobs with lower wage rates.

Furthermore, the acquisition of superior educational qualifications from documented migrants has reduced the employment rates of black South Africans. Evarratt (2011) alludes that stiffer competition has resulted in the continuous suffering of the unemployed natives, hence, indignation grows over time. The failures by the government to readdress the financial inequality through economic programmes, such as Black Economic Empowerment (BEE) programme, have been castigated as it has been merely a black elite project excluding most of the masses. The domino effect of wallowing in poverty has established the continuation of the violent spells of African victimisation.

Migrant Politicking in South Africa

Chiumbu and Moyo (2022) alludes that the insecure documented and undocumented migrants have been used for political mileage and scapegoating that has seen the eruption of Afrophobia attacks in Durban. Different political parties in the countries have reacted to anti-migration sentiments and acted in different ways. The ANC wants the enactment of effective borders to curtail counterfeit goods and drug peddling, the DA wants secure borders evident with former Johannesburg Mayor Herman Mashaba's sentiments, and the Economic Freedom Fighters (EFF) calls for unity with migrants. South Africa is a multicultural country, with high population of migrations, but unnecessary antagonism and hostility to migrants, haunt the country.

The resurgence of the violence has mainly been attributed to the lack of vibrant administrative implementation and enforcement of regulations and promulgation of policies. The reality is that violence is a daily feature but attention might not be drawn to it. The influence of Afrophobia is fuelled by the complex interplay of the past and present structure politically, socially, and economically (Misago, 2017). The failure of politicians to fulfil electoral promises and meet the expectations of the citizens has sparked resentment among the masses. This dissatisfaction has been redirected towards migrants, falsely portrayed as the root cause of government shortcomings. Politicians have resorted to making foreigners scapegoats. Governments at various levels have faltered in delivering services, extending from central to local administrations, and instances of perpetrators enjoying impunity and immunity from prosecution have been observed. These circumstances have instilled fear and trauma among foreign migrants living in South Africa.

Since the episodic 2008 Afrophobia attacks, promises for the establishment of distinct courts to try Afrophobia-related crimes were made but never actually materialised. These failures are resented majority of the respondents have immensely attributed that institutionalised violence unto foreign migrants is state-oriented through various channels from politics, police, and the home affairs department. Home Affairs and Police Departments have participated in the institutionalisation of Afrophobia through a state an exception allowing several irregularities. South African political parties have utilised migrant politicking to try and gunner votes from the electorate, notably the African National Congress (ANC), ActionSA, and EFF. The ANC and ActionSA have been calling for a stringent migration policy, while the EFF has displayed pro-migration behaviours and duly welcome foreign migrants as fellow "Africans and brothers".

The Nexus Between Economic Inequality and Afrophobia

The political economy of South Africa has necessitated the high escalation of crime levels and competition for marginal opportunities and limited opportunities for natives have initiated the violence from 2008 to 2018. There is stiff competition for jobs and every entrepreneur and business merchant aimed at profit maximisation hence, migrants, particularly undocumented, present the best opportunity for low wages and high performances. Economic competition has been the major catalyst for the recurrence of violence. The attacks are based on economic and class-based variables, which are expressed through the major triplex conundrum of unemployment, poverty, and inequality. These three shreds of evidence of poor governance have been the major catalyst for the eruption of Afrophobic violence that has rocked the ANC-led government since it attained pyrrhic victory over the Apartheid regime. The challenge of dismantling the anti-migration stance in the country is a formidable task, requiring the confrontation of a deeply ingrained 300-year-old system of colonial and apartheid domination in the journey towards establishing a democratic society.

The economic grievances have brewed and catalysed in the poor communities and townships where the effects of economic subjugation have been encountered. In addition, Okyere (2018) posits that most of the foreign migrants reside in low-cost housing facilities in the townships, where the disenfranchised reside, and, resent their feelings of being outclassed by migrants, socially and economically. The resentment has been castigated and attributed to the failure of the government to fulfil its promises, obligations, and commitment to empowering the local natives. The suffering of the local native has often been attributed to the labour laws and trade unions but there is a grave alteration between the political elites and the economic elites that have seen the failures of the political elites being scapegoated on African migrants, trade unions, and labour laws.

Economic inequity has prompted the disenfranchised native to resort to violence as *politics by other means* to also draw the attention of the government to their social and economic realities. Though there has been competition arising from the high rate of immigration into South Africa, some of the natives have been hostile due to their inferiority complex. Many of the locals have failed to empower themselves through investment grants and loans from local banks, unlike their counterparts who have no source of funding, as some of them have no proper legal documentation nor surety to acquire loans.

There has been concern about the level of entrepreneurial skills displayed by many migrants. They sometimes use instrumental marketing modus operandi to secure more customers hence greed, jealousy, and malevolence arising from the competition have intensified indignation of their socio-economic aspirations prompting general malfeasance. The current set of South African political classes has failed to economically empower the native people.

The Correlation of Afrophobia and Unemployment

As reflected in Fig. 15.1, the high unemployment rates in South Africa have presented fundamental challenges to the administration.

The citizens have resented their indignation through both peaceful and violent protests. Threats and tauter competition arising from educational qualifications and passion for the job has seen the native who used to enjoy menial labour jobs like gardening, domestic work, and construction lose their jobs to qualified migrant labourers. In many instances, some of them are overqualified and seek minimal wages to earn a living. The country records high unemployment rates, hovering around 25 to

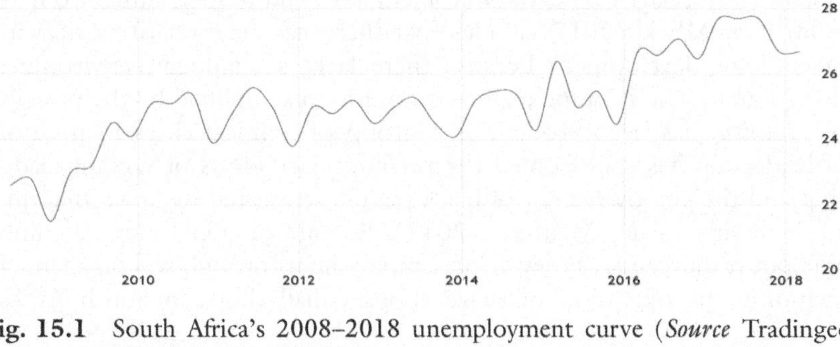

Fig. 15.1 South Africa's 2008–2018 unemployment curve (*Source* Tradingeconomics.com|Statistics South Africa)

28%, have generated a lot of resentment among the local population (Trading Economics, 2021). The rate of unemployment has increased due to the distribution of social grants, which tend to have created indulgence. In rural South Africa, many of the citizens have been threatened by the prosperity of migrants, many of whom are employed. Connolly (2009: 2) asserts that trade unions, like the Congress of South African Trade Unions (COSATU), have promised to uphold their supports for fair labour wages and respect the labour laws, but many industrialists have found a cost-efficient mechanism through cheap migrant labour that has little protection from the political elites and various government structures and departments.

A triplex conundrum of poverty, unemployment, and disenfranchisement coupled the economic inequality. South African industrial prowess has declined by more than 10% since the 1990 epoch, and the country has moved to be a mere consumer of industrial products; thus, the resources curse has trapped south African natives into poverty merely relying on government social grants (Mbeki, 2009). Afrophobic violence has mainly erupted in the townships and shack towns as lives have been compared between the natives and the migrants. This has engendered jealousness in many communities, which are the most affected by economic inequality and high unemployment; hence, it becomes a futile ground for violence to erupt. Since 1994, the frustration among the indigenous population has accounted for a succession of violent outbursts against foreign migrants. Concurrently, resentment within the townships, driven by complex economic challenges, has steadfastly fuelled advocacy for the victimisation of foreign migrants.

Furthermore, at least 70% of the triggers of Afrophobia-induced-violence are related to economic inequality and scapegoating from the politicians. Mbeki (2017) alludes that there has been relatively marginal ground for development because there lacks a conducive environment due to graft. The genuine expression of love, exemplified by the principle of *Ubuntu,* has been eroded, as a group of political elites in positions of leadership has transformed the revolutionary ideals of servant leadership and the empowerment of black people advocated by Steve Biko into a self-serving cartel (Mlangeni, 2017). Foreign migrants may be vulnerable but resourceful, as they create employment through several channels, including the operation of spaza shops (small shops in South African villages or remote areas). The principle of *Ubuntu* has been relegated to the political "dustbin" by political elites that find themselves attached to their interests at the mercy of both the black South African natives and foreign migrants, as highlighted by the black consciousness, African renaissance, and Pan-Africanism doctrines.

Pan-Africanism and the Diplomatic Implications of Afrophobic Violence

From the research findings obtained from the document review and as reflected on the Fig. 15.2, 10% of African countries reacted through diplomatic correspondents against the Afrophobia attacks. Malawi, Zimbabwe, and Zambia organised buses to repatriate those that wanted to return home, while issuing public notice denouncing the Afrophobia attacks in South Africa. In addition, Nigeria summoned its Ambassador in South Africa to report on the prevailing situation. Regional institutions also denounced the Afrophobia-induced violence. The other 90% did not react to the outbreak of recurring Afrophobic violence due to some reasons, namely the hegemonic prowess of South Africa on the continent and instability in countries such as the Central African Republic and Somalia. South Africa is a big investor in many countries whose citizens are affected by the Afrophobia violence, due to asymmetrical relations, few African countries are unwilling to sever relations with South Africa.

The consequences of Afrophobia have been detrimental as South Africa experienced hostile relations with countries in the Southern African Development Community (SADC) region, Malawi, Zambia, Zimbabwe Mozambique, and the continental powerhouse, Nigeria, have at different times, reconsidered their diplomatic relations with South Africa due to the victimisation of their citizens. Media coverage of the atrocities have been aired on television and print media, drawing attention from members of the AU and the international community (Table 15.1).

The upsurge of violence has immensely affected every sector of South Africa, as the international community has condemned the Afrophobia attacks through several diplomatic procedures, ranging from the issuance of diplomatic demarche as witnessed in the Nigerian response in 2017, while other states embarked on quiet and cohesive diplomacy. Zimbabweans protested at the South African embassy in Harare, the victimisation of their relatives who were attacked by marching and chanting the South African national anthem *Nkosi sikelela* in the quest to obtain

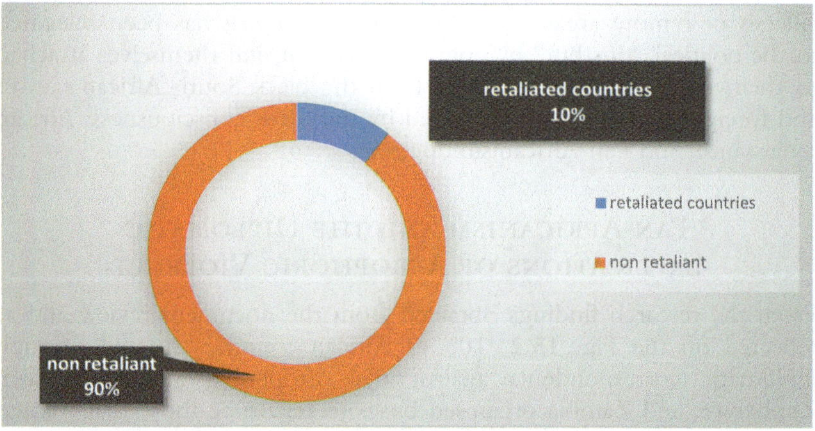

Fig. 15.2 Diplomatic reaction index (*Sources* Compiled by the authors)

answers and convey a hefty message to stop the attacks (Mundenga, 2015). The sporadic eruption of Afrophobic violence has often generated diplomatic tensions between South Africa and Zimbabwe. According to Gande (2015), former Zimbabwean President Robert Mugabe alluded that native South Africans are cowards who cannot slap a Whiteman's plaque, but they are bold to spill the blood of an African brother.

A quiet diplomatic initiative was adopted by the members of the diplomatic call from Zimbabwe, Malawi, and Zambia and provided transportation facilities to repatriate the migrants to safety. South African-owned companies faced sabotage in Zambia and Nigeria. A flurry of diplomatic engagements was undertaken during the 2019 Afrophobia attacks, as Geoffrey Onyema, the Nigerian Foreign Affairs Minister summoned the South African High Commissioner Bobby Moroe, to discuss the attacks and the status of Nigerians in South Africa.

Onyeji (2019) alludes that South African businesses in other African countries were negatively affected by the Afrophobia attacks. Citizens of some African countries, like Nigeria, retaliated and stormed Shoprite and PEP retail stores, and MTN offices, which were destroyed and forced to shut down their operations. Economic diplomacy is the most trivial and profitable for South Africa as Zimbabwe is a supermarket economy

Table 15.1 Afrophobia Attacks since 2008–2021

No	*Period*	*Province/Venue*	*Casualty*	*Reason*
1.	2008 Multiple Attacks in different provinces	Eastern Cape Gauteng, Durban, Cape Town, Mpumalanga, Northwest and Free State	62 people lost their lives, thousands were displaced, 342 migrants owned shops looted, 213 burnt	High crime rates, unemployment, competition for jobs, housing, and social amenities blamed on foreigners
2.	2009	Western Cape	2500 Zimbabwean farm labourers forcibly displaced from their dwellings	Job competition
3.	2012	Johannesburg, North West and Free State	Six attacks were reported and 42 shops looted and burnt. A handful of people were displaced. 273 People were Arrested by the police	Poor service delivery and high unemployment. NB these were legitimate protests that turned into Afrophobia attacks
4.	2013	Gauteng	A Mozambican National was tied up unto the back of polia ce van and dragged by 8 policemen. 4 Somalians and 2 Zimbabweans were murdered	Wrongful parking of Taxi along the road

(continued)

Table 15.1 (continued)

No	*Period*	*Province/Venue*	*Casualty*	*Reason*
5.	2015	Kwazulu Natal, Gauteng, Limpopo and Eastern Cape	7 people were killed of different nationalities namely Mozambique, Zimbabwe and South Africa. Migrant owned shops were vandalised and 2 Ethiopian brothers were set alight, In Durban G-section Umlazu and Kwamashu almost 2000 foreigners were displaced. In Grahamstown 500 were displaced and 300 shops and homes looted and destroyed	14-year-old had been shot during an armed robbery attempt by a Somali business owner in Soweto. The incident triggered episodic attacks and looting. Further King Goodwill Zwelithini's sentiments that foreigners should return back to their home countries also triggered attacks
6.	2016	Gauteng	Riots in Tshwane resulted in the attacking of foreigners and looting of foreign-owned shops	Dissatisfaction of ANC Municipal Election Nominees
7.	2017	Gauteng	Anti-migrant protests	Foreigners accuse of crimes, causing unemployment and being arrogant

Sources Compiled by the author and based on the information from these sources (News24, 2012; Patel & Essa, 2015; Ogo & Nwokike, 2021) for South African manufactured goods. South African industrial products have dominated Zimbabwean markets, as the depleting industrial productivity of Zimbabwe is being exposed.

The April 2015 Afrophobic attacks saw the recalling of the Nigerian Ambassador Kabiru Bala from Pretoria to Lagos, a move that shocked the South African administration. Furthermore, Nigeria withdrew from participating in the World Economic Summit that was being hosted in Cape Town, South Africa. The two African major powers have experienced punctuated diplomatic relations since 1994, but the reoccurrence of spontaneous violence targeting Nigerians in South Africa demanded cohesive diplomacy. This was coupled with a demarche issued to South Africa's embassy in Lagos in 2019, criticising the Afrophobic attacks and the *laise ferre* of the administration in combating them.

The demarche had an ultimatum calling for the intervention of the South African government to thwart the upsurge in the hate violence. South Africa has throughout the violence issued platitudinous speeches that downplayed the attacks as a crime and not xenophobia, which petrifies the home nations of African victims, notably Nigeria (Moyo, 2022). South Africa is witnessing a surge in violence and militant behaviour, as indicated by the widespread possession of firearms among civilians and an alarming increase in homicides (Hodzi, 2018).

South Africa lacks a robust diplomatic communication criterion that has foreseen diplomatic spats over the occurrence of waves of Afrophobic violence since 2008. South Africa has attributed the resurgence of violence to its long history of being a police state structurally and psychologically. The South African government further compounded its diplomatic relations with others, through the issuance of disturbing rhetoric about "your citizens are in our country". Though the country is a signatory to several protocol on migration with the obligation under the realm of international law to protect migrants and refugees, South Africa has concurrently failed to abide by these rules and protocols.

The economic diplomacy between the two continental powers, South Africa and Nigeria, has been negatively affected by Afrophobia. MTN, Multichoice, and Standard Bank, owned by South Africans, have suffered immensely. For instance, in 2015 MTN was slapped with punitive tax and fined for violating the Nigerian telecommunications regulations in their operations amounting to 5.2 billion naira (Akuki, 2017). Nigeria, a major source of income for MTN, contributes about to 37% of the continental mobile telecommunication company's revenue, and the country offers more subscribers than MTN possesses in its home country (Mainwaring, 2016).

The Economic Implications of Afrophobic Violence on Africa

The wave of Afrophobic attacks has been met with grave displeasure, coupled with fear and apprehension across the continent. Some African countries have enacted economic measures to force the government to curb violent attacks. Former Minister in the Presidency of the Republic of South Africa, Jeffrey Radebe, alluded that South African-owned businesses that contribute revenue have suffered huge losses. Revenue generation for international corporate companies headquartered in South Africa namely MTN, Standard Bank, Multichoice, and Shoprite have faced punitive retaliatory mechanisms in foreign countries where they operate. Infrastructural damage and looting of foreign-owned businesses have affected revenue collection by the South African Revenue Services, as migrants, who are business persons, feel insecure and vulnerable to the natives.

The epitome of the benefits of regional integration and the African integrating agenda are commerce and economics; however, the lingering socio-political nuances have impacted the central tenets of its developmental agenda, diplomatic prowess, and exportation of its Ubuntu philosophy. Diplomatic standoffs have been detrimental economically as boycotts on products of South African origin have been detrimental to its economic growth. Malawian government issued a presser against the South African administration and asserted that Pretoria must safeguard migrants or expect retaliation through trade repercussions as trade is conducted with mutually respected recipient states. Although the country is rich in minerals and has a vibrant industrial and financial prowess on the continent, no country can survive in isolation as interdependence is needed to ensure maximum profitability through the principle of comparative advantage. Issuance of travel warnings has been raised and plighted tarnishing the image brand South Africa, losses have been encountered in the tourism sector which is mostly dominated by African tourists in every 10 tourists 7 are Africans (Mundenge, 2015). Foreign migrants in

South Africa are vulnerable but resourceful as seen through their intellectual skills have managed to fund entrepreneurial projects that generate revenue and employment.

Remittance companies in South Africa, like *Hello Paisa, Mama Money*, and *Mukurudotcom*, have benefitted immensely as migrants remit money back to their home countries, using these platforms. The backlash of Afrophobia violence has also had adverse effects on the African continent, threatening Pan-African aspirations of continental integration, as nationalism continues to outwit the quest for African unity.

Conclusion

The chapter has contextualised the recurrence of attacks against foreign nationals in South Africa. No doubt, the Afrophobic attacks have impacted Pan-Africanism as well as diplomatic relations between South Africa and several African countries. The chapter has contextualised how economic and governance deficits in South African have aggravated the plights of majority South Africans. Furthermore, the continued neglect of the economic and social needs of the South African black population have been pivotal in triggering Afrophobia in South Africa. The chapter also highlighted how the escalation of Afrophobia attacks has also exposed the economic deprivation and heightened poverty among black South Africans.

The failures of the government to tackle socio-economic challenges have led to the unfair scapegoating of fellow African migrants. Unjust accusations, such as involvement in drug trafficking, contributing to poor service delivery, and exacerbating high unemployment, have been propagated by the media, politicians, and vigilante groups. The issues of Afrophobia, migrant politicking, and violence have been employed as methods of political communication, expressing frustration over the shortcomings of both central and local governments in South Africa.

As the initial excitement of majority rule subsided, the socio-economic challenges of the country became apparent, accompanied by issues of mismanagement, political strife, and conflicts that triggered a significant movement of migrants to South Africa. The expectations of the South African populace started to diminish in the face of these realities. Additionally, diplomatic tensions arose in response to manifestations of Afrophobic violence in the country. This chapter underscores that violence driven by Afrophobia, stemming from both domestic and external factors, poses a significant threat to the goals and ideals of not only the AU but also to African diplomatic relations, unity, and integration.

References

Akinrinde, O., & Tar, U. A. (2021). Political Economy and the Dialectics of Xenophobia in Post-Apartheid South Africa. *The Journal of African-Centered Solutions in Peace and Security, 4*(1), 50–63.

Akuki, A. (2017,March 2). Xenophobia: Threat to Nigeria-South Africa Trade Relationship. *The Independent Newspaper*. Retrieved from http://www.independent.ng/xenophobia-threat-tonigeria-southafrica-trade-relationship/

Bordeau, J. (2009). *Xenophobia*. The Rosen Publishing Group.

Campbell, E. K. (2009). *The Role of Xenophobia in Obligating Decisions Towards Transnationalism and Return Migration*. https://warwick.ac.uk.fac/soc/crer/events/African/confp_eugene_campbel.pdf

Chiumbu, S. H., & Moyo, D. (2022). "South Africa belongs to all who live in it": Deconstructing media discourses of migrants during times of xenophobic attacks, from 2008 to 2017. *Communicare: Journal for Communication Studies in Africa, 37*, 136–152. https://doi.org/10.36615/jcsa.v37i1.1586.

Connolly, R. (2009). 'South Africa Xenophobic Violence Condemned' *International News Green left Weekly #752*, 28 May 2008, http://www.greenleft.org.au/2008/752/38860. Assessed on November 10, 2022.

Consortium of Refugees and Migrants in South Africa (CoRMSA). (2008). *CoRMSA Report: Protecting Refugees, Asylum Seekers and Immigrants in South Africa*. http://www.migration.org.za/wp-content/upoads/2017/08/Protecting-Refugees-Asylum-Seekers-and-Immigrants-in-South-Africa.pdf

Evarratt. (2011). Xenophobia, State and Society in South Africa 2008–2010. *Politikon*, 7–36.

Gande, C. (2015). *Mugabe Attacks Zulu King, Urges South Africans to Stop Xenophobic Attacks*, www.voazimbabwe.com/a/Zimbabwe-mugabe-independence-day/2724959.html

Gumede, W. (2015, April 20). South Africa must confront the roots of its xenophobic violence. *The Guardian*, 1.

Hodzi, O. (2018). *Personal Communication via Email*, 17 June.

Landau, L. (2012). *Introducing the Demons in Exorcism the Demons within Xenophobia, Violence and Statecraft in Contemporary South Africa*. United Nations University Press.

Mainwaring, Ċ. (2016). Migrant Agency: Negotiating Borders and Migration Controls. *Migration Studies, 4*(3), 289–308.

Maimane, M. (2022). Here's How We Build a Resilient and Modern Economy that Rewards All, *Mail&Guardian*, 5 October. https://mg.co.za/opinion/2022-10-05-mmusi-maimane-heres-how-we-build-a-resilient-and-modern-economy-that-rewards-all/

Mbeki, M. (2009). *Architects of Poverty: Why African Capitalism Needs Changing*. PICADOR Africa.

Mbeki, M. (2017). CBNC AFRICA, *Youtube*. www.youtube.com.watch?v=G8o T1XjDjpA

Mhlanga, S. (2008, July 24). SouthAfrican Government to close xenophobia camps. *Reliefweb*. Accessed at https://reliefweb.int/report/south-africa/south-african-government-closexenophobia-camps.

Misago, J. P. (2017). Politics by Other Means? The Political Economy of Xenophobic Violence in Post-Apartheid South Africa. *The Black Scholar, 47*(2), 40–53.

Mundenga, T. (2015). 'Afrophobia in South Africa: A Drawback to Regional Integration and Development'. *Southern Africa in the New Millennium Discourse*, pp. 1–16, https://www.academia.edu/12940177/Afrophobia_in_South_Africa_A_Drawback_to_Region

News24. (2012). *Xenophobic Attacks-Pattern Changing*, www.news24.comSouthAfrica/News/Xenophobic-attacks-pattern-changing-20120724

Ogo, N. C., & Nwokike, K. I. (2021). *Nigeria and South Africa's Bilateral Relations: Controversial Origin and Practice*.

Oksana, Y. (2008). Xenophobia: Understanding the Roots and Consequences of Negative Attitude towards Immigrants. *The Counselling Psychologist Journal, 1*(37), 40–46.

Onyeji, E. (2019). *Nigeria Recalls Ambassador to SA*, www.premiumtimesng.com/new/headlines/350546/breaking-nigeria-recalls ambassador-to South-AFrica.html

Patel, K. & Essa, A. (2015). No Place Like Home: Xenophobia in South Africa, *Aljazeera TV*, https://interactive.aljezeera.com/aje/2015/xenopobiasouthafrica//#two

Peberdy, S. (2001). Imagining Immigration: Inclusive Identities and Exclusive Policies in Post-1994 South Africa. *Africa Today, 48*(3), 15–32.

Punch. (2019). Xenophobia: Nigeria Recalls High Commissioner to South Africa, shuns WES 4th September 2019. https://punchng.com/breaking-xenophobia-nigeria-recalls-ambassador-to-south-africa-shunswes/#:~:text=John%20Ameh%2C%20Abuja,South%20Africa%2C%20Ambassador%20Kabiru%20Bala.&text=The%20nation%20has%20also%20pulled,quoting%20a%20%E2%80%9Cpresidential%20source.%E2%80%9D

Sniderman, P. M., Louk, H., & Markus, P. (2004). Predisposing Factors and Situational Triggers: Exclusionary Reactions to Immigrant Minorities. *American Political Science Review, 98*(1), 35–49.

Smith, A. D. (1991). *National Identity*. Penguin Press.

Soyombo. (2008). Xenophobia in Contemporary Society: A Sociological Analysis. *Psychologia*, 94–104.

Tella, O. (2016). Understanding Xenophobia in South Africa: The Individual, the state and the International System. *Insight on Africa, 8*(2), 142–158.

Trading Economics. (2021). *South Africa unemployment Curve*, Retrieved from https://www.tradingeconomics.com

Tshaka, R. (n. d.). Afrophobia Versus Xenophobia in South Africa, www.unisa.ac.za/site/corporate/default/News-&-Media/AFrophobia-verus-cenophobia-in-South-Africa

CHAPTER 16

Insights from Niger Delta Coastal Communities on Decolonial Climate Adaptation

Fidelis Allen

Introduction

Decolonisation of climate adaptation refers to the use of indigenous and traditional knowledge by communities to cope with climate change. Decolonisation is both an ideology and a practice that seeks to dismantle unhealthy colonial values, structures, systems, and legacies in post-colonial states. It is also about a preference for alternative models of development in which ecological concerns, fairness, justice, well-being, and human security are evident.

The concept of decolonisation is a valuable tool for analysing development in the developing world. It describes the desired development

F. Allen (✉)
Department of Political and Administrative Studies, University of Port Harcourt, Port Harcourt, Nigeria
e-mail: allfidelis@protonmail.com

School of Criminology, Sociology and Social Policy, University of Leicester, Leicester, UK

A. O. Akinola and E. A. Liaga (eds.), *Development and Regional Stability in Africa*, https://doi.org/10.1007/978-3-031-56695-0_16

model. There is typically a crisis of ideological interpretations when it comes to the concept of development. As a world characterised by hegemonic and unequal power relations between Northern and Southern countries, the mere mention of colonialism, neo-colonialism, or western development models can send different messages to different people. Development is a change process in response to human security needs. As argued elsewhere, decolonial development models are desired for their adjudged capacity to achieve this objective through critical assessment of the existential realities and outcome of Eurocentric development models to strike a balance or make the preference for a model that is responsive to human security needs of citizens (Allen & Amadi, 2022). Such a model or set of models must be seen to be holistic in approach, touching on all dimensions of human existence, including ecological systems.

There is no shortage of stories about how climate change affects communities. According to the table below, hunger will increase in the Sudan Savanna region of Africa due to rising temperatures, unpredictable and decreasing rainfall. Based on World Food Programme data, 41 million people are facing hunger in West Africa and the Sahel because of climate change (UN News 8 April 2022). Floods, droughts, unpredictable rainfall, and erosion are becoming more common throughout the world and pose a threat to Africa (Pyhälä et al., 2016). The prevalence and impact of these problems on people's well-being, especially regarding the availability and affordability of food, are key concerns. It is crucial to adapt to these problems. Decolonial ways of doing it, understood in terms of traditional and indigenous knowledge and practices, have been acknowledged in the literature (see, for example, Daszkiewicz, 2022).

The impact of climate change on food production, consumption, and hunger between 2030 and 2050 in Africa south of the Sahara and Nigeria in particular shows a steep rise. The picture suggests a much larger problem for Africa since food insecurity remains one of the main characteristics of extreme poverty. The data show that Africa will be the most affected by climate change-induced food security problems (Fig. 16.1).

Coastal communities in the Niger Delta of Nigeria are vulnerable to floods, unpredictable rainfall, erosion, and excessive heat, as are many other regions in Africa. The economic, social, and environmental conditions that follow these disasters have implications for social cohesion and development of communities and the region at large. For example, these conditions continue to fuel insecurity and conflict. The assumption is that

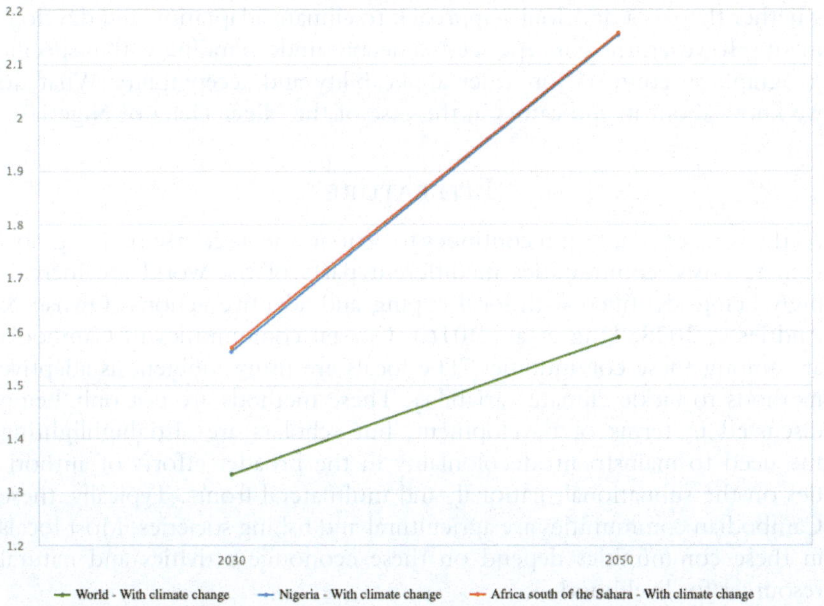

Fig. 16.1 Impact projections on food production, consumption, and hunger to 2050 (*Source* International Food Policy Research Institute)

the deployment and strengthening of local knowledge might be a vital component of what needs to be done for coping with these problems.

It must be noted that the idea of decolonising climate solutions in Africa does not in any way portray an uncritical rejection of Western solutions. In other words, it does not mean blind rejection of Western-oriented models of dealing with the climate crisis and development in Africa. Instead, it means careful integration of Western and indigenous knowledge or acknowledging and utilising indigenous models as alternatives when the processes and outcomes of Western models have proved incapable of improving people's living conditions in the post-colonial state. The concept of traditional or local knowledge is elastic and used in the analysis of non-African settings by non-African scholars (Chevallier, 2017). To be sure, scholars have highlighted how traditional and local knowledge systems are driving climate adaptation in several parts of the world. These efforts have hinted in a positive sense at the question of whether there is a decolonial approach to climate adaptation and development. However, the concept needs a deeper understanding within specific geographical contexts for wider applicability and acceptability. What do we know about its indicators in the case of the Niger Delta of Nigeria?

Literature

As the issue of adaptation continues to echo in the discourse on the global climate crisis, communities in different parts of the world are increasingly being identified with local coping and adaptive actions (Owusu & Andriesse, 2023; Ung et al., 2016). Coastal communities in Cambodia are among these communities. The locals are using indigenous adaptive methods to tackle climate variability. These methods are not only being discussed in terms of development, but scholars are also highlighting the need to mainstream decoloniality in the broader efforts of authorities on the subnational, national, and multilateral fronts. Typically, these Cambodian communities are agricultural and fishing societies. Most locals in these communities depend on these economic activities and natural resources for livelihood.

It is important to note. Scholars have used the concepts of coping and adaptation to convey different meanings although they are interconnected. Adaptation refers to strategies deployed in response to climate change that aims to reduce harm or negative impact. These measures sometimes are even expected to provide new opportunities (Ung et al., 2016). They can be anticipatory or proactive (Ung et al., 2016). In contrast, coping measures are short-term and reactive. As Ung et al. (2016) further argued, adaptation can be viewed as the extension of coping mechanisms or the taking of coping measures to the next level. Both can be initiated by people in the public and private sectors.

As far back as 2006, the Cambodian government had created the National Adaptation Programme of Action on Climate Change. Participatory principles were applied in the process that led to the establishment of this body in the sense that it involved local communities, policymakers, and stakeholders. It had to be that way because these communities are highly sensitive to climate variability. To deal with the associated risks, people needed to be adequately involved in policymaking. A report by the natural disaster committee of that country estimated the cost of disasters such as floods, destructive storms, and drought at hundreds of millions of United States dollars in 2011. This raised a serious concern from the government and communities. Ung et al. (2016) used self-efficacy theory to investigate the incidence of local knowledge and adaptive response to climate change and argued for a need to strengthen indigenous responses. Self-efficacy itself is a key conceptual tool in health research. Based on the theory's key hypothesis, when individuals assess their capacity to undertake a task in reaction to risk, they would do it to prevent or reduce impending harm (Bandura, 1997).

The Vanuatu Pacific example is equally revealing. Its rich heritage of local knowledge on climate adaptation has been explained (Granderson, 2017). Granderson argues that local knowledge in this region can be used to strengthen the resilience of the community. Granderson's analysis of local perspectives on the Pacific Island points to the direction of a legacy of application of local knowledge application in tackling the impact of environmental change. The following are some identifiable methods common in the region: water and food storage, collective pooling of resources for problem-solving, the elevation of settlement, superstitions, and religious ways of life, and predicting climate variability (Granderson, 2017).

North-Central Vietnam is another region of the world that provides an interesting case study. Local knowledge occupies a key position in its development discourse. This owes much to a growing culture of participatory resource governance among locals and authorities. Typically, local knowledge in this part of the country has suffered disdain and relegation by adherents to modernity. The analysis by Brunn and Ngoc (2018) on the significance of indigenous methods for adapting to natural disasters by rural people is instructive (2018). As they argued, there is a parallel reality of indigenous and Western adaptive responses to climate variability. The authors, however, mentioned a lack of requisite political context that promotes active resource management among locals. Vietnam will not be the last in this journey of identifying regions in the world where local knowledge has made important contributions to climate adaptive measures.

Scholars have analysed the case of coastal communities in West Africa. For example, Amadou et al. (2018) related the reality of local populations in Northern Ghana. This is an agriculture-based population, using land-use adaptive agricultural approaches to deal with climate problems. In the same vein, locals in Northern Mali are using the diversification of means of livelihood, migration, and institutional adjustments as strategies to adapt to severe ecological tragedies (Brockhaus et al., 2013). These are communities that rely on natural resources for survival.

In the Sudan Savannah of West Africa, specifically in Dassari, Benin, and Dana in Burkina Faso, local adaptation to climate vulnerability has taken root (Callo-Concha, 2018). However, there is a need for more commitment and pragmatism for the optimum performance of local knowledge. This is even more so to help reduce the risk of conditions capable of triggering violent conflict for those whose adaptive measures are antisocial. Temperatures have increased between 0.5 and 0.8 since 1970 in West Africa. Similarly, rainfall has decreased by at least 10% since 1950 (Callo-Concha, 2018).

In these communities, farmers can forecast weather conditions to make decisions about cropping seasons. They adapt with technologies although often with a feeling of no real sense of ability to adapt to climate change without being able to read weather situations. This is what matters to them. They insist on a combination of local or Western knowledge. The area in question is climate-sensitive agricultural systems that are known to produce cereal species as dominant crops due to their high tolerance nature.

Based on fieldwork experience in two villages in Tanzania, Naess (2013) identified three broad categories of components and examples of how local knowledge can support climate adaptation: biophysical and social exposure, sensitivity and variability, and adaptive capacity and adaptive capacity adaptation processes (see Table 16.1). The last component includes examples of the use of local observations in decision-making, perceptions of changing the behaviour of locals as defenders or destroyers of the environment, and insights into the importance of changing local institutions and cultures. Tanzania presents another case of how local knowledge can help climate adaptation, although it also has a challenging future here. Naess (2013: 101) explained the meaning of local knowledge as context-specific knowledge produced over the long term and utilised within the context. Traditional knowledge is used interchangeably with local knowledge. Adaptive actions aim to reduce the vulnerability of people to climate change. However, some challenges include sensibility to the environment, political and policy context, and capacity.

In the final analysis, Africa faces palpable climate-related disasters. Communities are responding with coping and adaptive measures. However not much is known about how this is unfolding and how local knowledge can interact better with political institutions as a matter

Table 16.1 How local knowledge can support climate adaptation

Component	*Examples*
Biophysical and social exposure	• Integration of local and scientific observations of climatic change[3, 49] • Indigenous weather forecasting to moderate the effects of variable rainfall[39, 50, 51] • Seasonal migration to minimize weather impacts[52] • Protection of water sources through taboos and designation of sacred sites[47] • Reducing exposure to environmental hazards[53]
Sensitivity to change and variability	• Management of common property[54, 55] • Use of crop varieties and mixes that provide yields in a wide range of climates[56] • Traditional soil and water management and conservation systems[57, 58] • Distribution of risks through social networks for food sharing • Allocation of pasture for livestock grazing[40] • Local institutions for managing sudden influxes of migrants[60]
Adaptive capacity and adaptation processes	• Using indigenous observations in decision making[3] • Insights into changing attitudes towards the role of people's resource management, as destroyers of the environment' or 'custodians of resources' • Insights into social differentiation of vulnerability and adaptation, including socially conditioned responses to external stressors • Insights into communication needs, e.g., cognitive processes that determine the update of seasonal forecasts[61, 62] • The significance of changing cultures and loss of traditional institutions[4]

Source Naess (2013: 101)

of decoloniality to increase its value for reducing the vulnerability of communities to the impact of climate change.

Methodology

The chapter focused on six coastal communities in three states of the Niger Delta, namely, Bayelsa Rivers and Akwa Ibom. In Bayelsa state, data was collected in Beletiama and Nembe in the local government areas of Brass and Nembe. In Rivers State, the study was conducted in Finima and Kono, in Bonny and Khana local government areas. In Akwa Ibom State, data was collected in Ibeno (Ibeno Local Government Area) and Okoroete (Eastern Obolo Local Government Area). The study used data collected by Health of Mother Earth Foundation of Nigeria through participatory research methods in a study of "climate change as a cause of conflict in coastal areas of West Africa" (Health of Mother Earth Foundation, 2022). I participated in the research component of that project and give the necessary credit to the Health of Mother Earth Foundation for the data-driven insights in this chapter.

The study deployed focus group discussion for data collection with a total of 60 participants selected through snowballing on a quota basis with 10 from each community. In addition, Twelve participants based on a quota of 2 per community were selected using the snowballing technique. These decisions were influenced by several factors, including insecurity in these communities. Participants were drawn from fishers, farmers, women, men, youth, and community leadership. A sense-making meeting organised for an initial joint analysis of the data collected from the field with research assistants and some of the participants from communities in attendance, helped strengthen the data's validity due to the study's participatory approach. Overall, data from transcripts of recorded discussions and field diary content were thematically analysed with ATLAS.ti.

The question of how people are coping or adapting to climate change yielded data that suggest the use of local knowledge or decolonisation of solutions to the problem. They are adapting in the local sense based on their extensive awareness and knowledge of the environment and climate. The problem, however, is that policymakers do not pay adequate attention to local solutions to climate change at the community level. Despite the threat that climate change poses to the well-being of people in Africa and the role that adaptation is expected to play in addressing the crisis, only little is known about the important place of local knowledge.

Case Studies: Bayelsa, Rivers, and Akwa Ibom of Nigeria

Bayelsa, Rivers, and Akwa Ibom are part of the nine oil-producing states in Nigeria, politically defined as the Niger Delta. This has not always been the meaning of the region. In a way, it speaks to the importance of the oil industry in any definition of this region in contrast to the enormous and rich biodiversity and general coastal features that previously characterised the region as part of the entire Gulf of Guinea states of Africa. The region was a key destination for early European slave trading activities and the shipment of conscripted slaves overseas. It later became a major centre for sourcing raw materials for the industrial revolution in Europe. The establishment of a protectorate and colony in 1906, and the eventual amalgamation of same in 1914 was the height of the appropriation of Nigeria by Britain under its imperial policy in the post-European Berlin-Conference era.

Bayelsa State

> "We fish in the ocean without a compass. We study the movement of the moon to know when to go out. Knowledge of the movement of fish is essential. Turbulence in the ocean is seasonal. It does not happen all the time".

This was how a former fisherman and native of Beletiama in the Brass Local Government Area of the state responded to a question on how he and his community people were coping with changes in the environment. It immediately raises the question of whether locals know their environment, changes, and how they are responding to continue to meet their needs.

There is a tacit portrayal of the ability of local fishermen to understand the environment of practice. Predicting the weather, no matter how inaccurately done, has a valuable positive impact on fishing and farming practices. It is a key aspect of the cultural and local knowledge infrastructure of the people, which has not been explored in the face of difficult economic conditions climate change is bequeathing. Reading local weather and being guided by it for safety and fishing at the right time is certainly not an accurate system for decision-making by modern standards. Furthermore, there have been insinuations in many quarters of how this type of knowledge continues to assist fishing populations, especially those without the capacity for the modern fishing tools and technology needed for decision-making about practice.

The issue here is that climate variability is intensifying and posing threats, especially to the extremely poor. The resilience of local people who face the challenge of lack of adequate presence of state authorities in matters of climate change will not wait to be consumed by climate events where they feel able to do something about such problems with whatever knowledge they have. However, modern knowledge systems discourage or fail to integrate it. They neither scrutinise local knowledge to determine its suitability for times in which people are in.

Like the rest of the coastal areas of the Niger Delta, oil company activities in Bayelsa State contribute a significant amount of CO_2 emissions to Nigeria's total profile which stood at 115, 280 as of 2019. This infamous testimonial of the Nigerian state is part of the cause of the global climate crisis. Greenhouse gases in the atmosphere are the cause of rising temperatures.

Sea level rise, flood, unpredictable rainfall patterns, excessive heat, and erosion are severe climate change issues in Bayelsa State. Together, they pose a threat to the survival of community people. Waiting for the government and non-governmental organisations to respond with adaptive programmes each time a disaster strikes, is reasonable, but that is inadequate and often too politically guided to yield good results. Fishing, farming, hunting, canoe carving, and palm wine (local gin producing), are key legitimate economic activities threatened and affected by climate problems. The impact on the practice of these occupations unfolds in different ways. For example, fisherfolk's ability to read the ocean's behaviour is failing due to the unpredictability of seasons. Harmattan seasons nowadays are shorter than expected. They interfere with the rainy season period. Fishermen and farmers understand the implications of these changes for the practice of their occupations. The data showed evidence of frustration with the impact of these changes on livelihood activities.

The shift from fishing and farming to other trades comes with many challenges, such as the lack of financial resources and skills needed for the shift. Likewise, migrating, a common adaptive decision people make, comes with challenges. People tend to leave their families behind when they first move. When flood and erosion are the issues, migrating due loss of living houses, requires movement by entire households. These adaptive measures involve a cost that must be considered. The capacity of victims to bear the cost can affect the outcome. Resilience is the critical element for survival to which the question of decolonisation of adaptation relates. Improving the level of resilience of community people is essential for effective adaptation. As the data showed, one of the adaptive measures taken by some fishermen in the Niger Delta is changing from the use of local boats without outboard engines to those with engines. Outboard engines are not manufactured locally, but they contribute to increasing fishermen's resilience. This upgrade in equipment use represents a mixture of local knowledge and Western knowledge. The move to distant seas for fishing was forced by the growing depletion of fish species in nearby water bodies due to overfishing or pollution.

One aspect of the changing climate in Bayelsa is the presence of nipa palms. These are subversive plants that locals believe to have no economic or ecosystem service-providing values. They are mostly defined by locals as destructive because they block waterways and mangroves. Mangroves, in contrast, are resources of great value for locals who see them as sources of medicine, fuel hoods, natural habitats for the reproduction of fish species, and much more known to be.

The locals were asked how they coped and adapted to the effects of climate change. Their responses included the following: use of outboard-powered seagoing boats, natural wisdom installation to guide when to fish, customised fishing nets, trading, poultry farming, skills development, and vocational training.

There are maladaptive measures people have taken as well. Most of them contribute to insecurity. Crime, in different forms including piracy, kidnapping, armed robbery, and cultism, is one of them. Many young people who chose these antisocial measures do so out of frustration with unproductive fishing and farming. The net result of all this, which includes unemployment, a lack of sufficient income during growing food insecurity, and a lack of government attention to the provision of basic social amenities, means that some would seek alternative livelihood through crime. Some have turned to illegal oil refining, a loathed business among those who value the environment more than money.

The Etiema, Agbakabiriyai, and Igbetaiwoama communities in the Nembe local government area have long-lasting cultures of wildlife conservation. The knowledge around this did not emanate from the West. They just know that this is valuable for the community's well-being in the long run. This practice has come under severe threat, as the maladaptive actions of many affected by climate change led them to disobey the community restrictions on economic activities in some parts of the environment. Flood, erosion, sea level rise, unpredictable rainfall, and heat waves, and their attendant resource scarcity, are specifically making some people pay lip service to regulations guiding fishing in specified areas. Although some of these rules have spiritual dimensions, their full implementation faces obstacles due to pressure from the changing climate. For example, commercial picking of is forbidden, but people in neighbouring communities ignore the spiritual consequences of indulgently using it for commercial purposes.

Africa lacks the resources to address the adaptation and mitigation of climate change. This was the point that the President of the African Development Bank, Akuwumi Adesina, recently highlighted at the Africa Adaptation Summit in The Netherlands (Olisa, 2022). He disclosed that Africa needs a total of $1.3 to $1.6tn between now and 2030 to be able to tackle climate change. It needs about $118bn to $145bn yearly to meet its Paris Agreement and nationally determined obligations. In the past year, only about 3% of the $100bn pledged by countries of the North to support developing countries to fight climate change annually was redeemed. Africa does not even have a mechanism to track the level of commitment of these countries to meet their promise. African leaders should keep local solutions as part of their alternatives at the level of adaptation.

Rivers State

In Rivers State, the study was carried out in Finima, Bonny local government area and in Kono, Khana local government area. Locals face the problem of devastating floods, thunderstorms, rise in sea level, erosion, and invasion by seas on the land. Despite adaptive efforts such as people seeking alternative sources of livelihood, migration, landscaping, and makeshift drainage, coping has been difficult. The adaptive capacity of locals must be built through interventionist financing of social amenities, and economic empowerment of the extreme poor from the victims' perspectives.

In Kono, locals are involved in landscaping to check erosion and protect houses from collapsing. They are also involved in planting special grasses that can withstand floods. These responses work regardless of the degree of the result. As such, they have the potential to help many communities if awareness is created and encouraged through a more systematic and productive approach. According to participants from these communities, this potential must be explored and effectively tapped.

Kono People

"We *change the way we plant. Sometimes, we allow farmland to stay for seven years, but this time for three years. We add fertilizer to cope*", was how one participant expressed the resilience of local farmers, transiting from nature-based farming practice to the use of fertilisers. Seven years is a long period to wait for flood-affected land to build momentum for the next farming season amidst growing food insecurity.

The Kono people have a culture of collective intervention. They raise funds through individual contributions to the construction of roads and drainages in the community as part of efforts to contain the impact of flooding. As also observed during the field study, a deep-rooted culture of care for one's neighbour in the community exists. For example, fishermen who return from the sea on specific days of the month can share part of their catch with neighbours. This is very comforting for people in the community struggling to cope with the impact of climate change.

The Kono Wiinua Mangrove Reserved Area is an amazing example of local initiatives in conservation. Logging and fishing activities are prohibited in this area. This practice is inconvenient for some fishermen who feel that the distances they must go fishing are too long. Even so, the community seems to have long settled for this practice based on good knowledge of the long-term benefits for the community through protection of fisheries species and guarantee resources for future generations. In the words of one participant,

> ...we are farmers and fishermen and you will find more fish around the mangrove area than you will find around the nipa palm areas. You find more fish, crabs, periwinkles, etc. So, we decided to preserve that area, let us see, and even if other areas have been devastated, let us keep it the way it is... When you look at the yield you get from the areas that have been devastated and this area that we protect, we will be able to draw a comparison.... You get more from here, but in the nipa area – no, you don't get as much. The fish do not thrive as much in the nipa area.

Likewise, in Bonny, *Finima Nature Park* is a protected area. The community is not permitted to fish or log in the area. But some fishers affected by climate disasters are not sure how this practice supports their livelihoods or benefits them in the short term. For example, they are unhappy with the impact of thunder and lightning and wish the area was not protected to prevent them from fishing. Finima is the *Thunder Belt* of the Niger Delta. *Thunder arrestors* have been provided by Nigeria's liquefied natural gas company operating there, but they were not functional at the time of this study. Their forebears had originally relocated from this location to where the natural gas company is located today because of thunder strikes. However, they were forced back by the Nigerian government due to the location of the company. In Bonny, fishermen are enlisting as members of local fisherman's unions to allow them to articulate collective positions on issues related to well-being and communicate the same to local authorities. Although there are no known substantial results from this development, signs indicate that this could be a way that fishermen could find a form of power to influence local authorities' responses on occupation-related issues.

How is house demolishing an adaptive or mitigation action? Some houses impede the free flow of water, thereby exposing the areas to worsening floods in the community because the houses block roads and pathways for floodwater evacuation. The local government in Bonny and the community leadership in the case of Kono are driving this in the hope of reducing the impact of climate change and helping people cope better with the situation. But this has its side effects. First, those affected by demolition may be unable to provide the financial resources needed for replacement without adequate compensation. Even when the community is magnanimous enough to provide alternative land for the victim, building on it is a responsibility the community will not do or has the resources to do.

The study observed the protection of the Bonny shoreline on the beach provided by the community to prevent sea encroachment. As one participant noted, *"shoreline protection has helped to maintain the area… else, it would be gone by now… For years now that they did that thing, nothing has happened. The place has remained intact"*.

The Rivers State government and the Nigeria Liquefied Natural Gas company are currently constructing a road, Bonny-Bodo-Road, to connect Bonny Island with the rest of the state. This project is considered a mitigation and adaptation measure due to its accompanying design and fitting drainage system.

Akwa Ibom State

> A) January to December... we need harmattan, but we cannot see it. B) "The change in harmattan season is affecting us, especially in fishing in the sense that as fishers, we like the sea breeze because it brings fish. This one blowing now is the ocean breeze..." C) We are suffering from water and every time we have a great water season there is always flooding in the community that destroys homes and properties, especially those close to water.

There are four main issues conveyed in these comments. They were made by three participants in two communities in Akwa Ibom State. First, is the issue of delayed harmattan seasons, which locals associate with difficulties and a lack of opportunities for productive fishing. Second, there is an understanding of the character of the season concerning fishing and farming. Third, is their knowledge of the direction of the wind, and the availability of fish in specific areas of the ocean. Finally, what happened or how did they experience the impact of floods on their well-being?

In Okorette, Eastern Obolo local government area of the state, the impact of flood, sea level rise, and heat waves are severe on the local farming and fishing population. Fishing is the main occupation of the people. Farming should be an alternative means of income, but both can be affected at the same time in various ways. The situation is the same as that of the Upenekang community in the Ibeno Local Government Area of the state.

Locals perceive unpredictable rainfall as an act of God for which they feel little or no real responsibility in terms of mitigation. They (Okorette community people) feel the government must construct an embankment at the river shores. They also believe the government should assist them with relief materials and funds to deal with problems caused by regular flooding. Floods typically cause havoc on homes and crops. They also believe that the government should provide potable drinking water, a big issue locals believe is needed to cope with climate events' social and economic consequences. Furthermore, channelling excessive water caused by rain and flooding through gutters is an expensive project that the government should handle.

Meanwhile, both communities face severe security issues such as piracy and armed stealing of boats with outboard engines. One of the coping methods fishermen have adopted to tackle the problem of low fish catch in nearby water areas is to move to distant sea and ocean, a step that requires better technology such as boats with outboard engines in contrast to canoes. Again, local canoes are not oceangoing vessels. These crimes, which are related to the impact of climate change through maladaptive responses of perpetrators, pose a threat to the survival of fishers. To address these security issues, people in the community want more presence of both states (navy, police, and army) and non-state security actors (popularly known as vigilantes).

Discussions

One striking aspect of the analysis is that local people are using local knowledge to make adaptive decisions in the six communities in the Niger Delta examined in this study. In other words, local knowledge supports adaptation and helps to reduce vulnerabilities no matter how insignificant the results have been. Second, the adaptative capacity of these communities remains weak and tilted towards criminal maladaptive components, compounding the problem of climate change. The sustainability of benefits from the integration of local knowledge is a key concern due to the nature of existing political institutions and limited external support for the use of such knowledge. This corroborates data obtained from the review of the literature, which showed that people in coastal communities affected by climate change have had a long-lasting mode of adaptive response from the point of view of local knowledge, defined in terms of decoloniality.

The local population migrate to other locations, seek alternative sources of income, acquire new skills and vocational training, trade, or do several things as forms of legitimate adaptation to climate change. Fishers and farmers specifically in some of the communities even pride themselves on knowing what to do in decisions about when and where to go for daily and seasonal fishing activities and planting and choice of crops that suit the changing environment. On the other hand, criminal activities such as piracy, kidnapping, the use of dynamite fishing techniques, armed robbery, illegal oil refining, and cultism or gangsterism are the main illegitimate adaptive areas of decisions people tend to make (See Table 16.2).

The debate on decolonisation of climate adaptation and mitigation measures is not about blind rejection of solutions based on Western knowledge. Instead, it includes the acknowledgement of the reality, possibilities, and value that local knowledge offers to local populations. The knowledge people have about their environment and the changes, their definition of the daily experiences, and methods for tackling the challenges resulting from the changes are crucial decolonial perspectives for proper response to the impact. Some scholars' attempts to define the decolonial approach to dealing with the problem of climate change in Africa and the rest of the developing world have suggested the integration of Western and local knowledge. The analysis includes a rejection of the historical misdeeds of Northern countries against the planet through the transatlantic slave trade, colonisation, and pillaging of African resources.

Table 16.2 Examples of local adaptive measures in the Niger Delta

Adaptive measures	*Challenges*	*Components*
Migration	Lack of resources; conflict	
Alternative sources of livelihood	Lack of resources, support from state institutions, lack of capacity from local institutions to support, and maladaptive actions	Petty trading, poultry business, skills development, vocational training, work, etc
Maladaptation	Maladaptation	Illegal oil refining; piracy, kidnapping, illegal logging of mangroves, use of dynamite fishing, armed robbery, and illegal picking of periwinkle
Modern technology/local technology	Lack of financial resources	Modern farming techniques and the use of improved crop varieties; use of boats with outboard engines; planting of special grasses to combat erosion; fisheries; local observation and understanding of weather conditions for decision-making; local embankment of shorelines, etc

All this enhanced the European industrial revolution and turned out to be the foundation of the current global climate crisis. Furthermore, decolonisation of climate policy is understood as the recognition of the context and unique situations of vulnerable communities with social, economic, environmental, or ecological concerns as critical elements of the survival and development of the capacity of communities to adapt to climate change (Daszkiewicz et al., 2022).

Coastal communities in the Niger Delta have one thing in common: locals understand that the environment is changing. They make valid observations about the environment, though they cannot explain by the standards of Western knowledge systems. Their experience with the oil industry's impact in terms of pollution greatly impacts their judgements about the environment. Despite all this, the local fishing and farming population continue to interact with nature in ways that support insights into the changing climate, though this happens mostly without their use of the concept of climate change. For example, they can tell the implications of delayed harmattan and rainy seasons for agriculture and fishing. They know the negative warnings about the environment when birds such as vultures are no longer sighted eating animal carcasses. They also read the direction of the wind at sea to understand when it is safe to go fishing, during which time they can also know where fish may be available.

It was very difficult for fishers to lose their bearing at sea before. Going nautical miles into the sea for fishing was safe with local knowledge of weather and direction for many. They had no modern compass, except natural local knowledge of time and direction. This wisdom may not always have been accurate, but it served these communities for ages when the climate started to take on more intense and unpredictable forms. The impact of climate change on people in coastal communities in the Niger Delta manifests itself in various forms, including human insecurity through social, economic, political, and economic conditions that sometimes fuel or trigger conflict (Daszkiewicz et al., 2022).

The Niger Delta represents a complex case of double tragedy. Nigeria's oil and gas establishment has posed a serious threat to creeks, air, mangroves, rivers, seas, and the ocean. Many coastal communities battling climate change effects also face the challenge of the destructive impact of oil facilities through regular spills. As a result, it is sometimes difficult to draw the line between oil-related and climate change issues. The additional burden these communities face now is the pollution arising from the activities of illegal oil refiners.

An interesting dimension of the decolonial discourse on climate change is rooted in the role of slavery, the Industrial Revolution, and colonialism. During these periods countries of the North created the foundation for the pollution of the earth with fossil fuels. The aggressive and unregulated quest and use of fossil fuels in Northern countries drove the Industrial Revolution and colonialism. Acknowledging and accepting to pay the debts arising from the pillage of developing countries by these countries has been argued to fit into the decolonial discourse. The net implication is that these countries should take the responsibility of financing adaptation and mitigation more seriously. It is instructive that in 2021 only 3% of these countries' commitment to their pledge of annual contributions of $100bn for tackling climate change in the developing world was realised. The lack of commitment on their part shows a lack of remorse for their role in the global climate crisis.

Conclusions

Overall, the chapter has examined the meaning of decolonisation of climate adaptation and development by exploring the literature to situate the experience of people in six communities in three states in the Niger Delta of Nigeria. This chapter contributes to the conceptualisation of the decolonial discourse of climate adaptation. The analysis reinforces the position of the literature that local knowledge matters in climate adaptation at the community level. Communities are practising decolonial climate adaptation. Migration, alternative means of livelihood, local embankment of shorelines, skills development and vocations, and community infrastructure development are among legitimate adaptive measures local communities are adopting. At the same time, these communities face many challenges.

Maladaptive measures such as piracy, kidnapping, illegal oil refining, and gangsterism are common. They are part of the challenges because of their broader impact on the peace of society. They even pose severe threats to human security. These are antisocial behaviours with the capacity to trigger violent conflict, indirectly resulting in making the climate crisis a complex problem. Food insecurity, poverty, unemployment, and the risk of violent conflict are all indirectly linked or part of the maladaptive measures. They are part of the challenges of decolonial climate adaptation, defined in terms of local knowledge to tackle the effects of climate change. The effectiveness of the role of local knowledge in climate adaptation is a function of many factors. For example, the nature of traditional institutions, cultural practices, political institutions' character, and communities' adaptive capacity are critical elements.

The fact that climate change is a global problem with unequal impact and the ability of communities to respond with adaptation means that local institutions, regional, continental, and international efforts justify deeper interactive processes with aspects of local knowledge that productively serve the interest of people to cope with impacts. The interaction of traditional knowledge with political and economic institutions at those levels entails a critical assessment of Western knowledge as a form of power. By simple logistic extension, it means careful mixing of Western and local knowledge systems and strengthening of the same.

Climate adaptation requires adequate financing which countries in the developing world are fundamentally lacking. The sum of $100bn which countries of the North have pledged as annual contributions for tackling climate change in the developing world will serve decolonial purposes if they make good on their pledges. A decolonial approach will further mean de-emphasising problematic solutions such as markets and minimising investments in fossil fuels while boosting investments in alternative renewable energy. This requires individual country efforts at making energy mix a core national energy and foreign policy goal. In the same vein, regional economic groupings, continental organisations such as the African Union, and United Nations Framework Convention on Climate Change (UNFCCC) are encouraging energy mix as part of the solution to the global climate crisis. It requires acknowledgement of decoloniality as a key element of ideas about the origin of the climate crisis, adaptation, and mitigation through participatory principles that capture the experiences and views of people in communities, climate justice networks, state authorities, and big businesses. The critical element in this analysis is the vulnerability of coastal communities and serious financial attention for adaptation, the strengthening of existing local approaches, and the integration of workable Western ideas to support the resilience and well-being of people.

References

Allen, F., & Amadi, L. (2022). Introduction. In F. Allen, & L. Amadi (Eds.), *Decolonising Colonial Development Models in Africa, a Postcolonial Critique* (pp. vii–xxvii). Lexington Books.

Amadou, M. L., Villamor, G. B., & Kei-Baffor, N. (2018). Simulating Agricultural Land-use Adaptation. *Agricultural Systems, 166*, 196–209.

Brown, O., & Crawford, A. (2008). *Assessing the Security Implications of Climate Change for West Africa: Country Case Studies of Ghana and Burkina Faso.* https://www.iisd.org/system/files/publications/security_implications_west_africa.pdf

Brockhaus, M., Doubt, H., & Localleti, B. (2013). Envisioning the Future and Learning from the Past: Adapting to Changing Environment in Northern Mali. *Environment, Science and Policy, 25*, 94–106.

Bandura, A. (2011). A Social Cognitive Perspective on Positive Psychology. *Revista de Psicología Social, 26*, 7–20.

Bandura, A. (1997). *Self-efficacy, The Exercise of Control.* W. H. Freeman and Company.

Brunn, O., & Ngoc, L. B. (2018). Local and Independent Knowledge for Disaster Prevention and Livelihoods Protection in North-Central Vietnam. *Journal of Vietnamese Studies,* 13(2), 74–101.

Chevallier, R. (2017). Integrated Community and Ecosystem-based Approaches to Climate Change Adaptation. *South African Institute of International Affairs Policy Insight*, 49, https://www.jstor.org/stable/resrep29519?seq=1

Callo-Concha, D. (2018). Famer Perceptions and Climate Change Adaptation in the West Africa Sudan Savannah: Reality Check in Dassari Benin, and Dana, Burkina Faso. *Climate, 6*, 44, https://www.mdpi.com/2225-1154/6/2/44

Daszkiewic, T. (2022). Food Production in the Context of Global Developmental Challenges. *Agriculture, 12*(6), 832. https://doi.org/10.3390/agriculture12060832

Daszkiewicz, C., Shawoo, Z., Nazareth, A., Coleoni, C., Kwamboka, E., Ghosh, E., Han, J. Y.-C., Inga, K., Tran, M., & Diaz-Chavez, R. A. (2022). *Shifting Power Through Climate Research: Applying Decolonial Methodologies.* Environment Institute. http://www.jstor.org/stable/resrep39740

Granderson, A. A. (2017). The Role of Traditional Knowledge in Building Adaptive Capacity for Climate Change: Perspectives from Vanuatu. *Weather Climate and Society, 9*, 546–5561.

Granderson, A. A. (2014). Making Sense of Climate Change Risks and Responses at the Community Level: A Cultural-Political Lens. *Climate Risk Management, 3*, 55–64.

Health of Mother Earth Foundation. (2022). *Climate Change as a Cause of Conflict in Coastal Areas of West Africa* (Research Report).

Naess, L. O. (2013). The Role of Local Knowledge in Adaptation to Climate Change. *Wires Climate Change, 4*, 99–106.

Owusu, V., & Andriesse, E. (2023). Local Differentiation and Adaptation to Climate Change Coastal Ghana. *Geographical Review, 113*(3), 337–358.

Pyhälä, A., Fernández-Llamazares, Á., Lehvävirta, H., Byg, A., Ruiz-Mallén, I., Salpeteur, M., & Thornton, T. F. (2016) Global Environmental Change: Local Perceptions, Understandings, and Explanations. *Ecology and Society, 21*(3), 1–29. http://www.jstor.org/stable/26269967

Ung, M., Luginaah, I., Chuenpagdee, R., & Campbell, G. (2016). Perceived Self-efficacy and Adaptation to Climate Change in Coastal Cambodia. *Climate, 4*(1), 1–16.

United Nations News. (2022). *Sub-Saharan Africa under Threat from Multiple Humanitarian Crises*, https://news.un.org/en/story/2022/04/1115922

World Bank. (2016). *Climate Change Knowledge Portal.* http://sdwebx.worldbank.org/climate portal/

Index

A. O. Akinola and E. A. Liaga (eds.), *Development and Regional Stability in Africa*, https://doi.org/10.1007/978-3-031-56695-0

SPRINGER NATURE

GPSR Compliance

The European Union's (EU) General Product Safety Regulation (GPSR) is a set of rules that requires consumer products to be safe and our obligations to ensure this.

If you have any concerns about our products, you can contact us on ProductSafety@springernature.com

In case Publisher is established outside the EU, the EU authorized representative is:

Springer Nature Customer Service Center GmbH
Europaplatz 3
69115 Heidelberg, Germany

The manufacturer's authorised representative in the EU is Springer Nature Customer Service Centre GmbH, Europaplatz 3, 69115 Heidelberg, Germany. If you have any concerns regarding our products, please contact ProductSafety@springernature.com

Printed and bound by CPI Group (UK) Ltd, Croydon, CR0 4YY
28/09/2026
02224074-0008